DAY BY DAY
VOLUME 3

Day by Day

VOLUME 3

The Bible Reading Fellowship

Text copyright © BRF 1995

Published by
The Bible Reading Fellowship
Peter's Way, Sandy Lane West
Oxford OX4 5HG
ISBN 0 7459 3259 0

First edition 1995
10 9 8 7 6 5 4 3 2 1

Acknowledgments

Good News Bible copyright © American Bible Society 1966, 1971 and 1976, published by the Bible Societies and Collins.

The Alternative Service Book 1980 copyright © The Central Board of Finance of the Church of England.

The Jerusalem Bible copyright © 1966, 1967 and 1968 by Darton, Longman & Todd Ltd and Doubleday & Company, Inc.

The New Jerusalem Bible copyright © 1985 by Darton, Longman & Todd Ltd and Doubleday & Company, Inc.

The *Revised Standard Version* of the Bible, copyright © 1946, 1952, 1971 by the Division of Christian Education of the National Council of the Churches of Christ in the USA.

The *New Revised Standard Version* of the Bible, copyright © 1989 by the Division of Christian Education of the National Council of the Churches of Christ in the USA.

The Holy Bible, *New International Version*, copyright © 1973, 1978, 1984 by International Bible Society. Used by permission of Hodder and Stoughton Limited.

Extracts from the Book of Common Prayer of 1662, the rights in which are invested in the Crown in perpetuity within the United Kingdom, are reproduced by permission of the Crown's patentee, Cambridge University Press.

The Holy Bible, *Living Bible Edition*, copyright © Tyndale House Publishers 1971, published by Kingsway.

Extracts from the *Authorized Version* of the Bible (The King James Bible), the rights of which are vested in the Crown, are reproduced by permission of the Crown's Patentee, Cambridge University Press.

New English Bible, © 1970 by permission of Oxford and Cambridge University Presses.

Revised English Bible © 1989 by permission of Oxford and Cambridge University Presses.

A catalogue record for this book is available from the British Library

Printed and bound in Slovenia

Contents

Introduction

Here is another volume of Bible readings and prayers to take you day by day through the whole year. All readings come from past issues of *New Daylight*.

If you start at the beginning, on New Year's Day, you will finish up at the end of the year with Bible readings for the season of Advent and Christmas. But if you start to read later on in the year, and still want to read about Easter and Pentecost at the right time, you can work out where you are by looking at the dates of Easter and counting backwards or forwards from there.

In 1996 Easter Sunday will be on 7 April; in 1997 on 30 March; in 1998 on 12 April and in 1999 on 4 April.

All the *Day by Day* readings are arranged in sections, and you will find the contents of each section set out on page 5. There are readings on The Practice of Faith—how to live out our faith in the world and to be 'the light of the world', which is what Jesus Christ told us we are. There are several weeks of readings from the Gospel of John and the Gospel of Luke. There are readings from the Psalms, and from various New Testament letters: Ephesians, James, 1 and 2 Timothy and Titus. There is the story of Ruth and the love story of Hosea from the Old Testament, and the book of Revelation from the New. All those readings are arranged to fit in with the Christian story as it runs through the year. As in *New Daylight*, Sundays are different, and are nearly always to do with Holy Communion or with praying.

The whole reason for our reading the Bible is to encounter the living God. As we read we shall hear the voice of God speaking to us—through all the different sorts of writings. Psalm 40 is what is known as a messianic psalm—pointing to the way the Messiah would act when he came. 'You have given me an open ear', it says—which means an ear that listens to the voice of God. It goes on: 'Then I said, "Here I am"; in the scroll of the book it is written of me. I delight to do your will, O my God; your law is within my heart' (Psalm 40:6–8, NRSV). It is when we really listen to the voice of God that we do the will of God—and the will of God is the salvation and the healing of the whole world and everyone who lives in it.

The Church of England Collect for the second Sunday in Advent (known as Bible Sunday) is a lovely prayer to use before we read.

Blessed Lord,
who caused all holy Scriptures
to be written for our learning:
help us so to hear them,
to read, mark, learn, and inwardly digest them
that, through patience, and the comfort
of your holy word,
we may embrace and for ever hold fast
the hope of everlasting life.
which you have given us in our Saviour Jesus Christ.

(ASB, page 426)

The practice of faith

The Christian faith is always lived out in practice—in the life of faith. And if it isn't being lived out then it's an empty faith, not a living faith.

The letter to the Hebrews says that 'faith is the assurance of things hoped for, the conviction of things not seen. Indeed, by faith our ancestors received approval...' (11:1–2)

They received it because of what they *did*—and the rest of that marvellous chapter 11 of Hebrews is about how the great heroes and heroines of faith from the very beginning lived out their relationship with the living God in the world.

This section of *Day by Day* is about how we can live out our faith. With Garth Hewitt we look at the letter of James—immensely practical on the way that real faith shows itself in real life. Then the book of Proverbs offers us the gift of Wisdom. The Wisdom through whom God made the worlds—and who, the New Testament tells us, is Christ himself: Christ the power of God and Christ the wisdom of God. There for us—to live the life of God in union with us, and to work the works of God in union with us. 'The life of God in the soul of man,' Henry Scougal called it—and it's a life that shows.

After the works of faith and the wisdom of God, Rosemary Green takes us through Paul's letter to Timothy—'my true son in the faith' he calls him at the start of the letter, and says to him later on, 'Don't let anyone look down on you because you are young, but set an example to the believers in speech, in life, in love, in faith and in purity.' The living faith that showed itself by its actions.

Finally, we spend a week with the prophet Habakkuk, who looked around him in dread at a world that seemed to be falling apart, but came from fear to faith as he contemplated the nature and the acts of the God in whom he had put his trust. 'The righteous live by their faith', he wrote—and we do. By faith in the living God—a faith whicht we live out in the world that God loves.

Struggle towards maturity

James, a servant of God and of the Lord Jesus Christ, To the twelve tribes in the dispersion: Greetings. My brothers and sisters, whenever you face trials of any kind, consider it nothing but joy, because you know that the testing of your faith produces endurance; and let endurance have its full effect, so that you may be mature and complete, lacking in nothing.

The letter of James comes straight in with 'persevere'—keep going, it will make you 'complete'. It's a down to earth book suggesting that through the struggle comes endurance and through endurance, maturity. Some people want to rush from one spiritual high to another and are deeply disappointed if there aren't easy answers. James points out that true spirituality comes through struggle and endurance but has the great joy of leading towards maturity and wholeness. Wisdom is needed and that comes through life's struggles. If we always had easy answers we would lack wisdom and we would not be complete.

But consider it *joy* when the trials come?! Isn't that going a bit far? I remember in 1982 visiting Uganda at a time of incredible violence. Killings were happening every day and every family had been touched. Yet in many of the Christians I did see joy—and if I had to sum up that trip with one word I think it would be 'joy'. I don't mean superficial happiness—there was none of that— but a resurrection faith rising amidst the crucifixion of the people.

The road to maturity and wholeness is a road we often don't want to take.

Christians want God to do it all and are tempted to stay as children. But God says 'No, you must become whole and adult. And the choices you make, and your struggles of life, and your saying "No" to the temptations will make you whole and adult.'

To think about

'We tried to be formed and held and kept by Christ, but instead He offers us freedoms: and now when I try to know His will, His kindness floods me, His great love overwhelms me and I hear Him whisper "surprise me".'

From a letter in a novel, Marriette in Ecstasy

Next time you're struggling over a difficult decision and you're begging God to tell you what to do, remember he may simply be saying 'Yes, I'm interested in what you're going to do as well, surprise me!'

GH

The gospel of equality

Let the believer who is lowly boast in being raised up, and the rich in being brought low, because the rich will disappear like a flower in the field. For the sun rises with its scorching heat and withers the fields; its flower falls and its beauty perishes. It is the same way with the rich; in the midst of a busy life, they will wither away.

Do you know the chorus which goes, 'And now let the weak say I am strong, let the poor say I am rich, because of what the Lord has done'? I have a friend who is a pastor who won't let this chorus be sung without a verse turning it the other way as well—'let the strong say I am weak, let the rich say I am poor, because of what the Lord has done'. Jesus came to break down the barriers of division. When I was in Lima, Peru, I came across a mountain called Monterico which means 'rich mountain' and on it there was a wall built to keep the poor away from the rich. There are walls of division all around our world and the gospel comes to remove them and to bring justice and equality.

This is both the excitement and the challenge of the gospel and of our God who turns the world's values upside down.

When I was a teenager I heard Martin Luther King preach at St Paul's Cathedral. He talked about right relationships and used a verse from Revelation, about the new Jerusalem that God was building in which 'its length and breadth and height are equal', and he said that the new city God was building would not be an unbalanced entity with caring virtues on one side and degrading vices on the other. The most noble thing about it would be its completeness, whereas the troubles of our world are due to incompleteness.

To think about

Is there an area in your life where you cling to prestige or power, in class or race or gender? If so, bring it now to God and ask him to remove this wall of division. Then say: 'Now let the rich say I am poor, let the strong say I am weak because of what the Lord has done.'

GH

It wasn't my fault

No one when tempted, should say, 'I am being tempted by God'; for God cannot be tempted by evil and he himself tempts no one. But one is tempted by one's own desire, being lured and enticed by it; then, when that desire has conceived, it gives birth to sin, and that sin, when it is fully grown, gives birth to death. Do not be deceived, my beloved. Every generous act of giving, and every perfect gift, is from above, coming down from the Father of lights, with whom there is no variation or shadow due to change.

There's a country song about falling into temptation with the lyric, 'The devil made me do it the first time—the second time I did it on my own.' And the second time the writer's found the culprit—but neither God nor the devil can be blamed for the first time. James makes it clear—we are enticed by our own desires, which give birth to the making of selfish choices and to wrong.

Generous choices and acts stem from God's motivation. Our own desires entice us and lead us to wrong choices and deeds which lead to death, in contrast to the struggles and trials which lead to endurance, to wisdom and right choices, and to the crown of life.

'Father of lights' is a strange and poetic phrase that seems to refer to God as Creator, the one who said, 'Let there be light'. This was the start of his giving good gifts. We are called to join God in being creative by resisting the selfish, greedy and eventually destructive desires and, instead, imitate the generous creativity that stems from God—that gives to others, puts them first and thinks of their needs. In a nutshell, loving our neighbour as ourself. We should start with that love that values and respects our own dignity, so that in turn we can show that same love to our neighbour. We tend to love ourselves better when we recognize the acceptance and warmth of God's love that doesn't change and always says, 'You are accepted—you are loved.'

Prayer

Creator God, Father of lights—whose character is unchanging—thank you for your generous love—give me a generous spirit that makes me a giving person rather than a greedy one. Amen.

GH

Stop speaking and listen!

You must understand this, my beloved: let everyone be quick to listen, slow to speak, slow to anger; for your anger does not produce God's righteousness. Therefore rid yourselves of all sordidness and rank growth of wickedness, and welcome with meekness the implanted word that has the power to save your souls.

'Quick to listen'—'I couldn't get a word in edgeways.' We all know the frustration of those conversations. But we can all end up being guilty of insensitivity by talking too much or simply not taking time to listen—to our children—to our partner—our friends—to the old person—to the difficult person...

'Slow to speak'—Are you someone who is tempted to rush in with an easy answer—or top the last person's story with something better! When I was a child, my father used to puzzle me by saying, 'empty vessels make the most noise'. Now I understand—and maybe, with a little more thought, will be slower to speak. Try and discipline yourself to keep quiet and genuinely to hear the other person. Maybe we wouldn't need so many counsellors if we would only listen to one another.

'Slow to anger'—There is a time for righteous anger on behalf of the powerless and voiceless. But our quick anger is often selfish and it's not God's anger. It's part of our refusal to listen or to see the other person's point of view or to learn lessons. I believe these three attributes are part of what it means to be humble, to be a servant. Don't dominate a conversation—or the other person. Allow them space.

This seems to be a route of good habits—that help us get rid of the wrong, stops the 'growth of wickedness' and allows the welcoming 'with meekness' of God's word. Interesting to note 'with meekness'—people often want it 'with power', but the way of Jesus is not to dominate—it is the way of humility that listens and learns and therefore does not rashly indulge in selfish anger.

Thought

A way to learn to listen is to set aside time each day for a few minutes of solitude and silence. Don't have an agenda, then you can be 'slow to speak' and God can refresh you in the stillness. And you can be 'quick to listen'—to his creation all around you, and to his word.

GH

13

Walk the talk

But be doers of the word, and not merely hearers who deceive themselves. For if any are hearers of the word and not doers, they are like those who look at themselves in the mirror; for they look at themselves and, on going away, immediately forget what they were like. But those who look into the perfect law, the law of liberty, persevere, being not hearers who forget but doers who act—they will be blessed in their doing.

I have a friend who is a country singer—George Hamilton IV. One day he was talking to me about Jimmy Carter, the former President of the United States. He said, 'Do you know what he is doing?—he is up a ladder with hammer and nails making homes for the homeless.' Then he added, 'He really walks his talk.' I love that expression. I had never heard it before and to me it is another way of expressing that we should be 'doers of the word'. It means to live out the gospel, not just talk about it. Jimmy Carter teaches Sunday school each week in his home church but he puts his faith into action in practical ways as a 'doer' and as a peacemaker. It is no good having a wonderful faith that satisfies us personally if we do not show love in action to those we meet—our faith in that case would be purely self-indulgent.

The word of God is like a mirror—it presents ideal human behaviour and shows us where we have fallen short just as a mirror would show untidiness or blemishes. So after reading God's word don't forget it—go and live it—go and 'walk the talk'. Then as the passage reminds us—you will be blessed.

A song lyric to reflect on

*Reach out in love
to a world that is hurting,
Bind up the wounds,
bring the Gospel of hope.
Care for the lonely,
show love in action,
Companions of Jesus
for the Kingdom of God.*

*We must walk the talk,
live the life
Moving this world
from darkness to light.
Showing each person what
God thinks they're worth
Linking arms together
around the earth.*

Garth Hewitt © Chain of Love music

GH

True spirituality

If any thinks they are religious, and do not bridle their tongues but deceive their hearts, their religion is worthless. Religion that is pure and undefiled before God the Father, is this: to care for orphans and widows in their distress and to keep oneself unstained by the world.

You often hear people saying, 'I want really lively *worship*', but what does that word mean? Its root is 'worth'—meaning reflecting the worth or value of God, and that worship must carry on outside church on Sundays—in the practical acts that reflect the worth and the character of God who is our parent—so caring for the orphans and rejecting the selfish, materialistic values of the world.

Within a world where there are one hundred million street children that no one cares for and countless refugees, how should you and your church express true spirituality and true worship? Future generations of Christians will be staggered that we allowed these huge injustices to continue between the rich world and the poor world—just as we were amazed that earlier Christians could countenance the slave trade.

Martin Luther King said 'The Christian gospel is a two-way road. On the one hand, it seeks to change the souls of men and thereby unite them with God; on the other hand, it seeks to change environmental conditions of men so that the soul will have a chance after it is changed. Any religion which professes to be concerned with the souls of men and is not concerned with the slums that damn them, the economic conditions that strangle them, and the social conditions that cripple them is an opiate of the people.'

Prayer

Lord lead us from selfish religion to a whole faith of true spirituality that reflects you and your priorities. Amen.

GH

God has no favourites

Then Peter began to speak: 'I now realise how true it is that God does not show favouritism but accepts men from every nation who fear him and do what is right. You know the message God sent to the people of Israel, telling the good news of peace through Jesus Christ, who is Lord of all. You know what has happened throughout Judea, beginning in Galilee after the baptism that John preached how God anointed Jesus of Nazareth with the Holy Spirit and power, and how he went around doing good and healing all who were under the power of the devil, because God was with him.'

'God does not show favouritism'—what a marvellous and reassuring statement that is! Here, St Peter is responding to his own experience of the Gentile Cornelius and his household, who were standing before him eager and ready to hear the gospel. He may have known in his head that the Jewish prophets looked forward to a day when all the nations would turn to the Lord, but he probably hadn't expected to live to see it. And yet here they were, Gentiles, but objects of God's love and concern.

God has no favourites! At times we, too, may be tempted to think he has. We may feel he prefers 'people like us'. Or of course we may feel sometimes that others are his favourites and that he clearly prefers them to us they get the 'goodies', we get the disappointments. Favouritism is always unpleasant, destructive and unkind, so it is hardly surprising that it is not part of God's nature.

In God's overall purpose for humanity, the great foundation truth is that he loves 'the world'. 'Whoever will' may come to him. 'Those who call on the name of the Lord will be saved.' He 'is not willing that any should perish, but that all should come to repentance'. Christ did not die 'for our sins only, but for the sins of the whole world'. However we feel about it, God's love encompasses everyone, everywhere, at all times... without favourites!

A prayer

As you, Lord, have no favourites, teach me what it means to see everyone, everywhere, as within the circle of your love.

DW

No favouritism

My brothers and sisters, do you with your acts of favouritism really believe in our glorious Lord Jesus Christ? For if a person with gold rings and in fine clothes comes into your assembly, and if a poor person in dirty clothes also comes in, and if you take notice of the one wearing the fine clothes, and say, 'Have a seat here, please,' while to the one who is poor you say, 'Stand there,' or, 'Sit at my feet,' have you not made distinctions among yourselves, and become judges with evil thoughts? Listen, my beloved brothers and sisters. Has not God chosen the poor in the world to be rich in faith and to be heirs of the kingdom that he has promised to those that love him? But you have dishonoured the poor.

Here James gives a further explanation for being 'doers of the word'. It leads to a fuller concern for the poor in the community. If we really believe in 'our glorious Lord Jesus Christ'—then the glory of the Lord should eclipse all our ideas of worldly rank or status. Acting with favouritism denies that we have put God and his glory first. There are certain Christian activities or organizations that sometimes favour the wealthy or powerful or people of status—with the view that if only they become Christians others will be influenced because these people are powerful.

James would see this as a denial of God's glory and of the Christian gospel. There is no status in Christ—no class distinctions. James is reflecting a very biblical view here. The Old Testament says that the poor have God's special care. Jesus says, 'Blessed are the poor'.

In Britain in recent times, the poor have got poorer in real terms and the rich richer—so the community has been tearing apart. This also reflects what has been happening worldwide in divisions between the rich world and the poor world. The gospel is the challenging, healing hope for a different way, a different kingdom, with different values, where huge inequalities are not condoned but where 'justice rolls down like a river'.

Prayer

Lord, may we see people through your eyes—to value all equally and to show this by our deeds of compassion and justice. Amen.

GH

17

Faith without works is dead

What good is it, my brothers and sisters, if you say you have faith but do not have works? Can faith save you? If a brother or sister is naked and lacks daily food, and one of you says to them, 'Go in peace; keep warm and eat your fill,' and yet you do not supply their bodily needs, what is the good of that? So faith by itself, if it has no works, is dead. But someone will say, 'You have faith and I have works.' Show me your faith apart from your works, and I by my works will show you my faith... Do you want to be shown, you senseless person, that faith apart from works is barren? Was not our ancestor Abraham justified by works when he offered his son Isaac on the altar? You see that faith was active along with his works, and faith was brought to completion by the works... You see that a person is justified by works and not by faith alone.

I was in a huge shanty town area of Lima, Peru, and visited a Catholic priest called Father Matthias and a nun called Sister Juanita. When asked what was their motivation, Father Matthias replied, 'To be faithful, and to be holy and to live the gospel in this place', waving his arm as he said this to indicate the shanty town. They were making Christ visible by deeds and they correctly saw this as holiness. Their brothers and sisters were 'naked and lacked daily food' and their faith was making them do something practical about it in providing health care, nourishment, job creation skills and so on to help the people combat the poverty.

Faith by itself in that situation would have been meaningless. We can believe all the 'right' and 'sound' doctrines but if we stop there our faith is dead. It is our works that not only reveal our faith but also point to the character of God. Without deeds of love and justice a person who calls themselves a Christian brings God into disrepute because they suggest he is not interested in the poor and needy. If he wasn't, he would be an unjust God—not worth worshipping.

Prayer

Lord, may we be people of good works, showing your just character to our broken world. Amen.

GH

Watch your tongue!

Not many of you should become teachers, my brothers and sisters, for you know that we who teach will be judged with greater strictness. For all of us make mistakes. Anyone who makes no mistakes in speaking is perfect, able to keep the whole body in check with a bridle ... Look at ships; though they are so large that it takes strong winds to drive them, yet they are guided by a very small rudder, wherever the will of the pilot directs. So also the tongue is a small member, yet it boasts of great exploits. How great a forest is set ablaze by a small fire! ... With it we bless the Lord and Father, and with it we curse those who are made in the likeness of God. From the same mouth come blessing and cursing. My brothers and sisters, this ought not to be so.

James is back on two themes he has already touched on—the tongue, and also that not many should be teachers in the Church. The reason why is that 'we who teach will be judged with greater strictness'. Why?—the capacity to lead astray—to influence people in wrong directions. It is power too, and the humble way of the servant is the rejection of power. So teachers and leaders in the Church must be very careful not to manipulate or dominate or allow their ego to get out of hand, or to think that they are too significant in God's plan! The gift of speaking or oratory is one we have seen abused in our century, from Hitler to tele-evangelists, but we have also seen it used to heal and to proclaim God's justice.

And we can use our tongue in two ways—to heal or to crack a racist joke; to bring peace or to spread rumours and gossip that bring divisions. We can use it to pray and to encourage people, or to curse people made in God's image and to put people down.

Reflect

Take time to be quiet and to think about your tongue—can you think of an incident where you have recently encouraged someone, or one where you have spoken hastily and caused pain. Pray for wisdom to think before speaking.

GH

A harvest of justice

Anyone who is wise or understanding among you should from a good life give evidence of deeds done in the gentleness of wisdom. But if at heart you have the bitterness of jealousy, or selfish ambition, do not be boastful or hide the truth with lies; this is not the wisdom that comes from above, but earthly, human and devilish. Wherever there are jealousy and ambition, there are also disharmony and wickedness of every kind; whereas the wisdom that comes down from above is essentially something pure; it is also peaceable, kindly and considerate; it is full of mercy and shows itself by doing good; nor is there any trace of partiality or hypocrisy. The peace sown by peacemakers brings a harvest of justice.

What is our ambition? Frederich Buechner has a rule of thumb for vocation, 'The place God calls you to is the place where your deep gladness and the world's deep hunger meet' (Frederich Buechner, *Wishful Thinking—A Theological ABC*, Harper and Row, New York, 1973, page 95). If only your 'deep gladness' is satisfied, it is probably selfish and if only the 'world's deep hunger' is met, you are probably not the person to be doing it!

Real wisdom leads us to doing good, to being peacemakers and to bringing a harvest of justice. If our churches become communities of peacemakers, we will have a harvest of justice that brings healing to a divided and hurt world. A harvest of justice—isn't this what our world needs—justice for the oppressed and forgotten—for the refugees—the street children—for the homeless—for the racially oppressed? Justice that points out as did the prophets of old the structural sin of systems that are crippling people. A harvest of justice would remove the huge inequalities as the healing gospel asserted the worth of everyone.

Meditate

Meditate on the words of Frederich Buechner and ask yourself, 'Is my deep gladness meeting the world's deep hunger?' Then read again the Bible passage above.

GH

Enmity with God

These conflicts and disputes among you, where do they come from? Do they not come from your cravings that are at war within you? You want something and do not have it; so you commit murder. And you covet something and cannot obtain it; so you engage in disputes and conflicts. You do not have, because you do not ask. You ask and you do not receive, because you ask wrongly, in order to spend what you get on your pleasures. Adulterers! Do you not know that friendship with the world is enmity with God? Therefore whoever wishes to be a friend of the world becomes an enemy of God . . . Submit yourselves therefore to God. Resist the devil, and he will flee from you. Draw near to God, and he will draw near to you. Cleanse your hands, you sinners, purify your hearts, you double-minded . . . Humble yourselves before the Lord, and he will exalt you.

Now James heads from peace to war and to what causes disputes. The root of the trouble is covetous and greedy cravings for things we have not got. And the reason we don't get what we ask for is that we ask for them for the wrong reasons. Like an Old Testament prophet here, he yells, 'Adulterers'—friendship with worldly or selfish values is against God. You're adulterers because you are worshipping false idols—of money, materialism, personal greed, of war to achieve these ends. Wars are to preserve the domination of one group over another or to satisfy the greed of one country—or the greed of the arms trade. There are those who have even tried to develop a spirituality of acquisitiveness—a prosperity doctrine that says God will make you rich. But that is to harness two enemies. Impossibly, it tries to combine a love of the idol of materi-alism and greed with love of the ways of God, and James speaks powerfully to this: 'Do you not know that friendship with the world is enmity with God?'

To think about

We must learn this invitation of Christ: 'Those who wish to come after me must renounce themselves' . . . renounce their comforts, renounce their personal opinions, and follow only the mind of Christ which can lead us to death but which will also surely lead us to resurrection.

Archbishop Oscar Romero

GH

Warning to the rich

Come now, you rich people, weep and wail for the miseries that are coming to you. Your riches have rotted, and your clothes are moth-eaten. Your gold and silver have rusted, and their rust will be evidence against you, and it will eat your flesh like fire. You have laid up treasure for the last days. Listen! The wages of the labourers who mowed your fields, which you kept back by fraud, cry out and the cries of the harvesters have reached the ears of the Lord of hosts. You have lived on the earth in luxury and in pleasure; have fattened your hearts in a day of slaughter. You have condemned and murdered the righteous one, who does not resist you.

Have you noticed how the 'rich' are always someone else? 'I'm not rich because I can show you people much richer'—when actually I am rich compared to so many people in our world. Many of us who live in Western societies have wealth beyond the wildest dreams of the majority on our planet, and our pursuit of wealth is destroying our planet.

There was a cartoon in the paper recently of a boat sinking. In the front were hoards of little people falling out but at the back sat a few gross, fat people—they were causing the boat to sink, but they were saying, as they pointed to the others, 'If only they would stop breeding.'

'Our riches have rotted' and our world is suffering because we in the Western world have over-indulged and misused the planet and oppressed the poor. In Nicaragua I met Father Miguel d'Escoto, who for many years was Foreign Affairs Minister for the Sandinista government. He said, 'The atmosphere in the West is toxic'—I think he meant something like this passage—our over-indulgence is destroying us. Then he added, 'There are not many Christians in the West because you keep Jesus nailed up inside you and don't live his way.' He then called on us to be 'fools for Christ' and to pursue the upside down values of Christ.

Thought and prayer

Where is Jesus in your life? Nailed up inside you or walking slightly ahead of you, leading you on a path of sacrifice that may be painful but it will also be deeply satisfying? Then pray, 'Go before me Lord... I will follow... even through the wilderness.' Amen.

GH

Walk in the light

This is the message we have heard from him and declare to you: God is light; in him there is no darkness at all. If we claim to have fellowship with him yet walk in the darkness, we lie and do not live by the truth. But if we walk in the light, as he is in the light, we have fellowship with one another, and the blood of Jesus, his Son, purifies us from all sin.

The message of Epiphany is encapsulated in one striking phrase in this reading: 'God is light.' This is the 'season of light'—the light that shone at Bethlehem is to illuminate the whole world. The star that shone for the Magi and drew them to the Saviour now shines to draw all people to him.

Jesus said that he was 'the light of the world' and he told his followers to 'let their lights shine' as reflectors of his light. But we may assume that the light of Christ is itself part of that infinite and holy light that is God himself a light in which there is 'no darkness at all'. For most of us, that raises problems! The Bible tells us that God dwells in 'light unapproachable', but sent his Son to bring that light into our world. More than that, God caused his light to 'shine in our hearts to give us the light of the knowledge of the glory of God in the face of Christ' (2 Corinthians 4:6).

The problem, in a sentence, is this: How can people like ourselves possibly receive in our hearts the blazing light of God himself? Surely our own 'inner darkness', the sin of which we are so painfully conscious, makes the very idea a blasphemy? The answer is in the rest of the passage: not by claiming that we have no sin (are without darkness), but by being forgiven through his Son Jesus. 'Living in the light' is living in relationship with the God of light, and that is only made possible by the Saviour who is himself 'the light of the world' and shed his blood to bring us 'out of darkness into his wonderful light' (1 Peter 2:9).

A prayer

God of light, help me through your Son to walk in the light and find peace through the forgiveness of my sin. Amen.

DW

23

The way to win

The proverbs of Solomon son of David, king of Israel: For learning about wisdom and instruction, for understanding words of insight, for gaining instruction in wise dealing, righteousness, justice, and equity; to teach shrewdness to the simple, knowledge and prudence to the young—Let the wise also hear and gain in learning, and the discerning acquire skill, to understand a proverb and a figure, the words of the wise and their riddles. The fear of the Lord is the beginning of knowledge; fools despise wisdom and instruction.

Last Saturday in *The Times* newspaper they set out the schools league tables. The schools whose pupils got most As came at the top of the league—and those with the least at the bottom.

Winners and losers. And it's exciting to win and disappointing to lose—or not to do as well as we'd hoped we would. But in our Western society we seem to have got our values wrong and to judge success by false criteria. The people of the ancient Middle East set great store by wisdom—which was about how to be a real winner in the game of life. Not in athletics or tennis or football, and not in the rat race of financial and social success. But how to live a good life and to be happy and fulfilled as a human being.

The Book of Proverbs is a detailed game-plan that looks at every aspect of human life—and shows us the way to live a happy life. It is about wisdom and about knowledge, but a far deeper and more profound knowledge than we need to pass exams or qualify to compete in 'Mastermind' on television. The knowledge that the Book of Proverbs teaches us starts off with the fear of the Lord, and that is the beginning of real knowledge. This knowledge is about knowing a person. About knowing the living, loving God who created us to have a relationship with him and also with all his other creatures. Human creatures in a loving relationship with their Creator and with the the whole of the creation.

A reflection

Reflect on what it means that 'the fear of the Lord is the beginning of knowledge'. Pray for a deeper awareness of the glory and the nature of God—so that you worship with delight and with awe the one who created you.

SB

Don't ignore me!

Wisdom cries out in the street; in the squares she raises her voice. At the busiest corner she cries out; at the entrance of the city gates she speaks: 'How long, O simple ones, will you love being simple? How long will scoffers delight in their scoffing and fools hate knowledge? Give heed to my reproof; I will pour out my thoughts to you; I will make my words known to you. Because I have called and you refused, have stretched out my hand and no one heeded, and because you have ignored all my counsel and would have none of my reproof, I also will laugh at your calamity; I will mock when panic strikes you . . . like a storm.'

The inspired Jewish Scriptures make Wisdom into a person—and, although they knew they spoke in symbols, the ancient Jews said that from the dawn of time God dandled two children on his knees, his Wisdom and his Word (and they knew too that God doesn't have knees). It was through wisdom that God made the worlds. Almost unbelievably, God wants to give us that same wisdom—which will transform the whole of our life—and pleads with us to listen.

We don't much like the idea of a God who laughs at us when things go horribly wrong because we refused to listen and refused the offer that God made. And the truth of the matter is that when God took human flesh he didn't laugh. He wept. Over the Jerusalem who refused to be gathered under his wings as he longed to gather her, as a hen gathers her chickens to herself to love them and protect them.

But God has given us the awesome gift of choice—and although he woos us like a lover, with all the wisdom that made the worlds at his disposal to know the best way to win us, he will never force us. If we don't want him—or wisdom—then we can live without either. Without wisdom and without God. Except that to be without God is, in the end, not to live but to die, cut off from the source of life, and to have suffered what the Book of Revelation calls 'the second death'.

A reflection

Reflect on the power of choice that God has given to us—and think about the results of making a right choice and making a sinful one.

SB

Don't be stupid!

Then they will call upon me, but I will not answer; they will seek me diligently, but they will not find me. Because they hated knowledge and did not choose the fear of the Lord, would have none of my counsel, and despised all my reproof, therefore they shall eat the fruit of their way and be sated with their own devices. For waywardness kills the simple, and the complacency of fools destroys them; but those who listen to me will be secure and will live at ease, without dread of disaster.

The best and wisest teacher in the world cannot make us learn if we don't want to. We have to have at least some thirst for knowledge—and then the knowledge has to enter into us in a way that affects our life. Really to know that fire is hot will make us wise enough not to burn ourselves—and also to be able to use it to cook with. Really to know that speed kills will mean that we don't drive too fast in the fog, in the motorway madness that causes pile-ups and kills people.

Waywardness really does kill—and a wayward person is 'disposed to go counter to the wishes or advice of others or to what is reasonable; wrong-headed, intractable, self-willed, perverse' (Shorter Oxford Dictionary). The simple people to whom Wisdom is calling out and warning to change their ways aren't simple with a childlike simplicity. They are culpably stupid. They suffer because of their stupidity and so do other people.

Yet we shouldn't despise them. We should pity them, with something of the divine pity. And align our wills with the will of God, who is continually calling out to them to change their ways. Our part of the task is to pray for them.

A way to pray

Think of the areas in your life where you are not very wise—and pray for wisdom. Then think of a person you know who is persistently stupid and simple—and pray for him, or for her. Then perhaps think of some more people who need to be prayed for in this way—and decide to commit yourself to pray for them regularly. As you pray for them, pray that God will enable you to know the pity he has for them even as he warns them and pleads with them to listen to his voice.

SB

Cry out for me!

My child, if you accept my words and treasure up my commandments within you, making your ear attentive to wisdom and inclining your heart to understanding; if you indeed cry out for insight, and raise your voice for understanding; if you seek it like silver, and search for it as for hidden treasures—then you will understand the fear of the Lord and find the knowledge of God. For the Lord gives wisdom; from his mouth come knowledge and understanding; he stores up sound wisdom for the upright; he is a shield to those who walk blamelessly, guarding the paths of justice and preserving the way of his faithful ones. Then you will understand righteousness and justice and equity, every good path . . .

In Proverbs 1 Wisdom was crying out for us to listen to her. Now she is telling us to cry out to her. Wisdom is like a relationship. It doesn't land on our laps full grown and ready made. It starts small, like a seed taking root—and we know that we want to grow the plant because we have seen it growing in other places and in other people, and it attracts us. On television recently there was a man who had a passion for fuchsias, and he had travelled to the heights of the Himalayas to search for unknown species of the plant that he loved. When we set out on that sort of search for wisdom the promise is that we shall certainly find it. But unless we really desire it we shall never set out. When God is speaking to the Jewish exiles in Babylon through the prophet Jeremiah this is what he says:

'I know the plans I have for you,' says the Lord, 'plans for your welfare and not for harm, to give you a future with hope. Then when you call upon me and come and pray to me I will hear you. When you search for me, you will find me; if you seek me with all your heart.'

Jeremiah 29:11–13

A way to pray

Spend a few moments reflecting on your own life . . . and then on the national life of your own country. Reflect on the tragic stupidity and folly of so many people. Will you commit yourself to search for wisdom, so that God can bless you and other people through you?

SB

A way of healing

My child, do not forget my teaching, but let your heart keep my commandments; for length of days and years of life and abundant welfare they will give you . . . Trust in the Lord with all your heart, and do not rely on your own insight. In all your ways acknowledge him, and he will make straight your paths. Do not be wise in your own eyes; fear the Lord, and turn away from evil. It will be a healing for your flesh and a refreshment for your body . . . My child, do not despise the Lord's discipline or be weary of his reproof, for the Lord reproves the one he loves, as a father the son in whom he delights.

In a fascinating book, *None of These Diseases*, a Christian doctor, S.I. McMillen, says how seriously we can damage our health by breaking various laws of God. The diseases we catch from sexual immorality are fairly obvious. But nasty things can happen to us when we consistently lose our temper and fly off the handle, or if we brood about the injury that someone has done to us.

If someone has not acted in a right way we don't necessarily have to let them get away with it. God promises to guide us—and Proverbs spells out the wise action for us to take. So we can trust—and obey—and remind ourself that when God tells us to do something (or not to) it really is for our good—a healing for our flesh and a refreshment for our body.

Perhaps a member of our family has behaved badly—or a bad driver has cut us up on the motorway and nearly caused an accident. If we are wise we shall be totally honest with God about our feelings—of fury, or of fear—and then pray for the other person and ourself.

Pray

Pray for a difficult member of your family, or a friend. First, that God will bless the person through the painful situation that has arisen. Then, for yourself, that God will give you the wisdom to know how to confront them, calmly and lovingly, and not smugly or in a superior way. Pray for the last bad driver you encountered (as a practice for the next one you meet!), that the Spirit of God will convict him of his sin (and dangerous driving is a serious sin).

SB

The paths of peace

Happy are those who find wisdom and those who get understanding, for her income is better than silver, and her revenue better than gold. She is more precious than jewels, and nothing can compare with her. Long life is in her right hand; in her left hand are riches and honour. Her ways are ways of pleasantness, and all her paths are peace. She is a tree of life to those who lay hold of her; those who hold her fast are called happy. The Lord by wisdom founded the earth; by understanding he established the heavens; by his knowledge the deeps broke open, and the clouds drop down the dew.

Every week in Britain the media is full of reports on the National Lottery. Sometimes no one wins the big prize, and then it accumulates and so does the desire of the gamblers for the money. Millions of gamblers—but perhaps only one big winner. And even if the big prize is shared, and even though there are a lot of much smaller prizes, not everyone wins: only a tiny percentage of the people who bought tickets.

God makes us a much better offer. Not just for a few people to win, but everyone. Everyone who listens and who wants to win the prize of wisdom and understanding, which is far better than pounds or dollars or deutschmarks. Wisdom will probably bring ordinary 'riches' along with it—because to run our lives wisely will almost always result in having enough money for all our needs (and even in difficult circumstances God promises to give us our daily bread if we pray for it).

When we have wisdom—and the only way to have it is through God, and through the indwelling of the Spirit of God—we know real happiness and a deep heart-peace. Our relationships are right and good—and day after day they get richer. Our relationship with God and our relationship with people.

A way to pray

Think about all the people who will lose their money in the National Lottery—and also about those who will win this week. Then reflect on the offer that God makes to every human being—and think about the happiness and the blessing that comes to us through wisdom. Pray for wisdom for yourself, and hold in the presence of God any particular people or situations for which you want it.

SB

Forgiveness

Peter went up to Jesus and said, 'Lord, how often must I forgive my brother if he wrongs me? As often as seven times? Jesus answered, 'Not seven, I tell you, but seventy-seven times.'

Seven is the number that symbolized perfection, so seventy-seven is surely a number that goes beyond counting. Just keep forgiving, said Jesus.

What a burden. Surely there must come a point when I can put up with injury and betrayal, deception and abuse no longer? But no, there isn't. God keeps forgiving you, so you must keep forgiving others, and there's no other option allowed.

Of course, I don't suppose for a moment that Jesus meant us to try to trust those who had proved themselves untrustworthy, or to stay with those who habitually beat us. But what he did mean is that those hurts must be written off, and no animosity carried.

There's a good reason for this, quite apart from the call to be like God (and we don't, for some strange reason, ever want God to give up on us). You see, nursing hatred hurts us a lot more than it hurts the person we hate. It makes us immune to love, it cuts others off from us and becomes a passion which consumes us. Failure to forgive should carry a government health warning.

Of course it's hard, but it becomes easier with practice. And that's the answer to the standard complaint, 'I could never forgive x', where x is the most horrendous crime imaginable. Perhaps not yet. But can you forgive the small insult, the being ignored by a friend, the thoughtless gesture that cuts to the bone? Start with these, and being like God can become a habit.

MM

The way to life

Hear, my child, and accept my words, that the years of your life may be many. I have taught you the way of wisdom; I have led you in the paths of uprightness . . . Do not enter the path of the wicked, and do not walk in the way of evildoers. Avoid it; do not go on it; turn away from it and pass on. For they cannot sleep unless they have done wrong; they are robbed of sleep unless they have made someone stumble. For they eat the bread of wickedness and drink the wine of violence. But the path of the righteous is like the light of dawn, which shines brighter and brighter until full day. The way of the wicked is like deep darkness; they do not know what they stumble over.

In a town near me there are two ways to get from the station to one of the local schools. One way is along the main road. The other is a pathway that runs between the back gardens of houses. It is much shorter, but the pupils are forbidden to take it because people have been mugged there—and what looks easy can end up being anything but. Like the two ways that Jesus talked about. The wide gate and the easy road that leads to destruction (or narrowness) and the narrow gate and the hard road that leads to life (and width and fulness).

The road to life is hard because all the time sin is advertising its wares on the hoardings along the way, and tempting and enticing us to try out its suggestions. But the way of wisdom and righteousness isn't just about resisting temptation and evil. It is about happiness and life in all its fulness—a shining happiness and the light of life, that gets brighter and brighter until we die—and then, on the other side, see the face of Christ who is the light of the world, and in whom there is no darkness at all.

A reflection

Reflect on the two ways—on the happiness of the right way and the sorrow of the wrong way. Pray that the Holy Spirit of God will give you light on your way—and reveal to you if there are any areas in your life where you are hiding away in the darkness.

SB

Death or delight?

The lips of a loose woman drip honey, and her speech is smoother than oil; but in the end she is bitter as wormwood, sharp as a two-edged sword. Her feet go down to death; her steps follow the path to Sheol. She does not keep straight to the path of life... Keep your way far from her, and do not go near the door of her house ... Drink water from your own cistern, flowing water from your own well. Should your springs be scattered abroad, streams of water in the streets? Let them be for yourself alone, and not for sharing with strangers. Let your fountain be blessed, and rejoice in the wife of your youth, a lovely deer, a graceful doe. May her breasts satisfy you at all times; may you be intoxicated always by her love. Why should you be intoxicated, my son, by another woman and embrace the bosom of an adulteress? For human ways are under the eyes of the Lord, and he examines all their paths.

Yesterday we looked at the two ways we have to choose between. Today we are looking at two women—the loose woman who is an adulteress, and the wife who is the cause of her husband's rejoicing and intoxication. Both those delights come from the satisfaction of the love-making which is the will of God. The foolish man makes love to the adulteress. The wise man makes love to his wife. When Proverbs was written everything was seen from the man's point of view. But today in the Western world we can apply the same principles to the way that a woman is to live her life. Adultery is equally wrong for man and for woman—though it has not always been seen that way. Sex is a gift of God— and he created us male and female in his own image. And the will of God for a man and woman within marriage is an intoxicating sexual relationship. The Song of Solomon spells that out in rich and sensual language.

A reflection

Spend some time reflecting on how you think about sexual love—and how you think God sees it. If there seems to be a difference of opinion—pray that you will see it God's way. And when you have half an hour to spare, read the Song of Songs and also chapter 2 of Hosea.

SB

Wisdom for all of us

Does not wisdom call, and does not understanding raise her voice? On the heights, beside the way, at the crossroads she takes her stand; beside the gates in front of the town, at the entrance of the portals she cries out: 'To you, O people, I call, and my cry is to all that live. O simple ones, learn prudence, acquire intelligence, you who lack it. Hear, for I will speak noble things, and from my lips will come what is right; for my mouth will utter truth; wickedness is an abomination to my lips. All the words of my mouth are righteous; there is nothing twisted or crooked in them. They are all straight to one who understands and right to those who find knowledge. Take my instruction instead of silver, and knowledge rather than choice gold; for wisdom is better than jewels, and all that you may desire cannot compare with her.'

God made the worlds through Wisdom, and he offers us that wisdom to run our personal and private worlds. Derek Kidner says this about Proverbs chapter 8: 'A chapter which is to soar beyond time and space opens at street-level, to make it clear, first, that the wisdom of God is as relevant to the shopping centre as to heaven itself; second, that it is available to the veriest dunce... third, that it is active in seeking us—so that our own search, earnest as it has to be, is a response, not an uncertain quest' (*Proverbs*, IVP).

The way to make the wisdom of God our own is to reflect and to pray.

A reflection

Think about your family and your friends. Be aware of any problems and difficulties. Pray for the people concerned and ask for wisdom. Think about your job (or lack of one). Reflect on the problems, and the opportunities. Pray for any people concerned and ask for wisdom. Think about your lifestyle—your diet and your drinking, your sexual behaviour, your leisure time. Pray for wisdom. Think about your spiritual life and pray that God will show you how healthy it is. Think about your prayer life, your relationship with God, your church-going, your Bible reading, the way you use your day off for renewal and refreshment or for catching up on work. Pray for wisdom to know how to live a richer spiritual life and to grow to Christian maturity.

SB

Fear God and hate evil!

The fear of the Lord is hatred of evil. Pride and arrogance and the way of evil and perverted speech I hate. I have good advice and sound wisdom; I have insight, I have strength. By me kings reign, and rulers decree what is just; by me rulers rule, and nobles, all who govern rightly. I love those who love me, and those who seek me diligently find me. Riches and honour are with me, enduring wealth and prosperity. My fruit is better than gold, even fine gold, and my yield than choice silver. I walk in the way of righteousness, along the paths of justice, endowing with wealth those who love me, and filling their treasuries.

God actively seeks to injure and overthrow evil and injustice because he hates it. So that is what we should be seeking to do as well. To be wise is to hate evil—and in order to hate it we have to be aware of it, and of those who do evil things, so that we can take whatever action is necessary to put things right. We mustn't bury our heads in the sand. God wants us to see, and to take action.

In a brilliant book, *The Psychology of Military Incompetence*, Norman Dixon analyses the performance of incompetent military leaders throughout history, and discovers that they all have one thing in common: an inability to receive new information and to process it and to act appropriately. The bad generals and commanders simply denied that the information given to them was true (and if its source was a 'lower-class' person then it couldn't possibly be true!). Thousands of soldiers died because of this evil stupidity (the total opposite of wisdom). Correct information is a necessary part of changing our life in the way that God wants it to be changed—and St Paul pre-dated *The Psychology of Military Incompetence* by nearly two thousand years: '...be transformed by the renewing of your minds' he wrote in Romans 12:2, and since our mind is something like a computer (though far more complex) that means to put some new software into the hardware and run a new program.

A prayer

Lord God, you hate everything that is evil (though you still love the evildoer). Help me to do the same—and to take action in your world to put things right.

SB

Mutual delight

The Lord created me at the beginning of his work, the first of his acts of long ago. Long ago I was set up, at the first, before the beginning of the earth. When there were no depths I was brought forth, when there were no springs abounding with water. Before the mountains had been shaped, before the hills, I was brought forth—when he had not yet made earth and fields, or the world's first bits of soil. When he established the heavens, I was there, when he drew a circle on the face of the deep, when he made firm the skies above, when he established the fountains of the deep, when he assigned to the sea its limit so that the waters might not transgress his command, when he marked out the foundations of the earth, then I was beside him like a master worker; and I was daily his delight, rejoicing before him always, rejoicing in his inhabited world and delighting in the human race.

In the soaring theological declaration of the Fourth Gospel, John writes 'In the beginning was the Word, and the Word was with God, and the Word was God. Without him was not anything made that was made . . .', and in Colossians, St Paul says that it was through Christ that 'God made the worlds . . .' So in the light of the Gospel revelation we can read this marvellous passage about the Wisdom who is the Word, the Christ of God, and discover the delight with which God made the worlds, and the delight which God has in his creation and in us. 'Delighting in the sons of men', it says—and he still delights in us, even though he often grieves over us. And the Wisdom who made the worlds will give us himself, and his own wisdom, to do our own work: to create a home, a garden, a symphony, a song, a meal, a letter, a table or a book.

A prayer

Lord Jesus Christ, you who are the power of God and the wisdom of God, give us your wisdom to remake our broken world, and to mend our broken relationships, and to know what the wisest thing is to do day by day as we live our lives in your beautiful and hurting world. Amen.

SB

Come & eat: life or death

Wisdom has built her house, she has hewn her seven pillars. She has slaughtered her animals, she has mixed her wine, she has also set her table. She has sent out her servant girls, she calls from the highest places in the town, 'You that are simple, turn in here!' To those without sense she says, 'Come, eat of my bread and drink of the wine I have mixed. Lay aside immaturity, and live, and walk in the way of insight . . .' The foolish woman is loud; she is ignorant and knows nothing. She sits at the door of her house, on a seat at the high places of the town, calling to those who pass by, who are going straight on their way, 'You who are simple, turn in here!' And to those without sense she says, 'Stolen water is sweet, and bread eaten in secret is pleasant.' But they do not know that the dead are there, that her guests are in the depths of Sheol.

It isn't that Wisdom doesn't offer an invitation to brilliant, intelligent and important people, and to the 'establishment' and the rulers of the land. But the invitation and the offer is to everyone. Two women offer two totally different invitations: the wise woman offers life, and the foolish woman offers death. The power of the feminine can attract—to the heights or to the depths. The invitation of Wisdom is to a feast of bread and wine, and those who eat it are alive with the life of God, growing up to Christian maturity, and knowing a deep heart-wisdom. The other woman also offers her guests a meal, but it is a clandestine affair in the darkness that doesn't want the light to shine on it. This meal and this way lead to death and destruction.

A reflection

Imagine a house built on seven pillars— on the teaching of Wisdom who is Christ. All of us who live in that house are blessedly happy (even if often we are sorrowful) because we are alive with the life of God. We can know how to live our lives, because Christ, who is the power of God and the wisdom of God, lives in us, just as we live in him. And in the safety of that house we are growing up to maturity, and to the measure of the stature of the fulness of Christ.

SB

He still eats with sinners

[Jesus] went away to the lake-side. All the crowd came to him, and he taught them there. As he went along, he saw Levi son of Alphaeus at his seat in the custom-house, and said to him, 'Follow me'; and Levi rose and followed him. When Jesus was at table in his house, many bad characters—tax-gatherers and others—were seated with him and his disciples; for there were many who followed him. Some doctors of the law who were Pharisees noticed him eating in this bad company, and said to his disciples, 'He eats with tax-gatherers and sinners!' Jesus heard it and said to them, 'It is not the healthy that need a doctor, but the sick; I did not come to invite virtuous people, but sinners.'

Jesus still eats at his table with sinners. At every service of holy communion we always confess our sins before we eat the bread and wine of the sacrament. The self-righteous have no place at the Lord's table. We always come as sinners— although forgiven sinners—and at the heart of our sinfulness is our failure to love. Someone hurts us or, even worse, hurts someone we love. Then we have to struggle with the pain and try to forgive and to love.

We may not have done many 'things which we ought not to have done', but we have almost certainly left undone a large number of 'those things which we ought to have done'. To take just one example, two-thirds of the world is full of hungry people—while our third of it struggles to lose weight. The problem seems so enormous that we want to turn away from it because we just don't know what we can do. But the risen Christ at whose table we eat and drink is also the source of all wisdom—and if we ask he will give us the wisdom to know what we *can* do.

'Follow me!' he said to Levi, and Levi did—one step at a time along the way, following the one who is the life and the truth and the way. So when we come to the table in the house of God we can pray first of all in deep thankfulness that he invites us to come, that he forgives our sins, and that that he feeds us with himself. Then we can pray, 'Lord, what would you have me to do?'—and know that he will certainly tell us.

SB

A special greeting

Paul, an apostle of Jesus Christ by the command of God our Saviour and of Jesus Christ our hope, To Timothy my true son in the faith: Grace, mercy and peace from God the Father and Christ Jesus our Lord.

If I, called Rosemary, were to open a letter and find it addressed 'Dear Judy,' signed by someone I had never met, I would think twice about reading it! But if Judy passes me her letter, saying, 'Read this,' I should not only want to read it, but also to know something about the writer, about why it was written and whether it had anything of particular interest to me. So let's investigate the opening words of Paul's letter to Timothy, a letter which has been passed to us to read.

Paul, the ex-Pharisee, used to be number one enemy of Jesus and exterminator of Christians. Now Paul is an apostle, ranked among those who had been constantly with Jesus for the last three years on earth, dedicated to serve God his saviour. What an amazing change! 'Through Christ', no longer his enemy but his *hope*. In Christian language, hope is not a word of vague desire but of confident expectation for the future.

'To Timothy, my true son in the faith.' Timothy had grown up in a godly home where he had learnt the scriptures from the time he was a small boy; his father was a Gentile, his mother a Christian Jewess. He probably became a Christian when Paul was first in his home town of Lystra (in eastern Turkey); and on Paul's second visit, Paul heard Timothy highly recommended and decided to take him along as companion and helper. The relationship was a warm one ('my true son in the faith'; 'my dear son' in 2 Timothy 1:2) and, as they travelled, Timothy grew in experience and responsibility. This letter was apparently written when he had been left in charge of the church in Ephesus.

'Grace, mercy and peace.' What encouraging words they are to wish on the recipient of any letter!

To think over

Choose one phrase from today's reading or one thought from today's notes that you want to remember. Chew over it for a few minutes; then pray 'Lord, thank you for that thought. May it seep right through into my life.'

RG

Transformed by grace

I thank Jesus Christ our Lord, who has given me strength, that he considered me faithful, appointing me to his service. Even though I was once a blasphemer and a persecutor and a violent man, I was shown mercy because I acted in ignorance and unbelief. The grace of our Lord was poured out on me abundantly, along with the faith and love that are in Christ Jesus.

Paul describes his old self in strong terms. 'I was a blasphemer... a persecutor... the worst of sinners.' That makes him all the more aware of God's goodness and generosity. 'I was shown mercy... The grace of the Lord was poured out on me abundantly...' Paul knew he didn't deserve God's grace, a free, totally unmerited gift. Grace is a hard word to grasp, because we experience little of it in everyday life. 'Free gift' says the advert—but not so free when we read the small print! In relation to God we often tend to believe either that, 'My own bit of goodness deserves God's favour,' or else, 'I'm not good enough for God to want me.' Both attitudes are wrong! God says to us, 'No, you're not good enough. No one but Jesus will ever be good enough. But I love you anyway. So open your heart to receive my generous love—receive *me*.'

I do some pastoral counselling; 'prayer counselling' we call it—not merely a one-to-one relationship, but with God there, linking us in a triangle. I encourage the person seeking help to talk to God about the difficulty and ask him how he wants to help. Amazingly often, the person has a mental picture while praying, a picture of Jesus standing in front with outstretched arms. The meaning is clear, without words. He says, 'Come—come to me as you are. "Come to me, all you who are weary and burdened, and I will give you rest"' (Matthew 11:28). However painful or disgraceful the burden, he wants to carry it. *That* is grace!

John Newton was a man who discovered the meaning of God's grace when he was in the slave trade. We can use the words of his hymn as a prayer:

Amazing grace! How sweet the sound
That saved a wretch like me.
I once was lost, but now am found,
Was blind, but now I see.

RG

Mercy for sinners

Here is a trustworthy saying that deserves full acceptance: Christ Jesus came into the world to save sinners—of whom I am the worst. But for that very reason I was shown mercy so that in me, the worst of sinners, Christ Jesus might display his unlimited patience as an example for those who would believe on him and receive eternal life.

'Here is a trustworthy saying.' Paul uses the phrase three times in this letter. If the statement to follow 'deserves full acceptance' it certainly deserves our careful consideration!

Few of us share the suddenness of Paul's conversion through his dramatic meeting with the risen Jesus on the road to Damascus, and we may not see the changes in ourselves as starkly as he did. How would you tell the story of your own journey of faith? What changes has Jesus made in your life? How has the Lord become real to you?

In my own life I had a good, traditional church background; baptized as a baby, regular churchgoing as a child (I see it as 'One Sunday on, one Sunday off!'). At boarding school there were chapel services twice a day and I was confirmed, voluntarily, when I was fourteen. But four years later I realized I was not the 'goody goody' I thought I was; I saw myself instead like a shiny apple with one just bad spot on the outside; only slightly blemished, you think, until you cut it open and find the maggots inside! So then I understood that Jesus came into the world, not just to save other sinners but to save me. I needed to ask for forgiveness and invite his Spirit into my life. That was my real start with Christ, forty-three years ago (and I know the date!). Since then there have been plenty of ups and downs—I have found the hard times the most influential in discovering more of God and in spring-cleaning my own life.

A prayer

Thank you, Lord, for your mercy and patience towards me. I don't deserve it; but I thank you for wanting to forgive me, to make yourself real to me and to give me your eternal life.

RG

God's purposes

I urge, then, first of all, that requests, prayers, intercession and thanksgiving be made for everyone—for kings and all those in authority, that we may live peaceful and quiet lives in all godliness and holiness. This is good, and pleases God our Saviour, who wants all men to be saved and to come to a knowledge of the truth. For there is one God and one mediator between God and men, the man Christ Jesus, who gave himself as a ransom for all men—the testimony given in its proper time. And for this purpose I was appointed a herald and an apostle—I am telling the truth, I am not lying—and a teacher of the true faith to the Gentiles.

Paul gives us plentiful food for thought in a few verses! I find four strands to pick out today. Our prayers—the intercessions in the Anglican liturgy take Paul's urging seriously. What about our private prayers? I suggest that sometimes, after reading the newspaper or watching the TV news, we spend a few minutes talking to God about the items we have read or seen. God's purposes—so great is his love that 'he sent his one and only Son into the world that we might live through him . . . he loved us and sent his Son as an atoning sacrifice for our sins' (1 John 4:9–10). He longs that everyone should come to know Jesus, who said of himself 'I am the way and the truth and the life' (John 14:6). Christ's place— Paul tells us clearly that Christ is the only mediator between God and people. We can picture the arms of the cross stretched out as a bridge wide enough to span the gulf between a holy God and sinful humans, a bridge we can cross. For in his life he came, not only to serve but 'to give his life as a ransom' (Mark 10:45) that through his death we might live. Paul's proclamation—Paul was thrilled to be herald, apostle and teacher, with the privilege of telling people the good news about Jesus.

An aid to worship

Jesus my Redeemer,
Name above all names,
Precious Lamb of God, Messiah,
O for sinners slain.

Melody Green

RG

The leader's character

Here is a trustworthy saying: If anyone sets his heart on being an overseer, he desires a noble task. Now the overseer must be above reproach, the husband of but one wife, temperate, self-controlled, respectable, hospitable, able to teach, not given to drunkenness, not violent but gentle, not quarrelsome, not a lover of money. He must manage his own family well and see that his children obey him with proper respect. (If anyone does not know how to manage his own family, how can he take care of God's church?) He must not be a recent convert, or he may become conceited and fall under the same judgment as the devil. He must also have a good reputation with outsiders, so that he will not fall into disgrace and into the devil's trap... In the same way, their wives are to be women worthy of respect, not malicious talkers but temperate and trustworthy in everything.

What would Paul have looked for if he were a selector at a conference to choose candidates for ordination training? Here are some of the questions he would ask: Is the person respected in the community? Is the spouse reliable and trustworthy? What impression do you have of the family life? Is it a hospitable home? What about his/her Christian maturity, character and relationships? And his/her attitudes to material possessions? Is there an ability to communicate the faith convincingly and comprehensibly?

As you read the characteristics listed here, think about the leader of your own congregation (vicar, minister or whatever title he or she has in your particular church!) Ponder the person's strengths and weaknesses—not to lead into destructive criticism, but to stimulate constructive intercession (remembering that there may be circumstances in the minister's life of which we are oblivious.) Give thanks to God for your leaders. Pray for as many aspects of their busy lives as you know about.

To think over

How can I express my appreciation to my minister? In what ways could I help?

RG

A living faith

This is a trustworthy saying that deserves full acceptance (and for this we labour and strive), that we have put our hope in the living God, who is the Saviour of all men, and especially of those who believe. Command and teach these things. Don't let anyone look down on you because you are young, but set an example to the believers in speech, in life, in love, in faith and in purity.

This is the third 'trustworthy saying' in this letter (see Wednesday and Friday). Let us look carefully at the key words. He is the *living* God, as vital and active in the world now as he was in creation, for Moses, for Elijah or for the apostles. This God is compassionate and powerful, described by Moses as 'a faithful God who does no wrong' (Deuteronomy 32:4). The *Saviour of all men* is the God who 'so loved that he gave his one and only Son, that whoever believes in him shall not perish but have eternal life' (John 3:16). God loves all people. He gave his Son to live and die for all people. But it is *those who believe* who find the reality of God as Saviour. This is the God in whom we put our *hope*, in whom we can rest our confidence.

This truth, which is the heart of the gospel, is exciting news. No wonder that Paul exhorted Timothy to command and teach these things! I pray that more of us, whether we are in the pulpit or the pew, may share both Paul's assurance and his excitement—to know the living God and to tell others about him.

Youth or maturity—both have their advantages and their disadvantanges!

But whether old or young, our behaviour and character win either respect or disapproval. Speech, life, love, faith, purity—that gives us a pretty comprehensive checklist. Pause to think about each of these words. Who we are and how we live: these are the tests we must pass if other people are going to listen to what we say about our faith.

For prayer

Ask the living God to increase your confidence in him. Talk to him about your 'speech, life, love, faith and purity', and ask him to show you what changes he wants to make.

RG

Words that feed us

Then Jesus was led up by the Spirit into the wilderness to be tempted by the devil. And he fasted forty days and forty nights, and afterward he was hungry. And the tempter came and said to him, 'If you are the Son of God, command these stones to become loaves of bread.' But he answered, 'It is written, "man shall not live by bread alone, but by every word that proceeds from the mouth of God."'

Many of us have developed our cooking skills to a fine art, and we can produce delicious and satisfying meals. Meals that satisfy our taste buds and our stomachs but not the hunger of our souls. 'Why do you spend your money for that which is not bread, and your labour for that which does not satisfy?' asks God through the prophet Isaiah, 'Hearken diligently to me, and eat what is good, and delight yourself in fatness' (Isaiah 55:2) .

Jesus knew that there was a far more important hunger than ordinary food could ever satisfy. He knew the profound satisfaction of that inner hunger when he did the will of God. After he had been talking to the Samaritan woman at Jacob's well his disciples (who had come back from their shopping expedition to buy food) said to him, 'Master, eat!'. But Jesus was eating food that wasn't physical food, and he said to them, 'I have food to eat of which you do not know' (John 4:32) .

Jesus countered the temptations of the evil one by quoting the Old Testament scriptures. But the words that proceed from the mouth of God are not only written words. There is a sense in which the whole world 'proceeds out of the mouth of God'. It came into being when he 'spoke', and he is still 'upholding the universe by his word of power' (Hebrews 1:3) . When we become aware of that we shall know a new delight and satisfaction in the way the world is, and discover a deeper knowledge of the nature of God even in the suffering of the world, because we have a suffering and a self-giving God.

And as we adore and worship Jesus, the living Word of God, who became flesh and dwelt among us, we shall be satisfied in the depth of our being, as we feed on God himself.

SB

Feeding the faithful

Until I come, devote yourself to the public reading of Scripture, to preaching and to teaching. Do not neglect your gift, which was given you through a prophetic message, when the body of elders laid their hands on you. Be diligent in these matters; give yourself wholly to them, so that everyone may see your progress. Watch your life and doctrine closely. Persevere in them, because if you do, you will save both yourself and your hearers.

Imagine the scene. Paul, Timothy and a group of church leaders praying together. The Holy Spirit gives one of them a clear message. So Timothy kneels in the middle of the circle while they lay their hands on him and pray for the Spirit to equip him. This scene is repeated in many of our churches today where there is expectant faith in the living God and in the Spirit's activity.

What was this 'gift' that Timothy received? I suspect that he was given a special ability in teaching Scripture. We need to understand the Bible, not merely for intellectual stimulus but so that our faith is nourished and our lifestyle moulded. 'Be diligent in these matters.' This is the only way to counteract the false teaching, prevalent in the first century and in the twentieth.

Nowadays our congregations are often fed with 'sermonettes' which do little to teach the Bible as God's truth to be grasped at depth and made relevant for our lives. Would you give your family a McDonald's burger for Sunday lunch—and no more food for a week? Of course not! If your church does not have a mid-week Bible study, could you start one? Even if there is no obvious leader, look for two or three others to meet in a home. Use one of the many available Bible-discussion guides (or even *New Daylight*; 'What has each of us learnt this week? Let's look at a bit more together ...')

A prayer

Blessed Lord, who caused all holy Scriptures to be written for our learning; help us so to hear them, to read, mark, learn and inwardly digest them, that, through patience, and the comfort of your holy word, we may embrace, and for ever hold fast the hope of everlasting life, which you have given us in our Saviour Jesus Christ. Amen.

RG

Caring for the vulnerable

Give proper recognition to those widows who are really in need. But if a widow has children or grandchildren, these should learn first of all to put their religion into practice by caring for their own family and so repaying their parents and grandparents, for this is pleasing to God. The widow who is really in need and left all alone puts her hope in God and continues night and day to pray and ask God for help. But the widow who lives for pleasure is dead even while she lives. Give the people these instructions, too, so that no-one may be open to blame. If anyone does not provide for his relatives, and especially for his immediate family, he has denied the faith and is worse than an unbeliever.

There was no welfare state in Paul's day! But—as so often down the centuries—the church was in the forefront in social action. Paul had thought out the principles carefully. He was concerned that there should be provision for those who really needed it; but he was also anxious that help from the church should not lead to an evasion of responsibility, either on the part of younger relatives (children and grandchildren in particular) or on the part of the widows themselves. His main concern here is that care should be undertaken by family members, as a way of expressing appreciation for the widows' past care for their families. How sad it is in our day when the elderly are ignored, and not given either practical or emotional support, even by their own offspring. Caring love is a mark of God's character and pleases him; ignoring the elderly is a mark of ungodliness.

'No widow may be put on the list of widows unless she is over sixty...' we read a little further on. Paul feared that those who were younger would squander their lives if they had no home responsibilities. There was, of course, no decent employment for a woman in those days. The temptation would be for prostitution as a means of support—that may well be what he means by 'living for pleasure'. Paul advocated re-marriage or practical service in the church as right alternatives in the society of his day.

For reflection

Social conditions have changed considerably in nineteen centuries. How are Paul's guidelines relevant in our own culture?

RG

Advice for employees

All who are under the yoke of slavery should consider their masters worthy of full respect, so that God's name and our teaching may not be slandered. Those who have believing masters are not to show less respect for them because they are brothers. Instead, they are to serve them even better, because those who benefit from their service are believers, and dear to them.

It would be seventeen centuries before William Wilberforce's vigorous campaign against the slave trade, and two centuries more before the end of apartheid in South Africa. In the first century, slavery was a deeply rooted part of the social system. Slaves were at the very bottom of the social ladder; in many homes they were treated little better than the cattle. But in Christ 'there is neither Jew nor Greek, slave nor free, male nor female' (Galatians 3:28). So in the Church they enjoyed equality of status, and there was a new bond of relationship between slave and master. But, says Paul, even if you meet your master in church on Sunday (or any other day!) you are not therefore to be casual in your work for him on Monday. Rather, out of your love and respect for him you can work even more diligently.

And what advice does Paul offer to the Christian slave with a non-Christian master? Even if you cannot respect your master for his beliefs or his behaviour, work in a way that honours God and commends him. Peter spells out this situation very clearly. 'Slaves, submit yourselves to your masters with all respect, not only to those who are good and considerate, but also to those who are harsh' (1 Peter 2:18). He goes on to show how Christ set us an example in receiving unjust treatment. I found Peter's words like a rope to hold me when I was a new Christian. My mother was *furious* with me for giving evidence in court against her careless driving. I read, 'When they hurled their insults at him [Jesus], he did not retaliate; when he suffered, he made no threats. Instead, he entrusted himself to him who judges justly' (1 Peter 2:23).

To think over

What difference does it make to our behaviour and relationships when we meet people in different contexts—for example, customer and shop assistant one day, in church or at a party the next?

RG

Beware!

If anyone teaches false doctrines and does not agree to the sound instruction of our Lord Jesus Christ and to godly teaching, he is conceited and understands nothing. He has an unhealthy interest in controversies and quarrels about words that result in envy, strife, malicious talk, evil suspicions and constant friction between men of corrupt mind, who have been robbed of the truth and who think that godliness is a means to financial gain.

Three times in this letter Paul warns Timothy of the danger of false teaching; in fact, it is the first topic he tackles after his opening greeting. 'Command certain men not to teach false doctrines any longer nor to devote themselves to myths and endless genealogies' (1:3–4); and later, 'The Spirit clearly says that in later times some will abandon the faith and follow deceiving spirits...' (4:1). On Monday we read Paul's plea to Timothy that Scripture should be pre-eminent in his teaching and in his life. It is when we fail to have biblical foundations for belief and behaviour—as, sadly, the church has often failed—that we fall prey to the false teachers who ignore, misinterpret or disobey God's 'sound instruction'. The Moonies; the Mormons; scientology; the 'New Age' movement; the community in Waco, Texas that hit the headlines last year: these are among the errors we have seen in the last decade.

Look at some of the consequences listed here if we do not submit to God's teaching. We see pride—without anything to be proud about! We see a desire to pick quarrels over minutiae. And it leads to the sectarianism that must cause deep grief to the heart of the One who prayed: 'Sanctify them by the truth; your word is truth...I pray also for those who will believe in me through their message, that all of them may be one...May they be brought to complete unity to let the world know that you sent me...' (John 17:17, 20–21, 23)

A prayer

O God, we pray that our Church leaders may expound your truth, and that they may set examples of godly lives for us to follow. And Lord, please show me the ways in which I am ignoring or disobeying your truth. Through Jesus Christ my Lord. Amen.

RG

The king of peace

When [Jesus] came in sight of the city, he wept over it and said, 'If only you had known, on this great day, the way that leads to peace! But no; it is hidden from your sight. For a time will come upon you, when your enemies will set up siege-works against you; they will encircle you and hem you in at every point; they will bring you to the ground, you and your children within your walls, and not leave you one stone standing on another, because you did not recognise God's moment when it came.'

Things have hardly changed, have they? Couldn't Jesus still stand overlooking Jerusalem, and weep for its possible violent fate? And if not Jerusalem, then Sarajevo, or Aden, or any one of a dozen cities in a score of war-torn lands which stretch around the world as I write. By the time you read this, the names of the cities may have changed again, but the despairing cry remains the same: 'If only you had known the way that leads to peace!'

Of course, Jesus was not just speaking of more sensible politics; the way that led to peace was the one that he was bringing. Shortly he would ride into Jerusalem on the donkey of peace, and proclaim for all to see that he was the king. (A king who came to a city in peace rode on a donkey; if he came in battle he rode on a war-horse.) But the king of peace would be crucified, and a generation later Jerusalem would fall in fire and blood to vengeful Roman legions.

Yet that was not the end. The apparent defeat of Jesus, the triumph of violence, led to the defeat of death. Yet even knowing the inevitability of his rejection, and the salvation it would make possible, Jesus wept over Jerusalem, and no doubt weeps still over the futility of human strife.

So in your prayers take time to weep with those who mourn, and to grieve over the folly of human sin, joining with the tears of Christ. But do not despair; for out of the ashes of human violence, God still can bring the victory of life and love, and the salvation bought for us by the king of peace.

MM

A strange judgment

The oracle that the prophet Habakkuk saw. O Lord, how long shall I cry for help, and you will not listen? Or cry to you 'Violence!' and you will not save? Why do you make me see wrong-doing and look at trouble? Destruction and violence are before me; strife and contention arise. So the law becomes slack and justice never prevails. The wicked surround the righteous therefore judgment comes forth perverted. Look at the nations, and see! Be astonished! Be astounded! For a work is being done in your days that you would not believe if you were told. For I am rousing the Chaldeans, that fierce and impetuous nation, who march through the breadth of the earth to seize dwellings not their own.

Habakkuk was a man of prayer and of vision. He looked at the world around him and he prayed passionately to God to help him to understand what was happening. It seems that Habakkuk prophesied between 609 and 597BC. King Josiah (one of the good kings of Israel) had died, and the reforms he had made had fizzled out. Pagan elements were corrupting the pure worship of God, and public morality was almost non-existent. Israel was turning away from her God. Sin, immorality and injustice were everywhere and the government in power was slack and indolent. The whole nation was in a state of religious, moral and political decline.

Habakkuk had been crying out to God about the whole situation yet God didn't seem to be answering. Perhaps we know something of what the prophet felt like as we have prayed for some agonizing situation in our own lives, the lives of people whom we love, or in the world. Why doesn't God intervene? Why doesn't he heal the sickness—of the person or of the nation? Why doesn't he strike down the wicked and violent men who are destroying people's lives and possessions? Why?

Then the answer comes from God to his prophet—but Habakkuk can hardly believe it. A godless nation is going to conquer the nation which is God's people—and this is the judgment of God. The corruption, immorality and rank injustice of the people of God would be the cause of their decline— and in the end those evils always lead to the downfall of a nation.

A way to pray

Think of the state of your nation, and your church, and pray accordingly.

SB

He sees everything

They all come for violence, with faces pressing forward; they gather captives like sand. At kings they scoff, and of rulers they make sport. They laugh at every fortress, and heap up earth to take it. Then they sweep by like the wind; they transgress and become guilty; their own might is their god! Are you not from old, O Lord my God, my Holy One? You shall not die. O Lord, you have marked them for judgment; and you, O Rock, have established them for punishment. Your eyes are too pure to behold evil, and you cannot look on wrongdoing; why do you look on the treacherous, and are silent when the wicked swallow those more righteous than they?

Habakkuk sees a people who are arrogant and utterly self-confident. Instead of worshipping the living God they worship their own might—yet the God who created them does nothing to stop it. They are his chosen instruments of judgment on his chosen people, who are also guilty of a failure in worship—and the people of God have no excuse for their actions.

The prophet Jeremiah was a contemporary of Habakkuk, and God speaks out through him against what is happening in the nation and says what he is going to do. ' "… I will stretch out my hand against the inhabitants of the land," says the Lord. "For from the least to the greatest of them, every one is greedy for unjust gain; from prophet to priest, every one deals falsely." '

Two thousand years ago, in between us and Habakkuk, Christ came into our world so for us there is a deeper knowledge of the nature of God. Habakkuk says that the eyes of God are 'too pure to behold evil', and that God 'cannot look on wrongdoing' . Yet he does look at it even though it grieves him to the depths of his holiness. In the end it broke his heart. And when the Word became flesh and dwelt among us God 'made him to be sin for us, who knew no sin, so that in him we might become the righteousness of God' (2 Corinthians 5:21) .

Perhaps today we are so aware of the vastness of the love and the mercy of God that we forget the awfulness and the horror of evil and sin.

A prayer

Lord God, please show me sin as you see it. Amen.

SB

Looking and watching

I will stand at my watchpost, and station myself on the rampart; I will keep watch to see what he will say to me, and what he will answer concerning my complaint. Then the Lord answered me and said: Write the vision; make it plain on tablets, so that a runner may read it. For there is still a vision for the appointed time; it speaks of the end, and does not lie. If it seems to tarry, wait for it; it will surely come, it will not delay. Look at the proud! Their spirit is not right in them, but the righteous live by their faith.

Recently I flew from Cyprus to England on a beautiful clear day and I had a window seat. As I kept looking down I saw the sea, then the great land mass of Europe, with the Swiss lakes and the Alps. Finally, we crossed the Channel and the white cliffs of Dover, and as we dropped down to land at Gatwick we flew over the little green fields and towns of Southern England. When I look out of my window now I can see just a small range of hills, and three small fields.

If we are going to understand the plans and purposes of God we need to see with a world vision and to do what Habakkuk did. 'I will stand on my watchpost . . . and watch, to see what he will say to me.' When we can manage to look at things from God's point of view we see differently. We see things in the light of eternity. We see that this life is very short and that that life goes on for ever. So that although this life is vitally important, it is only a small part of the whole.

God tells his anguished and praying prophet to write down what he says to him so plainly that anyone can read it just as a jogger will see the big words on a poster while running past. The vision that Habakkuk sees forms the rest of his prophecy and the bottom line of it is that whatever happens or doesn't happen 'the righteous live by their faith'—their utter confidence in the nature of the God in whom they have put their trust.

Reflect

We know that God works all things together for good with those who love him.

Romans 8:28

SB

Look out!

'Alas for you who build a town by bloodshed, and found a city on iniquity!' Is it not from the Lord of hosts that peoples labour only to feed the flames, and nations weary themselves for nothing? But the earth will be filled with the knowledge of the glory of the Lord, as the waters cover the sea. 'Alas for you who make your neighbours drink, pouring out your wrath until they are drunk, in order to gaze on their nakedness!' You will be sated with contempt instead of glory. Drink, you yourself, and stagger! The cup in the Lord's right hand will come round to you, and shame will come upon your glory! For the violence done to Lebanon will overwhelm you; the destruction of the animals will terrify you because of human bloodshed and violence to the earth, to cities and all who live in them.

'Alas for you', Habakkuk is saying, and in the original the word 'Alas', or 'Woe', is a warning of future sorrow. Jesus also warned of future sorrow and judgment, and in Luke's Gospel he speaks of woes as well as blessings in his Sermon on the Plain. A woe is 'a condition of deep suffering from misfortune, affliction, or grief; ruinous trouble' (Webster's Dictionary) and Habakkuk is warning of the judgment of God on those who hurt their fellow human beings.

If we take away the dignity of another person, the woe that lies ahead for us is that our dignity and our reputation will be taken away. Not immediately, but inevitably unless we see what we are doing and repent. Habakkuk's words could have been written about more than one nation in the Western world. In her commentary *Wrath and Mercy*, Maria Eszenyei Szeles writes: 'Debauchery and drunken orgies that know no bounds are one way to reveal what the good life and success can lead to. In such a situation the "big shot", in giving a party, goes to excess and ensures that his guests become drunk. He gets them to discard their clothes and rape one another. The word *hemah* means excitement, anger, erotic passion, sexual stimulation. Here we have a prophetic judgment upon demoralization' (page 40).

We may not like this bluntness. But the Bible treats things as they are—not as we would like them to be.

To think about

Do you believe that God will judge evil if the evildoer does not repent? When a person sins, who is responsible?

SB

Who do you worship?

What use is an idol once its maker has shaped it—a cast image, a teacher of lies? For its maker trusts in what has been made, though the product is only an idol that cannot speak! Alas for you who say to the wood, 'Wake up!' to silent stone, 'Rouse yourself!' Can it teach? See, it is gold and silver plated, and there is no breath in it at all. But the Lord is in his holy temple; let all the earth keep silence before him!

We put our trust either in the living God who creates all things or in something which has been created. God is the living, mighty God, who is the Lord of life. We in the Western world are too sophisticated to bow down to gold-plated idols of wood but we have other false gods, and right at the top of the list is money, or what the Bible calls mammon.

In the Sermon on the Mount Jesus said that 'No one can serve two masters; for either he will hate the one and love the other, or he will be devoted to the one and despise the other. You cannot serve God and mammon' (Matthew 6:24).

The Scottish Bible commentator William Barclay says that originally 'mamon was the wealth which a man entrusted to someone to keep safe for him. But as the years went on mamon came to mean, not that which is entrusted, but that in which a man puts his trust'. And surely, says Barclay, 'there is no better description of a man's god, than to say that his god is the power in whom he trusts;' and when a man puts his trust in material things, then material things have become not his support, but his god' (*The Gospel of Matthew*, The Daily Study Bible, The Saint Andrew Press, 1975, page 249).

A reflection and a prayer

Think about your own attitude to money and to material things. How much trust do you put in them for your happiness? Then think about God in his glory and pray.

A prayer of Habakkuk the prophet, according to Shigionoth.

O Lord, I have heard the report of thee, and thy work, O Lord, do I fear. In the midst of the years renew it; in the midst of the years make it known; in wrath remember mercy.

Habakkuk 3:1–2 (RSV)

SB

I will rejoice!

I hear, and I tremble within; my lips quiver at the sound. Rottenness enters into my bones, and my steps tremble beneath me. I wait quietly for the day of calamity to come upon the people who attack us. Though the fig tree does not blossom, and no fruit is on the vines; though the produce of the olive fails and the fields yield no food; though the flock is cut off from the fold and there is no herd in the stalls, yet I will rejoice in the Lord; I will exult in the God of my salvation. God, the Lord, is my strength; he makes my feet like the feet of a deer, and makes me tread upon the heights.

Early in my Christian life I read and loved a book called *Hind's Feet In High Places*. The title comes from the Authorized Version of that last verse: 'He makes my feet like hind's feet: he makes me to walk upon my high places.' The book was an allegory. The Shepherd had called Much-Afraid to go on a journey, and given her two companions to help her called Sorrow and Suffering. When she was desperate on the journey she called to the Shepherd, who came bounding down the mountain to help her. But on the way to the heights he asked her permission to extract out of her heart her deep desire for a husband (in the next book by the same author Much-Afraid married the man she loved, but she had to give him up first).

It seems that if we want anything, or anyone, too much, then God has to extract the desire like the pus of an abscess, because if it is allowed to remain it will harm us. Jesus didn't say to everyone he met, 'Sell what you have and give to the poor': only to the rich young ruler, because that desire and love had to be cut out of his heart if he was really to follow Jesus.

Whatever our human desolation and disappointment, we can rejoice and exult in the God of our salvation because of the God he is. When Much-Afraid arrived at the High Places, Sorrow and Suffering were transformed into Grace and Glory.

A prayer

Make my feet like hind's feet, Lord, and make me tread upon the heights. Amen.

SB

The way to life

This section starts with *Forgiveness* (on Sunday) and *The danger of busy religion* (on Monday), when Jesus takes a whip and drives the money changers out of the temple courts in Jerusalem. It ends over Holy Week and Easter with *God: Good Shepherd & Paschal Lamb.*

These are the weeks that run up to Easter through Lent—and for the first five of them David Winter takes us through chapters 2 to 14 of the Gospel of John, with Jesus telling his disciples that he is going to prepare a place for them, and that when he has done that he will come to them again and take them to be with him, 'so that where I am there you may be also'.

As ever, Thomas asks Jesus the crunch question: 'Lord, we don't know where you're going. How can we know the way.' The answer is that 'I am the way, the truth, and the life.' But the way to life is through death. So to prepare for the death we look at Lamentations, used since the earliest days of Christianity in the prayers of Holy Week. But Henry Wansbrough takes us through them in the week before Holy Week. Then (with me) we look at the nature of God-in-Christ: the good shepherd, who lays down his life for his sheep; the Lamb of God who takes away the sin of the world; and, at the heart of that revelation, on Easter Sunday—and for all eternity—'the Lamb upon the throne.'

Forgiveness

Jesus said, 'There was a man who had two sons. The younger of them said to his father, "Father, give me the share of the property that will belong to me." So he divided his property between them. A few days later the younger son gathered all he had and travelled to a distant country, and there he squandered his property in dissolute living. When he had spent everything, a severe famine took place throughout that country, and he began to be in need. So he went and hired himself out to one of the citizens of that country, who sent him to his fields to feed the pigs. He would gladly have filled himself with the pods that the pigs were eating; and no one gave him anything. But when he came to himself he said, "How many of my father's hired hands have bread enough and to spare, but here I am dying of hunger! I will get up and go to my father, and say, 'Father, I have sinned against heaven and before you; I am no longer worthy to be called your son; treat me like one of your hired hands.'" So he set off and went to his father . . .'

And of course, we know the outcome of the story; how his father ran to meet him and celebrated his return with joy. If there was only one parable that we could keep, it would surely be this one. And how we need its message.

Over the last few months, I have come to realize how many people in my church are hurt, and have hurt others. Many have committed serious sins, and are wracked with guilt. Others feel trapped in sins and are lost and confused. And I must admit I often feel that way myself.

And then the temptation is to say: I'll stay away from church until I get sorted out, or until I feel better. It rarely happens. Because the one thing that is really needed is forgiveness and the reassurance of love.

So Jesus gives us the story of the lost son. A reminder that God watches for our return, and is ready to reclothe us and celebrate; to restore our lost self-esteem and heal our damage with his love.

And it is no cheap forgiveness either. It does not ignore the pain and hurt and humiliation; but instead it takes that burden onto itself, for Jesus is our forgiveness made flesh, and in that flesh has borne our pains.

MM

The danger of busy religion

When it was almost time for the Jewish Passover, Jesus went up to Jerusalem. In the temple courts he found men selling cattle, sheep and doves, and others sitting at tables exchanging money. So he made a whip out of cords, and drove all from the temple area, both sheep and cattle; he scattered the coins of the money-changers and overturned their tables. To those who sold doves he said, 'Get these out of here! How dare you turn my Father's house into a market!' His disciples remembered that it is written, 'Zeal for your house will consume me.'

This is a strange and exciting incident in the life of Jesus one of the few recorded in all four Gospels. John puts it at the start of Jesus' ministry, marking out his priorities, as it were.

The money-changers were exchanging ordinary coins for temple currency, which could be used for religious purposes, and the salesmen were providing animals and birds for the sacrifices. So it could be said that they were providing a necessary service. But the overall effect (certainly as Jesus saw it) was to 'turn my Father's house into a market'.

The disciples remembered some words from Psalm 69: 'Zeal for your house will consume me.' And that seems to sum up the situation. For Jesus, the temple wasn't just a place where you fulfilled religious observances, offered sacrifices and carried out religious rituals. It was 'his Father's house', the place where you would expect to meet God.

And all this business activity—relatively harmless, perhaps—was a serious distraction from that. The Father's house was being turned into a place where things happened, rather than a place where he dwelt.

The Christian's 'temple', of course, isn't in Jerusalem, but wherever people worship God in Spirit and in truth. But there is still the danger of being so busy about our religion and its activities that we forget that in the end it is about meeting God himself

---

A prayer

Heavenly Father, deliver me from frantic religion and bring me to quiet faith.
Amen.

DW

Being born again

Now there was a man of the Pharisees named Nicodemus, a member of the Jewish ruling council. He came to Jesus at night and said, 'Rabbi, we know you are a teacher who has come from God. For no-one could perform the miraculous signs you are doing if God were not with him.' In reply, Jesus declared, 'I tell you the truth, no-one can see the kingdom of God unless he is born again.' 'How can a man be born when he is old?' Nicodemus asked. 'Surely he cannot enter a second time into his mother's womb to be born!' Jesus answered, 'I tell you the truth, no-one can enter the kingdom of God unless he is born of water and the Spirit. Flesh gives birth to flesh, but the Spirit gives birth to spirit.'

Birth is a mysterious process not so much the 'mechanics' of it, but the transition from one kind of existence to another. The baby leaves the warm, comfortable and secure world of the womb and is thrust into the noisy, anxious and dangerous world of human life. No wonder the effects of this traumatic experience lie deeply within our subconscious all through the rest of life.

Jesus used birth as a means of explaining to a devout Jewish religious leader, Nicodemus, what would be required for him, or anyone else, to 'see the kingdom of God'. The experience would be so total, so transforming and so completely new, that it could only be described as being 'born again'.

Nicodemus trips over the image. 'What do you mean?' he asks. 'Do you want me to go back into the womb and start again?'

Jesus repeats his original statement, but now in negative terms. You can't enter the kingdom of God unless you are 'born of water and the Spirit'. Kingdom-of-God people aren't born the earthly way ('of the flesh') but the heavenly way through water (baptism, perhaps) and the Spirit: it is a miracle of God, his gift like life itself. So being a Christian is about starting a new life in a new environment, with new interests, a new family and new values. We sell Christianity short if we make it less than that.

A prayer

Lord Jesus, help me today to experience this new life you have given me. Amen.

DW

The heart of love

For God so loved the world that he gave his one and only Son, that whoever believes in him shall not perish but have eternal life. For God did not send his Son into the world to condemn the world, but to save the world through him.

Here is probably the best-known verse in the New Testament, together with the one which follows it, which is nowhere near so well known. They both sing the same song, but, like good stereo, they perfectly complement each other. The first tells us why God sent his Son into the world. The second tells us why he didn't.

God so loved that he gave... That is the heart of love—giving. I still feel moved when I hear a bride or groom at a wedding holding a ring on their partner's finger and saying, 'All that I am I give to you.' It's magnificent. It leaves no room for negotiation. It has all the extravagance and illogicality of love itself

The world's love says, 'I love you and I want you and I'm going to have you.' Divine love says. 'All that I am I give to you.' God didn't talk about love, he gave us his Son. And he gave him, it says, so that all who believe in him can have 'eternal life'.

The other side of the coin, as it were, in the next verse, is just as attractive, though expressed negatively. God didn't send his Son into the world to condemn it. That is good news! Sometimes Christians have given the impression that this is precisely what he did do. But God doesn't desire the destruction of his creatures. He longs that they will turn to him and live. God didn't send his Son to condemn, but to save.

And in both cases it is the world—the *cosmos* in Greek—that is in question. All through the New Testament the 'world' is seen as God's enemy, rejecting his ways. And yet God didn't send his Son to condemn it, but to rescue it. That is the measure of his love.

A prayer

Lord, help me to know that I am loved by the only one who has the right to judge me. Amen.

DW

Working without stress

His disciples urged him, 'Rabbi, eat something.' But he said to them, 'I have food to eat that you know nothing about.' Then his disciples said to each other, 'Could someone have brought him food?' 'My food,' said Jesus, 'is to do the will of him who sent me and to finish his work. Do you not say, "Four months more and then the harvest"? I tell you, open your eyes and look at the fields! They are ripe for harvest. Even now the reaper draws his wages, even now he harvests the crop for eternal life, so that the sower and reaper may be glad together. Thus the saying "One sows and another reaps" is true.'

'Oh,' his wife said, 'he eats and drinks work.' It was not intended as a compliment. For most of us, work is a part of life, not the whole. But we also know that for some people it is the controlling drive in life 'meat and drink', as we say. Friends, families, hobbies (and certainly God) have to take second place.

In one sense—but only in one sense—Jesus was like that. 'My food is to do the will of him who sent me and to finish his work.' That was his over-whelming ambition. He had a clear priority: to do God's work and to complete it. Meals and sleep, even, took second place.

But the Gospels make it clear that this didn't turn Jesus into a 'workaholic', mainly because he saw 'his Father's work' in a more life-enhancing way than the workaholic. He was single-minded in accomplishing his task, but he also found time to sit by a well and talk to an alien woman about the nature of worship. He made time for the sick, the blind, the handicapped. He ate meals with disreputable people, observed the birds of the air, made space for prayer. Although he never seemed to waste time, he does not come across as 'busy'. Jesus never once said, 'I'm too busy,' or, 'Come back later,' because he always had time for what really mattered. It is a marvellous example: single-minded, but not at all obsessive.

A prayer

Lord, help me to live my life and do my work with this unhurried sense of priority. Amen.

DW

Believing and seeing

Once more [Jesus] visited Cana in Galilee, where he had turned the water into wine. And there was a certain royal official whose son lay sick at Capernaum. When this man heard that Jesus had arrived in Galilee from Judea, he sent to him and begged him to come and heal his son, who was close to death. 'Unless you people see miraculous signs and wonders,' Jesus told him, 'you will never believe.' The royal official said, 'Sir, come down before my child dies.' Jesus replied, 'You may go. Your son will live.' The man took Jesus at his word and departed. While he was still on the way, his servants met him with the news that his boy was living.

'Taking Jesus at his word' seems to have been the turning point of this story. The official had begged Jesus to come to Capernaum to heal his son, but Jesus declined, with what seems like a dismissive remark about people who require miraculous evidence before they can believe.

But the official didn't. That is the heart of the story. Jesus told him to go—'Your son will live.' And he went, taking Jesus at his word. And as he went ('while he was still on the way') he was brought the news that his son had recovered. The 'evidence', as it were, followed his faith rather than provided a basis for it. He was not like the people Jesus had criticized, who 'unless they see signs and wonders will never believe'.

Later in the Gospel, Jesus says to 'doubting' Thomas, 'Blessed are those who have not seen and yet have believed.' The patron saint of believers like that could well be this royal official, a man who simply took Jesus at his word.

That is very often the only 'evidence' we shall be given. His word should be enough: what he has promised he will fulfil. The Lord doesn't make empty promises. Faith precedes evidence—not always (there are remarkable exceptions), but as the norm. Blessed are those who do not see, who are not given proof, but who take God at his word.

A prayer

Lord, help me to believe where I cannot see, and trust where the only evidence is your word of promise. Amen.

DW

Being set free

One who was there [at the pool of Bethesda] had been an invalid for thirty-eight years. When Jesus saw him lying there and learned that he had been in this condition for a long time, he asked him, 'Do you want to get well?' 'Sir,' the invalid replied, 'I have no-one to help me into the pool when the water is stirred. While I am trying to get in, someone else goes down ahead of me.' Then Jesus said to him, 'Get up! Pick up your mat and walk.' At once the man was cured; he picked up his mat and walked.

Thirty-eight years is a long while to be paralysed. I think we can assume that the man in this story had long ago given up any realistic hope of being released from it. Doesn't his conversation with Jesus wreak of defeated resignation?

'Do you want to get well?' Jesus asks him—the question itself begs several others, doesn't it? And his reply is even more revealing: 'I have no-one to help me . . . others always get there first.' One can understand how he felt, but it is an answer full of defeat—of self-pity, even. It is hardly the bright confidence of someone who expects to be healed.

But healing was what he got—sudden, complete and dramatic. The stranger told him to get up, pick up his mat and walk. And he did.

The story has many further complications, as you can discover by reading the rest of the chapter. But the incident itself is marvellously relevant to everyone who feels 'paralysed', not just physically, but emotionally, morally or spiritually. Like him, we've often got a rational explanation as to why nothing can be done about it. In our heart of hearts we might not be able honestly to answer the question, 'Do you want to get well?'

But it was the presence and word of Jesus that made the difference, not the man's feelings, failure or faith. We are not to look inwards to our problems but outwards towards the one who says, 'Get up!'

A prayer

Lord, I do want to be whole but I have little confidence that it will happen. Please speak the word and make the difference. Amen.

DW

Window in the world

[Jesus] took Peter, John, and James with him and went up into the hills to pray. And while he was praying the appearance of his face changed and his clothes became dazzling white. Suddenly there were two men talking with him; these were Moses and Elijah, who appeared in glory and spoke of his departure, the destiny he was to fulfil in Jerusalem. Meanwhile Peter and his companions had been in a deep sleep; but when they awoke, they saw his glory and the two men who stood beside him.

Looking out of my study window the world seems drab. The bright spring green of the trees' new leaves seems dusty under an overcast sky, and the tarmac of the drive and the street beyond is dull grey. The traffic that passes has a patina of dust, and even the schoolchildren on their lunch break lack their normal liveliness.

On a day like this the weather seems a symbol of everyday life; a humdrum round of work, shopping, house cleaning, cooking—the gnawing worries which drag at our lives and the anxieties we feel for ourselves, our children and the world at large.

Then the sun breaks through, the leaves light up, tossing in the breeze to scatter dappled light over the pavement, light flashes from the chrome of the cars, a child laughs and dances over the shining road, and the world is transfigured.

In a time of prayer, Jesus broke through the barrier between the world as we see it in its drabness and the light and glory of God which holds all things in existence and is the true reality that underlies the world. The sleepy disciples looked up and saw Jesus not on the surface, but as he really was, filled with the glory of God, and at one with the saints of heaven.

Prayer does that. It opens a window in the world which lets us see into eternity, and be touched by the glory of God. And we too can pray.

MM

Inner blindness

I have testimony weightier than that of John. For the very work that the Father has given me to finish, and which I am doing, testifies that the Father has sent me. And the Father who sent me has himself testified concerning me. You have never heard his voice nor seen his form, nor does his word dwell in you, for you do not believe the one he sent. You diligently study the Scriptures because you think that by them you possess eternal life. These are the Scriptures that testify about me, yet you refuse to come to me to have life.

How do we know that Jesus is the one sent by God, and not just a deluded fanatic? That was the question the Jews of his time asked, and it was a reasonable one. They had endured any number of bogus prophets and false dawns. How was Jesus different?

And it's a modern question, too. There are many religions, many prophets and gurus, many claims on our belief and commitment. In what way is Jesus different from the rest?

He offers the Jewish crowd some answers. First, because of what he has done, what he calls 'the Father's work'. They had to ask themselves, as we should do the things Jesus did look like 'the Father's work'? Would a loving God of mercy and truth want to heal the sick, give sight to the blind, cleanse the leper, forgive sins? Does all of this have the ring of divinity about it? If the answer is 'yes', then Jesus is different.

Secondly, Jesus points them to the Scriptures (what we could call the 'Old Testament'). Unlike most modern people, the Jewish people of his day knew their Bible inside out. As he says, 'You diligently study the Scriptures.' But they were reading them with their minds closed. The very Scriptures they studied spoke of a coming Messiah who would preach good news to the poor, free the prisoners of sin, open the eyes of the blind and release the oppressed (Isaiah 61:1–2). And here it was happening before their very eyes and they refused (notice the word!) to recognize it. As the old saying goes, 'There's none so blind as those who will not see.'

A prayer

Lord, as I read the Scriptures help me to see beyond simply the printed words, to recognize your living Word to me. Amen.

DW

A better diet

When they found him on the other side of the lake, they asked him, 'Rabbi, when did you get here?' Jesus answered, 'I tell you the truth, you are looking for me, not because you saw miraculous signs but because you ate the loaves and had your fill. Do not work for food that spoils, but for food that endures to eternal life, which the Son of Man will give you. On him God the Father has placed his seal of approval.' Then they asked him, 'What must we do to do the works God requires?' Jesus answered, 'The work of God is this: to believe in the one he has sent.'

This whole chapter six of John's Gospel, beginning with the feeding of the five thousand, seems to be an extended meditation on the Eucharist. John, uniquely among the evangelists, has no account of the institution at that meal of what we call 'holy communion'. But it's hard to believe that he didn't see in these words of Jesus about 'heavenly food', about the 'bread of life' and especially about 'my flesh... and my blood' (v. 55), pre-echoes of the sacrament which came to mean so much to the first Christians.

Here, after the crowd had pursued him around the lake, Jesus is testing their spiritual perception. Are they following him in the hope of a permanent supply of free bread? Or are they prepared to put their trust in him and discover spiritual riches they have never dreamed of?

'Do not work for food that spoils'— they knew all about that! Hard work all day, every day, simply to feed themselves and their families. It was the pattern of their daily life. By the sweat of the brow they earned just enough to live. But here another, richer, diet is on offer—'food that endures to eternal life', available only through 'the Son of Man'.

'What work is required for this?' they asked. 'The work of faith,' replied Jesus believing in the one he has sent. Like the manna in the wilderness, or the food foretold by Isaiah (55:1) which would require no payment, bread comes to them from Jesus which cannot be earned, only accepted.

A prayer

'Sir, from now on, give us this bread'—
Amen.

John 6:34

DW

Life that lasts for ever

'No-one can come to me unless the Father who sent me draws him, and I will raise him up at the last day. It is written in the Prophets, "They will all be taught by God." Everyone who listens to the Father and learns from him comes to me. No-one has seen the Father except the one who is from God; only he has seen the Father. I tell you the truth, he who believes has everlasting life. I am the bread of life. Your forefathers ate the manna in the desert, yet they died. But here is the bread that comes down from heaven, which a man may eat and not die.'

These words of Jesus are well-known and full of profound meaning. They continue the theme of the 'living bread'—that's to say, bread that gives life. Of course, in one sense all food 'gives life', but Jesus has already made clear that he is talking about 'spiritual' or 'eternal' life and that this life is his gift to those who believe.

The idea of 'eternal life' is one to stretch the imagination. Its simplest meaning is 'life that lasts for ever', and there's no doubt that concept is included here. But eternal life is more about quality than length. It is life as God lives it, life with the stamp of eternity upon it.

And it doesn't start after we die, but right now. Notice the tenses in verse 47, 'he who believes [now] has eternal life [now]'. Or look on to verse 54, 'Whoever eats my flesh and drinks my blood has [now] eternal life'. Eternal life is a seed planted by the Spirit of God, the 'life-giver', which takes root in the human spirit and continues its life right on through the experience we call death and into eternity.

A prayer

Heavenly Father, who gave me the gift of life when I was born, help me to put my trust in the one you sent, Jesus, and experience the gift of eternal life now, and on into the life with you which you have prepared for those who love you.
Amen.

DW

Thinking spiritually

Aware that his disciples were grumbling about this, Jesus said to them, 'Does this offend you? What if you see the Son of Man ascend to where he was before! The Spirit gives life; the flesh counts for nothing. The words I have spoken to you are spirit and they are life. Yet there are some of you who do not believe.' . . . From this time many of his disciples turned back and no longer followed him. 'You do not want to leave, too, do you?' Jesus asked the Twelve. Simon Peter answered him, 'Lord, to whom shall we go? You have the words of eternal life. We believe and know that you are the Holy One of God.'

We have a reminder here that it wasn't easy for the disciples to follow Jesus (just in case we thought it was!). As devout Jews, taught never to consume blood, they had just heard him speaking of people drinking his blood and eating his flesh. Many of the crowd who followed him simply couldn't take this and drifted away. Even the disciples found it difficult, and Jesus recognized this.

His answer is interesting: change your whole way of looking at things. Stop thinking in wooden, literal terms and start thinking spiritually. The 'Son of Man' will return to heaven, so his body and blood, as it were, will no longer be on earth. In the spiritual realm they would be able to feed on him, to draw from him daily sustenance, strength and refreshment, but they would miss the point completely if they thought that he was speaking of some kind of cannibalism. His words about eating flesh and drinking blood shouldn't be taken literally but spiritually the 'flesh counts for nothing', it is 'the Spirit who gives life'.

It's an important lesson for us all. Sometimes we create difficulties about faith by thinking in essentially 'earthly' terms about 'heavenly' issues. The 'flesh' what we might call the crudely materialistic side of life must not be allowed to dominate our thinking. Like Peter and the Twelve, we have to recognize that Jesus has 'words of eternal life' life-giving words in a way no one else has. As the 'Holy One of God' his words are 'spirit, and they are life .

A prayer

Deliver me from the confined space of human thinking and help me to start thinking spiritually. Amen.

DW

The living water

On the last and greatest day of the Feast, Jesus stood and said in a loud voice, 'If anyone is thirsty, let him come to me and drink. Whoever believes in me, as the Scripture has said, streams of living water will flow from within him.' By this he meant the Spirit, whom those who believed in him were later to receive. Up to that time the Spirit had not been given, since Jesus had not yet been glorified. On hearing his words, some of the people said, 'Surely this man is the Prophet.' Others said, 'He is the Christ.' Still others asked, 'How can the Christ come from Galilee? Does not the Scripture say that the Christ will come from David's family and from Bethlehem, the town where David lived?' Thus the people were divided because of Jesus.

The Feast of Tabernacles is still one of the most popular among Jewish people. It comes in September, after the harvest time, and commemorates the time when the Jews lived in tents on the journey to the Promised Land. To mark it, simple booths are made and for the eight days of the Festival everyone lives in them—quite fun in a warm land like Israel! In the time of Jesus it had two other distinctive features—large candles, which were placed and lit in the courtyards; and the bringing in of great vessels of water from the Pool of Siloam for ritual washings.

It's clearly this latter ritual to which Jesus is referring. On the last day (a sabbath) no water was brought in, so Jesus 'in a loud voice' proclaims himself as a provider of 'living water' literally, running water, an endless supply, like a brook or spring. The one who offered them living bread now offers them living water not as an external gift but as a source within them. All we need for the full life can be found in him—nourishment for the inner being, bread to strengthen and water to cleanse and refresh. It's a beautiful picture, and John adds his own commentary: 'he meant the Spirit, whom those who believed in him were later to receive'.

A prayer

Lord, as you are bread for my soul and water for my dry spirit, help me to find all I need in you. Amen.

DW

Throwing the first stone

The teachers of the law and the Pharisees brought in a woman caught in adultery. They made her stand before the group and said to Jesus, 'Teacher, this woman was caught in the act of adultery. In the Law Moses commanded us to stone such women. Now what do you say?' . . . But Jesus bent down and started to write on the ground with his finger. When they kept on questioning him, he straightened up and said to them, 'If any one of you is without sin, let him be the first to throw a stone at her.' Again he stooped and wrote on the ground. At this, those who heard began to go away one at a time, the older ones first, until only Jesus was left, with the woman still standing there . . . 'Woman where are they? Has no-one condemned you?' 'No-one, sir,' she said. 'Then neither do I condemn you,' Jesus declared. 'Go now and leave your life of sin.'

Experts tell us that this story probably isn't part of John's Gospel, but no one disputes that it is part of the story of Jesus. Who could possibly invent it, including such marvellous detail as the doodling in the sand (what did he write?) and the oldest slinking away first, more conscious, I suppose, of past sins—or more willing to recognize them as such.

It's usually described as the story of the woman taken in adultery, and of course it is. But the heart of the story isn't Jesus dealing with her, but with her accusers. It's really a story about hypocrisy rather than adultery. The male accusers stand for outraged respectability. They wanted the letter of the law enforced. But even in that there was hypocrisy. It takes two people to commit adultery and the Law of Moses called for the stoning of both parties to it.

What Jesus put to them was perfectly reasonable. Let the sinless condemn the sinner. But faced with the stark equation, they can do nothing but slope off—the stones remain on the ground. And Jesus, who being sinless could have thrown the stones, didn't. He declined to condemn, but he told her to 'leave her life of sin'. Can anyone doubt that she did?

A prayer

Lord, deliver me from judging others and teach me how to judge myself.

DW

The wine of joy

On the third day there was a wedding at Cana-in-Galilee. The mother of Jesus was there, and Jesus and his disciples were guests also. The wine gave out, so Jesus' mother said to him, 'They have no wine left.' He answered, 'Your concern, mother, is not mine. My hour has not yet come.' His mother said to the servants, 'Do whatever he tells you.' There were six stone water jars standing near, of the kind used for Jewish rites of purification; each held from twenty to thirty gallons. Jesus said to the servants, 'Fill the jars with water', and they filled them to the brim. 'Now draw some off,' he ordered, 'and take it to the steward of the feast'; and they did so.

This is one of my favourite stories in the New Testament. It speaks of hope for all the dull, grey areas of life that plague us. No matter what Jesus is given, he brings transformation to it, and makes our ordinary lives into a glorious joy.

Here he is attending the wedding banquet, presumably of some friends, when the embarrassing social mishap occurs. The wine runs out. How often in our everyday lives does our resource run dry? We try to solve problems, struggling and grinding until we eventually give up. It is often then that God begins his work. Our small resource is flooded with his power.

Bishop Michael Marshall, on a visit to our church, said that God often speaks to us in dreams because that's when we interfere with what he's saying the least. I know that for me, in my busy life, I find God has to pull me up before I will allow him to act.

But that which thrills me most about this story is that Jesus changes so much water into wine. One hundred and eighty gallons of the finest, but shortest vintage. It speaks of the overflowing, overwhelming love of God.

The contrast that we are meant to see is of the ordinariness of this life compared with the tremendous wealth of the spiritual life in Christ. Love, joy, peace and the other fruits of the Spirit, transcendence, intimacy, depth, height, breadth and length of love, faith and grace and hope, protection, freedom, and acceptance are just the beginning of God's liberality. What a God we have!

As we drink wine today, may it mark the cost of God's love and symbolize all God's blessings.

GD

True freedom

To the Jews who had believed him, Jesus said, 'If you hold to my teaching, you are really my disciples. Then you will know the truth, and the truth will set you free.' They answered him, 'We are Abraham's descendants and have never been slaves of anyone. How can you say that we shall be set free?' Jesus replied 'I tell you the truth, everyone who sins is a slave to sin. Now a slave has no permanent place in the family, but a son belongs to it for ever. So if the Son sets you free, you will be free indeed.'

John has just reported (v. 30) that 'many put their faith in [Jesus]'—these were Jews who had come to believe that he is the one he claimed to be. Now Jesus sets out to them the great reward of the true disciple—freedom through the truth: 'You will know the truth, and the truth will set you free.'

What is certain is that error, untruth, can't 'set us free'. It may delude us for a while, or offer temporary relief from anxiety, but, if it isn't based on the truth, in the end it can only lead to disappointment. Jesus offered these new disciples the 'truth', though they didn't immediately find it very palatable. They might be descendants of Abraham, but they were also slaves to sin, which would deprive them of a 'permanent place' in God's family. But the Son and heir Jesus was clearly speaking of himself has the right to admit them to that family... and if he does, then they would be truly free as God's sons and daughters.

There is no substitute for the truth, however unpalatable we may find it to be, and nothing else can set us free. The only one who can set us free from the clinging chains of our own failure and guilt is the one God sent for that very purpose.

Many people think of religion as a kind of slavery (to dogma, or ritual, or laws and rules), but God sent his Son not to enslave people but to set them completely free. As Charles Wesley wrote, 'My chains fell off, my heart was free...'

A prayer

Son of God, set me free to live joyfully in your family. Amen.

DW

Sin and suffering

As he went along, [Jesus] saw a man blind from birth. His disciples asked him, 'Rabbi, who sinned, this man or his parents, that he was born blind?' 'Neither this man nor his parents sinned', said Jesus, 'but this happened so that the work of God might be displayed in his life. As long as it is day, we must do the work of him who sent me. Night is coming, when no-one can work. While I am in the world, I am the light of the world.' Having said this, he spat on the ground, made some mud with the saliva, and put it on the man's eyes. 'Go,' he told him, 'wash in the Pool of Siloam' (this word means Sent). So the man went and washed, and came home seeing.

The question raised by the disciples was based on the common view at that time that suffering was a direct result of sin. It's strange that this belief could have been held by those who had the book of Job in their sacred scriptures, but it is a deep-rooted human instinct to look for cause and effect. Someone sinned, and sin is wrong. So, as a direct result, someone suffered. The only question to be settled was, 'Whose fault was it? This man's—blind from birth—or his parents?'

The answer of Jesus is quite abrupt. 'Neither this man nor his parents sinned.' His handicap wasn't anybody's 'fault'. He gave a similar answer when asked whether some people who were killed by a collapsing tower were worse sinners than everyone else. His answer then was a categorical 'no'.

In this case the man's blindness was going to be taken by Jesus and used to display the 'work of God'. That fits in with St Paul's assertion that 'in all things God works for the good of those who love him' (Romans 8:28). God is able to take human suffering and pain—even injustice and evil—and out of them create 'good' for those who love him. The eye of faith will often see this in daily life. And, of course, we see it supremely in the cross of Jesus.

A prayer

Lord, help me so to love you that I may see your good purpose being worked out even through suffering.

DW

The only true test

They brought to the Pharisees the man who had been blind. Now the day on which Jesus had made the mud and opened the man's eyes was a Sabbath. Therefore the Pharisees also asked him how he had received his sight. 'He put mud on my eyes,' the man replied, 'and I washed, and now I see.' Some of the Pharisees said, 'This man is not from God, for he does not keep the Sabbath.' But others asked, 'How can a sinner do such miraculous signs?' So they were divided.

It's not clear whether Jesus broke the Sabbath simply by the fact that he had healed someone, or because, in the process of doing so, he mixed soil and saliva to make mud (presumably that was 'manual work'). Either way, it probably seems to us a footling objection and our natural reaction is to be irritated with these over-scrupulous Pharisees. We may even see them as examples of extreme hypocrisy.

But in fact most of us find it quite hard to accept that people who don't conform to our way of doing things can be instruments of God's work. We can be as quick as the Pharisees to cast doubts on the credentials of preachers, evangelists and healers whose methods or teaching we don't approve of. The Pharisees had a simple logic. God gave the Law of Moses. If this man doesn't keep it, then he can't be from God. It's simple, when you put it like that!

But others (also Pharisees, it seems) were not so sure. How could a 'sinner' do such miraculous signs?

They were not prepared to judge Jesus solely on doctrinaire grounds, but on the evidence of what he did. In his own words, 'You shall know them by their fruits.'

It sometimes seems that God delights to shock us by making use of the most unlikely people to do his work. Of course, not everyone who claims to be a 'miracle-worker' is from God. But when we see God demonstrably at work, let's be generous and give thanks ... whoever he has chosen to use for the purpose.

A prayer

Help me to recognize what is from you and to be grateful for your blessings, whatever way they come to me. Amen.

DW

One thing I know

The Jews still did not believe that he had been blind and had received his sight until they sent for the man's parents. 'Is this your son?' they asked. 'Is this the one you say was born blind? How is it that now he can see?' 'We know he is our son,' the parents answered, 'and we know he was born blind. But how he can see now, or who opened his eyes, we don't know. Ask him. He is of age; he will speak for himself.' . . . A second time they summoned the man who had been blind. 'Give glory to God,' they said. 'We know this man is a sinner.' He replied, 'Whether he is a sinner or not, I don't know. One thing I do know. I was blind but now I see!'

Each of the seven miraculous 'signs' in the Fourth Gospel has a whole network of ways in which it can be read and this one is no exception. By all means read it as a jolly good story—I love the sheer cheek of the formerly blind man! But we can also see it as a tragic parable of rejection of the light—Christ opens blind eyes, but the spiritually blind refuse to 'see'. Or we can see it as an affirmation of 'simple faith' as opposed to self-righteous religiosity.

Certainly the faith of the man who has been healed is simple. He professes not to understand all these sophisticated distinctions about Sabbath-breaking and who is, or is not, a 'sinner'. He declines to get into that debate at all 'I don't know whether he's a sinner, but I do know one thing . . . I used to be blind, but now I can see.' In the end, in sheer fury at his impudence, the Pharisees threw him out of the synagogue (v. 34), but the violence of their reaction shows that they had no other answer to the sheer logic of his position. They had doctrines they held. He had an experience which he couldn't deny. They studied the scriptures. His eyes had been opened by Jesus. They were God-fearing men, but he had experienced the work of God in his own life. God affirms the simple faith of a poor man but leaves the 'religious' stranded among the stumbling blocks of their own position.

A prayer

Lord, keep my faith simple, but not simplistic, and help me to value every experience of your love in my life.

DW

Called by name

'I tell you the truth, the man who does not enter the sheep pen by the gate, but climbs in some other way, is a thief and a robber. The man who enters by the gate is the shepherd of the sheep. The watchman opens the gate for him, and the sheep listen to his voice. He calls his own sheep by name and leads them out. When he has brought out all his own, he goes on ahead of them, and his sheep follow him because they know his voice. But they will never follow a stranger; in fact, they will run away from him because they do not recognise a stranger's voice.

I suppose everyone is familiar with the biblical picture of the 'good shepherd', even those of us who have never met a real live one. Certainly the twenty-third Psalm 'The Lord is my shepherd' could make some claim to being the best-known passage in the whole of the Bible. Here Jesus is describing his relationship with his followers in terms of a shepherd with his sheep, and, while the idea is not an easy one for our more urban culture, it is so vivid that even a child (or perhaps especially a child) could understand it.

The shepherd 'knows his sheep'. To the Middle-Eastern shepherd they weren't just a quantity of livestock but individual creatures, presumably with individual characteristics. By knowing them, he could guide and protect them effectively. That knowledge would cover their known weaknesses ('this one gets tired easily') and their self-destructive tendencies ('this one wanders off at nightfall'). It is tremendously reassuring that the Lord's knowledge of us is individual and personal.

And he leads them—though not in the manner of Western shepherds, who tend to follow the sheep, usually aided by a sheep-dog. He goes ahead, to ensure that he encounters any difficulty or danger before they do. He puts himself in the position of risk in order to guarantee the safety of the sheep. No wonder the sheep know his voice—they recognize his care for them and his wisdom that knows the best way. As the Psalmist reminds us, 'We are the sheep of his pasture' ... and the Lord is our shepherd.

A prayer

Teach me today to follow the one who knows the way and trust the one who knows me as an individual.

DW

The good shepherd

'I am the good shepherd; I know my sheep and my sheep know me—just as the Father knows me and I know the Father—and I lay down my life for the sheep. I have other sheep that are not of this sheep pen. I must bring them also. They too will listen to my voice, and there shall be one flock and one shepherd. The reason my Father loves me is that I lay down my life—only to take it up again. No-one takes it from me, but I lay it down of my own accord. I have authority to lay it down and authority to take it up again. This command I received from my Father.'

'I lay down my life for the sheep.' I think those who first heard these words would have understood what they meant on one level but would have had problems with their real meaning, if that makes sense! They knew that shepherds guarded the sheep, and in a country where there were wolves—and human predators, too—that could be a dangerous task. At night, the shepherd was alone with his sheep, probably far away from any buildings or village. He would lie across the entrance to the sheep-pen, barring entry to it with his own body. And if it came to it, he would be expected to defend those sheep, if necessary with his own life. The by-standers would have understood that.

But how would Jesus fulfil that role? How would he 'lay down his life for the sheep'? Who were his sheep, anyway (and especially who were these 'other sheep' in v. 16)?

It may seem obvious to us now. He would 'lay down his life' for the lost sheep of the house of Israel and also for 'the scattered children of God' in all the nations (see 11:52). His life wouldn't be 'taken' from him—it would be an act of sacrifice. And it would culminate in his 'taking it up again'—this would not be a kind of defeat, but a real victory over evil. The victory is the shepherd's, but the beneficiaries are the sheep.

A prayer

Good Shepherd of the sheep, guard me in my going out and coming in, from this time forth and for ever more. Amen.

DW

Longing for home

How lovely is your dwelling place O Lord God of hosts! My soul has a desire and longing to enter the courts of the Lord: my heart and my flesh rejoice in the living God. The sparrow has found her a home and the swallow a nest where she may lay her young: even the altar O Lord of hosts my King and my God. Blessed are those who dwell in your house: they will always be praising you.

A few years ago I went to America for a week on church business. As I set off from Gatwick I remember leaving my wife and one-year-old daughter, Helen, at the passport control. I flew to New York then travelled on to Boston by car. As I stopped for a break at a service area I bought a sandwich and sat outside in the garden eating it. Presently, along came a couple with a little girl about the same age as Helen. We chatted about why I was there, but as I watched the mother with the girl, I suddenly felt tremendously moved inside and terribly homesick. I longed to be with my family and back home.

Fortunately, the feeling went off shortly afterwards. If it hadn't, I would have simply turned around there and then and travelled the three thousand miles back as fast as I could.

There is nothing like being away from home to make us appreciate it. The psalmist is up in the north and not able to be with his spiritual family. He longs for the courts of the Lord and the living God with all his soul and body.

If we lived constantly with this aching longing we should probably get frustrated. Yet in a sense we do. Like the Israelites, we are on a journey. From time to time we feel the underlying frustration of being in the world but not of it. We are like foreigners in our own country; homeless, yet heirs of a mansion; bound to the earth, yet set free.

Some days I experience the difficulties of praying to an unseen God. I'm reminded of George Carey who once said, 'If God seems very distant, guess who moved.' When I visited America I enjoyed it very much but I was more glad to get home again. Every Easter Day I remind myself of how lovely God's dwelling place is and wear a badge on my jacket which proudly proclaims, 'Only visiting this planet.'

GD

When it's hard to believe

The Jews gathered around Jesus and said to him, 'How long will you keep us in suspense? If you are the Messiah, tell us plainly.' Jesus answered, 'I have told you, and you do not believe. The works that I do in my Father's name testify to me; but you do not believe because you do not belong to my sheep. My sheep hear my voice. I know them, and they follow me. I give them eternal life, and they will never perish. No one will snatch them out of my hand. What my Father has given me is greater than all else, and no one can snatch it out of the Father's hand.'

The answer Jesus gave here to the question, 'Are you the Messiah?' was not evasive, but direct. He had told them, not in words but in actions. In the name of God he had healed the sick and cast out demons. He had mirrored God's feeding of the children of Israel with manna by miraculously feeding the people with bread and fish. And he had done what only God could do, forgive sins.

But still they didn't believe! And gave the excuse that he hadn't 'told them plainly'. It's hard to know how much 'plainer' he could have been!

Jesus explained the real reason for their unbelief—'you do not belong to my sheep'. His sheep hear his voice. He knows them, and they know him. They follow him. It's this relationship which creates faith—not evidence, and not even 'plain words'. If we find we are full of doubts about Jesus, the reason is seldom lack of evidence. Far more often it is that we have drifted out of this relationship of dependent trust. Events, people, distractions, business, other re-lationships: it's things like that that make it hard for us to believe in Jesus as Lord and Christ. Sometimes, of course, we may need evidence, but more often we need to come back into the fold.

A prayer

Lord, when I find it hard to believe, draw me back into the fold, where I can hear your voice, recognize your love, and follow you. For your love's sake, Amen.

DW

The one you love is sick

Now a certain man was ill, Lazarus of Bethany, the village of Mary and her sister Martha. Mary was the one who anointed the Lord with perfume and wiped his feet with her hair; her brother Lazarus was ill. So the sisters sent a message to Jesus, 'Lord, he whom you love is ill.' But when Jesus heard it, he said, 'This illness does not lead to death, rather it is for God's glory, so that the Son of God may be glorified through it.' Accordingly, though Jesus loved Martha and her sister and Lazarus, after having heard that Lazarus was ill, he stayed two days longer in the place where he was.

'Lord, he whom you love is ill.' That was the message Martha sent to Jesus to tell him that his friend Lazarus was very sick. They appealed to him as a friend of the dying man: 'he whom you love is ill'.

It's a message we can also send to him when someone near us is ill, because the love of Christ knows no favourites. No one who came to him was turned away. They were all valued and loved. So we can say, 'Lord, the one you love is ill.'

But that didn't mean then, and it doesn't mean now, that Jesus was going to come rushing to the rescue! He was 'on the other side of the Jordan', perhaps twenty or thirty miles from Bethany. He could have been with Lazarus within six or seven hours—a day's walk. Yet 'he stayed two days longer in the place where he was'.

It is part of the mystery of God's response to human suffering that he doesn't always act in the way we would expect him to. It is not lack of love ('he whom you love is ill'). It isn't indifference to anguish or pain. And it isn't inability to do anything about it. Whatever else, the rest of this chapter, as we shall see, makes those three things clear. But he waited ... 'so that God's Son may glorified through it'. That is a mystery, incomprehensible to human minds, but part of a purpose known only to God: a purpose, in the end, of love.

A prayer

Lord, when the one we love is ill, help us to remember that that one is also loved by you, and that your purpose for them is a purpose of love. Amen.

DW

Indignation of bereavement

Martha said to Jesus, 'Lord, if you had been here my brother would not have died. But even now I know that God will give you whatever you ask of him.' Jesus said to her, 'Your brother will rise again.' Martha said to him, 'I know that he will rise again at the resurrection on the last day.' Jesus said to her, 'I am the resurrection and the life. Those who believe in me, even though they die, will live, and everyone who lives and believes in me will never die. Do you believe this?' She said to him, 'Yes, Lord, I believe that you are the Messiah, the Son of God, the one coming into the world.'

'If you had been here, my brother would not have died.' Down the centuries we can still feel the rebuke in Martha's words. How could you delay coming, and so let him die? It's just another variation on the words one often hears from those who have just been bereaved: 'Why her? Why did God let it happen?'

But Martha was also a woman of faith. Look at her next words: 'But even now I know that God will give you whatever you ask of him.' That 'even now' is the crucial part of the sentence. 'Even now', days after the death, Jesus could do something, because of his special relationship with God.

Even now. The phrase combines an element of desperation ('at this eleventh hour, hope almost gone') and of faith. She believed that in that moment of despair and darkness there was hope in the person and power of Jesus. She believed that Jesus was the Messiah, the Son of God.

Martha's faith, expressed in a moment of despair and desperation, was to be rewarded in the most spectacular way. But even before that happened one can detect a change in her. Her simple faith in Jesus, the one to whom God will give whatever he asks, has already begun to bring an inward peace, an experience she wants her sister Mary to share (see v. 28—'The Master is here and is calling for you'). Perhaps already her 'if only' and 'why him?' doubts are beginning to be resolved.

A prayer

When I am near to despair, or voicing angry questions, doubting your love, give me a faith like Martha's, that holds on to the known, and hopes for the unknown.
Amen.

DW

Trapped in grave-clothes

Then Jesus, again greatly disturbed, came to the tomb. It was a cave, and a stone was lying against it. Jesus said, 'Take away the stone.' Martha, the sister of the dead man, said, 'Lord, already there is a stench, because he has been dead four days.' Jesus said, 'Did I not tell you that if you believed, you would see the glory of God?' So they took away the stone. And Jesus looked upward and said, 'Father, I thank you for having heard me . . .' When he had said this, he cried with a loud voice, 'Lazarus, come out!' The dead man came out, his hands and feet bound with strips of cloth, and his face wrapped in a cloth. Jesus said to them, 'Unbind him, and let him go.'

The story of the raising of Lazarus includes three verbal commands. Each comand is an important part of what the story tells us about the process by which human beings can emerge from the darkness of spiritual death into the light of eternal life. That seems to be the 'secret message' of this sign.

The first command is, 'Take away the stone' (v. 39). The stone was the visible sign of death and burial, the great barrier that divided the body of Lazarus from the world of the living. The possibility of new life could only exist once the stone had been removed. Jesus, the 'lamb of God', had been sent to 'take away [literally, bear off] the sin of the world'—the evil that separates us from the life of God.

Then, 'Lazarus, come out!' Presumably Lazarus could have opted to stay in the burial chamber. He had to respond to the call of Jesus and claim the new life that was being offered. Eternal life has to be received; it is never forced on us.

When Lazarus staggered out into the light of day he was still wrapped in the trappings of death. 'Unbind him, and let him go,' was the third command. Only when the dead man is free of that which relates to death will he truly be alive.

For us, too, there are 'grave-clothes' to be removed—the bindings of the 'old nature'. Only when they have been stripped away will we really be free to live the risen life.

A prayer

Lord, remove the barrier of sin, bring me into life, and deliver me from those things from my past which hold me back.
Amen.

DW

The price of unity

The chief priests and the Pharisees called a meeting of the council, and said, 'What are we to do? This man is performing many signs. If we let him go on like this, everyone will believe in him and the Romans will come and destroy both our holy place and our nation.' But one of them, Caiaphas, who was high priest that year, said to them, 'You know nothing at all! You do not understand that it is better for you to have one man die for the people than to have the whole nation destroyed.' He did not say this on his own, but being high priest that year he prophesied that Jesus was about to die for the nation, and not for the nation only, but to gather into one the dispersed children of God.

As John observes, Caiaphas spoke prophetically—a greater truth than he realized. Because Jesus would indeed die not only for the Jewish nation, but 'to gather into one the dispersed children of God'.

How could the death of Jesus 'gather dispersed people together' and make them 'one'? Well, think of disputes that we ourselves have been involved in. What keeps them going is the stubborn refusal of either party to sacrifice anything. They simply stand there shouting 'No surrender!' and 'No compromise!' If the separated parties are ever to come together, somebody has to take a daring and costly first step, and give up something.

In Jesus, God took that 'first step'. He didn't wait for us to admit we were in the wrong. If he had, he'd still be waiting. He sent his Son to take that costly first step and give up something: and the 'something' he gave up was his life. God took the initiative by making the sacrifice.

'One man' did indeed die 'to bring together the scattered people of God and make them one'.

Now that the first step has been taken, it's up to us to take the second, and respond to it. It takes two to make a separation and it takes two to end it.

A prayer

Heavenly Father, help me to respond to what Jesus has done by rejecting everything that separates me from you, and from others. Amen.

DW

Extravagant gestures

Six days before the Passover Jesus came to Bethany, the home of Lazarus, whom he had raised from the dead. There they gave a dinner for him. Martha served, and Lazarus was one of those at the table with him. Mary took a pound of costly perfume made of pure nard, anointed Jesus' feet, and wiped them with her hair. The house was filled with the fragrance of the perfume. But Judas Iscariot, one of his disciples (the one who was about to betray him), said, 'Why was this perfume not sold for three hundred denarii and the money given to the poor?' ... Jesus said, 'Leave her alone. She bought it so that she might keep it for the day of my burial. You always have the poor with you, but you do not always have me.'

Buying her jewellery you can't really afford... getting the disc jockey to play a special record on his birthday... hiring an airship with a streamer proclaiming 'I love Sarah!'—the history of devotion is the history of extravagant gestures!

Mary, the sister of Lazarus, chose a very expensive gesture to show her love for Jesus. The perfume she poured over him was worth a year's wages—in modern terms, something like £10,000.

What she did was extravagant, of course. The money could indeed have fed the poor or clothed the naked. But sometimes a great love demands an irrational expression. I don't believe that Mary cared less about the poor than Judas, but at this moment all she wanted to do was express her overflowing gratitude to Jesus. And Jesus, whose concern for the poor was beyond dispute, expressed his approval.

It may well be that Mary, the sister of Lazarus, is one and the same person as Mary Magdalene—it's possible to read the evidence that way. Perhaps her gratitude was not only for the raising of Lazarus, but for the forgiveness of her sins. Whatever its reason, it couldn't be contained. Wouldn't it be marvellous if just sometimes we could forget our inhibitions and in a gesture of spontaneous gratitude do 'something beautiful' for him?

A prayer

Give me the priceless gift of gratitude, and help me to express it with love and spontaneity. Amen.

DW

Get clean and get rich

'To the angel of the church in Laodicea write: "This is the message from the Amen, the faithful and true witness, who is the origin of all that God has created. I know what you have done; I know that you are neither cold nor hot. How I wish you were either one or the other! But because you are lukewarm, neither hot nor cold, I am going to spit you out of my mouth! You say, 'I am rich and well off; I have all I need.' But you do not know how miserable and pitiful you are! You are poor, naked, and blind. I advise you, then, to buy gold from me, pure gold, in order to be rich. Buy also white clothing to dress yourself and cover up your shameful nakedness. Buy also some ointment to put on your eyes, so that you may see. I rebuke and punish all whom I love. Be in earnest, then, and turn from your sins. Listen! I stand at the door and knock; if anyone hears my voice and opens the door, I will come into his house and eat with him, and he will eat with me." '

Self-righteousness and smugness are so destructive and death-dealing that Christ wants us to get rid of them. If we are self-righteous we are also proud. Two marks of a healthy Christian life are a deep heart-knowledge of the enormous love of God for each one of us and a knowledge that each one of us is a sinner. A forgiven sinner—but never without sin. And to have had our sins washed away through the blood of Christ, and to know that day after day we have to confess some more sins, puts an end to any illusion of self-righteousness.

Will you pray that God will show you if you are self-righteous and sinful in any area of your life? Then open yourself up to him—and let him come in to that place, or in to that relationship. So that your self-righteousness can be transformed into the righteousness of Christ. So that you see what he sees, and so that your sin can be covered. So that you can be rich with the love and forgiveness of the God of love.

SB

The only way to life

Now among those who went up to worship at the festival were some Greeks. They came to Philip, who was from Bethsaida in Galilee, and said to him, 'Sir, we wish to see Jesus' . . . Philip went and told Andrew; then Andrew and Philip went and told Jesus. Jesus answered them, 'The hour has come for the Son of man to be glorified. Very truly, I tell you, unless a grain of wheat falls into the earth and dies, it remains just a single grain, but if it dies, it bears much fruit.'

There's a pulpit in a church in north London where a text confronts the preacher who climbs its steps. It simply says, 'Sir, we would see Jesus.' It echoes, of course, the request of these Greeks, probably proselyte Jews, certainly seekers after the truth. They were looking for the right person and asked the right question.

But Jesus answered it with words about his impending death—his 'glorification', as this Gospel calls it. A solitary grain of wheat has no future unless it falls to the ground and 'dies' in the soil. But if and when it does, it multiplies over and over again.

Those who seek Jesus must recognize him in the crucified Saviour of Golgotha. It is only through his death that new life can occur, and be multiplied. The prophet from Nazareth was restricted in space and time, and could only touch the lives of those around him at that point in history. The Lord of the cross and empty tomb, on the other hand, reaches out through space and time to touch countless millions with forgiveness and eternal life. The lonely seed died, but from it has come an enormous harvest.

It probably wasn't the answer the Greeks expected, or wanted. But it was the truth. There was no way to life except through death. It's true for seeds, and it's true for us.

A prayer

Heavenly Father, I thank you for the Son of man, who was glorified by his death for us. As I seek him, may I tread the way of his cross, knowing that only through his death can I find true life. Amen.

DW

A voice from heaven

'Now my soul is troubled. And what should I say—"Father, save me from this hour"'? No, it is for this reason I have come to this hour. Father, glorify your name.' Then a voice said from heaven, 'I have glorified it, and will glorify it again.' The crowd standing there heard it and said that it was thunder. Others said, 'An angel has spoken to him.' Jesus said, 'This voice has come for your sake, not for mine. Now is the judgment of this world; now the ruler of this world will be driven out. And I, when I am lifted up from the earth, will draw all people to myself.'

John does not include in his Gospel any mention of Christ's agony in Gethsemane, when he prayed that he might be spared the cup of suffering: 'nevertheless, your will, not mine, be done'. But here is John's 'Gethsemane', because here, too, Jesus considers asking his Father to 'save him from this hour'. Here it is not so much God's will as his 'glory' that is paramount: 'Father, glorify your name.'

And his name would be glorified, in the strangest way imaginable: through the death of his Son. The earthly throne of God's Son was a crude wooden cross, his crown a circle of piercing thorns. Yet with them he won the greatest victory of history, the defeat of evil itself. That is 'glory'.

The incident with the voice from heaven is fascinating for its description of human reactions to the miraculous. Some said 'it thundered'—they were the rationalists, ready with a plausible explanation. Others said 'An angel has spoken to him'—in other words, if there had been a miracle that was fine ... but it was nothing to do with them. Its message was for someone else.

In fact, as Jesus makes clear, it was a message for them: 'This voice has come for your sake.' By shutting their minds to it, they would miss the whole point of the glory that was coming.

A prayer

Lord, when you speak to me—through word or sign—may my ears be open to hear and my will to obey whatever you are saying to me. Amen.

DW

Spiritual self-appraisal

Then Jesus cried aloud: 'Whoever believes in me believes not in me but in him who sent me. I have come as light into the world, so that everyone who believes in me should not remain in the darkness. I do not judge anyone who hears my words and does not keep them, for I came not to judge the world but to save the world. The one who rejects me and does not receive my word has a judge; on the last day the word that I have spoken will serve as judge.'

This is a passage about a difficult subject—judgment. Those who 'see' Jesus (presumably he means those who see what he had done, like raising Lazarus) were in fact 'seeing' God at work. Consequently, to 'see' Jesus but not 'see' the work of the Father is to miss the point of all he had come to do.

Jesus had already made it clear (see 3:17) that he had been sent to be the Saviour of the world, not its judge. But this did not mean that there was no judgment or that evil would remain undefeated. God hasn't gone soft on sin! But Jesus did not come to judge. His proper title is 'Saviour'. He does not judge people, but what he says and does judges them, because the way they react to his words and actions determines whether they accept or reject him. If they 'reject him and do not accept his word' (v. 48), then that very word will condemn them. It's a sobering thought.

Many people think of God as an awesome judge, sitting on a lofty throne rewarding some of his creatures and punishing others. Jesus offers us here a different understanding of judgment: we judge ourselves. It's rather like what they call 'self-appraisal' nowadays. We judge ourselves not so much by our actions as by our reactions. How we receive the 'word' of Jesus will be our judgment.

A prayer

Heavenly Father, you sent your Son to be the Saviour of the world. Help me to 'see' him, to believe in him and to receive what he has said and done for me, so that I may know him as Saviour and worship him as Lord. Amen.

DW

The real nature of love

Now before the festival of the Passover, Jesus knew that his hour had come to depart from this world and go to the Father. Having loved his own who were in the world, he loved them to the end . . . And during supper Jesus, knowing that the Father had given all things into his hands, and that he had come from God and was going to God, got up from the table, took off his outer robe, and tied a towel around himself. Then he poured water into a basin and began to wash the disciples' feet and to wipe them with the towel that was tied around him.

Mary made an extravagant gesture of love when she poured thousands of pounds worth of perfume over the feet of Jesus. It was splendid, spectacular, 'over the top'. But at least no one could doubt her devotion.

Here Jesus also makes an extravagant gesture of love—'he loved them to the end' probably means 'to the fullest possible extent'. The medium he used was more down to earth than Mary's—not perfume, but plain cold water. But again it was applied to feet and again he lovingly dried them—not with his hair, like Mary, but with a towel.

Feet are not usually thought of as objects of beauty! They work hard for us, and in the process they get calloused and sore, and they sweat. The disciples were waiting for the household slave to offer them the usual courtesy of a cool bath for their feet before the meal began. When no servant appeared, the Son of God (who 'knew that the Father had put all things under his power') took on that role. The hands of the one who came from God tended to their sweaty, blistered feet.

And in this way he showed his love 'to the fullest possible extent'—in the simplest and humblest action of domestic service, one within the capability of any of us. Not grand gestures, not magnificent acts of self-sacrifice, but simple and loving service most fully demonstrates the real nature of love.

A prayer

Lord, show me how to demonstrate your love in the humble and simple things of life, for Jesus Christ's sake. Amen.

DW

The test of love

**Jesus said, 'I give you a new commandment, that you love one another...
By this everyone will know that you are my disciples, if you have love for
one another.' Simon Peter said to him, 'Lord, where are you going?' Jesus
answered, 'Where I am going, you cannot follow me now; but you will
follow afterward.' Peter said to him, 'Lord, why can I not follow you now? I
will lay down my life for you.' Jesus answered, 'Will you lay down your life
for me? Very truly, I tell you, before the cock crows, you will have denied
me three times.'**

The disciples are gathered in the upper room, and the atmosphere is sombre. Jesus is talking as though some great crisis lies just ahead, a crisis that will involve his leaving them and 'going away'. And although he speaks of a new 'Counsellor' or helper who will come to their aid, they are clearly worried and perplexed.

It is in this context that we must see both the 'new commandment' and the warning to Peter. They must learn to love each other, because only then would they be able to fulfil his mission in his absence. Their love for one another would unite them, and their unity would convince the world and bring it to faith in him. It was true then, and it's true now, that the most attractive thing about the Christian Church is the love its members show to each other; and conversely that the most unattractive thing about the Church is when they don't.

The warning to Peter is stark. His profession of love—even to the point of death—is challenged. As it happened, he was prepared to die for Jesus. At least, he took a sword and was prepared to fight the soldiers who came to arrest him, which would probably have cost him his life (see 18:10). But he caved in before an apparently less serious threat, denying that he knew Jesus when challenged by a servant girl.

Sometimes we are better able to withstand the big test than the little one. Sometimes physical courage is easier than emotional or spiritual courage. What Peter didn't know was himself. Unsurprisingly, Jesus knew Peter better than Peter did!

A prayer

Lord, help me to love others, and to love you, with a love that doesn't boast or make huge claims, but flows from gratitude and trust. For Jesus' sake. Amen.

DW

Knowing the way

'Do not let your hearts be troubled. Believe in God, believe also in me. In my Father's house are many dwelling places. If it were not so, would I have told you that I go to prepare a place for you? And if I go and prepare a place for you, I will come again and take you to myself, so that where I am there you may be also. And you know the way to the place where I am going.' Thomas said to him, 'Lord, we do not know where you are going. How can we know the way?' Jesus said to him, 'I am the way, and the truth, and the life. No one comes to the Father except through me.'

This well-known passage is about a journey. Jesus is 'going away' to prepare a place for his disciples, so that eventually they can be with him. It's a picture of long-distance travel in the ancient world, where a servant went ahead to find the next night's resting place and prepare beds and a meal. Jesus would be the one going ahead; the disciples, in due time, would follow. But Thomas is mystified. It was all very well Jesus going on ahead to prepare this 'resting place', but as they had no idea where he was going, how would they ever find it?

His answer may or may not have helped Thomas, but it should be clear to us. Jesus himself is the way to the place where he is going—he is, if you like, the path there, the map, the means of discovery. He had come to earth to show us the way to the Father, and that was where he was about to go.

But he is not only the 'way', the means by which we get there. He is also the one who has gone ahead on the journey. It is a very reassuring thought that on the journey which we dread more than any other—the one that takes us from this life to the life beyond death—Jesus has gone ahead, and is waiting for us at the resting place.

A prayer

Lord, take from my heart anxiety and misgiving about the journey that lies ahead. Strengthen me with the promise that Jesus has gone on ahead, that he is preparing a place, and that one day I shall be where he is now. Amen.

DW

The suffering servant

We had all gone astray like sheep, each taking his own way, and Yahweh brought the acts of rebellion of all of us to bear on him. Ill-treated and afflicted, he never opened his mouth, like a lamb led to the slaughterhouse, like a sheep dumb before its shearers he never opened his mouth.

Traditionally this Sunday turns the attention of Christians from the preparation to the reality. Lent is a period of preparation for the renewal in us of the Passion, death and resurrection of Christ. At Passion Sunday attention turns to these events themselves. If we are consciously to join in these basic events of our salvation, we need to enter into Jesus' own thoughts.

At the last supper, as he blessed the cup of the new covenant, Jesus said it would be 'poured out for many'. This precious saying shows that he saw his action in terms of the suffering servant of the Lord. Other sayings in the course of his ministry point in the same direction, that he will be 'a ransom for many', that he 'came not to be served but to serve'. At the baptism and the transfiguration, the voice from heaven declares him, 'my beloved Son, in whom I am well pleased'. This is an allusion to the first of the songs of the servant in Isaiah.

In the words of Jesus there are enough allusions to these songs to justify the suggestion that these songs form the background of Jesus' thought, both in his ministry and more especially in his road to the cross. He saw himself as the servant of the Lord foretold by the prophet in these four songs. The fourth especially concentrates on the rejection, humiliation and death of the Lord's servant as a willing victim, to bring Israel back to God. The servant had a mission from the Lord to lead Israel back through suffering willingly undergone. The servant had a mission as the embodiment of Israel to bring God's light to the nations and lead them to commit themselves to the Lord. In both these capacities Jesus saw himself as he was brought to his Passion.

In his turn, Paul sees himself as the servant of Christ. So, too, all Christians are the servants of Christ, committed to following him through suffering to glory.

HW

First Lamentation (1)

How deserted she sits, the city once thronged with people! Once the greatest of nations, she is now like a widow. Once the princess of states she is now put to forced labour.

The tragedy of the Babylonian exile bit deep into the soul of Israel. Jerusalem was the city of God, the city where God dwelt among human beings. In the temple they could be close to God, could pray to him and dedicate themselves to him. The king at Jerusalem was God's anointed; God had promised to treat him always like a loving father, even when he needed correction.

Now all that was ended. The Babylonians had sacked Jerusalem and despoiled the temple. The last king saw his sons killed before being blinded and dragged off to exile. When they reached the waters of Babylon, all the Israelites could do was weep as they thought of Jerusalem. There was no thought that God had deserted them. No, they had deserted God and been taken away from his company and his protection through their own fault, their own faithlessness.

These five poems, the Lamentations, are songs of mourning composed soon after the sack of Jerusalem. The greatest figure of these last days of Jerusalem was the prophet Jeremiah, and there was a tendency, both in Judaism and in Christianity, to link any writing of that time with him (just as anything ancient in Egypt tends to be linked to that well-known figure, Cleopatra). So for many

centuries Jeremiah was thought to be the author of these Lamentations.

The sensation of being deserted by God comes to all of us at one time or another. We search our consciences. Is it because I have been unfaithful? Unfaithful in prayer, not giving him time or attention? Unfaithful in action, by behaviour which separates myself from him? Unfaithful in intention, putting my own selfish concerns and interests first, in ways incompatible with the commitment to God which I have undertaken? These are certainly important soul-searchings. But the book of Job and the parable of the payment of the vineyard workers show that God is accountable to no one. He gives what he wills to whom he wills, and we cannot ask him to justify his actions. If he wishes me to feel his absence for whatever reason, it is ultimately for my own good, and always out of love for me.

To think about

Our hearts are restless till they rest in you.

St Augustine

HW

First Lamentation (2)

Jerusalem has sinned so gravely that she has become a thing unclean. All who used to honour her despise her, having seen her nakedness; she herself groans aloud and turns her face away . . . All you who pass this way, look and see: is any sorrow like the sorrow inflicted on me, with which Yahweh struck me on the day of his burning anger?

The tragedy which struck Jerusalem is seen by Christian tradition to be repeated in the sufferings of Christ. Christ is the new Israel, the complete fulfilment of the chosen people. He takes up in himself the history of the chosen people, so that what happened to them may be seen as a foretaste of what happened to him. Their passion and rejection is seen as prefiguring his rejection and his Passion. Israel suffered at the hands of foreigners, the Babylonians, just as Jesus suffered at the hands of foreigners, the Romans. They were cast out of the city, just as he was. Only they were reaping the harvest of their sins, whereas he was the sinless one.

Since the earliest days of Christianity, the Lamentations have been used in the Christian prayers of Holy Week. Like a great ancient church or cathedral, they are hallowed not only in themselves but also by the Christian devotion of centuries. The fact that a church has for centuries been a place of prayer and devotion gives it a certain sacred character; it has been 'consecrated' by that devotion, by the affection and dedication expressed there by Christians through the ages. In the same way these passages of Scripture have become more sacred for Christians by their application to the Passion of Christ. Especially the second of these two verses has been used to apply to Jesus on the cross. Perhaps Matthew already alludes to it, when he writes of the passers-by who looked at the crucified Jesus and jeered at him. The very ancient Christian lament, sung on Good Friday at the veneration of the cross, uses the verse to contrast Jesus' unlimited generosity and self-sacrifice with human selfishness. In the monastic prayer of the Church the Lamentations are read at the night office for the last three days of Holy Week. Perhaps best known of all is the aria in Handel's *Messiah*.

For meditation

Behold, and see if there be any sorrow like unto my sorrow.

HW

Second Lamentation

In his anger, with what darkness has the Lord enveloped the daughter of Zion! He has flung the beauty of Israel from heaven to the ground, without regard for his footstool on the day of his anger.

What is this talk of anger? Is it really true after all that the God of the Old Testament is a God of anger and revenge? Is it reserved to the New Testament that God should be seen as a God of love? Not always, even in the New Testament, has God been regarded as purely a God of love. Medieval theologians took the image of sacrifice so far that in discussing the crucifixion they could speak of the Father venting on his Son the wrath which was due upon all humanity, the Father thrusting the knife into the heart of his Son, the Son suffering the pains of the damned.

Such thoughts are repulsive. The hypocrisy of a God who sponsors forgiveness, and yet secretly himself exacts the full penalty from an innocent victim, would be loathsome. Still worse that the victim is his own Son, who has during his life expressed such prayers of devotion and lived for the will of his Father alone.

The crucifixion must be the moment of purest love and union between Father and Son. 'My God, my God, why have you forsaken me?' is only the beginning of a psalm which goes on to thank God for his protection and final victory. How, then, did it happen? The loving Father gave to Adam, the crown of his creation, the gift of free will, so that Adam could love him freely. Down the ages Adam has systematically misused this power. So both Father and Son were trapped in the net of human perversity and blindness.

What do the prophets, and this sorrowing poet of the Lamentations, mean by the anger and the jealousy of God? His jealousy is that he will brook no rival. Israel—and all his followers—must be dedicated uniquely to God. In the troubled times before the exile, this meant that no alliance with Egypt or Assyria was tolerable: such alliances inevitably meant accepting the foreign gods, too, as powerful protectors. So these final days of Lent and the approach of Holy Week give all Christians a chance to re-examine our own fidelity. Have we rival gods? Do we form alliances with idols whose worship jars against our Christian commitment to God alone?

A prayer

Lord Jesus, you suffered for us on the cross. Grant me the same unflinching fidelity to your Father.

HW

Third Lamentation

Yahweh is good to those who trust him, to all who search for him. It is good to wait in silence for Yahweh to save. It is good for someone to bear the yoke from a young age, to sit in solitude and silence when it weighs heavy, to lay one's head in the dust—maybe there is hope.

The Hebraeo-Christian tradition is not alone in valuing suffering as a means of learning. 'Wisdom comes by suffering,' said the Greeks too. The Greek myths are full of stories of those who were brought to their full moral stature by suffering, such as Oedipus and Orestes. In the Bible suffering is valued because it leads the sufferer back to God. Especially from the exile onwards—as shown in these poems—the poor and the oppressed were seen as God's favourites. They could not rely on their own resources and must turn to him in all their needs; they could only wait in silence and hope for deliverance from him. This is the mainspring of spirituality after the exile.

In the Christian tradition, too, Mary is the spearhead of the poor of the Lord, relying on him, totally dependent on and obedient to him. Jesus himself is from among the poor, a despised Galilean, bringing his message to outcasts. He warns the rich and successful that their riches and their success are a danger, distracting them from reliance on God. His own disciples fail in every conceivable way, slow to understand his message, too frightened to stay with their master in his suffering, and after his death merely skulking away in hiding.

Their remorse at their failure must have pained them and made them wiser and more eager to follow when the strength of the Spirit came to fortify them.

When pain and suffering come from the Lord, they are often in precisely that mode which we find unbearable. We protest. We rebel. We cannot understand. Anything but this! A bereavement, a humiliation, loss of independence, a total failure, a physical or mental sickness. Even Paul suffered the agony of some scourge that he asked three times to be removed from him. That too was part of his learning, that he must sit and wait, intensifying his dependence on the Lord.

A thought

I know that my Redeemer lives, and that he will rise up last. After my awakening he will set me close to him, and from my flesh I shall look on God.

Job 19:25–26

HW

Fourth Lamentation

The children of Zion, as precious as finest gold—to think that they should now be reckoned like crockery made by a potter! ... Once her young people were brighter than snow, whiter than milk, rosier than coral their bodies, their hue like sapphire. Now their faces are blacker than soot, they are not recognised in the streets, the skin has shrunk over their bones, as dry as a stick.

A grim picture of the transformation from prosperity to disaster, using the image of skin-colour to convey the change from the tender, lissom skin of flourishing young people to the drawn leathery hide of terminal starvation. One is reminded of the images of modern war and destruction.

How could a loving Father so correct his children? He had promised to David that if his descendants did wrong, he would punish them 'with a rod such as men use, with blows such as mankind gives' (2 Samuel 7:14) . And yet, even this punishment was a corrective, and did indeed bring Israel back from their neglect and their idol-worship to a realization of the source of their being. Had they not been brought back, they could well have become just another backward, Near Eastern hill-tribe. As it was, they went forward: before the exile their devotion to God had been largely institutional and national. From the exile dates the increased awareness of an intensely personal bond, a commitment of the heart, of each individual. They can no longer rely on the institutions of Israel, temple, cult and kingship.

Looking back from our historical distance, we can see how extraordinary was God's care of his people, and how close they came to being absorbed or losing their religious purpose. The ten tribes of Israel in the north disappeared from history. No other special faith survived the Babylonian captivity. Again at the time of the Maccabees, a century and a half before Christ, a desire to be like other nations almost cost the Jews their special heritage. Again they were corrected and strengthened by persecution.

If I look back over my life, I can see times when the Lord corrected me in ways which at the time were painful, and seemed unnecessary or meaningless. Yet I came out of them strengthened and even perhaps less unfaithful.

To meditate on

I shall punish their offences with the rod ... but I shall never withdraw from him my faithful love.

Psalm 89:32–33

HW

Fifth Lamentation

Our ancestors sinned; they are no more, and we bear the weight of their guilt . . . Joy has vanished from our hearts; our dancing has turned to mourning . . . Make us come back to you, Yahweh, and we will come back. Restore us as we were before! Unless you have utterly rejected us, in an anger which knows no limit.

It was during the exile, soon after the composition of this lament, that Israel came to see personal responsibility in a new light. Each of us is responsible only for personal sins, not for those of our ancestors.

Yet there is still some truth in the saying that we bear our ancestors' guilt and, more important, we pass on our own guilt to future generations. Moral failure may not be in the genes. If alcoholism were passed down in the blood from one generation to the next, the moral failure of the first generation would be all the greater and that of the later generation correspondingly less. But the evil that we do does redound on those around us and those that follow us. Our attitudes, our example does have an effect for good or evil, and to that extent we can share in the guilt of others.

This lament, however, dares to ask God to bring us back to himself God's justice is not like human justice. It is more that God is true to himself. He exercises judgment not according to our behaviour but according to his nature. On Sinai God declared himself to be a God of mercy and forgiveness, and this is the conception of God which echoes down the scriptures. His justice is that he must be true to his nature of mercy and true to his promises of mercy. His justice is seen also as his salvation, his power to save and his will to forgive. It is this which gives the poet confidence to demand that God should make us come back to him. However conscious we are of sin, joy cannot permanently vanish from our hearts if we keep before our eyes the nature of God.

A prayer

Let me hear the sound of joy and gladness, and the bones you have crushed will dance.

Psalm 51:8

HW

The Lamb of God

The next day [John the Baptist] saw Jesus coming toward him, and said, 'Behold, the Lamb of God, who takes away the sin of the world! . . . I myself did not know him; but he who sent me to baptize with water said to me, "He on whom you see the Spirit descend and remain, this is he who baptizes with the Holy Spirit." And I have seen and borne witness that this is the Son of God.' The next day again John was standing with two of his disciples; and he looked at Jesus as he walked, and said, 'Behold the Lamb of God!'

Most of us don't like to think about lambs going to be slaughtered—perhaps herded into lorries, frightened, and sometimes thirsty because proper provisions aren't always made for them. We choose our lamb in tidily butchered joints in the shop or the supermarket and eat it roasted with redcurrant jelly or mint sauce. The slaughter of lambs isn't part of our thinking. But it was very much part of Jewish thinking and when John the Baptist spoke about the Lamb of God the people would have thought immediately about the lambs that were killed in the temple and the Passover lambs that were killed and eaten at the Feast of Passover (which we shall look at tomorrow) .

The people must have been puzzled if they really thought about what this strange prophet was saying. Pointing to a man, and saying, 'Behold the Lamb of God', They wouldn't have understood. Not until much later, when the Lamb of God had died on the cross for the sin of the world and the eleven apostles had gone out into the world to preach the good news about the forgiveness of sins and the death of Christ. Sin is a difficult subject to think about and not a fashionable one. But whether we like it or not it is present in our world, and it is a killer. It destroys relationships and lives like a polluted and poisoned river of hate.

A project and a reflection

When you listen to the news today, consider how many of the news items are events caused by human sin. Then consider the words of Jesus: '. . . out of the heart of man come evil thoughts, murder, adultery, fornication, theft, false witness . . .'

SB

The Passover

The Lord said to Moses and Aaron ... 'Tell all the congregation of Israel that ... they shall take every man a lamb ... Your lamb shall be without blemish ... and you shall keep it until the fourteenth day of this month, when the whole assembly of the congregation of Israel shall kill their lambs in the evening. Then they shall take some of the blood, and put it on the two doorposts and the lintel of the houses in which they eat them. They shall eat the flesh that night, roasted ... It is the Lord's passover. For I will pass through the land of Egypt that night, and I will smite all the first-born in the land of Egypt, both man and beasts; and on all the gods of Egypt I will execute judgments: I am the Lord. The blood shall be a sign for you, upon the houses where you are; and when I see the blood, I will pass over you ...'

Yesterday for my Sunday lunch I had roast lamb, and as I smelt it cooking, and then ate it, I thought about the Israelites eating their Passover lambs first on the night of their exodus from Egypt, and then through the years at every Feast of Passover.

There is a cost to living and for us to live other living things than ourselves have to die (whether animal or vegetable). There is also a cost to forgiveness. 'The wages of sin is death' (Romans 6:23) a spiritual death which is a broken relationship and separation from God. For the relationship to be put right again the one who was sinned against has to bear the pain of the sin and offer love and friendship to the sinner. Every sin against another person or creature is a sin against God, and after he has committed adultery with Bathsheba and had her husband murdered David cries out, 'Against thee, thee only have I sinned.'

And it is only God who can forgive sin and take it away in the ultimate sense. He does it by taking the pain of it into his own body and holding out the arms of love to the sinner. But there is a terrible cost.

Reflect

Behold the Lamb of God, who takes away the sin of the world.

SB

The good shepherd

Get you up to a high mountain, O Zion, herald of good tidings; lift up your voice with strength, O Jerusalem, herald of good tidings, lift it up, fear not; say to the cities of Judah, 'Behold your God!' Behold, the Lord God comes with might, and his arm rules for him; behold, his reward is with him, and his recompense before him. He will feed his flock like a shepherd, and he will gather the lambs in his arms, he will carry them in his bosom, and gently lead those that are with young.

When many of us read these words from Isaiah we hear inside our heads the marvellous aria from Handel's *Messiah*. As I listen to it now (in my head) my heart lifts up with delight that this is our God and through the words we can do what Isaiah told us to do: 'Behold your God!' When we look we see God as a shepherd who looks after the flock, and who loves it so much that he dies for it. That is what Jesus said and when the Word became flesh he spoke about the nature of God by using all the Old Testament imagery that came out of their pastoral, sheep-keeping nation.

The other day when I was looking out of my study window at the Shetland sheep who live three fields away the owner came out and separated one sheep and its lamb from another mother and baby and gave to each pair a little heap of food. Special food for each one, and the shepherd knew just what they needed. We might be doubtful about that when we apply it to God and feel that 'This I can definitely do without!' But the Lord who is our shepherd can make any circumstances of our life into nourishing food for our soul, however bitter it tastes to eat. We can know the presence of God with us in all our circumstances and then every moment can be a sacrament (what Pierre de Caussade called the sacrament of the present moment) in which we know and encounter the living God who creates us and loves us.

Reflect

'His reward is with him.' 'Fear not Abraham, I am your shield and your exceeding great reward.' 'How much more will your heavenly Father give the Holy Spirit to them that ask him.'

SB

The wrathful shepherd

Thus says the Lord God, Behold, I am against the shepherds; and I will require my sheep at their hand, and put a stop to their feeding the sheep; no longer shall the shepherds feed themselves. I will rescue my sheep from their mouths, that they may not be food for them. For thus says the Lord God: Behold, I, I myself will search for my sheep and will seek them out . . . I myself will be the shepherd of my sheep, and I will make them lie down, says the Lord God. I will seek the lost, and I will bring back the strayed, and I will bind up the crippled, and I will strengthen the weak, and the fat and the strong I will watch over; I will feed them in justice.

The other day on television I saw a gentle-faced mongrel dog that was so thin it could hardly stand. Its owner had starved it and beaten it and kept it tied up—and the Royal Society for the Prevention of Cruelty to Animals had rescued it. I felt very angry with the owner.

There is a school of thought in Christianity which says that God never gets angry. But the Bible and our own experience tell us how false that belief is. The wrath of God is the other side of the coin of the love of God. How could a loving person not be implacably opposed to actions which hurt and destroy both people and creatures? The loving person doesn't stop loving the person who does harmful and hurtful things—but love wants the sinner to repent and turn away from his or her sin and be forgiven.

Ezekiel spoke out the wrath of God against the shepherds of Israel—the teachers and leaders who were supposed to be looking after the people of God. But they weren't: they were looking after themselves. There was a religious hierarchy which was disgracefully failing in its task. So the God who passionately minds about the welfare and the happiness of the sheep would come and do the job himself.

Reflect

Think about the nature of the God whom we worship. Reflect on the wrath of God and why he gets angry. Then reflect on the love of God, and the actions that a good shepherd takes in looking after the flock. Turn your response into prayer.

SB

Eating the lamb of God

The Jews then disputed among themselves, saying, 'How can this man give us his flesh to eat?' So Jesus said to them, 'Truly, truly, I say to you, unless you eat the flesh of the Son of man and drink his blood, you have no life in you; he who eats my flesh and drinks my blood has eternal life, and I will raise him up at the last day. For my flesh is food indeed, and my blood is drink indeed. He who eats my flesh and drinks my blood abides in me, and I in him . . . I came that they may have life, and have it abundantly. I am the good shepherd. The good shepherd lays down his life for the sheep.'

Jesus' hearers would have been horrified. They were forbidden to eat animal blood—let alone human blood or human flesh. Their scriptures told them the truth that 'the life of the flesh is in the blood' (a truth it took hundreds of years for the medical profession to discover) and their whole sacrificial system was about creatures being killed and their blood drained out—and sometimes poured out on to the earth and sometimes sprinkled over the people.

What Jesus did on that first Maundy Thursday evening was to set up for all time the great sacrament of the Eucharist, or Holy Communion—and to eat his flesh and to drink his blood was to share in 'the benefits of his death and passion'. '. . . In Christ God was reconciling the world to himself, not counting their trespasses against them, and entrusting to us the message of reconciliation' wrote St Paul in 2 Corinthians 5:19. In 1 Corinthians he said that 'Christ, our paschal lamb, has been sacrificed. Let us, therefore, celebrate the festival . . .' (1 Corinthians 5:7–8) There is a sense in which we celebrate it at every Eucharist because every service of Holy Communion looks back to that Passover night when Jesus set up the sacrament—and to his death on the cross which is at the heart of it.

A reflection

Think about the nature of the one whose body and blood you eat and drink in the sacrament. Think about the paschal lamb, sacrificed and then roasted and eaten with bitter herbs. Think about the Lamb of God, who had come to Jerusalem to be slaughtered, and to take away the sin of the world.

SB

The sin bearer

He was despised and rejected by men; a man of sorrows, and acquainted with grief; and as one from whom men hide their faces he was despised, and we esteemed him not. Surely he has borne our griefs and carried our sorrows; yet we esteemed him stricken, smitten by God, and afflicted. But he was wounded for our transgressions, he was bruised for our iniquities; upon him was the chastisement that made us whole, and with his stripes we are healed. All we like sheep have gone astray; we have turned every one to his own way; and the Lord has laid on him the iniquity of us all. He was oppressed, and he was afflicted, yet he opened not his mouth; like a lamb that is led to the slaughter, and like a sheep that before its shearers is dumb, so he opened not his mouth.

Christianity is the only religion in the world which tells us of the suffering God—and the God who suffers is the only God there is. The first Christians recognized in Jesus the suffering servant of the Lord whom Isaiah wrote about. In Acts chapter 8 the Ethiopian eunuch is reading Isaiah 53 and wondering who the prophet is writing about, and beginning with verses 7 and 8 Philip 'told him the good news of Jesus'.

It says in Isaiah 53 that the suffering servant of God bore our griefs and our sorrows and that God laid all our sins and iniquities upon him. That means that every individual in the world can know the forgiveness of God through the sin-bearing of the Lamb of God who takes away the sin of the world. Yet although he takes away our sin he doesn't take away our griefs and our sorrows. He bears them but that doesn't mean that all the pain is his and that our pain disappears. It does mean that in our grief and in our sorrow we can know the presence with us of the suffering Christ, suffering with us.

A way to pray

Hold in the presence of God anything that is making you sad and sorrowful and just stay in silence for a few moments. Then hold in his presence the sadness of another person or another situation and pray for that.

SB

He looks for the lost one

Now the tax collectors and sinners were all drawing near to hear him. And the Pharisees and the scribes murmured, saying, 'This man receives sinners and eats with them.' So he told them this parable: 'What man of you, having a hundred sheep, if he has lost one of them, does not leave the ninety-nine in the wilderness, and go after the one which is lost, until he finds it? And when he has found it, he lays it on his shoulders, rejoicing. And when he comes home, he calls together his friends and his neighbours, saying to them, "Rejoice with me, for I have found my sheep which was lost." Just so, I tell you, there will be more joy in heaven over one sinner who repents than over ninety-nine righteous persons who need no repentance.'

Two couples I know have both lost one of their children. The son of one has died. The daughter of the other has left home to 'live it up' with men, sex, drink and drugs. A prodigal daughter—and for her parents to be lost is the same in their experience as for her to be dead. Both couples have other children—just as the man in Jesus' story had other sheep. Ninety-nine of them. But they didn't fill the place of the one who wasn't there any more. The first couple know that one day they will see their son again, because he was a Christian and that is what Jesus promised his followers. For the parents of the prodigal daughter it is a sort of living death. A bleeding wound that never heals and that always hurts. Both sets of parents are waiting not knowing what will happen in the future. The parents of the son who has died can wait in hope for the resurrection morning. The parents of the prodigal daughter can wait in hope too, because they know what God is like.

In this much loved chapter 15 of Luke Jesus tells us about three things that are lost: a sheep, a coin and a prodigal son. God is the Father who waits for his son to come home again, and then runs out to meet him with his arms wide open. Then there is great rejoicing, because 'This your brother was dead, and is alive; he was lost, and is found.'

Reflect

What are you waiting for in hope?

SB

The Lamb upon the throne

And between the throne and the four living creatures and among the elders, I saw a Lamb standing, as though it had been slain . . . and he went and took the scroll from the right hand of him who was seated on the throne. And when he had taken the scroll, the four living creatures and the twenty-four elders fell down before the Lamb, each holding a harp, and with golden bowls full of incense, which are the prayers of the saints; and they sang a new song, saying, 'Worthy art thou to take the scroll and to open its seals, for thou wast slain and by thy blood didst ransom men for God from every tribe and tongue and people and nation, and hast made them a kingdom and priests to our God, and they shall reign on earth.'

Today we shall hear the story of the first Easter morning, and listen to the glorious words which tell us about the resurrection of Jesus Christ from the dead and the joy and bewilderment and disbelief of those first disciples. But the resurrection of Christ happened once in time—and the appearances and the empty tomb were events experienced and seen by the ones who were there in the beginning. For us the present reality is not that today Jesus rises again from the dead but that he rose on that first Easter morning.

It was the risen Christ whom John saw in the series of visions which form the book of Revelation. Earlier in this vision John has been weeping, because he has seen a scroll sealed with seven seals containing God's future plans for the earth, and no one has been found worthy to open the scroll. But John is told not to weep, because 'the Lion of the tribe of Judah, the Root of David, has conquered' so he can open the scroll. Yet when John looks he sees a Lamb. The purposes of God can go forward, but only because the Lamb has been slain and Christ has died for the sin of the world . . .

A song of praise

Forever You will be
The Lamb upon the throne
I gladly bow the knee
And worship You alone.

Noel and Tricia Richards
Copyright © Thankyou Music 1987

SB

Loving and feeding

When they had finished breakfast, Jesus said to Simon Peter, 'Simon, son of John, do you love me more than these?' He said to him, 'Yes, Lord; you know that I love you.' Jesus said to him, 'Feed my lambs.' A second time he said to him, 'Simon, son of John, do you love me?' He said to him, 'Yes, Lord; you know that I love you.' Jesus said to him, 'Tend my sheep.' He said to him the third time, 'Simon, son of John, do you love me?' Peter felt hurt because he said to him the third time, 'Do you love me?' And he said to him, 'Lord, you know everything; you know that I love you.' Jesus said to him, 'Feed my sheep.'

The English word 'love' in this passage is a translation of two sorts of loving, the sort of love that friends love each other with, and the sort of love that God loves us with and that we are to love God and our neighbour with. The love that the two great commandments talk about. 'Do you love me with that sort of loving?' Jesus asks Peter, twice, and each time Peter replies 'Lord, you know I love you with the love of a friend.' But then Jesus asks him 'Do you love me with the love of a friend'—and presumably Peter is grieved that he should question even that sort of loving.

Yet each time Peter tells Jesus that he does love him (and it must have reminded him of the three times he denied him) he is given a commission. To feed the lambs and the sheep, and to tend them. The just-born ones in a flock need different food from the adults—and in a good church they will get it. Simple teaching for beginners. The teaching on the deep things of God for the grown-ups, to enable them to grow up into Christ and into maturity.

Reflect

Think about Peter's three-fold denial of Christ—and his new awareness of his weaknesses. Think about this three-fold commission that the risen Christ gives to him. Then think about your own weaknesses and the weaknesses of the leaders in your church, and in the Church as a whole. Then pray—and thank God that his strength is made perfect in our weakness, and that he can use us just as we are, weaknesses and warts and all.

SB

Cost and confidence

Therefore gird up your minds, be sober, set your hope fully upon the grace that is coming to you at the revelation of Jesus Christ. As obedient children, do not be conformed to the passions of your former ignorance, but as he who called you is holy, be holy yourselves in all your conduct; since it is written, 'You shall be holy, for I am holy.' ... You know that you were ransomed from the futile ways inherited from your fathers, not with perishable things such as silver or gold, but with the precious blood of Christ, like that of a lamb without blemish or spot.

A man I know believes that now he is a Christian he cannot sin, and that therefore whatever he does isn't sin. That false belief is a sort of Gnosticism, which says that since the body is unimportant it doesn't matter what we do with it. But for Christians the body is very important, because through it we live out the whole of our life to the glory of God.

Unlike Gnostics, Christians believe that God values the mind and body together; and here Peter is saying to us, 'Use your mind', 'Think!' And that ties up with what St Paul said. 'Be transformed by the renewing of your mind.' We need to reprogram our minds (which in some ways are like computers) so that the information in them is correct. And to delight God and obey the greatest commandment of all is to love God with all our heart, soul, strength and mind. So thinking about the truth is part of our worship. Some of our thinking must be about the cost of our forgiveness to God-in-Christ—and the shedding of the precious blood of Christ like that of 'a lamb without blemish or spot'. When we consider that, how can we think of going back to our former ignorance and passions? We may sometimes slip back into them, and fall into serious sin, but then we confess our sins, and know that if we do he is faithful and just and will forgive us our sins and cleanse us from all unrighteousness.

Reflect

Reflect on your own confidence in God and consider what it rests on. Reflect on the cost to God of our forgiveness—and on the reason why he was willing to pay the price.

SB

Playing God's music

Servants, be submissive to your masters with all respect, not only to the kind and gentle but also to the overbearing. For one is approved if, mindful of God, he endures pain while suffering unjustly. For what credit is it, if when you do wrong and are beaten for it you take it patiently? But if when you do right and suffer for it you take it patiently, you have God's approval. For to this you have been called, because Christ also suffered for you, leaving you an example, that you should follow in his steps. He committed no sin; no guile was found on his lips. When he was reviled, he did not revile in return; when he suffered, he did not threaten; but he trusted to him who judges justly. He himself bore our sins in his body on the tree, that we might die to sin and live to righteousness. By his wounds you have been healed. For you were straying like sheep, but have now returned to the Shepherd and Guardian of your souls.

Bishop Wilfred Wood tells a story of a priest he knew who had his hi-fi equipment stolen. So he went to buy some more, and took a favourite record with him to play as a test. To his astonishment, he heard things in the music that he had never heard before. They had been there all the time, on the record, but since his old equipment hadn't played them he had never heard them. He reflected that it is like that for us in the Christian life. The world doesn't always see and hear all the music and the glory of the life of Christ, because Christians aren't living it out in the whole of its beauty and holiness.

Today's passage shows us just how high a level we are called to live at. We baulk at it. It seems outrageous to submit to an overbearing master. Surely we should be protesting? And yes, in a way we should. But perhaps the answer is that for our self we have to submit and on behalf of other people we have to protest.

Reflect

Read the passage from Peter again. Who do you know who lives it out so that the music of the life of Christ is heard in our discordant world? How good a piece of hi-fi equipment are you, for the music of God to be played on?

SB

The heavenly marriage

Then I saw a new heaven and a new earth; for the first heaven and the first earth had passed away, and the sea was no more. And I saw the holy city, new Jerusalem, coming down out of heaven from God, prepared as a bride adorned for her husband; and I heard a loud voice from the throne saying, 'Behold, the dwelling of God is with men. He will dwell with them, and they shall be his people, and God himself will be with them; he will wipe away every tear from their eyes, and death shall be no more, neither shall there be mourning nor crying nor pain any more, for the former things have passed away.' And he who sat upon the throne said, 'Behold, I make all things new.'

There is a glorious and beautiful tangle of mixed metaphors in the Bible. God is the good shepherd—and the good shepherd gives his life for the sheep. Jesus is both the shepherd and the Lamb of God who takes away the sin of the world. God is the husband of his people—and now a holy city is coming down out of heaven like a bride adorned for her wedding and the wedding will be the marriage supper of the Lamb.

Heaven is union and communion with God-in-Christ—a union far more intimate than any human marriage. But the human marriage can tell us things about the heavenly one. The prophet Hosea loves and marries an unfaithful and adulterous bride and then buys her back from slavery and goes on loving her. In the Song of Songs there is an enormous and mutual delight of the Lover and the Beloved, the bridegroom and the bride, and Jews and Christians have always seen in this a picture of the love relationship that there is between God and his people. When we are in love what we most want is to be in the presence of the beloved—and to make love is to express physically what we feel in our whole being. The biblical metaphors about the wonder and the glory of heaven point to a blissful union that is beyond any human union and a consummation beyond believing.

A way to pray

Reflect on human marriage, and let it show you something of the relationship between Christ and his Church.

SB

The glory of heaven

And I saw no temple in the city, for its temple is the Lord God the Almighty and the Lamb. And the city has no need of sun or moon to shine upon it, for the glory of God is its light, and its lamp is the Lamb. By its light shall the nations walk; and the kings of the earth shall bring their glory into it, and its gates shall never be shut by day and there shall be no night there; they shall bring into it the glory and the honour of the nations. But nothing unclean shall enter it, nor any one who practices abomination or falsehood, but only those who are written in the Lamb's book of life.

We don't seem to spend much time thinking about heaven. 'Well, we don't know anything about it, so how can we?' someone will say. But in fact we can know something about it and when the day comes for us to face our own dying we shall be glad if we have spent some time contemplating the subject. 'Eye has not seen, neither has entered into the heart of man, what God has prepared for them that love him,' people quote from 1 Corinthians 2:9. But although they stop there St Paul didn't. He went on: 'but God has revealed them to us by his Spirit'. And if we reflect on the Bible passages which tell us about the future life, the Spirit will reveal to us something of the glory that lies ahead for us.

God will be there—everywhere—the Lord God almighty and the Lamb: and the Spirit of God will be living in each one of us. In this life we know and experience what St Paul wrote of as 'Christ in you, the hope of glory'—and when we get to heaven the glory of the Spirit of Christ in us will shine out of us. All of us glorious, and all of us unique and different. All of us worshipping and knowing and adoring God the Father who made the world, and Christ the Son who died for the world. Nothing will be hidden there, because the light of God will shine everywhere.

Reflect

Read the passage again, and reflect on the pictures and images that you see as you read. Pray that the Spirit of God will reveal to you what God has prepared for those who love him.

SB

The water of life

Then he showed me the river of the water of life, bright as crystal, flowing from the throne of God and of the Lamb through the middle of the street of the city; also, on either side of the river, the tree of life with its twelve kinds of fruit, yielding its fruit each month; and the leaves of the tree were for the healing of the nations. There shall no more be anything accursed, but the throne of God and of the Lamb shall be in it, and his servants shall worship him; they shall see his face, and his name shall be on their foreheads. And night shall be no more; they need no light of lamp or sun, for the Lord God will be their light, and they shall reign for ever and ever.

Yesterday morning I arranged a bowl of honeysuckle, and the lovely pink and yellow flowers and green leaves on their twining stems hung over the edge of the vase. But in the evening some of the flowers and leaves had gone limp, and I saw that they were out of water. So I plunged them deep into a bowl of cold water—and this morning they have revived. No living thing can survive without water. Our bodies are 80 per cent water—and without ordinary water our bodies die. But there is a more serious death than the death of our bodies, and without the water of life our souls die. Our soul is our true self—the person God created us to be—and we can only be our true self in a relationship with God.

When he spoke to the thirsty Samaritan woman at the well Jesus said, 'If you knew the gift of God, and who it is that is saying to you "Give me a drink" you would have asked him and he would have given you living water.' If we drink that water it becomes in us 'a spring of water welling up to eternal life'. The river that flows from the throne of God is like the river that Ezekiel saw in his vision in the temple—and the river of life flows out of the place in the temple where the sacrifices were made.

A way to pray

Imagine the river that flows from the throne of God. Sit by it, and swim in it, and pray.

SB

Waiting

The work of God incarnate in Jesus was finished—and the work of God incarnate in the followers of Jesus through the Spirit was about to start. But not immediately. There was a time to wait—after the death and resurrection—for the great festival of harvest, which is what Pentecost is. The grain of wheat had fallen into the ground and died—and now there would be more grains of wheat. More disciples—millions of them, finally. But for now the few had to wait for Whitsuntide.

Jesus had breathed his Spirit into them (and that's where our first Sunday in this section starts) but they still had to wait for the great outpouring of the Spirit. In between they would have prayed, and thought about the incredible things that had happened. As Jews, they would have reflected on their faith as they had lived it out before the coming of their Messiah—and thought about the future.

For the next six weeks we can do something rather like that. For four weeks we look at the Old Testament, and for two at the New. The Psalms with Douglas Cleverley Ford for the first and the sixth week. The book of Ecclesiastes with Graham Dodds for the second and third weeks—the book that begins with meaninglessness and the vanity of human life and ends up with God as our judge on the day of our death. And with our need to fear God and to keep his commandments: 'for this is the whole duty of man.'

We know that it is both 'our duty and our joy'—but then we now more of the nature of God than the writer of Ecclesiastes did, because we know him through Christ.

That's how the Jew Paul knew him, and we spend our fourth and fifth weeks studying his second letter to Timothy. 'Paul, an apostle of Jesus Christ by the will of God, according to the promise of life that is in Christ Jesus', it starts—and Rosemary Green takes us right through to the end of it, with Paul's worship of Christ (the Christ he once persecuted) in the words 'To him be glory for ever and ever! Amen.'

'Even so I send you...'

On the evening of ... the first day of the week, the doors being shut where the disciples were, for fear of the Jews, Jesus came and stood among them and said to them, 'Peace be with you.' When he had said this, he showed them his hands and his side. Then the disciples were glad when they saw the Lord. Jesus said to them again, 'Peace be with you. As the Father has sent me, even so I send you.' And when he had said this, he breathed on them, and said to them, 'Receive the Holy Spirit. If you forgive the sins of any, they are forgiven; if you retain the sins of any, they are retained.'

Sometimes we think of mission as something that is done by missionaries—special people who go abroad and into the slum areas of our great cities (the state of which God is very much less than pleased about, but that is not the subject of this note). Every Christian is a missionary—because Christ has sent every one of us into the world to tell it the good news about the love and the forgiveness and the nature of God, and to live it out before their eyes, in the same way that the Father sent Jesus into the world. The Revd Professor J.G. Davies, editor of and contributor to *A Dictionary of Liturgy and Worship*, wrote this in his article in that book on 'Mission and Worship':

'The two chief Christian liturgical acts, baptism and the eucharist, can themselves be understood in terms of mission ... Baptism is ordination to the royal priesthood and acceptance into the covenant, both priesthood and covenant being understood in terms of mission. The eucharist renews both the ordination and the covenant. Baptism, with its pattern of life and death, initiates us into mission. The eucharist re-establishes us in this pattern. Baptism includes us in the obedience of Christ and so in his mission. The eucharist renews our commitment to God and so to mission' (SCM Press © 1972).

So whenever you go to the Eucharist, reflect on those truths. They are expressed in the beautiful post-communion prayer: 'Father of all ... May we who share Christ's body live his risen life; we who drink his cup bring life to others; we whom the Spirit lights give light to the world...'

SB

Daily thanksgiving

It is good to give thanks to the Lord, to sing praises to thy name, O Most High; to declare thy steadfast love in the morning, and thy faithfulness by night, to the music of the lute and the harp, to the melody of the lyre. For thou, O Lord, hast made me glad by thy work; at the works of thy hands I sing for joy. How great are thy works, O Lord! Thy thoughts are very deep! The dull man cannot know, the stupid cannot understand this.

Yes, I did. I gave thanks to the Lord soon after I awoke this morning. I can't say I sang praises, and certainly there was no accompaniment of lute and harp. One of my deficiencies—I have many—is that I can't play any musical instrument—but I went over in my mind causes for thanksgiving. I try to do this at the beginning of each day. There is always something for which to praise God, though apparently quite small, trivial. And at night before I go to sleep I run over in my mind the good things that have happened, frequently most ordinary things, like the garden machinery mechanic who said he would call to collect my mower for servicing and he did! Our Psalm today says, 'It is good to give thanks to the Lord, to sing praises to thy name, O Most High.' And then this 'the dull man cannot know, the stupid cannot understand this'. We are far more likely to be well in body and mind if we give proper place to thanksgiving in our lives. Discontent and ingratitude pull us down.

A few weeks ago I nearly 'came a cropper' on this resolve to keep the good and lovely things in mind; I thought I would let the garden go a bit this year. And then my eye caught a little cluster of snowdrops blooming merrily outside my study window and I was rebuked. They were praising God in their way. And it will not be long after Easter before that blackbird starts filling the garden with his song as he does every spring (is it the same one?) even though he will find some of the branches in the silver birch tree lopped off where he usually perches. So I will make a point of making my garden as decorative as I can. God has given us good and lovely things and we praise God, the Creator, by caring for them and rejoicing in them, and are better people for doing so.

***

Prayer

Lord, I praise you for the good things you have given me—my garden, lovely flowers, the kindness of neighbours and the love of some particular people, but above all for the wonder of Easter with its message of newness of life.

DCF

Light dispels the darkness

Blessed are the people who know the festal shout, who walk, O Lord, in the light of thy countenance, who exult in thy name all the day, and extol thy righteousness. For thou art the glory of their strength; by thy favour our horn is exalted.

About the end of the first week in January a friend telephoned me. The call was simply for a chat. I was pleased. 'Isn't it lovely,' she said, 'already the evenings are lighter.' I couldn't help smiling to myself because actually at the end of the first week in January there is only an increase in daylight of about ten minutes or less. But she was happy. She lives in the country and keeps about a dozen cows and a few geese. What was pleasing her was the extra time each day to lock up the animals and do all that has to be done before dark.

Have you noticed that almost the first words in the Bible are about light? 'The earth was without form and void, and darkness was upon the face of the deep... And God said, "Let there be light"; and there was light. And God saw that the light was good; and God separated the light from the darkness.' (Genesis 1:2–3). The darkness was not capable of stopping what God intended doing, he overcame the darkness, he separated it from the light and then his creative work went forward apace.

Perhaps you are going through a dark patch just now. A few days ago a man heavily engaged in business called on me. We got talking and I realized how hard it was for him to see ahead in the murky world of today's commerce. Your dark patch may be different: health not so good as it was; a family problem; declining income; increased expenditure. Listen to this! God is not overcome by darkness, he separates it out, and light appears, and the work progresses.

The darkness that closed in around the cross on Good Friday did not last. It was real but it was scattered on Easter Sunday morning. The sun streamed into the empty tomb. And before the day was out, the faces of the bewildered disciples were lit up with joy, good to see. It was in the light and the joy of Easter that the Church was born, grew and went forward, proclaiming the light of the world.

Read the verses again. For 'festal shout' read 'song in the heart'. And in the last verse read the NEB, 'through thy favour we hold our heads high'.

Prayer

Lord, let me hold my head high today, not because I am proud but because I have a song in my heart. I believe the message of Easter—God has banished the darkness, even the darkness of death.

DCF

The tongue and the heart

Come and hear, all you who fear God, and I will tell you what he has done for me. I cried aloud to him, and he was extolled with my tongue. If I had cherished iniquity in my heart, the Lord would not have listened. But truly God has listened; he has given heed to the voice of my prayer.

A notice in a delicatessen window read: 'Have you tried our tongue sandwiches? They speak for themselves.'

Perhaps you don't think that is funny! Never mind, but it caught my attention because I have been reading the letter of James in the New Testament and he has a great deal to say about the tongue, our tongues, much of it rather frightening. 'Think of ships: large they may be, yet even when driven by strong gales they can be directed by a tiny rudder... So with the tongue. It is a small member but it can make huge claims... We use it to sing the praises of our Lord and Father, and we use it to invoke curses on our fellow men who are made in God's likeness... My brothers this should not be so.'

The Psalmist in today's verses used his tongue well. God was extolled with it. God's praises were on his lips (NEB). He had also banished iniquity from his heart. He had been in trouble and cried aloud to God for help and God heard his cry and did great things for him, so he used his tongue to call people to come and hear of his deliverance. This is what we have to note, the heart and tongue are connected. If our heart is thankful to God we shall use our tongue well. If our heart is angry with God we shall use it to do harm. It is possible to tell what a person's heart is by the way the tongue is used. There is such an instrument as a kindly tongue and such an instrument as an evil tongue. A kindly tongue can do an astonishing amount of good and an evil tongue can do an astonishing amount of evil. We have to be very careful with our tongue. This applies especially to Christian congregations. Churches can be ruined by gossip. There is a simple rule of thumb—if you can say something good about another person, say it, if not, hold your tongue.

And now what about the newspapers and the news bulletins on television and radio? They seem to like to tell us the bad news which, let us face it, does exist. This is where we Christian people should come in. We shouldn't add to the world's sorry tale of woe by talking about nothing else. We should use our tongue to tell of the good things, some of which have come our way.

Prayer

Lord, let the Church proclaim good news, especially the good news of Easter.

DCF

The earth is the Lord's

The earth is the Lord's and the fullness thereof, the world and those who dwell therein; for he has founded it upon the seas, and established it upon the rivers.

A few days ago I met a lady who said she was very sad. I braced myself wondering if perhaps she had lost some member of the family. But no, she was sad because her gander whom she had looked after and loved for nearly nine years had died. I trod carefully because 'townee' that I am really, I wasn't sure I knew what a gander was. Of course I ought to have remembered the nursery rhyme 'Goosey goosey gander' but my nursery days are a long way back now. A gander is a male goose and this lady loved hers. It was part of her life.

I haven't any animals to look after myself but I can see how much they contribute to people's happiness. And I believe God meant it to be like this. If you read the story of the creation in Genesis you will notice the order of events there. First light separated from darkness, then living space, the vegetation, then living creatures which includes birds and animals (ganders too!), and then, not till all was ready, were man and woman created. Thus all was set for their welfare and pleasure. So the words of our Psalm, 'The earth is the Lord's and the fullness thereof.' So the text in 1 Timothy 6:17 'God... giveth us richly all things to enjoy.' I know we can abuse God's creation, we can be cruel to animals, we can turn the country-side into a desert—that is another matter and it is wicked—what I want to empha-size today is not that but rejoicing for all the good things God has given us.

Christians should not have their eyes closed to beauty, they should not be unresponsive to the lovely things there are in the world, they should be ready to laugh at funny things and sing when possible and certainly listen to singing. Christians should not be narrow, tight-lipped and loveless. Christians must be open—to people, to God's world (he made it): 'The earth is the Lord's and the fullness thereof.'

The other day I was told of a dog which had to be taken to the vet for a nasty operation on his back requiring an anaesthetic. He obviously disliked it intensely but as soon as he 'came round', up on his feet again he walked to where he knew his lead had been placed, picked it up in his mouth and went to his mistress, saying in effect, 'I'm ready now, let's go and enjoy ourselves.' Is there a lesson for us here?

Prayer

Lord, make me a happy person, happy in myself, happy so as to make others happy who come across my path through the faith we have in the risen Christ.

DCF

Learn to wait patiently

I waited patiently for the Lord; he inclined to me and heard my cry. He drew me up from the desolate pit, out of the miry bog, and set my feet upon a rock, making my steps secure. He put a new song in my mouth, a song of praise to our God. Many will see and fear, and put their trust in the Lord.

I have had to cut back the hedges on the drive in front of my house to make more room for the car coming in and out. I am rather sorry about this, the green has all gone leaving clipped bare wood. Apart from ripping out the whole hedge and planting something else or installing a wooden fence there is nothing for it but to wait patiently. In time there will be new growth and fresh green. 'In time' are the operative words. Anything to do with a garden requires patience. You can't sow seeds today and have flowers tomorrow. To be in a hurry with a garden is useless. Is this a lesson we have to learn too in our relationship with God? As I write this note there keeps ringing in my head that lovely aria: 'O rest in the Lord, wait patiently for him and he will give thee thy heart's desire.' But we are so impatient in our modern world. We want instant results. Hardly has any event taken place than we want not only instant reporting of it on radio, television and in the newspaper, we want informed comment. We can't wait to see things in perspective. Speed is the key word to-day. Even new buildings have to be put up almost overnight. There is no time to settle, no time to take stock.

The Psalmist knew better. Something had gone wrong for him. Somehow he was stuck, he just could not get going. And the place, or situation was not only desolate but depressing, it was dirty, a miry bog. And he cried out to God to pull him out and set him free. He was desperate. Even so, and this is the point to notice, even in that awful hole *he waited patiently* for the Lord. And his wait was not in vain. It never is with nature, nor with God. In due time the results appear, the garden greens over again, this Psalmist was lifted out of that dreadful hole and had his feet set on a rock.

And then he started to sing. It was a new song. I guess he lifted up his voice before he cleaned his muddy boots. And people heard him. They marvelled and what they saw and heard made them put their trust in the Lord for themselves. Let us hope and wait patiently for him, the God who will not let us down.

Prayer

Lord, we wait for the vision of your glory which we believe will come to us, for this is the message of Easter—resurrection and life.

DCF

Our foundation stone

Open to me the gates of righteousness, that I may enter through them and give thanks to the Lord. This is the gate of the Lord; the righteous shall enter through it. I thank thee that thou hast answered me and hast become my salvation. The stone which the builders rejected has become the head of the corner. This is the Lord's doing; it is marvellous in our eyes. This is the day which the Lord has made; let us rejoice and be glad in it. Save us, we beseech thee, O Lord! O Lord, we beseech thee, give us success!

If I have been too 'homely' in these notes—lighting them up (I hope) with everyday illustrations to bring out the meaning for us now—today, I am going to plunge back into Hebrew history.

First let me ask for your imagination. Behind this Psalm is the day when the Jewish people returned from their long years of exile in a foreign land. They laid a foundation stone of the new temple they were going to build, to replace the one that the invaders had destroyed. It looked a puny little piece of stonework set there on the site and the builders turned their noses up at it. Would there ever be a temple? Doubts were widespread.

But a temple was built using that humble piece of stonework in the foundation. And the day came for its opening and dedication. There was a grand procession and a gathering of priests there to receive it. 'Open to me the gates of righteousness, that I may enter through them and give thanks to the Lord' was the call. And the answer from within, 'This is the gate of the Lord; the righteous shall enter through it.'

And then this commentary in the light of all the prayer that had been offered up for this new building, the focus of their faith: 'I thank thee that thou hast answered me, and hast become my salvation.' And then they looked at that humble little piece of original stonework now part of the foundation of the new temple: 'The stone which the builders rejected has become the head of the corner. This is the Lord's doing; it is marvellous in our eyes.'

Is it any wonder we sing this Psalm at Easter? Jesus was insulted, despised and crucified. Who would believe that a worldwide faith would be built on him as the foundation? But it has happened and it is 'marvellous in our eyes'.

Prayer

Lord, let the Church never lose the sheer wonder of the resurrection of Jesus.
The foundation stone of our faith lies here
Let us clap our hands and sing.
'This is the day which the Lord has made;
Let us rejoice and be glad in it.'

DCF

Married bliss

I heard what sounded like a vast crowd, like the noise of rushing water and deep roars of thunder, and they cried: 'Alleluia! The Lord our God, sovereign over all, has entered on his reign! Exult and shout for joy and do him homage, for the wedding-day of the Lamb has come! His bride has made herself ready, and for her dress she has been given fine linen, clean and shining.' (Now the fine linen signifies the righteous deeds of God's people). Then the angel said to me, 'Write this: "Happy are those who are invited to the wedding-supper of the Lamb!"' And he added, 'These are the very words of God.'

A friend of mine was separated from her fiancé for nearly two years when he went abroad. For various reasons they could not marry before he went, and it wasn't easy for her (or for him). But all the time she wore the ring he had given to her: a single, sparkling diamond set in gold, and it reminded her of the promises they had made to each other, and the happiness that lay in the future. The two of them looked forward to their wedding— believing that it would take place, and cheering themselves up in their separation by the hope of what lay ahead.

It is rather like that for us as Christians. Ephesians 1:13–14 talks about us being 'sealed with the promised Holy Spirit, which is the guarantee of our inheritance until we acquire possession of it to the praise of his glory'. The inheritance is God himself, and the sealing is like an engagement ring except that it is far better, because it is the actual presence of the Spirit of God within us. So we can know something of the relationship now but the consummation won't be until then. Then there will be a marriage and a mutual indwelling, with a mutual delight and pleasure that goes on for ever. At the marriage supper of the Lamb who was slain, and whom the whole of heaven and earth will worship and adore:

'Worthy is the Lamb who was slain, to receive power and wealth and wisdom and might and honour and glory and blessing!' And I heard every creature in heaven and on earth and under the earth and in the sea, and all therein, saying, 'To him who sits upon the throne and to the Lamb be blessing and honour and glory and might for ever and ever!' And the four living creatures said 'Amen!', and the elders fell down and worshipped.

Revelation 5:12–13 (RSV)

SB

Where is meaning?

The words of the Teacher, son of David, king of Jerusalem: 'Meaningless! Meaningless!' says the Teacher. 'Utterly meaningless! Everything is meaningless.' What does man gain from all his labour at which he toils under the sun? Generations come and generations go, but the earth remains for ever. The sun rises and the sun sets, and hurries back to where it rises. The wind blows to the south and turns to the north; round and round it goes, ever returning on its course. All streams flow into the sea, yet the sea is never full. To the place the streams come from, there they return again. All things are wearisome, more than one can say. The eye never has enough of seeing, nor the ear its fill of hearing. What has been will be again, what has been done will be done again; there is nothing new under the sun.

The other day I invited a sculptor to come to church with a piece of his work. It was one of those circular outdoor clothes driers that you can hang washing on. But instead of washing, the sculptor had hung loaves of bread, made of different everyday materials. The interesting thing about it was the congregation's reaction to it. It stood provocatively in the middle of the church. For some it was confusing, it said nothing and they couldn't see any meaning in it at all. For others it was like being transported into Africa and longing for bread. As they looked at it, and felt it, the meaning poured out onto them.

In these first few verses of Ecclesiastes, the teacher is tired. Old Ecclesiastes is exhausted because he cannot see meaning anywhere. In work, life and nature he sees nothing new. The sun, the wind and the streams continue their endless, relentless course. He feels like a prisoner caught outside of nature. Like those who are prisoners outside of any society or community, he cries out, 'Everything is meaningless!'.

Today the philosophical debate that Ecclesiastes indulged in has a real and violent struggle attached to it. In the townships of Africa, in the back streets of South America, in our own communities human beings are experiencing the violence that accompanies an ultimately meaningless existence. It is into this setting that God sent his Son, and sends you and me to bring renewal to the things that have grown wearisome.

Prayer

Renew us by your Spirit
Inspire us with your love
And unite us in the body of your Son,
Jesus Christ our Lord.

GD

Straightening the twisted

I, the Teacher, was king over Israel in Jerusalem. I devoted myself to study and to explore by wisdom all that is done under heaven. What a heavy burden God has laid on men! I have seen all the things that are done under the sun; all of them are meaningless, a chasing after the wind. What is twisted cannot be straightened; what is lacking cannot be counted. I thought to myself, 'Look, I have grown and increased in wisdom more than anyone who has ruled over Jerusalem before me; I have experienced much of wisdom and knowledge.' Then I applied myself to the understanding of wisdom and also of madness and folly, but I learned that this, too, is a chasing after the wind. For with much wisdom comes much sorrow; the more knowledge the more grief.

Children sometimes play with pipe cleaners. It's great fun opening a new packet, all beautifully straight and clean. They bend them into new shapes until it's time to put them away. But trying to get them back to what they were is impossible no matter how hard they try. Once they've been twisted they can never really become straight again.

Adam and Eve sinned in the garden of Eden. Because sin twisted them they could never regain the lovely innocence of walking with God. They felt empty, and it's the echo of this isolation from God that Ecclesiastes is experiencing. He tries to solve it by increasing in wisdom. But the emptiness of Eden needs human beings in their wholeness to fill it, not abstract wisdom. And the hole in human beings can only be made whole again by God.

Sage-like wisdom is rather impressive but sometimes frustrating. I've been in Bible groups where we've struggled for an answer to some question. Near the end of our discussion the 'sage' pipes up and gives his or her understanding. In one sense it's great to have an impressive mind feed us with pearls of wisdom. Yet there's an unreality about it—something is missing.

Indeed I want God to be infinitely wise, but I also want to know him in my heart. Wisdom alone cannot help me, it only leaves me isolated like Adam and Eve outside the garden. I need God to come to me.

Meditate

Wisdom unsearchable, God the invisible
Love indestructible in frailty appears
Lord of infinity, stooping so tenderly
Lifts our humanity to the heights of His throne.

G. Kendrick, 'Meekness and Majesty',
© Thankyou Music

GD

When I surveyed

I thought in my heart, 'Come now, I will test you with pleasure to find out what is good.' But that also proved to be meaningless . . . I denied myself nothing my eyes desired; I refused my heart no pleasure. My heart took delight in all my work, and this was the reward for all my labour. Yet when I surveyed all that my hands had done and what I had toiled to achieve, everything was meaningless, a chasing after the wind; nothing was gained under the sun.

I have an eerie feeling about this passage. It makes me feel like a hamster going round and round a wheel. What was true for Ecclesiastes over two thousand years ago seems to have come round again. He denied himself nothing. His permissive society is outlined elsewhere in this chapter. Work, art, building projects, luxury, wealth, music and sex are all within his power to achieve. Ecclesiastes can even dominate other nations by controlling these things and it doesn't take much to think of those today who do exactly that. But where does it get him or us?

I'm sure hamsters, like people, want to enjoy life—after all pleasure is God-given. But being caged up is only a small part of the enjoyment they could have in their natural habitat. I may act like a hamster sometimes, but as the frustration rises I find myself leaping off the wheel, withdrawing to a corner and asking some questions. What is the pleasure in this? Where is it all leading to? The nub of the quest for Ecclesiastes is whether pleasure or happiness could take the place of God. He found his answer—'everything was meaningless'.

There's a whole philosophy worked out along the lines of trying to make everyone happy. This is not the way of the cross. When Jesus appeared to the disciples after the resurrection he showed them his hands and his side. That brought meaning to all they then did.

It's sad that pleasure can be so hollow when in other circumstances it can be so satisfying. As I examine what I do, I have to come to the conclusion, like the hymn-writer, that unless I do it in the light of the cross it simply counts as loss.

Prayer

*When I survey the wondrous cross
On which the Prince of glory died,
My richest gain I count but loss,
And pour contempt on all my pride.*

Isaac Watts

GD

The toil of the worker

So I hated life, because the work that is done under the sun was grievous to me. All of it is meaningless, a chasing after the wind. I hated all the things I had toiled for under the sun, because I must leave them to the one who comes after me. And who knows whether he will be a wise man or a fool? Yet he will have control over all the work into which I have poured my effort and skill under the sun. This too is meaningless. So my heart began to despair over all my toilsome labour under the sun. For a man may do his work with wisdom, knowledge and skill, and then he must leave all he owns to someone who has not worked for it. This too is meaningless and a great misfortune. What does a man get for all the toil and anxious strivings with which he labours under the sun? All his days his work is pain and grief; even at night his mind does not rest. This too is meaningless.

One of the most wide-ranging effects of Adam and Eve sinning in the garden is that work became toil. In Genesis, God says quite plainly to Adam that because of sin, 'cursed is the ground because of you; through painful toil you will eat of it'. Work, whether secular or sacred, is toil and Ecclesiastes experiences the pain of it.

However there is more to his lament than simply, 'it hurts'. Ecclesiastes is interested in what is the ultimate end of work. He sees that it may all be undone by his successors which aggrieves him even further.

I get nervous as a passenger in a car. I once went for a drive in North London with a rally driver. He was the most experienced driver I had ever met and yet I was still nervous. The fact is I just like being in control. If it wasn't for the beautiful beaches and wonderful sunshine in a holiday destination I should never be able to fly. The further aggravation for Ecclesiastes is that he cannot control the future. He has to leave it and trust it to his heirs.

Many of us plough much energy into work. It even reaches into our dreams. Yet Ecclesiastes is right—if work is our god, then our god becomes meaningless because there is no ultimate purpose to it.

Question

Am I working to live, or living to work?

GD

No time like the present

There is a time for everything, and a season for every activity under heaven: a time to be born and a time to die, a time to plant and a time to uproot, a time to kill and a time to heal, a time to tear down and a time to build, a time to weep and a time to laugh, a time to mourn and a time to dance, a time to scatter stones and a time to gather them, a time to embrace and a time to refrain, a time to search and a time to give up, a time to keep and a time to throw away, a time to tear and a time to mend, a time to be silent and a time to speak, a time to love and a time to hate, a time for war and a time for peace . . . [God] has made everything beautiful in its time. He has also set eternity in the hearts of men; yet they cannot fathom what God has done from beginning to end.

This rhythmic ebb and flow of time can be seen in two ways. There is chronological time from the Greek word *chronos*—time that rolls on and on seemingly never ending. It was, it is and it will be. Then there is specific time like a birthday or a moment of truth. This derives from the Greek word *kairos*. As this passage unfolds, it is clear that there are moments when there is an appropriate action to take, and yet, the eternal clock is ticking away in the heart. In both experiences we cannot exist outside of God. Even an understanding of time does not mean we can fathom what God is doing. We need a relationship with him to make the appropriate response every moment just as much as we need him to take care of our ultimate eternal destiny.

Problems will come along from time to time. We cannot stop them. If we live as it were 'in the past' we shall not be able to face them. If we live, as some try, in the future, we shall only worry about them because the future is uncertain. We can only spend time in the present and there is no better way than to invest it in God.

Meditate

O God our help in ages past,
Our hope for years to come,
Be thou our guard
while troubles last,
And our eternal home.

Isaac Watts

GD

When two becomes three

Again I saw something meaningless under the sun: There was a man all alone; he had neither son nor brother. There was no end to his toil, yet his eyes were not content with his wealth. 'For whom am I toiling,' he asked, 'and why am I depriving myself of enjoyment?' This too is meaningless—a miserable business! Two are better than one, because they have a good return for their work: If one falls down, his friend can help him up. But pity the man who falls and has no-one to help him up! Also if two lie down together, they will keep warm. But how can one keep warm alone? Though one may be overpowered, two can defend themselves. A cord of three strands is not quickly broken.

Winston Churchill once went on holiday up to Scotland. Whilst he was swimming in a lake he found himself in difficulties. A young man dived in, swam out to him and saved him. Winston's parents were so grateful for saving their son's life that they paid for the young Scottish man to study at medical school. In time the man became one of the best known research medics, discovering penicillin. His name was Alexander Fleming. In later life Winston Churchill became ill when he met Stalin and Roosevelt and it was penicillin that saved his life.

Stories like that are quite amazing because they tie up our lives together in a way that is more than coincidence. Someone has termed those experiences 'Godincidences' because God seems to be at work in a very apparent way. But the story also depends upon the human relationships within it. Each person played his part, gratitude was expressed and hard work in medical school enabled Alexander Fleming to make his discovery.

Ecclesiastes suddenly becomes very positive about relationships and how strong a bond is made between two people, especially when the third cord, God is involved. The loneliness of Adam and Eve, banished from the garden, out of sorts with each other and their environment is 'a miserable business'. But life with the creator 'is not quickly broken'. The three cords entwine like the Trinity banishing the dark loneliness of the soul.

Task

Observe a three corded rope or plait.

Pray

That which God has joined together, let not man divide.

GD

True bread

Jesus then said to them, 'Truly, truly, I say to you, it was not Moses who gave you the bread from heaven; my Father gives you the true bread from heaven. For the bread of God is that which comes down from heaven, and gives life to the world.' They said to him, 'Lord, give us this bread always.' Jesus said to them, 'I am the bread of life; he who who come to me shall not hunger, and he who believes in me shall never thirst.'

My favourite quotation is St Augustine's, 'Lord, you have made us for yourself, and our hearts are restless till they find their rest in you.' It's what Jesus is on about here. By calling himself the bread of life, he is claiming to be that which satisfies all our deepest longings, as food calms the pangs of hunger. To feed our souls on him is to be at last at peace.

And yet we may well wonder if it is true. Christians seem to have deep longings which their faith never makes up for. Loneliness, troubled marriages, anxiety for children, all these and more are part of our normal life. And not only does faith often seem a poor substitute, but we pity (and sometimes fear) those who rechannel all their frustrations into religion.

I don't think, though, that Jesus intended us to be free of life's troubles. What he promises is something else—a sense that under the storms of life is a deep calm which can never be shaken, an awareness of the presence of God which allows us to see all our other experience as secondary.

Also, I don't believe that Jesus was offering a magical cure. It's not a matter simply of saying 'I believe' and waiting for the heavenly peace to descend. It's a matter of digesting the bread of life; of letting Christ become a part of us in every aspect of our life. Our whole Christian life is a process of feeding and nourishing ourselves in him, through worship, prayer, learning and meditation.

In our communion, this process is dramatically symbolized. As we digest the bread and wine, we pray that we will similarly be pervaded by the presence of God. And eventually we will. Jesus truly is the bread of life, but that bread is no quick junk-food snack. It is a leisurely banquet which takes all our life to assimilate; and then truly satisfies our every need.

MM

The image on the coin

Whoever loves money never has money enough; whoever loves wealth is never satisfied with his income. This too is meaningless. As goods increase, so do those who consume them. And what benefit are they to the owner except to feast his eyes on them? The sleep of a labourer is sweet, whether he eats little or much, but the abundance of a rich man permits him no sleep. I have seen a grievous evil under the sun: wealth hoarded to the harm of its owner, or wealth lost through some misfortune, so that when he has a son there is nothing left for him. Naked a man comes from his mother's womb, and as he comes, so he departs. He takes nothing from his labour that he can carry in his hand. This too is a grievous evil: As a man comes, so he departs, and what does he gain, since he toils for the wind? All his days he eats in darkness, with great frustration, affliction and anger.

We're told elsewhere that the love of money is the root of all evil but this first phrase of Ecclesiastes somehow rings true in a more everyday sense to me. 'Whoever loves money never has money enough.' The fact is that money can be addictive. Perhaps it should carry a government wealth warning! Although in itself it is neither good nor bad, so often we tend to crave it. Another problem arises when we have to manage it. Then we have to take risks on the stock exchange or in investments. We can sit back and feel that our money is working for us, so that we can rest on our laurels. We find ourselves worried, even losing sleep about how it's doing. 'The sleep of the labourer is sweet ... but the abundance of the rich man permits him no sleep.'

Jesus handled money and taught the Pharisees and Herodians how to handle it. 'Give to Caesar what is Caesar's and to God what is God's.' The coin bears the image of the ruler to whom it belongs. Humans, like a coin, bear the image of the ruler to whom they belong—God. We are born with the image of our parents, earthly and heavenly, and when we depart God will look for his image again.

Task

Look at a coin, note what is on it and ask—who does this belong to?
What imprint am I carrying for others to see? How can I reflect God's glory today?

GD

Stillborn life

A man may have a hundred children and live many years; yet no matter how long he lives, if he cannot enjoy his prosperity and does not receive proper burial, I say that a stillborn child is better off than he. It comes without meaning, it departs in darkness, and in darkness its name is shrouded. Though it never saw the sun or knew anything, it has more rest than does that man—even if he lives a thousand years twice over but fails to enjoy his prosperity. Do not all go to the same place?

As part of our midweek Communion we have a Bible study. The other day we contrasted this whole chapter with Psalm 139. What a contrast!

In Psalm 139, David gives thanks to God for the fact that he is 'fearfully and wonderfully made'. He was 'woven together' and a great plan was ordained for his life. This child of God has awe, beauty and purpose to his life.

Ecclesiastes, trying to see if there is any meaning to life without God, couples a man in his prime siring a hundred children with a child born dead. To him, even the stillborn child is better off if the man cannot enjoy his prosperity.

This grotesque imagery is startling and shows the horrible misery of life without God's framework. C.S. Lewis sometimes talks of hell as a place of greyness which seems to turn a human being into a non-person. The torment is that the non-person realizes that life with God was once a possibility, but now the opportunity has been missed. By denying God, so the chance of enjoying his prosperity is gone too. Ecclesiastes is right there and would rather that he was

not living or even that he never existed than face this awful hell.

I have known people in mental hospitals who long for non-existence, it hurts so much to be alive. They would prefer never to have been born. I also know people who live life to the full. A friend once spoke in church about his conversion. He said, 'I don't know what Jesus has done but I know that the blues are bluer and the greens are greener.'

Pray

For all those in hospitals or in the community who see only greyness.

GD

The two sides of authority

Since a king's word is supreme, who can say to him, 'What are you doing?' Whoever obeys his command will come to no harm, and the wise heart will know the proper time and procedure. For there is a proper time and procedure for every matter, though a man's misery weighs heavily upon him. Since no man knows the future, who can tell him what is to come? No man has the power over the wind to contain it; so no-one has power over the day of his death. As no-one is discharged in time of war, so wickedness will not release those who practise it.

In four broad brushstrokes Ecclesiastes paints the limitations of living under ultimate authority. In the final two sentences of the passage he speaks of our powerlessness in the face of the wind (or spirit), and death. He points to the 'press gang' inevitability of those who have to go to war, and the prison of those who practise evil. These boundaries of human experience act in two ways.

There are times, I confess, when I wish I wasn't a Christian. Times under God's ultimate authority when I could do without the constant struggle with Christian standards. Why can't God just solve all my problems? I feel squeezed by the world, which attracts me, and God, whose authority is supreme. If I wasn't a Christian, life would be so much easier.

And yet this struggle is inevitable. It's like being squeezed on a train in the rush hour or caught frustratingly in a maze. Simon Magus, in the Acts of the Apostles, tried to gift-wrap and sell the Holy Spirit until Peter confronted him. I, too, am arrested by God and put in my place. I have eventually to come to the conclusion, like Ecclesiastes, that God is God and I am human.

On the other hand that's exactly what I always wanted God to be. Even though my life is in his hands, I feel strangely self-controlled. He speaks of riskiness and curiously I feel completely safe. He tells me that with him nothing is going to be the same again and oddly it feels familiar. God is supreme and I am his creation and I rejoice that I can begin to know the unknowable.

Meditate

God is an infinite circle whose centre is everywhere and whose circumference is nowhere.

Augustine of Hippo

GD

The fly in the ointment

The quiet words of the wise are more to be heeded than the shouts of a ruler of fools. Wisdom is better than the weapons of war, but one sinner destroys much good. As dead flies give perfume a bad smell, so a little folly outweighs wisdom and honour. The heart of the wise inclines to the right, but the heart of the fool to the left. Even as he walks along the road, the fool lacks sense and shows everyone how stupid he is. If a ruler's anger rises against you, do not leave your post; calmness can lay great errors to rest.

Sometimes in school assemblies I use this illustration. I hold up a white card with a small spot on it and ask the pupils, 'What do you see?' Almost inevitably they say, 'a spot'. We then go on to ask ourselves why only a spot and not the white surrounding it. It may seem a little trivial in one way but it is symbolic of the way that we tend to look for the small blemishes in life rather than the pure goodness of it. The 'one sinner', the 'dead flies' and the 'little folly' are all examples of how something quite small tends to pollute the greater good.

I often find in counselling that I am trying to help someone get themselves in perspective. There is usually lots of good in a person, but that one stain of sin overwhelms them. How often we find the press criticized for homing in on the tiny 'juicy' part of a story. Yet that's exactly what sells newspapers. Attempts are made to produce good news newspapers, but often they are bland and fail to attract our attention.

Ecclesiastes writes of how the heart inclines. In the context 'the right' was associated with salvation, protection and support, whereas 'the left' implied disfavour and incompetence. The way our heart inclines will show us up to be either wise or a fool. It's easy to criticize some of the press for only printing bad news. It's just as easy for us to criticize others impetuously and often inaccurately. Ecclesiastes encourages calmness which will lay mistakes to rest and Paul requests us to let the peace of Christ rule in all situations.

Think

It's better to keep your mouth shut and be thought a fool, than open it and remove all possible doubt.

Anon

GD

Giving in to God

Cast your bread upon the waters, for after many days you will find it again. Give portions to seven, yes to eight, for you do not know what disaster may come upon the land. If clouds are full of water, they pour rain upon the earth. Whether a tree falls to the south or to the north, in the place where it falls, there will it lie. Whoever watches the wind will not plant; whoever looks at the clouds will not reap. As you do not know the path of the wind, or how the body is formed in a mother's womb, so you cannot understand the work of God, the Maker of all things. Sow your seed in the morning, and at evening let not your hands be idle, for you do not know which will succeed, whether this or that, or whether both will do equally well.

At long last Ecclesiastes has begun to draw some conclusions about his quest. He has tried to examine life 'under the sun', in God's framework, but he has not found satisfaction in many of the gods of life. His conclusion is that in the light of all the misery of a life without God, why not find him and accept him?

Ecclesiastes encourages us to throw our lot in with God because at some point he will win anyway. To come to this point we sometimes need, like the prodigal son, to reach the lowest of the low. Dark clouds, storms and hurricanes predictably cause destruction. Unforeseen accidents like trees falling also cause grief. Whether foreseen or unforeseen, circumstances will affect our lives. The only solution is to invest ourselves in God.

In ancient times, owners needed to cast their bread upon the waters when they traded. They sent merchandise out in the ship and it could often be years before they received their profit, so long were the voyages. In the same way Ecclesiastes is suggesting that we throw our all in with God our maker and the reward will be given to us one day. I find it hard to think in the long term, especially in this age of immediacy. Thankfully God doesn't!

Prayer

Be thou my vision,
O Lord of my heart,
Be all else but naught to me,
save that thou art;
Be thou my best thought
in the day and the night,
Both waking and sleeping,
thy presence my light

Mary Byrne and Eleanor Hull

GD

Remember before you forget

Remember your Creator in the days of your youth, before the days of trouble come and the years approach when you will say, 'I find no pleasure in them'—before the sun and the light and the moon and the stars grow dark, and the clouds return after rain; when the keepers of the house tremble, and the strong men stoop, when the grinders cease because they are few, and those looking through the windows grow dim... Then man goes to his eternal home and mourners go about the streets... Now all has been heard; here is the conclusion of the matter: Fear God and keep his commandments, for this is the whole duty of man. For God will bring every deed into judgment, including every hidden thing, whether it is good or evil.

For me, putting things off is an art form. I find it amazing how long it takes me to do something if I don't do it immediately. A letter can sit on my desk or get buried in the filing cabinet or underneath some other papers for ages until it eventually surfaces to stare me out. Of course, embarrassment follows because it should have been done last month but now it's too late to answer it without a most humble apology.

Ecclesiastes exhorts us to remember God in our youth. In other words, not put it off. A San Francisco preacher was once evangelizing in a rally in 1906. He ended his message by inviting his congregation to come back the following night for information on how to respond to his message and become a Christian. The next day the San Francisco earthquake struck and many people died. For some the response was too late.

Ecclesiastes now comes to his ultimate conclusion. The only and whole duty of man is to fear God and keep his commandments. I'm always struck when the summary of the law is read in Holy Communion. We respond, 'Amen. Lord, have mercy.' God demands all of me and knows I cannot give it. And so the deeply profound words follow. 'God so loved the world that he gave his only Son Jesus Christ to save us from our sins, to be our advocate in heaven, and to bring us to eternal life.' Now we remember our creator and our redeemer.

Meditate

Thank you, O my Father,
for giving us your Son,
And leaving your Spirit
till the work on earth is done.

GD

Speak out

Scripture says, 'I believed, and therefore I spoke out', and we too, in the same spirit of faith, believe and therefore speak out; for we know that he who raised the Lord Jesus to life will with Jesus raise us too, and bring us to his presence, and you with us. Indeed, it is for your sake that all things are ordered, so that, as the abounding grace of God is shared by more and more, the greater may be the chorus of thanksgiving that ascends to the glory of God.

Believe, yes, that's all right. But speak out? That sounds like the embarrassing business of evangelism, or witnessing, or whatever we call it. It's something that many shy away from, out of fear or false humility. Yet for Paul, belief and proclamation were two sides of the same coin. There could be no secret, personal and private religion. There was only the response to God's call: a call to salvation and to mission.

Part of the problem is the way we separate our worship, prayer and devotion from our witness. Perhaps that can work when we are on our own, but never when we are in public. The way we live our lives, the extent to which our behaviour is shaped by our awareness of God, our relations with others by his love, and our conversation by his understanding—are all testimony to the faith we have.

Even more than that, our worship is a proclamation of the faith. In 1 Corinthians 11, Paul wrote that each celebration of Holy Communion is a proclamation of the Lord's death. At the very least, this means that the fact of our church worship is a statement to the world at large of the importance to us of God.

And the public celebration of the Eucharist is even more than that. It is saying that at the heart of our faith and worship is the death and resurrection of Jesus.

There's no getting away from it. To believe is to speak out, in one way or another.

MM

Faithfulness in hidden things

Paul, an apostle of Jesus Christ by the will of God, according to the promise of life that is in Christ Jesus. To Timothy, my dear son: Grace, mercy and peace from God the Father and Christ Jesus our Lord. I thank God, whom I serve, as my forefathers did, with a clear conscience, as night and day I constantly remember you in my prayers. Recalling your tears, I long to see you, so that I may be filled with joy. I have been reminded of your sincere faith, which first lived in your grandmother Lois and in your mother Eunice and, I am persuaded, now lives in you also.

Faithfulness in prayer. Time and again in Paul's letters he shows himself as a man of unceasing prayer who had a deep love for this 'dear son'. We more readily think of him as a man of bold activity than as a man of quiet, constant prayer but his praise and intercession as he moved into pagan territory and as he prayed for the churches must have affected the whole Roman empire as much as his travelling and preaching did. We rarely know what difference our prayer makes. Take heart, you who are elderly or ill, maybe feeling useless for God; your intercession is vital. Take heed, you who are in the front-line of activity; times of prayer are times of power; they are easily squeezed out but essential for effectiveness.

Faithfulness in parenting. I wish I had not waited until my children were grown to recognize a very important truth. Being a parent is the most important job in the world, with the incalculable influence for good or ill in the most formative years of a person's life. But we are neither trained to be parents, nor paid; the unspoken message is that parenting is not worth much. Look at Timothy, and the effect on him of a godly mother and grandmother. His early years laid the foundations for his later years of faith and usefulness.

Pray

Pray for the Christian homes in our land; pray for the broken homes and the unwanted children; pray for the children who grow up knowing nothing about Jesus; pray for the children in your own family and for your influence on them.

RG

Holy boldness

For this reason I remind you to fan into flame the gift of God, which is in you through the laying on of my hands. For God did not give us a spirit of timidity, but a spirit of power, of love and of self-discipline. So do not be ashamed to testify about our Lord, or ashamed of me his prisoner.

On Monday we saw that Timothy grew up in a home where there was real faith in God. By the time he was a young man he had appropriated this faith for himself and he joined Paul and Silas as companion and apprentice (Acts 16:1–3). Perhaps it was when he was commissioned for leadership that Paul laid his hands on him and specifically prayed for God's Spirit to empower him and give him gifts for ministry. Timothy appears to have been by nature shy and reticent; many of us can identify with him in that. 'But you have the gift of the Holy Spirit resident in you,' says Paul. So allow that Spirit to show itself, that your natural shyness may diminish and that you may look outward with the confidence of God's love and power; not an overbearing power, but one that is subject to the Spirit whose fruit is 'love, joy, peace, patience, kindness, goodness, faithfulness, gentleness and self-control' (Galatians 5:22–23) .

'So do not be ashamed to testify about our Lord.' In many so-called Christian countries there is tremendous ignorance about our faith. We who follow Jesus need to be increasingly sure of what we believe and to be ready to explain the difference it makes to us to know Christ.

'But I don't know how to start to talk about my faith!' Is that your comment? Here are some suggestions: (1) Put into words, for yourself, how your faith in Christ became a living reality. (2) Read today's newspaper. What do you think is God's outlook on today's news items? (3) How have you seen God answering prayer? Then get together with a Christian friend and share your thoughts. You might like to read *Good News and How to Share It* by Michael Green (published by BRF).

A prayer

Lord Jesus, please give me opportunities to talk about my faith in you, and the boldness to seize those opportunities.

RG

Faithful to the gospel

Join with me in suffering for the gospel, by the power of God, who has saved us and called us to a holy life—not because of anything we have done but because of his own purpose and grace. This grace was given us in Christ Jesus before the beginning of time, but it has now been revealed through the appearing of our Saviour, Christ Jesus, who has destroyed death and brought life and immortality to light through the gospel. And of this gospel I was appointed a herald and an apostle and a teacher. That is why I am suffering as I am. Yet I am not ashamed, because I know whom I have believed, and am convinced that he is able to guard what I have entrusted to him for that day. What you have heard from me, keep as the pattern of sound teaching, with faith and love in Christ Jesus. Guard the good deposit that was entrusted to you—guard it with the help of the Holy Spirit who lives in us.

A faithful God. Paul is utterly confident in the God he serves. 'I know whom I have believed.' That is not just the knowledge of intellectual assent; it is the knowledge of personal relationship. He knew a God who had brought him through riots, stoning, shipwreck and trial. Past experience gave him assurance for the future. Many phrases in these verses describe God's character and the way he takes the initiative with us. 'The power of God... his own purpose and grace... given us in Christ.' God's purposes are rooted in eternity ('from the beginning of time') and also in history ('now been revealed')

And what has Christ done? He has saved us. He has destroyed death. His resurrection has opened the gate beyond death into life and immortality. Pause for a moment to meditate on the immensity of God's faithfulness and salvation.

A faithful response. Paul was whole-hearted in his response to this faithful God. He was suffering in prison; but he did not mind. He could still live the holy life to which he was called; and he could still proclaim the truth about Jesus that so thrilled him.

My prayer

Take my life, and let it be consecrated,
Lord, to Thee.

RG

A faithful encourager

You know that everyone in the province of Asia has deserted me, including Phygelus and Hermogenes. May the Lord show mercy to the household of Onesiphorus, because he often refreshed me and was not ashamed of my chains. On the contrary, when he was in Rome, he searched hard for me until he found me. May the Lord grant that he find mercy from the Lord on that day! You know very well in how many ways he helped me in Ephesus.

I am writing this on a balcony over-looking a sandy Australian beach, watching an early morning swimmer. There is a dark shape in the water behind him; I thought at first it was a large lump of seaweed, but now see it is his black labrador. The dog is almost submerged but still perseveringly following his master. What a picture of Onesiphorus! Paul was in prison, needing friends more than he had ever needed them. While others deserted him, Onesiphorus arrived in Rome, searched for him, visited him, brought him encouragement by word and action. That was typical of Onesiphorus. 'You know in how many ways he helped me in Ephesus.' He is clearly one whose life was spent in bringing encouragement to others. That is a quality some people seem to have by nature; it is part of their God-given make-up. In Romans chapter 12 Paul writes of the spiritual gifts God gives his people. 'We have different gifts, according to the grace given us' gifts to be used in faith and love to help others. Encouragement is included in the list of gifts. 'If [a person's gift] is encouraging, let him [or her, of course!] encourage.' I covet that gift. For many years my words tended to criticize before they affirmed; now I am learning to give positive approval before—if necessary—making any negative comments. And I see that even the latter should be made in a way that seeks to build up rather than to destroy.

To think over

How do I think about... talk about... speak to... other people? Do my words build up and encourage, bring warmth and hope? Or do they leave others feeling worthless, discouraged or angry? Let us pray together that our words and our actions may bring joy and hope in a discouraged world.

RG

Faithful in hardship

You then, my son, be strong in the grace that is in Christ Jesus. And the things you heard me say in the presence of many witnesses entrust to reliable men who will also be qualified to teach others. Endure hardship with us like a good soldier of Christ Jesus. No-one serving as a soldier gets involved in civilian affairs—he wants to please his commanding officer. Similarly, if anyone competes as an athlete, he does not receive the victor's crown unless he competes according to the rules. The hardworking farmer should be the first to receive a share of the crops. Reflect on what I am saying, for the Lord will give you insight into all this.

What marvellous assurance Paul had! I would not want all the things I say to be passed on; would you? But he was sure of the quality of his teaching; he wanted others to know it, to remember it, to share it. 'What you heard from me, keep as the pattern of sound teaching' (2 Timothy 1:13). That was good strategy. Teach those who will be able to teach others, Paul tells Timothy. It is good advice for those in leadership, to invest time in training others for spiritual ministry. Many of our churches suffer from an overworked 'one-man band' who tries to do everything alone, rather than equipping lay people for service.

Paul gives us three pen-pictures of single-mindedness. The first is a soldier. In our prayer book service the newly baptized person is charged to 'fight valiantly under the banner of Christ against sin, the world and the devil, and continue his faithful soldier and servant to the end of your life.' We are enrolled in his army, dedicated to please and obey Jesus our commanding officer.

Nothing should distract us from that aim. The second picture is an athlete. Do you remember Ben Johnson, the Canadian sprinter who lost his gold medal and was banned from competition for taking steroids? Our aim is not to win by any means, but to obey. The third picture is that of a farmer. Hard work and perseverance receive a reward. For a Christian the reward may not come until we meet our Master and hear his commendation, 'Well done, good and faithful servant.'

RG

Faithful in speech

Keep reminding them of these things. Warn them before God against quarrelling about words; it is of no value, and only ruins those who listen. Do your best to present yourself to God as one approved, a workman who does not need to be ashamed and who correctly handles the word of truth. Avoid godless chatter, because those who indulge in it will become more and more ungodly. Their teachings will spread like gangrene. Among them are Hymenaeus and Philetus, who have wandered away from the truth. They say that the resurrection has already taken place, and they destroy the faith of some. Nevertheless, God's solid foundation stands firm.

Our words are powerful weapons—for good or evil, to build up or to destroy; Paul writes of both. The word of truth—God's truth—builds us up; the picture here is of a workman who uses the tools of his trade skilfully and effectively. In the same way God's 'workmen' need to understand and use the Bible correctly. But Paul warns us of ways in which we can use words negatively: quarrelling; gossip; talk that ignores God's standards or his way of looking at things. They are all destructive. In our day we read lurid stories in the tabloid newspapers, see violence and illicit sex on television; these are among our modern 'godless chatter'. It spreads like poison. Gangrene is a strong word; Paul uses it to shake us into recognizing the destructive power of idle words. I am reminded of the World War II slogan in England: 'careless talk costs lives'. It is interesting to notice that only thirty years after Jesus' death, some people's faith was being undermined by those who were teaching falsely about the resurrection; in that case it was the resurrection of Christians. In our day the faith of many has been undermined by those who have denied the truth of the incarnation and resurrection of Jesus. May we be good workmen who handle God's word correctly, who understand it, obey it and share it with others.

To think about

With the tongue we praise our Lord and Father, and with it we curse men, who have been made in God's likeness. Out of the same mouth come praise and cursing. My brothers, this should not be.

James 3:9–10

RG

The presence of God

Who shall separate us from the love of Christ? Shall tribulation, or distress, or persecution, or famine, or nakedness, or peril, or sword? As it is written, 'For thy sake we are being killed all the day long; we are regarded as sheep to be slaughtered.' No, in all these things we are more than conquerors through him who loved us. For I am sure that neither death, nor life, nor angels, nor principalities, nor things present, nor things to come, nor powers, nor height, nor depth, nor anything else in all creation, will be able to separate us from the love of God in Christ Jesus our Lord.

The last verse of this passage is one of the sentences which are read at the start of the Anglican funeral service. In our church, it tends to come just as the coffin comes to rest at the front. Then I turn to face the congregation, and wonder how many really believe it. Probably not all that many. I dare say that most (at least of those who hear it) would like very much to believe it, at least at that moment. But I am sure, that in the midst of deep distress and grief, such words ring hollow.

In fact, although Paul's words chime triumphantly, they have no power in themselves to bring comfort or hope. It is only when they find an echo in our own experience that they strengthen and console.

Paul could write those tremendous sentences because he knew them to be true. He had faced the possibility of death; he had known hunger and peril, and come face to face with the powers of evil; and he had found that God's love had never deserted him. And he was able to recognize that fact because he had made a long habit of faith and prayer.

To put it simply, recognizing God is a matter of practice. We may well believe that he is always with us, but only by continually setting aside time for him—time in which we not only speak, but listen to him—can we truly know his presence.

When you think about it, it makes sense. Who else would we expect to know well without ever communicating? If we need to spend time with *people* to get to know them, surely the same will be true of God?

When we do spend time with him, though, we discover the same thing as Paul: when troubles come, we find that we are not facing them alone. We *know* that God is there.

MM

A faithful lifestyle

Flee the evil desires of youth, and pursue righteousness, faith, love and peace, along with those who call on the Lord out of a pure heart. Don't have anything to do with foolish and stupid arguments, because you know they produce quarrels. And the Lord's servant must not quarrel; instead, he must be kind to everyone, able to teach, not resentful. Those who oppose him he must gently instruct, in the hope that God will grant them repentance leading to a knowledge of the truth, and that they will come to their senses and escape from the trap of the devil, who has taken them captive to do his will.

Flee. Pursue. These words imply movement and determination. Being a Christian can be compared with riding a bicycle; if we stop, we will fall off. Static, passive, dormant are not words Paul would ever want to use of a Christian. We can list first the things from which we are to run, and then those we are to follow. Flee the evil desires of youth... Pursue righteousness, faith, love, peace, kindness, forgiveness (to replace resentment). These are all qualities Paul attributes in Galatians 5:22 to the Holy Spirit's work in us. But we do not just sit back and say, 'Oh, the Spirit will change me.' I must cooperate with him in behaviour as well as in prayer.

What about those who go in the opposite direction? Paul is uncomfortably clear. They are in the devil's trap. He has taken them prisoner though they do not realize it. How different from the freedom we have in Christ, and our obedience which responds to his love! That is why we, the Lord's servants, should be gentle but firm in explaining what we believe to those who—often unknowingly—are not merely heading in the wrong direction but are stuck in the spider's web.

A prayer to use

Lord, please strengthen me to pursue all that is good, that I may work out in my life the fruit that the Spirit is working in me. I pray that in all my relationships I may commend you by my life and by my lips.

RG

Selfish and unfaithful

But mark this: There will be terrible times in the last days. People will be lovers of themselves, lovers of money, boastful, proud, abusive, disobedient to their parents, ungrateful, unholy, without love, unforgiving, slanderous, without self-control, brutal, not lovers of the good, treacherous, rash, conceited, lovers of pleasure rather than lovers of God—having a form of godliness but denying its power. Have nothing to do with them.

Paul is very up-to-date. Whatever country you are in you will almost certainly find in today's news stories that illustrate most, if not all, of the ungodly traits Paul lists here. Selfishness and self-aggrandizement; greedy and dishonest dealings in business; teenage rebellion; slander in news comments or in the law court; brutality, violence, hedonism; all these mark our modern age. Why? Because we have had a 'form of godliness' in our religious practices but have 'denied his power'. Jesus warned his followers that the immorality of Noah's day and of Lot's would still be prevalent at his second coming. Judgment fell then, and judgment will fall again, on the immoral (Luke 17:26–37).

Have you ever heard it said 'I can worship God in the open air I don't need to go to church'? Creation is indeed a marvellous aid to worship, so long as we worship the Creator, not his creation. But that worship alone does not bring us into relationship with the living God. And we can go to church Sunday by Sunday but still not allow the Spirit of God access into our lives with his power and his love. In one congregation we belonged to Margaret told us all that she had been going to that church regularly for sixty-four years but she had only just discovered Jesus as her personal saviour. Let there not be an empty shell of godfearing or of churchgoing without the living power of Christ to transform us.

What will this transformation mean? Think of the opposites to Paul's list of ungodly traits. Instead of loving ourselves we will put others first; instead of grasping for money we will be generous; boasting and pride will be replaced by humility and self-effacement.

For meditation

Continue through Paul's list and think of the opposites. Then pray that we may so allow the Holy Spirit to work in our lives that his character matures in us.

RG

Faithfulness to scripture

But as for you, continue in what you have learned and have become convinced of, because you know those from whom you learned it, and how from infancy you have known the holy Scriptures, which are able to make you wise for salvation through faith in Christ Jesus. All Scripture is God-breathed and is useful for teaching, rebuking, correcting and training in righteousness, so that the man of God may be thoroughly equipped for every good work.

Christian lives that are grounded in the Bible have a solid base. Paul gives us good reasons for his strong adherence to scripture. For him, of course, that meant the Old Testament. I wonder if he suspected that less than fifty years later his own writings would be officially included in scripture; certainly he was sure that he was writing with the Lord's authority.

(1) 'All Scripture is God-breathed.' The breath (the *pneuma*, the Spirit) used human writers to speak God's message. The writers were not God's dictating machines; they were biographers, story-tellers, historians, poets, who used their individual personalities to write the truths that the Spirit was, as it were, whispering in their ears. (2) 'They are able to make you wise for salvation in Christ Jesus.' The Old Testament looked forward to this salvation and much of the Jewish ritual illustrated it; the gospels demonstrate it; the Acts recount it; the epistles explain it. Our ideas about salvation will be pure speculation if we do not listen to what the Bible teaches. (3) It is 'useful for teaching' (AV, 'doc-trine'). Not only our understanding of salvation, but of God's character, his purposes for humankind and his relationship with us; all these are to be learnt from scripture. A preacher's responsibility is to teach faithfully from this book and to show its relevance to everyday life. (4) It is useful for 'rebuking, correcting and teaching in righteousness'. It shows us how to live. The Bible re-proves us when we have wandered off God's main road for our lives; it then shows us the way back to that road and how to stay on track.

Collect for St Simon and St Jude's Day

Almighty God, you have built your Church upon the foundation of the apostles and prophets with Jesus Christ himself as the chief cornerstone. So join us together in unity of spirit by their doctrine, that we may be made a holy temple acceptable to you.

RG

God's humanity

Then [Jesus] took [the disciples] out as far as the outskirts of Bethany, and lifting up his hands he blessed them. Now as he blessed them, he withdrew from them and was carried up to heaven. They worshipped him and then went back to Jerusalem full of joy; and they were continually in the Temple praising God.

For many Christians, the ascension seems to be faintly embarrassing. The resurrection is OK. The virgin birth can at least be coped with. But we know that heaven is not literally 'up there'. And so we spend a lot of time explaining that Jesus did not literally float off into the sky.

As if that weren't enough, we may find it hard to see the point of the ascension. We know Jesus was raised and transformed at Easter. Is there any need to have the bit about going into heaven? Yes, there is. Because it says something very important about the incarnation and the nature of God.

We may tend to think of God's becoming a human being as a kind of slumming. God the Son comes down from heaven, is born of Mary, and then goes home again, leaving his humanity behind. But the ascension tells us differently. It is about Jesus the man (who is God) being taken into God. Humanity is not left behind. It becomes a part of God.

To put it another way, the incarnation is not temporary. God has chosen to join himself intimately with his creation, so that there is now a human aspect to God. In Jesus, humanity has been forever joined to divinity.

If all that sounds rather fancy and intellectual, look at it this way. God has not merely come to share our nature, but invited us (in a sense) to share his. Of course, we cannot become God—but as we are joined to Jesus through faith, we find that God himself is not a stranger, but is (at least in part) one of us.

That means that when we pray, and bring our hopes and fears, troubles and joys to God, he understands them personally. Not just because he knows all about them, but because he, in his humanity, can feel them too. There is a part of God which is forever human.

MM

Faithful witness

Do your best to come to me quickly, for Demas, because he loved this world, has deserted me and gone to Thessalonica. Crescens has gone to Galatia, and Titus to Dalmatia. Only Luke is with me. Get Mark and bring him with you because he is helpful to me in my ministry. I sent Tychicus to Ephesus. When you come, bring the cloak that I left with Carpus at Troas, and my scrolls, especially the parchments.

'Only Luke is with me.' We usually think of Luke the doctor or Luke the biographer. But here we see Luke the faithful friend. It is interesting to trace in Acts the 'we' passages when Luke was one of the group travelling with Paul. No package holiday tour for him! He had shared extensively in Paul's missionary journeys, with their uncertainties and their riots; he was there in the shipwreck on Malta and now was there for Paul in prison. Friends who stick with us through thick and thin are precious but how often friends evaporate, sometimes through no fault of our own. I have a friend who stayed in an abusive marriage because of her Christian principles. Four years ago her husband walked out for another woman—and she has found that many social invitations from long-standing friends have ceased, when in her time of loneliness friends are most needed. Take some time to think about the friendships that have slipped; forgive those who have hurt you, and consider whether there are any old friends to whom you should make amends—perhaps by a letter, a phone call, an invitation or an apology.

Paul's other companions had scattered. Crescens, Titus and Tychicus had probably all gone on pastoral visits to encourage the Christians in various churches. The big disappointment was Demas. Earlier Paul had called him 'my fellow-worker' (Philemon 24); now he had deserted Paul for an easier life. The same happens today when Christians' early enthusiasm for Jesus crumbles under the pressures and temptations of life. But Mark, whose earlier lack of stickability had angered Paul (Acts 15:37–39) was now considered a help. Thank God for the changes he makes in us.

For prayer

Luke; Mark; Demas. Do they remind you of any of your friends? Pray for them, and ask God what he wants you to do for them.

RG

The faithfulness of God

At my first defence, no-one came to my support, but everyone deserted me. May it not be held against them. But the Lord stood at my side and gave me strength, so that through me the message might be fully proclaimed and all the Gentiles might hear it. And I was delivered from the lion's mouth. The Lord will rescue me from every evil attack and will bring me safely to his heavenly kingdom. To him be glory for ever and ever. Amen.

The passion of Paul's life was to spread the good news about Jesus. It was not just that he was sure the message was true. He was sure of Christ himself. He knew him. 'I know whom I have believed, and am convinced that he is able to guard what I have entrusted to him for that day' (2 Timothy 1:12). He was utterly sure of the Lord's faithfulness; past, present and future. He had experienced Christ's presence and strength through all the uncertainties of a tough missionary life. He knew the Lord had rescued him in times of human and Satanic attack and he was confident of eternity.

Are you as sure of God as Paul was? As sure as Moses? He said, 'He is the Rock, his works are perfect, and all his ways are just. A faithful God who does no wrong, upright and just is he' (Deuteronomy 32:4). We have a God who makes no mistakes. But when everything seems to be against us we find it hard to be sure. We ask, 'Why me? What have I done to deserve this? Where is God? Does he really love me?'

I once met a woman whose five-year-old son had a fatal illness. One day as she prayed she saw, in her mind, Jesus walking towards her. To her surprise she found herself thumping him. She had never recognized how angry she was with God about her child. His reply? In her 'prayer picture' he simply hugged her, held her tight. What a lovely way to communicate his love and the assurance that he really was holding her and her family in their painful situation!

A prayer

Father, please help me to trust you more fully as the faithful God who holds me tight in all circumstances.

RG

Enemies become friends

We are ruled by the love of Christ, now that we recognize that one man died for everyone, which means that all share in his death. He died for all, so that those who live should no longer live for themselves, but only for him who died and was raised to life for their sake . . . When anyone is joined to Christ, he is a new being; the old is gone, the new has come. All this is done by God, who through Christ changed us from enemies into his friends and gave us the task of making others his friends also. Our message is that God was making all mankind his friends through Christ. God did not keep an account of their sins and he has given us the message which tells how he makes them his friends. Here we are, then, speaking for Christ, as though God himself were making his appeal through us. We plead on Christ's behalf: let God change you from enemies into his friends! Christ was without sin, but for our sake God made him share our sin in order that in union with him we might share the righteousness of God.

This Sunday we are reflecting on the creation of the world and on the new creation. Today we go on contemplating the new creation—and the new life that we have through God-in-Christ. 'We are the body of Christ,' we shall almost certainly say if we go today to the Eucharist, and at Communion—as well as in the whole of our spiritual life—we feed on God. Through the bread and wine of the Eucharist, the body and blood of Christ. We look back to our dying with Christ at the start of our Christian life symbolized through the sacrament of baptism, and we remember that now we have a new life.

We know something now of the resurrection life that is the life of Christ—and the whole of the Communion Service remembers the cost and reminds us of the glory. Death and resurrection—and the transforming of enemies into friends. It is very good news—and God has given us the task of sharing it with all the people who don't know it. In this Decade of Evangelism we can pray that God will guide us to the particular people he wants us to pass the message on to—and if God guides us then we shan't have to force it.

SB

What we were meant to be

O Lord, our Lord, how majestic is thy name in all the earth! When I look at thy heavens, the work of thy fingers, the moon and the stars which thou hast established; what is man that thou art mindful of him, and the son of man that thou dost care for him? Yet thou hast made him little less than God, and dost crown him with glory and honour. Thou hast given him dominion over the works of thy hands; thou hast put all things under his feet.

I read through this Psalm in my study but the day was so lovely that I took my Bible out in the garden. A bird was obviously enjoying the day too, over and over again he sang his little song. Yes, it was easy this morning to rejoice in God's creation: 'O Lord, our Lord, how majestic is they name in all the earth.'

Perhaps David wrote this Psalm at night (the sun is not even mentioned in verse 3) or at least in the memory of those nights when he was a shepherd watching over his sheep in the fields. He looked up and marvelled at the spectacle of the full moon and the stars shining like lamps, great and small in the night sky (and they are particularly impressive in the Middle East). Yes, God's majesty really is visible in his creation.

But read on. Where do we humans come into all this? The Psalm says God thinks about us and cares for us. Yes, I like that. The thought will help me get along today. But what is this? 'Thou hast made him little less than God.' I have recently been catching up on my European history and feel like amending the Psalm to read, 'Thou has made him a little (only a 'little')

lower than the devil!' The terrible story of man's long *inhumanity* to man goes on and on today. What we see is *fallen humanity*. What the Psalmist saw however was man as he was meant to be— almost a god in the world, a surrogate lord (so to speak) of all creation. Sometimes he looks more like a destroyer of all creation!

But there came into the world One who more than fulfilled what we are meant to be, and in God's good time will be, through him who is our redeemer— Christ the Lord (Hebrews 2:6–8). That time is not yet, but meanwhile turn away from the troubles in the world, go out and look up at the full moon and the stars and, when day breaks, if you are fortunate enough, listen to that bird singing his heavenly little song: 'O Lord, our Lord, how majestic is thy name in all the earth!'

Prayer

Lord, we praise your name for all the wonder and the beauty you have given us. May we not only see it, but care for it.

DCF

Knowing God's name

The Lord is a stronghold for the oppressed, a stronghold in times of trouble. And those who know thy name put their trust in thee, for thou, O Lord, has not forsaken those who seek thee. Sing praises to the Lord, who dwells in Zion! Tell among the peoples his deeds! For he who avenges blood is mindful of them; he does not forget the cry of the afflicted.

Yesterday was a lovely day, so I forsook my desk and spent the time in the garden instead. Today is different, there is a howling wind, rain is pouring down. Isn't life a bit like that? There are smooth patches and rough patches. How do we react when we pass from the smooth into the rough? How do we react when we pass from the rough out into the smooth again? Read today's verses once more. They will tell us how King David reacted. He was back in Zion, what a mercy! But when the Amalekites and the Philistines were hounding him all over the country he wondered if he ever would be at home again. But it happened, and he lifted up his voice and sang 'Sing praises to the Lord, who dwells in Zion! Tell among the peoples his deeds!' This is how he reacted.

And this is the lesson he learned for the future, and we can learn. 'Those who know thy name put their trust in thee, for thou, O Lord, hast not forsaken those who seek thee.' I love those words and have made them my own over the years. I have had my rough patches and smooth patches too. I guess we all have, but even on the dark days for some people the clouds lift even then, those are the ones who know God's name. To know God's name is to know who he is, to know his character.

Recently a lady greeted me in the supermarket. I was embarrassed as I couldn't remember who she was and felt I ought to know. She saw the look of puzzlement on my face and revealed her identity and where we had met. What a difference knowing her name meant! We chatted happily after that.

Do we know the name of God? Or is he only a traditional figure, reverenced in the sphere of religion? Perhaps God allows rough patches to crop up in our lives sometimes to drive us out of our religious formality so he becomes a living reality, One to whom we turn and trust; and he does not forsake us when we do. And when we enter into the smooth patches we will bear our witness as David did when the Philistines and Amalekites retreated. 'The Lord is a stronghold for the oppressed, a stronghold in times of trouble.'

Prayer

Lord, you are my refuge in time of trouble. Let me never forget to hide in you.

DCF

Atheism

Why dost thou stand afar off, O Lord? Why doest though hide thyself in times of trouble? For the wicked boasts of the desires of his heart, and the man greedy for gain curses and renounces the Lord . . . all his thoughts are, 'There is no God.' . . . The hapless is crushed, sinks down, and falls by his might. He thinks in his heart, 'God has forgotten, he has hidden his face, he will never see it.' . . . Thou dost see; yea, thou dost note trouble and vexation, that thou mayst take it into thy hands; the hapless commits himself to thee; thou hast been the helper of the fatherless.

This is one of the very few anonymous Psalms; unlike most of them it has no title so we cannot know who wrote it nor what occasion caused it to be written. This much however is abundantly clear. Some godless man, boastful and ruthless, was parading his atheism, and terrifying his poor and defenceless neighbours, lying in wait for them as if he were a lion lurking in his covert and stealthily watching. To see this going on 'under his nose' revolted this Psalm writer. He was nauseated and couldn't help but cry out, 'Why dost thou stand afar off, O Lord?' But what about this tyrant? He boasted that there is no God, so he could do what he liked, there was none to hinder him. God wouldn't see because he can't see. No harm therefore would happen unto him.

Now what the Psalmist is portraying for us is not so much the man who says there is no God—that is atheism pure and simple—but the man who asserts that there is no *personal* God. Haven't we met this ourselves? God is 'the First Cause', God is the 'Ground of our Being', God is the sum total of existence, now more, God *is* existence. This is the philosopher's God. He is not one who does anything. He just is. He certainly does not interfere in the world nor in the affairs of human beings. This then is the awful thought, to deny a personal God comes in the end to deny the existence of any God at all.

But does this matter? Perhaps not in the short run. The atheist can continue placidly smoking his pipe and weeding his garden; but suppose atheism gets a hold on a whole country or a whole community . . . then it won't be long before tyranny rears its cruel, ugly head and the humble and poor will bear the brunt. This is what the Psalmist saw and wishes us to see. It is frightening.

Prayer

Lord, I believe that you do see and care. Let me not be laughed or argued out of this faith.

DCF

Individual piety enough?

In the Lord I take refuge; how can you say to me, 'Flee like a bird to the mountains; for lo, the wicked bend the bow, they have fitted their arrow to the string, to shoot in the dark at the upright in heart; if the foundations are destroyed, what can the righteous do'? The Lord is in his holy temple, the Lord's throne is in heaven; his eyes behold, his eyelids test, the children of men. The Lord tests the righteous and the wicked, and his soul hates him that loves violence. On the wicked he will rain coals of fire and brimstone; a scorching wind shall be the portion of their cup. For the Lord is righteous . . .

This Psalm isn't easy to follow at first, so let me open it out. Absalom, King David's son, was preparing an open rebellion against his father and against the kingdom. He intended taking over the reins of government and was arming his followers. David's entourage had learned what was afoot and advised him to flee to a place of safety, no doubt with his government. David however decided to stay put, 'In the Lord I take refuge' (v. 1). But his advisers came back at him. There is no time to lose! Absalom is ready to launch his offensive, 'for lo, the wicked bend their bow, they have fitted their arrow to the string' they are ready to shoot and they will, in the dark (vv. 2–3). It is all very well for you O King, boldly and bravely to stand your ground, but if the whole fabric of our country is crumbling *what can one man achieve*? King David listened but responded by confessing his trust in God who reigns on high. God will reward both the righteous and unrighteous according to their deeds (vv. 4–7). The Psalm doesn't tell us what happened, but Absalom launched his attack and David was forced to flee. After

terrible struggles he was restored to his kingdom.

But what has all this to do with us? Is it simply a piece of ancient history? No, not quite. The key text for us is in verse 3: 'if the foundations are destroyed, what can the righteous do?' What can individual faith and individual goodness achieve if there are no foundations, if there isn't the back-up of a *moral community*? Christians should help to build up this foundation: what will we accomplish on our own, without a *strong* Church behind us? We should be concerned for the community, for the foundations which have been built up and maintained. But we must not lose faith in the God who calls us to faithfulness, even when it seems individual piety is not enough.

Prayer

Lord, strengthen all that makes for a moral basis in our country and for the unity and health of the Church.

DCF

Hope in gloom

Help, Lord; for there is no longer any that is godly; for the faithful have vanished from among the sons of men. Every one utters lies to his neighbour: with flattering lips and a double heart they speak. May the Lord cut off all flattering lips, the tongue that makes great boasts, those who say, 'With our tongue we will prevail, our lips are with us; who is our master?' Because the poor are despoiled, because the needy groan, I will now arise,' says the Lord; 'I will place him in the safety for which he longs.' The promises of the Lord are promises that are pure, silver refined in a furnace on the ground, purified seven times. Do thou, O Lord, protect us, guard us ever from this generation. On every side the wicked prowl, as vileness is exalted among the sons of men.

We prefer happy, joyful songs. This is understandable, but life isn't all jolly, and if our Christian worship doesn't sometimes touch us at the sombre points with a message it is failing. This Psalm is a complaint but it does manage to rise above the gloom once or twice and confidence takes hold.

What is the trouble? It is the decadence that has crept in among God's people. Perhaps this Psalm was written when David's kingdom was established and the temple worship was splendid with entrancing music supported by professional singers. On the surface then everything was splendid but underneath the beautiful and orderly façade—'Everyone utters lies to his neighbour; with flattering lips and a double heart they speak.' The state religion has grown corrupt. Nothing was what it seemed.

And yet it could not be wholly corrupt because some worshippers were aware of that corruption. There was still a faithful remnant and if there was hope anywhere, it lay with this minority. They heard God's voice and they believed his promises made and purified in times of affliction. And they prayed to God to protect them from the generation which was acting so vilely.

This is a picture of Church decadence. Does it *in any way* relate to us? Read, if you have the nerve, the history of the Christian Church—a sorry story of a Church corrupted too often by power. At the heart of the corruption is what is said with the lips and what is actually carried out. They do not tally, so truth falls to the ground and the faithful are scarcely to be found any more (v. 1).

Yes, a sad Psalm, but God will turn our heaviness into joy.

Prayer

Lord, let us not lose our hope. In your good time the truth will be established.

DCF

Jealousy

O Lord my God, in thee do I take refuge; save me from all my pursuers, and deliver me, lest like a lion they rend me, dragging me away, with none to rescue. O Lord my God, if I have done this, if there is wrong in my hands, if I have requited my friend with evil or plundered my enemy without cause, let the enemy pursue me and overtake me, and let him trample my life to the ground, and lay my soul in the dust. Arise, O Lord, in thy anger, lift thyself up against the fury of my enemies; awake, O my God; thou hast appointed a judgment. The Lord judges the peoples; judge me, O Lord, according to my righteousness and according to the integrity that is in me.

When we take part in public worship, we begin by confessing our sins, for we are sinners, we admit it. But are there not times when it is right and proper to confess not our sins but our integrity? The Psalmist certainly thought so.

If David wrote this Psalm (and it is probable) then someone clearly had 'his knife in him'. The heading to the Psalm fixes on Cush, a Benjaminite, but who he was no one knew. My guess is that he was one of King Saul's minions and Saul certainly had his 'knife in David'. I think I know why. David was good-looking, gifted in poetry and music, physically strong and skilled in military tactics. People were fascinated by David. Saul was jealous of David. David had done nothing wrong, he was just himself.

I remember sitting in a splendid public building when many distinguished people were present. On the far side of the hall sat a lady who meant to be noticed and had dressed accordingly. Unfortunately for her she spotted another lady also beautifully dressed, through more modestly, who happened to look up catching the other in the act of observing her. That did it! She was having no rivals, and as soon as the proceedings were over she sought her out in the crowd with the express purpose of embarrassing her. She did it with great subtlety. Why? Jealousy.

David was the victim of King Saul's jealousy. He had done nothing wrong. There were no sins to confess. Was he right then to confess his integrity? Of course he was. There are times when we can rightly stand up before God, confident that God will justify us, but we must remain humble as we protest our innocence or we shall spoil everything.

Prayer

Lord, keep me from jealousy lest I treat people unfairly and put myself in the wrong.

Read the verse again.

DCF

The wind of the Spirit

When Jesus was talking to the Pharisee named Nicodemus, who had come to him by night, he told him of the need to be born of the Spirit. The Spirit who was like the wind. 'The wind blows where it chooses,' he said to Nicodemus, 'and you hear the sound of it, but you do not know where it comes from or where it goes' (John 3:8, NRSV).

Later on, after the events of Good Friday and Easter Day, when the day of Pentecost had come, 'the disciples heard a sound come from heaven like the rush of a mighty wind'—and the church that is the body of Christ was born. Pentecost is the birthday of the Church—and that is the day on which this section of *Day by Day* begins.

Then we look at St Paul's letter to the Galatians, in which he tells them pretty sharply that they are getting the Christian life wrong. 'How can you be so foolish? You began by God's Spirit; do you now want to finish it by your own power?' They can't, of course, and neither can we. Graham Dodds takes us through Galatians for two weeks, and then looks at the fruit of the Spirit—and in particular at love, joy and peace.

Blown along

When the Day of Pentecost had come, the disciples were all together in one place. And suddenly a sound came from heaven like the rush of a mighty wind, and it filled all the house where they were sitting.

If you were asked, 'What is the Holy Spirit?' probably you would find the question difficult to answer. We can visualize God the Creator for all around us is the created order, powerful and beautiful. We can visualize God the Son, for did not Jesus live and work in our world; people saw him and even touched him. But the Holy Spirit is different, you can't see a spirit. You can't touch a spirit. So what is the Holy Spirit?

The Holy Spirit is God at work in our world. The Holy Spirit is the means or the agent by which God is active in our midst now. It is a creative Spirit, a powerful Spirit, a Spirit which leaves nothing as it was before. The Hebrews had a distinctive word for it—*ruach*, the word for wind, but not a gentle zephyr inviting us to walk along the seafront, but a mighty, gusting force of which we had better be careful.

In 1987 we had such a wind here in South-East England. In one night it virtually destroyed my garden, taking me a year to replace and replant it. That wind was *ruach* all right. I shall not forget. And, of course, it blew powerfully on the day of Pentecost. It gave birth to the Christian Church. In no time it changed from being a dozen apostles in Jerusalem and some other men and women gathered around their nucleus, into an outgoing, thrusting movement soon, very soon, to claim attention and followers way out beyond Jerusalem, in Samaria, Antioch, across the sea to Cyprus, then to Greece and then even to Rome, that sophisticated, energetic city of a million inhabitants. It is impossible to explain how such an astonishing movement tool place in so short a time from its so humble origin in out-of-the-way, troublesome Palestine, without the Holy Spirit, the rushing mighty wind.

And how does it enter into a situation in the first place? The answer is when men and women take the bold step of believing in Jesus as the Son of God. The need then is not to thwart the Spirit but to be open to him, willing and ready to be led, or, if you like 'blown along'.

Prayer

Father, I commit myself to you through Christ your Son and I know your Spirit is with us. Help me, help the whole Church to be open to him, your Holy Spirit, in all that we do and say.

DCF

Paul's passion

In order to set us free from this present evil age, Christ gave himself for our sins, in obedience to the will of our God and Father. To God be the glory for ever and ever! Amen. I am surprised at you! In no time at all you are deserting the one who called you by the grace of Christ, and are accepting another gospel. Actually, there is no 'other gospel', but I say this because there are some people who are upsetting you and trying to change the gospel of Christ. But even if we or an angel from heaven should preach to you a gospel that is different from the one we preached to you, may he be condemned to hell!

My main church building in Walcot, Bath, is St Swithin's, the parish church. It prides itself on being Georgian. Built in 1777, it's a lovely rectangle with a gallery and an impressive east wall. The only trouble is that, somewhere along the line, someone (probably the Victorians) added all sorts of extras. It's not so much the pulpit or lectern that cause the imbalance, nor the Rector's and Curate's stall that face each other. Georgians built things symmetrically, but someone has stuck a wooden vestry in one corner at the front destroying the visual impact. Whether it's a carbuncle or architectural vandalism, it's there, added on, extra to requirements.

The Galatians had something of the same problem. The gospel had been changed and things were added, making another gospel. Paul doesn't say straight away what has happened, but its clear he's mad about what's gone on. His passion is for truth and a gospel given by God is the truth. So if someone changes it he feels he has every right to condemn them to hell.

Someone once asked me what I get mad about. The question made me think for some time before I replied. The thing is I don't get really mad about anything very often. Am I apathetic or just able to control my feelings? It could be either. Jesus chose his moments to show his anger and Paul follows suit here. There are some things so important it is right to defend them. Surely our world would be a better place if righteous anger was vented and destructive anger was controlled.

Prayer

Stir up, we beseech thee, O Lord, the wills of thy faithful people.

Collect for the 25th Sunday after Trinity, ASB

GD

The captain's choice

But God in his grace chose me even before I was born, and called me to serve him. And when he decided to reveal his Son to me, so that I might preach the Good News about him to the Gentiles, I did not go to anyone for advice, nor did I go to Jerusalem to see those who were apostles before me. Instead, I went at once to Arabia, and then I returned to Damascus. It was three years later that I went to Jerusalem to obtain information from Peter, and I stayed with him for two weeks. I did not see any other apostle except James, the Lord's brother.

I always remember my experience of games at school. At senior school it was very organized and professional, but in the juniors we had the humiliating ordeal of choosing teams. We, my classmates and I, would line up against a wall and the two captains would begin choosing. My heart pounded, not because I wanted to be on a particular side, but rather because I didn't want to be the last to be chosen. How far down the list would they go before it was me that they wanted? The tension was unbearable, but of course I didn't show it. I stood, pretending to agree with all the choices made, internally getting more and more desperate to join one team or the other.

The early experiences of life tend to etch themselves indelibly on the rest of our lives. This can make it all the harder later on to discover that God doesn't pick sides. God doesn't judge his creation in that way. He chooses life for each of his children, life in all its abundance. He sent his Son to forgive the world, and the entire world is forgiven, every last one of us. The trouble is that some do not accept the choice to join his team and so miss out on the game altogether.

Like other Bible characters, Paul has discovered that he has been chosen by God, personally, intimately, secretly and particularly. This experience of God is what Paul will not allow the Galatians to distort. It is wonderfully true, incredibly moving, and is as real today as it was then.

Praise

For each child is special,
accepted and loved,
a love gift from Jesus
to his Father above

Graham Kendrick

GD

That man?—a Christian!

At that time the members of the churches in Judea did not know me personally. They knew only what others were saying: 'The man who used to persecute us is now preaching the faith that he once tried to destroy!' And so they praised God because of me. Fourteen years later I went back to Jerusalem with Barnabas, taking Titus along with me. I went because God revealed to me that I should go. In a private meeting with the leaders I explained the gospel message that I preach to the Gentiles. I did not want my work in the past or in the present to be a failure.

I've always thought that Ananias was a brave man. He was the man whom God called to lay hands on Paul after his Damascus Road experience. In recent times it would have been like being called to Hitler's office to baptize him. No wonder the early Church received such a lift from Paul's conversion.

God does things in the Church and around it to encourage us. Whether it's the conversion of someone famous or a troubled situation come right, God often gives us a sign of his presence when we most need it. Some of us are better at seeing these things than others. When I was a curate I worked with a man who was brilliant at seeing things as they really appear. Whilst I was using all my intuition and seeing the potential of situations, he could point out what seemed obvious yet I had missed completely. There's a place for both kinds of people but it's often in these latter observations that the Church is encouraged the most.

One of the cries of our modern Church is 'if only we knew what is going on we'd be so encouraged'. Testimonies of ordinary people are so important. When Paul was converted it was so encouraging to the Church. Yet when anyone turns to Christ it is of great inspiration to the local Christians. A new person has become a child of God, a new creation. Not only is it encouraging it may also complete God's plan. As someone has said, 'God knows how many people will eventually accept him as their Lord, and it may just be that the person you lead to him will complete the number and we shall all rise to be with him in the skies.'

Meditate

Either in a group or on your own, list some encouragements of the last few days and rejoice in them.

GD

Not gods, but disciples

They [the spies in Paul's band] saw that God had given me the task of preaching the gospel to the Gentiles, just as he had given Peter the task of preaching the gospel to the Jews. For by God's power I was made an apostle to the Gentiles, just as Peter was made an apostle to the Jews. James, Peter and John, who seemed to be the leaders, recognized that God had given me this special task; so they shook hands with Barnabas and me, as a sign that we were all partners. We agreed that Barnabas and I would work among the Gentiles and they among the Jews . . . but when Peter came to Antioch, I opposed him in public, because he was clearly wrong.

I bet Antioch was tense when Peter and Paul met. These two giants of the early Church now seem to us to be spiritual leaders of such magnitude it's difficult to ever imagine them doing anything wrong. Yet they were not gods, they were disciples, and disciples have a habit of making mistakes from time to time.

Peter was never the most thought-out of people. He leapt onto the water before any of the others. He was all for stopping Jesus going to the cross, earning him the famous rebuke 'get behind me Satan'. He even denied his Saviour.

Paul was no lightweight either. His career as a liquidator of Christians was very successful and he certainly didn't pull any punches when he spoke. So it was likely to be quite a disagreement when it happened.

But we also hear Paul speaking of the great unity between them all, how they shook hands and agreed to work together. It all reminds me of my college days. There we would argue strongly over theological points for quite prolonged periods, sometimes it could seem like major disagreements.

The difference between doing this in a worshipping community and in secular life cannot be underestimated. We may disagree strongly as we discuss, but I've found that those who come together in worship and prayer find a unity that is not found in secular society. It's not a 'giving in'; it's an integrity which is born out of the Spirit.

Pray

Almighty and everliving God we beseech thee to inspire continually the universal Church with the spirit of truth, unity and concord: And grant that all they who do confess your holy name may agree in the truth of thy holy Word, and live in unity and godly love.

GD

Spiritual apartheid

Before some men who had been sent by James arrived there, Peter had been eating with the Gentile brothers. But after these men arrived, he drew back and would not eat with the Gentiles, because he was afraid of those who were in favour of circumcising them. The other Jewish brothers also started acting like cowards along with Peter; and even Barnabas was swept along by their cowardly action. When I saw that they were not walking a straight path in line with the truth of the gospel, I said to Peter in front of them all, 'You are a Jew, yet you have been living like a Gentile, not like a Jew. How, then, can you try to force Gentiles to live like Jews?'

I remember my student days with much relish. They were the greatest days of freedom and fun. My wife (only an acquaintance at the time) was the CU President at the music college we attended and I was the Prayer Secretary. This gave me the opportunity to engineer us being prayer partners, and so our relationship developed.

We not only prayed together but we also joined a little local church close to my digs. It was a great church in many ways and we loved the leader. However, it became clear that there was going to be a problem about Holy Communion. Even though we shared the same faith, they wanted us to be baptized. It was a strict policy of baptism, not only into the denomination but also into their fellowship. We didn't either want to, or feel it was right. I shall never forget the evening service where Communion was passed along the pews from person to person until it reached us and we were missed out. The hurt and pain for everyone was too much, and with tears we left the fellowship.

Peter knew full well that there was no rule in the gospel about Gentiles needing to be circumcised before one could eat with them, yet still he refused to share their table. No wonder Paul takes him to task. However, before we join Paul in his condemnation we too need to examine ourselves. Do we shun those who have not been confirmed or totally immersed or are a different colour or come from a lower social class?

Often those who are shunned don't kick up a fuss or speak out. They slip out of the fellowship quietly in disappointment, to their own loss and the church's.

Think

Who have I not seen in church recently?
Why not?

GD

Bolt-on faith

How can you be so foolish! You began by God's Spirit; do you now want to finish by your own power? Did all your experience mean nothing at all? Surely it meant something! Does God give you the Spirit and work miracles among you because you do what the Law requires or because you hear the gospel and believe it? Consider the experience of Abraham; as the scripture says, 'He believed God, and because of his faith God accepted him as righteous.' You should realize then, that the real descendants of Abraham are the people who have faith.

We have a fortnightly *Book of Common Prayer* Holy Communion service. During it I say a phrase in the prayer of consecration about Jesus' death on the cross. It goes like this: '[Jesus] who made there [by his one oblation of himself once offered] a full, perfect and sufficient sacrifice, oblation, and satisfaction, for the sins of the whole world.' Apart from it being quite a mouthful it's also difficult to understand, even after some time. But what it means is that Jesus did everything that was or would ever be needed for our salvation.

Paul knew that; even the Galatians knew that. So he bursts in with this rude rebuke, 'You idiots!' as J.B. Phillips translates it. Having been given the Holy Spirit they had now returned to trying to live by the Law again. Even though he's tough on them it's clear from the context that Paul knew they had been duped by the evil one. Still, sometimes the 'short sharp shock' is the only way to wake them up.

Many people in churches around the world think that Christianity is about feeling accepted and good. This 'feel-good' factor is important but it can easily turn into flabby Christianity. The nice fellowship, the well-managed service, the tidy sermon with the three points can lose the cutting edge of the Spirit. In other words, living by rote is much easier than living by the Spirit. Or is it?

Christianity is about following a person, relating to him and living with him. He has done all that is needed for us to live a fulfilled life. Yet from time to time we insist on bolting on to our faith new laws and weird rules.

Task

Write down in pencil what the eleventh and twelfth commandments are for your life or church. Then rub them out!

GD

Trinity Sunday

In the year that King Uzziah died I saw the Lord sitting upon a throne, high and lifted up; and his train filled the temple. Above him stood the seraphim; each had six wings: with two he covered his face, and with two he covered his feet, and with two he flew. And one called to another and said: 'Holy, holy, holy is the Lord of hosts; the whole earth is full of his glory.' And the foundations of the thresholds shook at the voice of him who called, and the house was filled with smoke.

Today is the day when we become lost in mystery, in admitting that God truly is beyond all human understanding, and must simply be accepted, worshipped and adored.

And yet we must try to understand, for our minds are God's creation, and are part of our equipment for worship and service.

God, we say, is three persons in one being. God is Father, Son and Holy Spirit. We say it, and yet cannot truly understand. (Jehovah's Witnesses call and say, ah, $1 + 1 + 1 = 3$, so you really worship three gods. No, we say, $1 \times 1 \times 1 = 1$, so we worship only one God. But this is meaningless.) The real point of the doctrine of the Trinity lies in our experience of God.

God reveals himself to us in Jesus Christ, through whom we have salvation. Try as we might, there is no truly satisfactory category for this revelation other than God himself. In Jesus we see the presence of God.

Yet we know that Jesus points us to our heavenly Father, source of all life and love, our strength and our redeemer.

Father and Son promise us their presence and transforming power in our lives, a power which convinces us of sin, equips us for service and warms our hearts with the certainty of God's love. A power which argues with us and challenges us, a power called the Holy Spirit, who is nothing less than God, but is neither entirely Father nor Son, but points us to both.

So we continue to wrestle with the concept, but we live the reality as we worship and serve God our Father, through the saving grace of God the Son, in the power of God the Holy Spirit.

MM

All one or alone

And so the Law was in charge of us until Christ came, in order that we might then be put right with God through faith. Now that the time for faith is here, the Law is no longer in charge of us. It is through faith that all of you are God's sons in union with Christ Jesus. You were baptized into union with Christ, and now you are clothed, so to speak, with the life of Christ himself. So there is no difference between Jews and Gentiles, between slaves and free men, between men and women; you are all one in union with Christ Jesus.

A real eye-opener for me when I was seventeen was walking into Keswick during Convention week. There seemed to be hundreds of stalls all selling books, tapes and other Christian artifacts. At the end of the week my Bible was usually covered in stickers publicizing 'Jesus Christ, the real thing' like the Coke advert, or 'Carpenter from Nazareth needs joiners'. It was great stuff and I loved it. But most striking of all was the big banner always there every year, 'All one in Christ Jesus'.

Together, we crowded into the tent lapping up the teaching. Even though the usual twenty-minute sermon was extended by at least 300 per cent, our youth group would debate the talk well into the night, often through to dawn. Singing together, praying together, helping each other, we had great times, good fun, real friends. For the first time in my life I really felt at one with God. If only it could stay like that.

Unfortunately somewhere down the line since then I've been influenced. Influenced by unseen forces that have spoilt the unity and tried to separate me from other Christians. I've developed some prejudices towards some kinds of Christians. Some, who don't agree with me, I've written off. Some, I've even thought would be better if they joined another church or even faith. What happened?

When I was baptized I was given a new set of clothes but someone stole some of them. I forgot to put them on one day and someone came along and lifted them. I was so embarrassed I dared not ask for new ones, so I hid, and that's when I began to distance myself from others and wish they were not even around. I became alone in Christ Jesus rather than 'all one'.

Meditate

'He became what we are that he might make us what he is.'

Athanasius

GD

Slaves of the spirits

The son who will receive his father's property is treated just like a slave while he is young, even though he really owns everything. While he is young, there are men who take care of him and manage his affairs until the time set by his father. In the same way, we too were slaves of the ruling spirits of the universe before we reached spiritual maturity. But when the right time finally came, God sent his own Son. He came as the son of a human mother and lived under the Jewish Law, to redeem those who were under the Law, so that we might become God's sons.

The chilling images of George Orwell's *1984* have remained with me since I read the book. Whilst it's true that the explicit slavery revealed by Orwell did not have its direct equivalent in the reality of that year (at least not in Britain), yet there are now millions of sons and daughters of nations who live in unseen slavery. The children of many countries are drafted into armies. There is still a huge juvenile population subjected to prostitution. Horrendous conditions exist in many places for those imprisoned by forced child labour.

Paul contrasts this slavery and freedom of all people in stark terms. The slave lives subject to powers far beyond his or her control. There is no chance that freedom can be won because he or she lives under the authority of the ruling spirits of the universe.

When Paul uses this phrase 'the ruling spirits of the universe' he is speaking about two things. Firstly he means the basic elementary ideas of the world and secondly he means the pagan elemental forces associated with de-mons or evil spirits. Both these ideas are relevant to us today. We need to examine the philosophies of the world and reflect on their measure of godliness or godlessness. We also need to counter the renewed interest in pagan forces. All over the country (especially in schools) there is an increased interest in the occult.

As John Calvin said, 'We are subject to the men who rule over us, but subject only in the Lord. If they command anything against him, let us not pay the least regard to it.'

Pray

For the work of those sent to bring release to the captives.

GD

My Father

To show that you are his sons and daughters, God sent the Spirit of his Son into our hearts, the Spirit who cries out, 'Father, my Father.' So then, you are no longer a slave but a son or daughter. And since you are what you are, God will give you all that he has for his heirs. In the past you did not know God, and so you were slaves of beings who are not gods. But now that you know God—or, I should say, now that God knows you—how is it that you want to turn back to those weak and pitiful ruling spirits? Why do you want to become their slaves all over again?

Those who have a rough experience with their earthly fathers often say that because of that they find the fatherhood of God difficult. But they may be seeing things the wrong way round when they say it. To interpret our relationship with God in the light of our earthly relationships is upside down. Our earthly parents are supposed to be a reflection of God the Father's care for his children.

Having said this, of course, there are many people who nevertheless find it hard to relate to God as Father. He may seem distant or cruel or even bad. For those who have been abused by their own father, to think of God like this is bound to raise some painful memories.

Although I've always got on well with my father I can relate to this problem in another way. For years I was brought up in a Catholic school which for the most part I enjoyed. I'm very grateful to the nuns who gave me so much, and imparted the reality of God to me. But in one way they failed. Every time I got into trouble I had to confess my sin to the Mother Superior. She would deal out the punishment which was inevitably something to do with praying. I'd have to say the Rosary or the Angelus or some other prayer. Unfortunately I was left with the impression that saying prayers is to do with punishment.

It has taken me years to try to see prayer in another way. It wasn't until I experienced intimacy with God that I found prayer to be anything other than a duty. Only after that can I say the Spirit of God's Son has truly entered my heart.

Think

What does a true father do for his children?

GD

Free freedom

Freedom is what we have—Christ has set us free! Stand, then, as free people, and do not allow yourselves to become slaves again ... As for us, our hope is that God will put us right with him; and this is what we wait for by the power of God's Spirit working through our faith. For when we are in union with Christ Jesus, neither circumcision nor the lack of it makes any difference at all; what matters is faith that works through love.

Everyday traps are not all that easy to spot. It's often not until someone or something makes us aware of being caught in a trap that we realize it. When I questioned some of my congregation about the traps they had fallen into in their lives, they said that it was one of the most difficult things to discover in the Christian life. I also asked them what kind of traps they had experienced. 'Living to please others, especially parents', one said, 'Feeling that everyone is against me', said another. We listed other prisons including thinking everyone is better than me, or worse than me. Becoming too rigid or too superficial about God was high on the list. But the one which everyone agreed with about church life was the trap of being stuck in one kind of churchmanship.

I remember my diocesan bishop, Rt Revd Jim Thompson, preaching once about 'isms' that entrap us. He sited some instances: Evangelicalism, Catholicism, Liberalism. We live in the comfort of thinking we have freedom and the 'real' truth. We pull up the drawbridge and defend the ramparts. But true freedom according to Paul is 'faith that works through love'. He doesn't mention any styles of churchmanship.

Experiencing overwhelming freedom is not usually an everyday event. It can happen when we initially find Christ but more often than not it's a slow gradual process of discovery. One lady I know said that for years the relationship with her son had been difficult. She even found herself not wanting him around. Then she confessed her feelings of failure to her husband and God woke her up some days later with a new love for her son. There was a sudden new freedom, long-awaited and gratefully received. It seems that our confession of being trapped is at least half way to freedom.

Think

The basic test of freedom is perhaps less in what we are free to do than in what we are free not to do.

Eric Hoffer

GD

Hidden fruit

What human nature does is quite plain. It shows itself in immoral, filthy, and indecent actions; in worship of idols and witchcraft. People become enemies and they fight; they become jealous, angry, and ambitious. They separate into parties and groups; they are envious, get drunk, have orgies, and do other things like these. I warn you now as I have before: those who do these things will not possess the Kingdom of God. But the Spirit produces love, joy, peace, patience, kindness, goodness, faithfulness, humility, and self-control. There is no law against such things as these.

I'm often surprised by how similar we all are and yet how much we hide from each other. Someone said 'the most personal is the most universal' and this seems to be true. When I dare to preach about something that I find hard in the Christian life I always find people who come up afterwards and say, 'You know, I feel exactly like that, too.'

But we so often miss all the wonderful qualities of life. We miss them because they are often done quietly, behind the scenes and don't attract attention. Like fruit on a tree they are often hidden so that we really have to look. I discovered an enormous harvest of pears which had been nestling near a fence when I picked some from our tree yesterday. They were much better and bigger than the rest but I didn't know they were there until I began picking.

So it is with following Jesus. Until a person begins the work of following him, much of the riches of God are concealed. This is partly because God is the God of surprises and partly because he wants us to grow closer to him.

James Jones tells in his book on suffering about walking past a school and hearing a child crying on the other side of the wall. It was a few moments later that he realized that it was his little girl and his instinct was to get there as quickly as possible to help her. But he refrained. Someone else was looking after her and he had to leave another to do the comforting.

God doesn't always jump in and rescue us. He allows us to find the hidden fruit of his Spirit through each other. This means that we have two quests. First, to explore and find his fruit, and secondly to allow others to see it on us.

Pray

May I be known by your fruit.

GD

Boasting about the cross

The people who are trying to force you to be circumcised are the ones who want to show off and boast about external matters . . . As for me, however, I will boast only about the cross of our Lord Jesus Christ; for by means of his cross the world is dead to me, and I am dead to the world. It does not matter at all whether or not one is circumcised; what does matter is being a new creature. As for those who follow this rule in their lives, may peace and mercy be with them—with them and with all God's people!

We've largely given up singing action choruses when the Sunday School are present in church. The children have taught the adults something very important. What happened was that the services always included an action chorus, one where we sang and did hand movements to illustrate the words. Sometimes there would be two or three together. Slowly but surely the children opted out of doing the actions leaving all the adults flapping about reliving their childhood days. When some of the children were asked why they didn't join in, they said it was because they didn't understand the songs, actions or no actions.

What Paul is saying in his parting comments of the epistle is, if you don't understand the meaning, don't do the actions. The inner understanding and life of a Christian is what matters, not what happens outwardly. Circumcision signifies outwardly that great things have happened, but the important thing is what has gone on inside. Our children instinctively became bored with the outward actions because they didn't understand the inward truths.

Boasting about something so horren-dous as the cross seems bizarre. But Paul is really boasting about the immense love of God. In comparison, those who boast about religious status boast about nothing.

His personal experience of knowing this love of God has made him a new creation. For him, this is the crux of faith, to become a new creation. When we join him in discovering this faith we are no longer bound. Rather, we are made new, whole, vibrant and living in Christ. God has given us the opportunity to be changed inside. May our outward actions reflect the changes he makes.

Pray

Change my heart O God, make it ever true,
Change my heart O God, may I be like you
You are the potter, I am the clay,
Mould me and make me, this is what I pray.

Eddie Espinosa

GD

Praise the Lord

Praise the Lord.Praise God in his sanctuary; praise him in his mighty heavens. Praise him for his acts of power; praise him for his surpassing greatness. Praise him with the sounding of the trumpet, praise him with the harp and lyre, praise him with tambourine and dancing, praise him with the strings and flute, praise him with the clash of cymbals, praise him with resounding cymbals.

Let everything that has breath praise the Lord.

Praise the Lord.

If we want to know where to praise God, the answer is everywhere. God is in his sanctuary—and God is everywhere. 'Where can I go to escape your presence?' asks the writer of Psalm 139 and the answer to that is 'Nowhere!' Because wherever we go God is there. That isn't a reason for dread (except for the right sort of holy awe), but for delight. We praise him on earth—and we join our praise 'with the whole company of heaven'. Our reason for praising him is that he is God—and that he is a God of love. He is the creator of the whole earth and he made all things. You and me, the seas and all the creatures who live in them, the sky and all the living things that fly in it, and the earth and all its plants and creatures. As well as all the stars in the galaxies of the Milky Way.

And God the creator is also God the redeemer—so with all the means we have at our disposal we praise him. Sometimes noisily, sometimes quietly. In every way we want, and in every way we choose. And not just human creatures. 'Let everything that has breath praise the Lord.' My blackbird who runs round on my grass, praises the Lord simply by being a blackbird. Sometimes singing its heart out. Sometimes sunning itself on the earth with its wings spread out and its beak wide open. Perhaps our task as a royal priesthood is to gather up all the creatures and all things and praise God through our delighting in them. But I think they existed to the praise of the glory of God during all the time before man and woman existed on the earth. And in the glory of heaven they will be praising God together with us and the angels.

SB

The fruit of the Spirit

'Be on your guard against false prophets; they come to you looking like sheep on the outside, but on the inside they are really like wild wolves. You will know them by what they do. Thorn bushes do not bear grapes, and briars do not bear figs. A healthy tree bears good fruit, but a poor tree bears bad fruit. A healthy tree cannot bear bad fruit, and a poor tree cannot bear good fruit. And any tree that does not bear good fruit is cut down and thrown in the fire. So then, you will know the false prophets by what they do.'

Imagine a large full tree. Some of its branches seem to soar into the air reaching up to the sky. Some branches reach out to neighbouring trees. They stretch out to try to touch another living part of nature. Some other branches cannot be seen with a glance. They need to be searched for, discovered by walking into the foliage. On these branches is the fruit of the tree.

The fruit of God's Holy Spirit is similar. Love, joy and peace are the Godward fruit, they reach up to heaven. They reflect the very essence of God almighty. Then there's the neighbourly fruit. Patience, kindness and goodness reach out to others in the world. This kind of fruit will be necessary to live together. The third category might be termed the inward fruit. Faithfulness, gentleness and self-control all describe the quality of life we live. They are not usually seen straight away in a person's life. They take time to be observed for they come from deeper down.

When Jesus says, 'By their fruit you will recognize them,' it challenges me. I often see these kinds of qualities in ordinary everyday sort of people. The plumber who came the other day is an example. He showed great kindness and patience to us as he mended our boiler. He's not a churchgoer, or so he says, and yet he demonstrated that much fruit grows in his life. It challenges me not to categorize people but it also makes me more aware of what is or is not distinctive about my lifestyle.

Pray

May Almighty God open our hearts to the riches of his grace that we may bring forth the fruit of the Spirit in love and joy and peace. Amen

Taken from the Collect for Pentecost 8, ASB

GD

The greatest love

'I am the real vine, and my Father is the gardener. He breaks off every branch in me that does not bear fruit, and he prunes every branch that does bear fruit, so that it will be clean and bear more fruit. You have been made clean already by the teaching I have given you. Remain united to me, and I will remain united to you. A branch cannot bear fruit by itself; it can do so only if it remains in the vine. In the same way you cannot bear fruit unless you remain in me . . . The greatest love a person can have for his friends is to give his life for them.'

This great saying of Jesus about love comes in the context of his sayings about the fruit of the vine. It's therefore no wonder that love is the first of Paul's fruit in his list in Galatians.

Thinking of dying is not pleasant. Thinking of dying for someone else is just as morbid, and yet at least it has some merit. The sacrifice that is made is not a waste. It goes to allow someone else to live.

I went to the Fleet Air Arm museum recently and saw the exhibition which included the last letters of kamikaze pilots to their wives or mothers. It was very distressing to read their thoughts the night before they set out on their mission. And yet it was clear that at least some of them believed in what they were doing.

Most of us would have to think hard before we took a decision to die for someone. Maybe if that someone was a member of our family we might consider it. But for someone unknown to us, we would be likely to refuse. And yet all the way through history, men and women have died so that others might live. They have laid down their own lives for someone else. The greatest of the people who did this was Jesus. His sacrifice brought about forgiveness and eternal life, the two greatest gifts we can possess.

From time to time we shall not be able to avoid sacrificing some things which we hold dear. This is the nature of life. But when I do forgo myself I pray that it is not unnecessary, that someone, somewhere will gain the benefit, as I have gained my Lord's.

Think

You can give without loving but you cannot love without giving.

Amy Carmichael

GD

The complete joy

'If you remain in me and my words remain in you, then you will ask for anything you wish, and you shall have it. My Father's glory is shown by your bearing much fruit; and in this way you become my disciples. I love you just as the Father loves me; remain in my love. If you obey my commands, you will remain in my love, just as I have obeyed my Father's commands and remain in his love. I have told you this so that my joy may be in you and that your joy may be complete.'

I met a man some years ago now who was just bursting with joy. He wasn't overpowering. He was just simply full of God's joy and no matter how I felt, he seemed to make me feel better. The interesting thing is that he didn't smile much, he didn't laugh greatly, he was quite serious and thoughtful, quiet and dignified. Yet he had a freedom and a joy which was terribly infectious.

On the other hand I've met many people who superficially look as though they are trying to be joyful. They have constant grins on their faces come what may. They drop their favourite pen on the floor. It breaks and they say, 'Praise the Lord', as much as to try to convince themselves as anyone else. They deny the sad feelings in others, saying to them, 'never mind', when minding is actually very important at that moment.

There's all the difference in the world, and heaven, between this first type of people and the second. Joy begins deep, deep down. It may begin with a profound need like immense guilt or it may begin with deep hurt. When forgiveness or healing occurs, what wells up is unmistakable joy.

Joy that comes from these kinds of places is the most attractive thing to those outside Christ. Many people see through superficial smiles and rather shallow happiness, but joy is very different. A member of my congregation stood up on Easter Day and spoke of the tragedy of being abused as a child and later in life being involved in an affair. As her husband sat in the front row she told of his forgiveness and God's and the joy she received. It was written all over her face. Her testimony affected many people that morning and her joy was complete as she vowed to remain in God's love.

Meditate

Joy is the serious business of heaven.

C.S. Lewis

GD

Passing peace

It was late that Sunday evening, and the disciples were gathered together behind locked doors, because they were afraid of the Jewish authorities. Then Jesus came and stood among them. 'Peace be with you,' he said. After saying this, he showed them his hands and his side. The disciples were filled with joy at seeing the Lord. Jesus said to them again, 'Peace be with you. As the Father sent me, so I send you.' Then he breathed on them and said, 'Receive the Holy Spirit.'

The usual thoughts about peace are a cosy fireside, the TV and, as the T-shirt puts it 'No Problems'. Yet is this what peace is really about? Consider the office worker who portrays no worries or cares, but inside is going through a horrendous divorce which is cutting him up. Think of the calm exterior of the commuter on the train in the morning who fights back the intense tears of loneliness of a life spent in abject isolation. Most of the world lacks real peace in their lives, even if they are lucky enough not to live in the myriad of war zones.

Peace is not the absence of war, it is the positive experience of Jesus in our lives. The disciples were terrified in their upper room. They knew that soon the Jews would come for the followers of Jesus after his crucifixion. It is in their hour of need that Jesus comes back, and gives them two kinds of peace.

The first is the peace that calms and brings them joy. It's a peace that says 'it's alright'. Like a parent holding a child after a nightmare or a celebration after an illness. It's a peace that elates and makes us so grateful.

The second is the peace of commission. It's a peace that sends them out to tell, more likely to shout, 'Jesus is alive'. What seemed like hell has turned to heaven. What was so black and awful has now changed out of recognition— it's love, it's joy, it's peace!

When we pass the 'Peace' in church, it is the peace that passes all understanding. It is peace like the first disciples knew when they met the risen Lord. It is a peace that makes us want to go and tell everyone that Jesus lives.

Reflect

Think of all the situations you can that require peace. Which of these has God given you peace to pass on? How will you do it today?

GD

The life of God

That which was from the beginning, which we have heard, which we have seen with our eyes, which we have looked at and our hands have touched—this we proclaim concerning the Word of life. The life appeared; we have seen it and testify to it, and we proclaim to you the eternal life, which was with the Father and has appeared to us. We proclaim to you what we have seen and heard, so that you also may have fellowship with us. And our fellowship is with the Father and with his Son, Jesus Christ. We write this to make our joy complete.

On my wall there is a painting of a church, with pillars and arches, and beyond it a greeny-blue sea surrounded by pale brown hills. It is the Church of the Beatitudes, built by the Sea of Galilee, and when I look at the painting I find myself looking beyond the church to the sea, and reflecting on the things that happened there once. I have never seen the Sea of Galilee, or seen the man who taught on its shores with my physical eyes, but I know that somehow I am part of the Christian story which started two thousand years ago and is still going on.

It was so that we could all be part of the story that John wrote this letter. He had seen Jesus, and so had some of his fellow Christians. So they could paint a picture in words—about the historical manifestation of the Eternal. 'The Word became flesh and made his dwelling among us' it says in the Gospel of John—and this letter is proclaiming the Word of life. The message is that the Eternal Word appeared, or was made manifest—which means 'readily perceived by the senses and especially by the sight, and also easily understood or recognized by the mind' (Webster's Dictionary). So John could write that they had 'heard' and 'seen' and 'touched' the incarnate Word. Now they were telling other people the truth and the wonder of the message, so that all of us can share in the same life and the same joy.

A way to pray

Read the passage again, and pray that you will know more and more of the reality of fellowship with the Father and with his Son, Jesus Christ—and experience more and more of the power and the joy of eternal life.

SB

The message of God

This is the message we have heard from him and declare to you: God is light; in him there is no darkness at all. If we claim to have fellowship with him yet walk in the darkness, we lie and do not live by the truth. But if we walk in the light, as he is in the light, we have fellowship with one another, and the blood of Jesus, his Son, purifies us from all sin.

I have just had two burglar lights installed, and on the first night they were fitted the friends who were having dinner with me said 'Stop talking! Look!' And there in the light was a most beautiful fox—probably looking for some more of the kidneys which I had cleared out from my freezer the day before.

The light shows us what is there. A fox or a burglar in my security lights. Good or evil in the light of God, whose nature and being is light. The nature of light is to shine, and it is the nature of God to reveal himself. He did it perfectly in Jesus. 'The true light that gives light to every man was coming into the world' says John in his Gospel, and it happened when the Word became flesh—the Word who was with God in the beginning, and the Word who was a person alive with the life and the light of God: 'In him was life, and that life was the light of men...' (John 1:9 and 4). The light of the love of God (because the being of God is also love) shows us ourselves as we really are. Sinners. But all the time greatly loved—and all the time having the guilt of our sins washed away through the blood of Christ. As we walk in the light we shall know the love of God for us, and also the beautiful moral perfection and purity of the God whose name is Holy. Then we shall change, and be more and more like him.

To reflect on

We who ... contemplate the Lord's glory, are being transformed into his likeness with ever-increasing glory, which comes from the Lord, who is the Spirit ... For God, who said "Let light shine out of darkness," made his light shine in our hearts to give us the light of the knowledge of the glory of God in the face of Christ.

2 Corinthians 3:18; 4:6

SB

Two books:
Ruth & Revelation

The book of Ruth and the book of Revelation are very different, but at the centre of both of them is the Lord of the whole earth—seen in the glory of heaven and in the day-to-day circumstances of his people's lives.

Ruth is a Gentile woman who has discovered the God of Israel. Once married to a Jew, but now widowed, she follows her Jewish mother-in-law back to her home in Bethlehem, saying to her, 'Where you go, I will go . . . your people shall be my people, and your God my God.'

Marcus Maxwell takes us through the lovely story of Ruth (and she is in the genealogy of 'Jesus, the Messiah' at the start of Matthew's Gospel) and also through chapters 4 to 11 of the book of Revelation.

The vision that God gave to John on the Isle of Patmos takes us behind the scenes. It reveals to us that through all the changing scenes of life our God is with us—working through all things to draw us to himself. Even the disasters and the destruction in our world are a way to God—and a way for God to wake us up from our lethargy and speak to our hearts. As C.S. Lewis put it: 'God whispers to us in our pleasures, speaks in our conscience, but shouts in our pains: it is His megaphone to rouse a deaf world' (*The Problem of Pain*, chapter 6).

Those in authority

I urge, then, first of all, that requests, prayers, intercession and thanksgiving be made for everyone—for kings and all those in authority, that we may live peaceful and quiet lives in all godliness and holiness. This is good, and pleases God our Saviour, who wants all men to be saved and to come to a knowledge of the truth. For there is one God and one mediator between God and men, the man Christ Jesus, who gave himself as a ransom for all men—the testimony given in its proper time. And for this purpose I was appointed a herald and an apostle—I am telling the truth, I am not lying—and a teacher of the true faith to the Gentiles.

The Epistle for today picks up the theme of 'those in authority'. The writer tells Timothy, a relatively young (thirty-year-old!) church leader, that prayers should be said 'first of all' for 'kings and those in authority'. When we think that the 'kings' he must have had in mind would have included the Roman Emperor and all those other local monarchs we read about in Acts (Agrippa, Festus and so on), we can appreciate that it is not necessary to approve of them in order to pray for them.

All authority comes from God—that's Paul's argument in Romans 13:1. God is on the side of law and order. He wants us to lead 'peaceful and quiet lives' (v. 2). The opposite of order is anarchy and lawlessness, and that contradicts the divine pattern of human life. We should pray for those who have authority because it is a fearful responsibility and because, in so far as they are maintaining an ordered and lawful society, they are doing God's work.

Of course that doesn't mean that we have to collude with evil, or that Christians can never oppose anyone in authority. John the Baptist opposed Herod. The apostles refused to obey a legal order to desist from preaching the gospel (Acts 4:19–20). But it does mean that we recognize the value of lawful authority and only oppose it when we are sure it is setting itself up against the will of God. And, all the while, we pray.

A prayer

Lord God, you have called us to live in peace with one another. Bless the peacemakers and give wisdom to all those in authority, that they may seek your will and honour your way. For Jesus Christ's sake. Amen.

DW

Tragedy

In the days when the judges ruled, there was a famine in the land, and a certain man of Bethlehem in Judah went to live in the country of Moab, he and his wife and two sons. The name of the man was Elimelech and the name of his wife Naomi, and the names of his two sons were Mahlon and Chilion; they were Ephrathites from Bethlehem in Judah. They went into the country of Moab and remained there. But Elimelech, the husband of Naomi, died, and she was left with her two sons. These took Moabite wives; the name of the one was Orpah and the name of the other Ruth. When they had lived there about ten years, both Mahlon and Chilion also died, so that the woman was left without her two sons and her husband.

We know stories like this quite well. They occur as thirty-second human-interest points in news reports of famines and disasters. We are fleetingly moved, and the news switches to the fortunes of the pound against the dollar.

The Book of Ruth is not a news 'sound bite'. It does not let us turn away from the tragedy, but takes us further into the anguish of disaster. It is a needed reminder that the stories which pass fleetingly across our awareness are about real people, who are as important to themselves and to God as are we.

Naomi is the focus of the story, and the disaster is her disaster. At first she is introduced as the wife of Elimelech—like all women of her time, she is important only in relation to a man. In the next verse, she seems to stand as a person in her own right; Elimelech dies and is described as Naomi's husband. But Naomi is a person of importance because she still has her two sons. When they die, she is given no name—'the woman' was left without men to support her and to give her worth. By leaving out her name, the story-teller shows that she has become a non-person. Disaster has stripped her not only of kin, but of worth and dignity.

Think

When we face adversity, one of the great temptations that comes with it is to lose our self-respect. But we should not, for we are still valued by God.

MM

Loyalty

Then she started to return with her daughters-in-law from the country of Moab, for she had heard in the country of Moab that the Lord had considered his people and given them food . . . But Naomi said to her two daughters-in-law, 'Go back each of you to your mother's house. May the Lord deal kindly with you, as you have dealt with the dead and with me. The Lord grant that you may find security, each of you in the house of your husband.' Then they wept aloud again. Orpah kissed her mother-in-law, but Ruth clung to her . . . Ruth said, 'Do not press me to leave you or turn back from following you! Where you go, I will go; where you lodge, I will lodge; your people shall be my people, and your God my God. Where you die, I will die—there will I be buried. May the Lord do thus and so to me, and more as well, if even death parts me from you!' When Naomi saw that she was determined to go with her, she said no more to her.

With her life and hopes in tatters, Naomi tries to send her daughters-in-law away, to search for a new life, and new husbands. Eventually, Orpah agrees, but Ruth vows to remain with her mother-in-law.

Ruth's declaration of love and loyalty is beautiful and total. She will throw in her lot with Naomi, come what may. And almost incidentally, she accepts Naomi's God. She turns her back on her former life and steps out in faith in a way which is almost unparalleled in the Bible. Even the disciples' response to Jesus' call or Abraham's response to God cannot measure up to this, for Ruth has received no direct calling, and no promise of future prosperity.

Instead, she allies herself with a hopeless cause, and gives herself fully, with no hope of reward. Even Naomi seems hardly to appreciate Ruth's sacrifice. The bereaved mother has failed to isolate herself from all love and friendship, but as yet she does not respond to it. Ruth's love is met with silence, but eventually that love will be her salvation.

God seems to be in the background for most of this story, but the pattern of his love is seen in Ruth. Naomi has almost challenged God to live up to the standards of her daughter-in-law ('may the Lord deal kindly . . . as you have dealt'). For Christians, Ruth's self-offering is a perfect reflection of the love of God.

Pray

For all who sacrifice their future for the love of others.

MM

Desolation

So the two of them went on until they came to Bethlehem. When they came to Bethlehem, the whole town was stirred because of them; and the women said, 'Is this Naomi?' She said to them, 'Call me no longer Naomi, call me Mara, for the Almighty has dealt bitterly with me. I went away full, but the Lord has brought me back empty; why call me Naomi when the Lord has dealt harshly with me, and the Almighty has brought calamity upon me?' So Naomi returned together with Ruth the Moabite, her daughter-in-law, who came back with her from the country of Moab. They came to Bethlehem at the beginning of the barley harvest.

The arrival of Naomi is a major event in the small town of Bethlehem, but whatever welcome she may have received is rebuffed. Naomi is still lost in bitterness and grief, and tells her old neighbours to change her name from 'Pleasant' to 'Bitter'.

There are few of us who have never felt desolated, by grief or abandonment, by failure or illness. And at times like that, we may lash out at the friendliest gesture, and reject all offered comfort, trying to retreat into a world of silence where our pain can be nursed and turned almost into perverse pleasure.

That is when love is most needed, not to invade (at first) that private world of sorrow, but to stand by and be ready to cast light and hope.

And when we are rejected by the pain of others, we too must stand by with the promise of hope, for the moment when pain eases, and life can once again be sought.

In our story, Naomi has not yet spoken to Ruth, but she is still with her, bringing the promise of help.

In the same way, the writer of Revelation pictured Jesus standing outside the door, waiting to be admitted, for no denial of ours can turn aside the reality of his love, and no clinging to death can deny the hope of resurrection.

So Ruth comes with Naomi to Bethlehem as the fields stand ready for harvest. Desolation comes to abundance and will eventually be overwhelmed by the offer of life.

Reflect

Christians are called to take up a cross, but beyond the cross is always resurrection.

MM

As it happens . . .

Now Naomi had a kinsman on her husband's side, a prominent rich man, of the family of Elimelech, whose name was Boaz. And Ruth the Moabite said to Naomi, 'Let me go to the field, and glean among the ears of grain, behind someone in whose sight I may find favour.' She said to her, 'Go, my daughter.' So she went. She came and gleaned in the field behind the reapers. As it happened, she came to the part of the field belonging to Boaz, who was of the family of Elimelech. Just then Boaz came from Bethlehem . . . Then Boaz said to his servant who was in charge of the reapers, 'To whom does this young woman belong?' The servant . . . answered, 'She is the Moabite who came back with Naomi from the country of Moab.'

Where is God in this story? It has been a story of disaster, and of bitterness, and as so often at such times, God seems distant. He has mainly been mentioned virtually as an enemy, as Naomi sees her personal tragedy as God's harshness towards her.

But look at the strange string of chance happenings which is building up. Ruth and Naomi happen to arrive at the barley harvest, when it is possible for the poor to make a living by gathering the dropped grains. Ruth just happens to go to the area cultivated by Boaz, a relative of Naomi's by marriage. Boaz happens to come out to inspect the work at that point, and happens to catch sight of Ruth.

As we look back over our lives there are stretches where we can see quite clearly that God is at work. Yet could we see it at the time? Usually not. God is at work with Ruth and Naomi, and he is at work with us, too. Spotting his work is the trick!

Yet whether we see him or not, he is there and, later on, all may well become clear (as it certainly will in heaven). Our job now is to trust him, and remember that no matter how far away he may seem, he is really just as close as ever, and no doubt very busy with our lives.

Reflect

Are there any parts of your own story where it is now clear that God was at work? Thank him for them, and thank him for the times when he seemed invisible, but still was with you.

MM

Good reports

Then Boaz said to Ruth, 'Now listen, my daughter, do not go to glean in another field, or leave this one, but keep close to my young women . . . I have ordered the young men not to bother you. If you get thirsty, go to the vessels and drink from what the young men have drawn.' Then she fell prostrate . . . and said to him, 'Why have I found favour in your sight, that you should take notice of me, when I am a foreigner?' But Boaz said to her, 'All that you have done for your mother-in-law since the death of your husband has been fully told me . . .. May the Lord reward you for your deeds, and may you have a full reward from the Lord, the God of Israel, under whose wings you have come for refuge!' . . . At mealtime Boaz said to her, 'Come here and eat some of this bread, and dip your morsel in the sour wine.' So she sat beside the reapers, and he heaped up for her some parched grain. She ate until she was satisfied, and she had some left over. When she got up to glean, Boaz instructed his young men, 'Let her glean even among the standing sheaves, and do not reproach her. You must also pull out some handfuls for her from the bundles and leave them for her to glean, and do not rebuke her.'

One suspects that Ruth wasn't a bad looker, from the attention that Boaz heaps on her. But we're not told that. What we are told is that he had heard of her faithfulness and care to Naomi.

It sounds like old-fashioned moralizing to say that the way we behave speaks much louder than all that we say, but old-fashioned or not, it remains true.

Whatever Ruth may have looked like, her character shone. Already, she was the talk of the town, and her love for Naomi draws out love and respect from others.

Not only that, but it lays the foundation for her own future happiness and success. We often hear that the only way to get ahead is to be tough and ruthless. But it is not true. Practising love pays much higher dividends, and pays them where it counts.

Think

What report do people hear of you? And what reaction do you draw out from others?

MM

Recovery

So she gleaned in the field until evening. Then she beat out what she had gleaned, and it was about an ephah of barley. She picked it up and came into the town, and her mother-in-law saw how much she had gleaned. Then she took out and gave her what was left over after she herself had been satisfied. Her mother-in-law said to her, 'Where did you glean today? And where have you worked? Blessed be the man who took notice of you.' So she told her mother-in-law with whom she had worked, and said, 'The name of the man with whom I worked today is Boaz.' Then Naomi said to her daughter-in-law, 'Blessed be he by the Lord, whose kindness has not forsaken the living or the dead!' Naomi also said to her, 'The man is a relative of ours, one of our nearest kin.'

So after all, Naomi is not without relatives, she is not abandoned by God and she once again can take an interest in life. From the woman whose name was Bitter, Naomi once again begins to emerge, seen through her grief and desolation by Ruth. The concern of her daughter-in-law, and the obvious help that Ruth has been given draws Naomi back to life.

For the first time in the story, Naomi mentions God kindly, and recognizes that, after all, his love has not deserted her and her daughter-in-law. In fact, as we have seen, it has not deserted her at all. Like Job, Naomi has suffered, and, like Job, has been brought to see the faithfulness of God.

But unlike the story of Job, Naomi's shorter tale does not pretend to give a glimpse into the working of God's mind. Disaster has struck, inexplicable as always. And the response can only be one of two—to accept and keep on trusting, or to retreat into bitterness. Neither offers explanations, but one offers life and comfort.

Pray

Father, we do not understand why disasters strike, but give us the faith to know that you work through them, and will bring recovery and hope.

MM

The light of the world

God in his mercy has given us this work to do, and so we are not discouraged. We put aside all secret and shameful deeds; we do not act with deceit, nor do we falsify the word of God. In the full light of truth we live in God's sight and try to commend ourselves to everyone's good conscience. For if the gospel we preach is hidden, it is hidden only from those who are being lost. They do not believe, because their minds have been kept in the dark by the evil god of this world. He keeps them from seeing the light shining on them, the light that comes from the Good News about the glory of Christ, who is the exact likeness of God. For it is not ourselves that we preach; we preach Jesus Christ as Lord, and ourselves as your servants for Jesus' sake. The God who said, 'Out of darkness the light shall shine!' is the same God who made his light shine in our hearts, to bring us to the knowledge of God's glory shining in the face of Christ.

A way for us to reflect on today's passage is to apply it to our own life—and to be drawn into worship as we contemplate the wonder and the nature of the Good News. We may not all be preachers in the strict sense, but each one of us is a light in the world. So pray that the Spirit will bring into the light anything that you have hidden in the darkness—so that your light will shine more brightly. Think about the people you know from whom the gospel seems to be hidden. Pray for them— that they will start to hate the darkness they are living in, and long for the light. Pray that they will see the glory of the light of Christ, who is the exact likeness of God—'a friend of sinners', and 'a man of sorrows'. Reflect on the glory of God—shining in the face of Christ, and praise God for the day when he called you out of darkness into his marvellous light (even if you don't know what day it was) and made you a new creature and a new creation—just as millions of years ago he commanded the light to shine in the darkness and created the worlds.

SB

Plotting

Naomi her mother-in-law said to [Ruth], 'My daughter, I need to seek some security for you, so that it may be well with you. Now here is our kinsman Boaz, with whose young women you have been working. See, he is winnowing barley tonight at the threshing floor. Now wash and anoint yourself and put on your best clothes and go down to the threshing floor; but do not make yourself known to the man until he has finished eating and drinking. When he lies down, observe the place where he lies; then, go and uncover his feet and lie down; and he will tell you what to do.' She said to her, 'All that you tell me I will do.'

Now that Naomi is back in action, her thoughts turn to the future. Ruth, aided by Boaz, has kept starvation from the door. But now the barley harvest is over, and plans must be laid.

Boaz is a near kinsman, and so can act as 'redeemer'. According to the law of Israel, it is the right and responsibility of the strong relative to guard the rights and property of the weaker family members. Whether that would extend to marrying a widow of a relative is debatable (it would in the case of a brother). This, however, is what Naomi has in mind. Once again, she is looking for a husband for Ruth, for only by marriage can Ruth move out of the trap of dependence and poverty.

So far, Ruth has shown no interest in marriage, either in her own land, or to any eligible young man of Bethlehem. Her self-appointed task has been to care for Naomi. But now she agrees.

So the plan is laid; Ruth must present herself to Boaz, and let him do the rest. Is it love? We are not told. The point is that these two women are doing all in their power to use the rules of their society to their own ends. They refuse to be passive objects or victims. Instead, they act. And certainly, so far at least, God has been with them.

Reflect

There is nowhere in the Bible that says God helps those who help themselves. But there is truth in it. God provides opportunities, and we seize them in faith.

MM

God's voice

So she went down to the threshing floor and did just as her mother-in-law had instructed her. When Boaz had eaten and drunk, and he was in a contented mood, he went to lie down at the end of the heap of grain. Then she came stealthily and uncovered his feet, and lay down. At midnight the man was startled, and turned over, and there, lying at his feet, was a woman! He said, 'Who are you?' And she answered, 'I am Ruth, your servant; spread your cloak over your servant, for you are next-of-kin.' He said, 'May you be blessed by the Lord, my daughter; this last instance of loyalty is better than the first; you have not gone after young men, whether poor or rich.'

Things do not go exactly according to plan. According to Naomi, Boaz will take charge. But Ruth is not a woman to let others take charge. She has resisted Naomi's attempts to send her away and she has taken control of the two women's fortunes as provider and carer. Now again, she takes the initiative.

Instead of presenting herself submissively to a prospective lord and husband (and the sexual overtones of this night meeting are clear) she challenges Boaz. Literally, she says, 'Spread your wing over me.' Boaz has said that she sought refuge under the wings of God. Well, then, says Ruth, be the wing of God. Take up your responsibility and act as God's agent.

It illustrates one of the great dangers of prayer. 'May the Lord reward you,' prayed Boaz, and Ruth, who of all in the story embodies the love of God, replies, 'Be God's blessing to me.' When we pray for others' needs, we have to watch out. God may make us the answer to those needs!

Pray

Father, whose needs am I the answer to?

MM

A time to wait

'And now, my daughter, do not be afraid, I will do for you all that you ask, for all the assembly of my people know that you are a worthy woman. But now, though it is true that I am a near kinsman, there is another kinsman more closely related than I. Remain this night, and in the morning, if he will act as next-of-kin for you, good; let him do it. If he is not willing to act as next-of-kin for you, then, as the Lord lives, I will act as next-of-kin for you. Lie down until the morning.' . . . She came to her mother-in-law, who said, 'How did things go with you my daughter?' Then she told her all that the man had done for her, saying, 'He gave me these six measures of barley . . .' She replied, 'Wait, my daughter, until you learn how the matter turns out, for the man will not rest, but will settle the matter today.'

Is Boaz being cagey, hoping to pass the responsibility off onto someone else? Probably not, as we shall see. The fact that there is another kinsman may well explain why Boaz, generous though he was, did not immediately act to help Ruth and Naomi; that was the duty of a closer relative, who was apparently reluctant to be their redeemer.

Now that Ruth has goaded him, he promises action, the 'worthy man' recognizing a worthy woman, and with that recognition seeing a future wife.

Ruth returns to Naomi, who now says that all that remains is to wait. Through bold action, and seizing God's opportunities, the story has been brought close to its end.

Waiting is always difficult, especially for someone like Ruth, who is one to act. Yet in doing God's will there is often a need to wait. When we are always in motion, always keen to be up and doing, it is all too easy to miss out on what God is up to. True wisdom lies in knowing when to act and when to wait for God. If we are prepared to wait (in prayer) God's opportunities for action come along. If we are always bustling, there is every chance of missing them.

Pray

Take some time today to stop acting, and wait prayerfully. Spend a little time being quiet with God, and see whether he shows you a new opportunity.

MM

The failed redeemer

No sooner had Boaz gone up to the gate and sat down there than the next-of-kin, of whom Boaz had spoken, came by. So Boaz said, 'Come over here, friend; sit down here.' And he went over and sat down. Then Boaz took ten men of the elders of the city, and said, 'Sit down here'; so they sat down. He then said to the next-of-kin, 'Naomi, who has come back from the country of Moab, is selling the parcel of land that belonged to Elimelech. So I thought I would tell you of it, and say: Buy it in the presence of those sitting here, and in the presence of the elders of my people. If you will redeem it, redeem it; but if you will not, tell me, so that I may know; for there is no one prior to you to redeem it, and I come after you.' So he said, 'I will redeem it.' Then Boaz said, 'The day you acquire the field from the hand of Naomi, you are also acquiring Ruth the Moabite, the widow of the dead man, to maintain the dead man's name on his inheritance.' At this the next-of-kin said, 'I cannot redeem it for myself without damaging my own inheritance. Take my right of redemption yourself, for I cannot redeem it.'

The whole tone of the story now changes. We are away from the concerns of women and in a man's world, where women are seen as prospective bearers of sons, and the concern is for inheritance and the preservation of male names. (It comes as a surprise to find that Naomi has land to sell, though presumably she and Ruth were unable to work it on their own, and it could not have helped them until the next harvest.)

Boaz presents a totally different picture here. His concern is apparently for property and inheritance, whereas he had promised Ruth to be a redeemer, not to her father-in-law's name, but to her.

But Boaz knows what he is doing. He has spoken of inheritance and property, and hooked his fish. The legal redeemer is happy to expand his property, but not to create a family which will take it away again in the name of Elimelech. So the one who should have been the redeemer fails in his duty, and is not even worth naming.

Think

What fears prevent us from doing as we should?

MM

Customs

Now this was the custom in former times in Israel concerning redeeming and exchanging: to confirm a transaction, the one took off his sandal and gave it to the other; this was the manner of attesting in Israel. So when the next-of-kin said to Boaz, 'Acquire it for yourself,' he took off his sandal. Then Boaz said to the elders and all the people, 'Today you are witnesses that I have acquired from the hand of Naomi all that belonged to Elimelech and all that belonged to Chilion and Mahlon. I have also acquired Ruth the Moabite, the wife of Mahlon, to be my wife, to maintain the dead man's name on his inheritance, in order that the name of the dead may not be cut off from his kindred and from the gate of his native place; today you are witnesses.'

As we saw yesterday, Boaz's ploy seems intended to ensure that he in fact ends up with Ruth. It suggests that although Boaz conforms strictly to law and tradition, his real intention is otherwise. He promised to redeem Ruth, not any land, and although he speaks very piously of continuing the name of the dead men in Naomi's family, in fact the descent of his and Ruth's son is reckoned through Boaz, not Mahlon.

I suspect that Boaz is being subversive. Ruth's and Naomi's concern is not to maintain a family name, but to ensure their own future. So although the encounter at the gate is conducted by men, in the terms approved by a male-dominated society, the women's concerns are what really set the agenda.

Ruth especially has behaved in a radical and unconventional way, but she has neither the power nor (perhaps) the notion to change the whole system of Israel. Yet it is clear from the story that that system had serious flaws as far as women were concerned. Perhaps the message for us is that there is no need to give in to things we cannot change. Within the system there are ways of working against it with the help of God. And look at how God has helped Ruth to buck the system. God, it seems, was more revolutionary than his people suspected. And, no doubt, still is.

Reflect

Just because things have always been that way does not mean that they are God's way.

MM

Descendants

So Boaz took Ruth and she became his wife. When they came together, the Lord made her conceive, and she bore a son. Then the women said to Naomi, 'Blessed be the Lord, who has not left you this day without next-of-kin; and may his name be renowned in Israel! He shall be to you a restorer of life and a nourisher of your old age; for your daughter-in-law who loves you, who is more to you than seven sons, has borne him.' Then Naomi took the child and laid him in her bosom, and became his nurse. The women of the neighbourhood gave him a name, saying, 'A son has been born to Naomi.' They named him Obed; he became the father of Jesse, the father of David.

So this story about women comes to its triumphant conclusion. The women have prevailed against fortune and despite the expectations of their culture. Ruth has a son, and by proxy so does Naomi. Ruth has secured her own future, and, despite the intervention of the men of the city, it is the women of Bethlehem who have the last word, proclaiming that one daughter-in-law is worth seven sons.

It is God, of course, who has been active all along, not by miracle or word of a prophet, but by the normal processes of life. We do not need miracles, we do not need more revelation than we have been given (though they're great when they come). All we really need is faith, and the vision to see and courage to grasp the chances that God sends.

And then there is the final sting in the tail. Obed is the father of Jesse, the father of David. Where would Israel have been without the boldness of the unconventional foreigner, Ruth? At a time when Israel was pursuing racial and religious purity, setting its barriers firmly in place, the story of Ruth was a timely reminder that God loves and uses the outsider as well as the pious insider.

In an age of racial tension, clashes of cultures and fear of the stranger, in an age of continuing sexual discrimination, in the twentieth century after Christ, we still need the story of Ruth.

MM

The evidence for faith

For I handed on to you as of first importance what I in turn had received, that Christ died for our sins in accordance with the scriptures, and that he was buried, and that he was raised on the third day in accordance with the scriptures, and that he appeared to Cephas, then to the twelve. Then he appeared to more than five hundred brothers and sisters at one time, most of whom are still alive, though some have died. Then he appeared to James, then to all the apostles. Last of all, as to one untimely born, he appeared also to me.

Obviously some of the people in the church at Corinth were having doubts about the resurrection of the dead. Friends—fellow-believers—had died, and there was no sign of the great day of resurrection for which they had been looking. St Paul's answer is to take them back to basics! The whole Christian faith, the very heart of the gospel itself, is the resurrection of Jesus. Had they forgotten the message that saved them?

He wrote this letter in about AD54, so this is almost certainly the earliest account we have of the resurrection stories—the Gospels were written between ten and thirty years later. Not only that, but Paul is harking back to what he was told when he became a Christian, which was a few years after the first Easter. Why, he says, most of those first witnesses are still alive... you can ask them, if you don't believe me! This is the approach of a man who is sure of the evidence. And what he is arguing is that Jesus who died and was buried was raised from the dead and seen by many, many reliable witnesses, on many different occasions.

St Paul does not see the resurrection merely as an internal spiritual event, but as an objective reality. This really happened, at a point in time and a place in history, and it was seen by flesh-and-blood witnesses. That was to be the basis of their faith in the resurrection—not only of Jesus, but of all those who are 'in Christ' (v. 22).

A prayer

Lord, at this Easter season, strengthen my faith in your power to give eternal life to those who trust in your Son. Amen.

DW

The ruler of all

After this I looked, and there in heaven a door stood open! And the first voice, which I had heard speaking to me like a trumpet, said, "Come up here and I will show you what must take place after this." At once I was in the spirit, and there in heaven stood a throne, with one seated on the throne! And the one seated there looks like jasper and carnelian, and round the throne is a rainbow that looks like an emerald. Around the throne are twenty-four thrones, and seated on the throne are twenty-four elders, dressed in white robes, with golden crowns on their heads. Coming from the throne are flashes of lightning, and rumblings and peals of thunder and in front of the throne burn seven flaming torches, which are the seven spirits of God; and in front of the throne there is something like a sea of glass, like crystal.

The main section of Revelation begins with a vision of God, though God himself is barely described—a blaze of brilliance like the flash of jewels. God is indescribable, and John is not foolish enough to try. But one thing is certain; this is the God who rules over all. Round the throne is a rainbow, the sign of God's trustworthiness which was given to Noah. This is the God of salvation, in whom we can put our trust, the focal point of our faith.

Indeed, he is enthroned in the midst of the church (the twenty-four elders). Here, says John, is the reality of the church. Not the struggling little congregations of ancient Rome, or of modern Britain, but the white-robed people of God, in whose midst is the shining glory of God, and whose feet are lit by the seven lamps which signify the Holy Spirit (seven is the number of perfection).

All this is normally hidden from our sight, and it is easy to become downcast as we struggle to be the people of God in a hostile world. But the deeper spiritual reality is still there; in our midst is the faithful God, who has taken us for his own and who rules over all.

A prayer

Open our eyes, Lord, to the reality which lies behind the church we see, and give us grace to make that reality visible to others.

MM

Lord of creation

Around the throne, and on each side of the throne, are four living creatures, full of eyes in front and behind: the first living creature like a lion, the second living creature like an ox, the third living creature with a face like a human face, and the fourth living creature like a flying eagle. And the four living creatures, each of them with six wings, are full of eyes all round and inside. Day and night without ceasing they sing, "Holy, holy, holy, the Lord God the Almighty, who was and is and is to come."

If you want some idle amusement, try to draw the creatures described in Revelation! It's almost impossible. The reason, of course, is that they are symbols, meant to be understood by reading, not by seeing. Traditionally, these four creatures are seen as the four evangelists, Matthew, Mark, Luke and John, and you'll see them in a stained glass window in most churches. But that's an unlikely explanation.

Much more probable is that they represent all of creation, animals and people. And all through creation, God is present, aware of what is going on (the eyes) and receiving its praise.

The Bible is full of the picture of creation praising God, and it's a picture we lose at our peril. The human attitude, and especially the modern Western one, is that creation exists for our use or abuse, and has little other significance. Of course, today it is fashionable to be "green", to sport Greenpeace stickers and use recycled paper toilet rolls, but we must go further than this. The world is God's creation, not ours, and deserves our respect not because it is useful, or because we endanger ourselves by abusing it, but because it is valuable in its own right, as the work of God which sings his praise with every new day.

It is worth noting that John sees the creature with a human face as part of creation, not as something separate. Much of the problem of our modern attitude to the world stems from the fact that we see ourselves as something other than the world. Nature is not only something we admire—it is also something we are a part of.

A question

What can Christians do to help the world recover a biblical view of creation? What can you do?

MM

True worship

And whenever the living creatures give glory and honour and thanks to the one who is seated on the throne, who lives for ever and ever, the twenty-four elders fall before the one who is seated on the throne and worship the one who lives for ever and ever; they cast their crowns before the throne, singing, "You are worthy, our Lord and God, to receive glory and honour and power, for you created all things, and by your will they existed and were created."

John's opening vision of the spiritual realities climbs to a peak of worship. All creation worships God, and the elders who are the church join in, throwing down their crowns as offerings to God.

In many of our churches, the communion service echoes this scene, as we join "with angels and archangels and all the company of heaven, saying, Holy, Holy, Holy…" And the point is worth making again and again. In our worship, poor though it may often be, we are united with all who give praise to God. Our halting prayers and often unenthusiastic hymns become a part of the continual cry of praise to our creator and redeemer. Perhaps if we thought more carefully about those words we say, our prayers would be surer and our singing lustier.

Yet there is an even more important aspect of worship in our passage. How often do we hear someone say, "That service did nothing for me"? Of course, if all worship does nothing for me, there is a serious problem either with the worship or (more probably) with me.

But the keynote of worship is not personal fulfilment but offering. The elders cast their crowns (which God has given them) before him. Worship is the giving of ourselves to God's service. All the songs and prayers and sermons in the world do not make worship until the singers give themselves to God. In our worship we recognize that all we have comes from God and rededicate it and ourselves to him. Perhaps we should think about that too. When we are prepared to give more in our worship, we receive more, for we come closer to the worship of heaven.

A meditation

You are holy, enthroned on the praises of Israel.

Psalm 22:3

MM

The key to victory

Then I saw in the right hand of the one seated on the throne a scroll written on the inside and on the back, sealed with seven seals; and I saw a mighty angel proclaiming with a loud voice, "Who is worthy to open the scroll and break its seals?" And no one in heaven or on earth or under the earth was able to open the scroll or to look into it. And I began to weep bitterly because no one was found worthy to open the scroll or to look into it. Then one of the elders said to me, "Do not weep. See, the Lion of the tribe of Judah, the Root of David, has conquered, so that he can open the scroll and its seven seals." Then I saw between the throne and the four living creatures and among the elders a Lamb standing as if it had been slaughtered . . .

Now we begin the first of several visions which spell out the history of the world. The first centres on the mysterious scroll, and the breaking of its seven seals. Just when it seems no one can open it, John is told that the victorious Lion has won the right by his victory. And then John looks, and sees a Lamb.

If we are to understand one of the central points of Revelation, we have to see the importance of that strange vision. The conquering Lion, symbol of might, ferocity and power, is in fact a Lamb that has been slaughtered.

Jesus has altered the categories of human thought. For us, victory is something to be won by force, by overwhelming our opponents. But not for Christ. For him, victory comes by being overwhelmed, by accepting all that a sinful world can do to him. By absorbing the full impact of evil, and emerging (not unscathed—never that, but still triumphant) on the other side.

This is the true pattern of Christian living. To meet evil and enmity with love, to accept not only the good that is offered us, but the evil too. To accept it and absorb it, and so neutralise its power. It's a tall order, and it can be done only in the strength given by the Lamb that was slain.

A reflection

The blood of the martyrs is the seed of the church.

Irenaeus of Lyons

MM

A song to Jesus

Then I looked, and I heard the voice of many angels surrounding the throne and the living creatures and the elders; they numbered myriads of myriads and thousands of thousands, singing with full voice, "Worthy is the Lamb that was slaughtered to receive power and wealth and wisdom and might and honour and glory and blessing!" Then I heard every creature in heaven and on earth and under the earth and in the sea, and all that is in them, singing, "To the one who is seated on the throne and to the Lamb be blessing and honour and glory and might for ever and ever!" And the four living creatures said, "Amen!" And the elders fell down and worshipped.

So you thought the worship in Revelation chapter 4 was impressive? Now the songs of praise swell to an unthinkable volume, as John pulls out all the stops in an attempt to describe the sheer might of the praises of heaven. Why has the volume suddenly been turned up?

In the last chapter, the praises of heaven focused on God the creator. The one who made us demands our praise and our love. But the reason for worship goes far beyond that. He is not only our creator, he is our redeemer.

If anything can go beyond the glory of creation, surely it is the amazing news that the love of God reaches out to those who have rejected him. It is one thing for him to love what he has made. It is another for him to love what has been perverted and soiled. Yet he does. In one version of the communion service in the Church of England, the confession of our sins is followed by the singing of 'Glory to God in the highest'. This is how it should be. Confession which does not result in praise is not really seeking forgiveness, but wallowing in guilt. For when we understand our sinfulness, we come closest to recognizing the overpowering love of the one who has come to us in our need, and himself paid the price for our wrong-doing.

The praises of heaven and earth are surely loudest for God the Redeemer.

Hark! the songs of peaceful Sion
Thunder like a mighty flood;
Jesus out of every nation
Hath redeemed us by his blood.

W. C. Dix

MM

The task of the redeemed

[The four living creatures and the elders] sing a new song: "You are worthy to take the scroll and to open its seals, for you were slaughtered and by your blood you ransomed for God saints from every tribe and language and people and nation; you have made them to be a kingdom and priests serving our God, and they will reign on earth."

We skip back a few verses now, to the song of praise which accompanies the Lamb's acceptance of the scroll. The focus is still on Jesus, the Lamb who died for our redemption. But it draws out an important part of what he has done: he has created a new people of God, to be a kingdom and priests.

The term "kingdom of God" is a slippery one, and in the New Testament as a whole it refers to more than merely the church. But it always includes the church. Whatever we see as the whole scope of the kingdom, we know that we are a part of it. Perhaps the best understanding of it is to say that wherever God's authority is acknowledged, there is the kingdom.

There is another side to that. It means that we who are called to be the people of God (the saints) must be people who recognize God's rule over us. It isn't enough to pay lip-service to God as "Lord" (Jesus had hard words about that—see Matthew 7:21) but to let him be truly in charge of our lives. The book of Revelation is all about how God is really in charge, no matter how things may appear. But those who worship him must go one further, and gladly accept that he is their Lord. That means putting him first, whether or not it is convenient. God cannot be someone to fill in the empty or boring bits of our lives. He must be the one fixed point around which all the rest of our concerns revolve.

When that becomes true, we are able fully to be the second picture we are given of the church—a people who are priests, called to be go-betweens who bring God close to others.

A prayer

Lord, make me a channel of the love you died to bring to all, as you reign in my life and, through it, in others.

MM

Shine and be salty

'You are the salt of the earth. But if the salt loses its saltiness, how can it be made salty again? It is no longer good for anything, except to be thrown out and trampled by men. You are the light of the world. A city on a hill cannot be hidden. Neither do people light a lamp and put it under a bowl. Instead they put it on its stand, and it gives light to everyone in the house. In the same way, let your light shine before men, that they may see your good deeds and praise your Father in heaven.'

In the summer my mother would sit in the garden with a big bowl of salt on one side of her and a heap of runner beans on the other. My father had grown them on his allotment, and she was slicing them up and layering them with salt for us to eat in the winter. The salt stopped the beans decaying—and the task of the Christian Church is to stop the decay and corruption of the world we live in. But salt can lose its saltiness. Then there is corruption—and the putrid, horrible smell of evil, violence and injustice.

The Church is also the light of the world. But our light can grow dim, and in the Western world I think it has. Then the darkness gets deeper. If a local or a national church refuses to repent then the Christ who is the light of the world will come to us and take away the candlestick that holds the light—and that church will be only a name in the pages of history. But we can repent and turn back to the Christ who is the head of the Church, and respond to the words that he spoke to the church of Laodicea, which was 'wretched, pitiful, poor, blind and naked', and wasn't aware of it: 'Here I am! I stand at the door and knock. If anyone hears my voice and opens the door, I will come in and eat with him, and he with me' (Revelation 3:20, NIV).

Next time you go to communion, will you think about the Church as the salt of the earth and the light of the world. Then, as you receive bread and wine, receive the One who knocks at the door and longs to come in and renew and revive the Church which is his body and his bride.

SB

The horses of chaos

Then I saw the Lamb open one of the seven seals, and I heard one of the four living creatures call out, as with a voice of thunder, "Come!" I looked, and there was a white horse! Its rider had a bow; a crown was given to him, and he came out conquering and to conquer. When he opened the second seal . . . out came another horse, bright red; its rider was permitted to take peace from the earth, so that people would slaughter one another; and he was given a great sword. When he opened the third seal . . . I looked and there was a black horse! Its rider held a pair of scales in his hand, and I heard . . . a voice . . . saying, "A quart of wheat for a day's pay, and three quarts of barley for a day's pay, but do not damage the olive oil and the wine!" When he opened the fourth seal . . . I looked and there was a pale green horse! Its rider's name was Death, and Hades followed with him; they were given authority over a fourth of the earth, to kill with sword, famine, and pestilence, and by the wild animals of the earth.

At last the seals are opened, and the future begins to unfold. On one level, this is a vision of the time of terror before the Last Day, but on another it is a description of life as it often is on earth.

The horses would be recognised by John's readers; the threat of invasion by the horse-archers of Parthia to the east, civil war, poor harvests and plague. All had happened in living memory, and more of the same could be expected again.

Things haven't changed much. We still live in a world of wars, insurrections, hunger and disease. The poor still find it hard to eat, while the wealthy have no shortage of oil and wine, or whatever are the modern luxuries.

Yet, says John, God remains in charge. He does not send the evil but, where evil occurs, it is worked into his plan, so that in the end his purposes will be triumphant.

A prayer

Bring before God the suffering of the world, and ask not for understanding but for faith in the one who turns all things to his purposes.

MM

Ultimate offerings

When he opened the fifth seal, I saw under the altar the souls of those who had been slaughtered for the word of God and for the testimony they had given; they cried out with a loud voice, "Sovereign Lord, holy and true, how long will it be before you judge and avenge our blood on the inhabitants of the earth?" They were each given a white robe and told to rest a little longer, until the number would be complete both of their fellow servants and of their brothers and sisters, who were soon to be killed as they themselves had been killed.

This is the first mention of an altar in the Revelation, and it drives home the picture of heaven as a temple. The martyrs, who have given their lives for the sake of the gospel, are under the altar—they are sacrifices who have given their all for God. We tend to think of martyrs as people who lived a long time ago, and who now mainly decorate stained-glass windows. There is a slight air of romance about them, and an air of unreality. But a few moments' thought shows that this is nonsense. There have been more Christian martyrs in this century than probably in the rest of Christian history. We can probably think of some famous names, such as Janani Luwum of Uganda, and Archbishop Romero of El Salvador. And besides such well-known martyrs there are thousands who have given their lives in South America, South Africa, the Middle East, Eastern Europe and so on. Today's reading says that such deaths are not in vain. They help to bring closer the final triumph of God. We are not told exactly how that works, though the term "martyr" (witness) suggests one way—their steadfast faith calls others to join them in following Christ.

On another level, today's reading tells us that suffering is not in vain. Behind it lies the plan of God, into which we can gain only glimpses, but which still governs the world. Once again, we are told that even when things seem to be at their very worst, God is in charge.

A prayer

Pray for all who are persecuted for their faith, and for those who are called to make the ultimate offering to God.

MM

The wrath of the Lamb

When he opened the sixth seal, I looked, and there came a great earthquake; the sun became black as sackcloth, the full moon became like blood, and the stars of the sky fell to the earth as the fig tree drops its winter fruit when shaken by the gale. The sky vanished like a scroll rolling itself up, and every mountain and island was removed from its place. Then the kings of the earth and the magnates and the generals and the rich and the powerful, and everyone, slave and free, hid in the caves and among the rocks of the mountains, calling to the mountains and rocks, "Fall on us and hide us from the face of the one seated on the throne and from the wrath of the Lamb; for the great day of their wrath has come, and who is able to stand?"

The first five seals gave us a glimpse into the world's suffering; war, civil unrest, famine, disease, the martyrdom of God's people. These were not special signs of the end of the world, but its normal course. It is in a suffering world that we are called to follow Christ, and to affirm that, despite all appearances, God is in charge.

It is possible to say that God is in charge because of the one who opens the seals—the Lamb who was slain is the one who makes sense of history. Only in the light of the cross, where God himself is revealed as suffering with and for his people, can we claim that God may be seen in a troubled world.

The sixth seal at last reveals the end, when God's judgment must be faced by all. It is the great who will most fear the wrath of God. Those who have power and have not used it in God's way, to support justice and compassion, must in the end come face to face with the enormity of their failure.

The love of God cannot be doubted, in the light of the death of Jesus. But that love can only have effect where it is accepted. When it is rejected, by rich or poor, there can remain only judgment.

A meditation

This is the judgment, that the light has come into the world, and people loved darkness rather than light...

MM

The army of the Lord

After this I saw four angels standing at the four corners of the earth, holding back the four winds of the earth so that no wind could blow on earth or sea or against any tree. I saw another angel ascending from the rising of the sun, having the seal of the living God, and he called with a loud voice to the angels who had been given power to damage earth and sea, saying, "Do not damage the earth or the sea or the trees, until we have marked the servants of our God with a seal on their foreheads." And I heard the number of those who were sealed, one hundred and forty-four thousand, sealed out of every tribe of the people of Israel . . .

If you've ever been visited by the Jehovah's Witnesses, you'll know that they have a lot to say about the 144,000; the elite of the Witnesses who will actually go to heaven, rather than live on a gloriously renewed earth. But that interpretation is hard to read out of the text. So what does this number mean?

There are two clues. Firstly, "Israel" almost certainly does not refer to Jews, but to Christians. In the New Testament, the church is often seen as the new Israel, a new people of God, formed not by birth into a particular nation or race, but by faith in Christ. Of course, there are no tribes in the church, but that is our second clue. This is a conscription, of a certain number from each tribe, just as Israel's army was formed in times of holy war.

What John is saying is that the church is the army of God, called to fight on behalf of the gospel. It is a picture of the church engaged in spiritual warfare. We are sometimes puzzled by the difficulties that we face in our Christian life. Why is it so hard at times? Here is the answer. We are in a real conflict with the powers of evil. We have seen some of the troubles that beset God's people, and many more will be revealed as we read on. But we are not just to be passive sufferers. We are called to fight back in the name of God.

A question

What weapons are we given for the spiritual warfare we are called into?

MM

Strange weapons

After this I looked, and there was a great multitude that no one could count, from every nation, and from all tribes and people and languages, standing before the throne and before the Lamb, robed in white, with palm branches in their hands. They cried out in a loud voice, saying, "Salvation belongs to our God who is seated on the throne, and to the Lamb!" ... Then one of the elders addressed me, saying, "Who are these, robed in white, and where have they come from?" I said to him, "Sir, you are the one that knows." Then he said to me, "These are they who have come out of the great ordeal; they have washed their robes and made them white in the blood of the Lamb..."

John has heard the number of those sealed by God but, when he looks, he sees that the number was only symbolic. In fact, there is a crowd beyond counting. They are the whole church—all the people who belong to God (which is what the seal means; a mark of ownership), but at the same time they are seen as martyrs. They wear robes which are white because they have followed the path of suffering like Jesus, and shed their blood like him.

If the church is called to be the army of God, it is a strange army indeed. Our way of fighting evil is to be like Jesus. We are not called to shed the blood of our enemies, but our own. The footsteps of Jesus led to Calvary, and those who walk in his footsteps can expect something of the same. The Christian approach to evil is to repay it with good—to absorb the hurt that is aimed at us, and to return forgiveness. It is the hardest part of the Christian life, but it is the only way to prevent the spread of evil. When we do wrong to those who wrong us, we increase the amount of wrong-doing, and the circle of violence and hatred spirals on.

A small example happened during a recent stewardship campaign at our church. Most members responded well, but some were rude and hurtful to their visitors. "How do we respond?" asked the visitors. Our adviser said, "Like Jesus."

A prayer

Father, it is hard to accept hurt and wrong. Give me strength to return love for hatred, compassion for bitterness and help for injury.

MM

Silence

When the Lamb opened the seventh seal, there was silence in heaven for about half an hour.

The opening of the seven seals on the Lamb's scroll revealed the plan of history. It was a history of disasters and suffering; a realistic history that fits well with the world as we know it. It was a history in which God's people could expect to suffer too; both with the normal suffering of the world, and with the added problems of bearing witness to the gospel. The history of the world ends with the judgment of God, when neither wealth nor worldly power will be protection.

Through all this, God's people have been marked out with the seal of God. They do not have magic to protect them from the pains of the world, any more than Jesus did. But they do have the presence of God, his strength and his comfort. And they have the promise of eternal life.

Then the final seal is opened, and there is silence. The history of the world is over. It doesn't mean that there is nothing more. As we shall see, there is an eternity more, but it is not something that we can see clearly from here.

The point is that though we catch glimpses of the life to come, in the Bible, in our prayers and our worship, it is not the main focus of our life. We are called to live out our faith here and now, in the world as it is. Heaven is for later.

Meanwhile, Christian discipleship is about how we witness to Christ at work, in the relationships we have with our employers and workers. It is about how we behave at home, in the care and respect we show for our families and friends. It is about the lifestyle we follow, and the respect we have for the world God made.

I have known Christians who were deeply "religious", their heads in heaven, but whose earthly lives were a mess, with troubled marriages and pointless conflicts at work. That is not Christianity; it is mere escapism.

A reflection

Where does your earthly life show the presence of Christ? And where does he need to be invited in?

MM

Go where you are wanted

After this the Lord appointed seventy-two others and sent them two by two ahead of him to every town and place where he was about to go. He told them, 'The harvest is plentiful, but the workers are few. Ask the Lord of the harvest, therefore, to send out workers into his harvest field.'

We can waste time where we aren't wanted—and Jesus tells us not to. He was training a group of his followers to travel ahead of him into all the towns and places where he was planning to go. They were to heal the sick and tell the people about the kingdom of God (which at that stage must have meant telling them all the things that Jesus had told them up to date). They didn't know then the good news of the death and resurrection of Jesus. But if a town didn't welcome them they weren't to hang around.

Jesus said some very tough things and he wasn't always tender. We don't always go by the book when we think about him or tell other people about him. He gives us choices—and if we make the wrong choice he does not stop us. Instead, he lets us work out the consequences of it in our lives. It may be that further down the line we shall make the right choice. But he doesn't argue with us. The judgments of God are always intended to bring us to repentance and—in the love of God—there is a judgment built in to every sin. If we won't have the love and forgiveness of God, then we shall have his wrath and his judgment. But the will of God, is that

people should repent—so they need to be told the good news. In this Decade of Evangelism it is still true that the harvest is plentiful and that the workers are few. But he has told us what to do about that. 'Ask the Lord of the harvest, therefore, to send out workers into the harvest field.' Ask, and go on asking—and ask what we ourselves can do in the harvest field for God.

SB

The meeting of heaven and earth

I saw the seven angels who stand before God, and seven trumpets were given to them. Another angel with a golden censer came and stood at the altar; he was given a great quantity of incense to offer with the prayers of all the saints on the golden altar which is before the throne. And the smoke of the incense, with the prayers of the saints, rose before God from the hand of the angel. Then the angel took the censer and filled it with fire from the altar and threw it on the earth; and there were peals of thunder, rumblings, flashes of lightning, and an earthquake.

Prayer is one of the great mysteries of the Christian life. Sometimes God seems to do what we ask, and at other times he does not. And when he does, is that because he was going to do it anyway? And if he was not, can we then claim to be able to change God's mind for him? That certainly seems a rather odd notion.

Perhaps one helpful way of looking at the problem is to say that God takes our prayers into account, along with many other things, when he is working out his plans for the world. Our actions certainly affect what goes on in the world; our whole lives can change because of the decisions we make. Yet, wherever we end up because of our actions, God works us into the plan and takes us forward. And the same happens with our prayers.

In this vision, John sees the prayers of God's people mingling with the worship of heaven, and the result of both is that God's plan for the world moves on another stage.

Whatever the "mechanism" of prayer may be, today's reading shows us that prayer is never pointless. It is the point where our lives and worship blend with the life of heaven, and together both help to shape the course of history, in ways great and small. When historians look back and try to plot the factors that led to certain events, there is one important one they can never see. But it is there all the same; the prayers of God's people.

So never give up on prayer. It plays a greater part than you may imagine.

MM

Call to repentance

Now the seven angels who had the seven trumpets made ready to blow them. The first angel blew his trumpet and there came hail and fire, mixed with blood . . . and a third of the earth was burned up . . . The second angel blew his trumpet and something like a great mountain, burning with fire, was thrown into the sea . . . A third of the living creatures in the sea died and a third of the ships were destroyed. The third angel blew his trumpet, and a great star fell from heaven . . . A third of the waters became wormwood, and many died from the water because it was made bitter. The fourth angel blew his trumpet, and a third of the sun was struck, and a third of the moon . . . a third of the day was kept from shining, and likewise the night.

Now we meet one of the strange things about the book of Revelation. After the visions of the seven seals come the seven trumpets. Is this what comes after the silence of the seventh seal? I don't think so. There is more to come after the End—and we will reach that in due time—but now John gives us another look at the history of the world. The first set of visions focused on the church in the face of suffering and persecution, and its hope for the future. Now John repeats the story, from the viewpoint of unbelievers.

The first four trumpets herald natural disasters—the kind we see on the news, and send donations for their relief. (Don't be misled by those who see prophecies of nuclear war and such; John intended his book to be understood by readers of his own time.) But they have a deeper meaning. The language reminds us of the plagues of Egypt in the time of Moses and, like them, these disasters are a call to repentance.

Human life is fragile. It can be snuffed out by accident or by disease. Yet we never think much of what that means. For John, the frailty of life is a reminder of our need to place our hope not in the things of this world but in God. More of that tomorrow.

A prayer

Father, help me to value most those things which last forever—the love, faith and hope which are ours in Jesus Christ.

MM

Severe kindness

Then I looked, and I saw an eagle crying with a loud voice as it flew in midheaven, "Woe, woe to the inhabitants of the earth, at the blasts of the other trumpets that the three angels are about to blow."

Yesterday we saw that John presents the disasters of the world as God's call to faith. Life is too fragile to be lived only in this world. That is why unbelievers are called "the inhabitants of the earth" in Revelation. Their hope and values are all set on the temporary world, and not on the eternal hope of God. But is it the action of a loving God to allow the wholesale slaughter of people, just so that the survivors may have a chance to repent?

There are at least two answers to that. The first is to point out that John is not presenting an answer to the age-old problem of suffering. Rather, he is saying that, since we live in a world in which disaster is prone to strike savagely and unexpectedly, those who put all their eggs in this world's basket are living disastrously. In the face of the world as it is, the pressing problem is not about the why of suffering but our response to it. In the end, we are faced with the choice of futility or faith. We face a meaningless world of pain, or we face a mysterious world which is still governed by God.

The second answer goes on from there. The very problem as we often pose it is part of the attitude that John is against. We are tempted to see death as the ultimate disaster precisely because we see this life as all that there really is. But in fact, all people die. When and how are almost unimportant compared to that fact. The real question is, "How do we face the certainty of death?" If we see it simply as the great ending, to be postponed as long as possible, then we are, in the end, without hope. If we see it as the gateway to eternal life, there may well be reasons for putting it off, but they are like reasons for putting off a joyful journey. Duty and love of family and friends may keep us here but, in the end, we are bound for a better place.

MM

The powers of darkness

And the fifth angel blew his trumpet, and I saw a star that had fallen from heaven to earth, and he was given the key to the shaft of the bottomless pit; he opened the shaft of the bottomless pit, and from the shaft rose smoke like the smoke of a great furnace, and the sun and the air were darkened with the smoke from the shaft. Then from the smoke came locusts on the earth, and they were given authority like the authority of scorpions of the earth. They were told not to damage the grass of the earth or any green growth or any tree, but only those people who do not have the seal of God on their foreheads. They were allowed to torture them for five months, but not to kill them, and their torture was like the torture of a scorpion when it stings someone . . . They have as king over them the angel of the bottomless pit: his name in Hebrew is Abbadon (Destruction) and in Greek he is called Appollyon (Destroyer).

As if the natural disasters of the world were not enough, the fifth trumpet reveals a world of spiritual evil, as demonic locusts are released from the depths of hell to torment those who lack the protection of faith in Christ.

Here the devil makes his first appearance. There are two errors we can make about the reality of spiritual evil; to disbelieve in it, and to overestimate it. John wants his readers to realize that there is indeed a demonic evil, and it is to be fought and resisted by prayer. Without the power of Christ we are helpless before it. Yet it is not an all-powerful opposite to God. The devil has power only because, like the other evils of the world, he is allowed it for a time, by God.

The other point to remember is that supernatural evil is only powerful because human beings give it a foothold. The locusts have human faces (verse 10) because, in the end, human beings have the responsibility for sin. 'The devil tempted me' is never an excuse.

A meditation

Like a roaring lion your adversary the devil prowls around, looking for someone to devour. Resist him, steadfast in your faith.

1 Peter 5:8, 9

MM

Cry havoc!

Then the sixth angel blew his trumpet, and I heard a voice from the four horns of the the golden altar before God, saying to the sixth angel who had the trumpet, "Release the four angels who are bound at the great river Euphrates." So the four angels were released, who had been held ready for the hour, the day, the month, and the year, to kill a third of humankind. The number of the troops of cavalry was two hundred million; I heard their number.

Once again, John refers to Roman fears of an invasion from the Parthian empire, with its feared regiments of horse-archers. But there is more to the vision. The invading armies are of overwhelming size, and reflect the Old Testament symbolism of evil, as "invaders from the north". Against this tide of evil, there seems no hope, for its size means that any victory against it can only be temporary; the powers of evil can call on limitless reinforcements.

There is an important truth here. Time and again, people tell me that the world is slowly getting better. They point to evils of the past which are no longer with us, and to improvements in medicine and standards of living. Yet with every advance for good there seems to be a corresponding increase in evil. The collapse of communist tyranny in Europe brought civil war and famine. Small-pox has disappeared but the spectre of AIDS has raised a more terrible threat. Technology has eased the lives of many, yet the greatest concentration of military power ever seen was unleashed in the Gulf only last year.

We are not on a steady climb to Utopia. We are in a ceaseless fight against evil, in which ground won is all too easily lost. All this may seem depressing and, if this were the whole story, it would be. There is another kind of victory, won by Jesus, and that is what we are leading up to. But for now, the fight goes on, and there can be no complacency.

A prayer

Father, when the evil in the world seems limitless, open our eyes to see the greater hope and the greater triumph of your love in Jesus. And, in that hope and love, strengthen us for the fight.

MM

Hardness of heart

The rest of humankind, who were not killed by these plagues, did not repent of the works of their hands or give up worshipping demons and idols of gold and silver and bronze and stone and wood, which cannot see or hear or walk. And they did not repent of their murders or their sorceries or their fornication or their thefts.

With the sounding of the six trumpets, we have seen horror piled on horror, all of it reflecting the evils of the real world. Yet the final verdict seems one of despair. No one repented and turned to God. Instead they stayed with their own false gods, made by themselves.

John has put his finger on the essence of sin. It is not the individual sins of murder, fornication etc., but the single great sin of idolatry. Not just the literal worship of idols, but setting up oneself or one's possessions as the greatest thing in life. Sin, in essence, is putting anything else in the place of God.

We see it so often, as political systems, economics, work, family, hobbies, all take pride of place in the life of nations or people. Few are evil, most are good, but all can become idols when they take the place of God.

Often it seems that the very signs which John presents as warnings turn people away from God. For the trumpet sounds can surely be heard even now in the world, in war and crime, pollution, political corruption, oppression and disaster. Yet we ignore them, not because we do not hear them but because they pose problems which seem too big to cope with. The world seems harsh and terrible, so people escape into their own small concerns, which so rarely concern the God who offers their one true security. At the same time they do nothing to ease the pains of the world.

So is there no hope? Yes, there is and, before the final trumpet blows, John will turn to the last hope; the witness of the church.

A thought

What threatens to become (or already is) an idol for you? Offer it to God, and let it take its proper place under him.

MM

Doing love

One of the teachers of the law came and heard them debating. Noticing that Jesus had given them a good answer, he asked him, 'Of all the commandments, which is the most important?' 'The most important one,' answered Jesus, 'is this: "Hear, O Israel, the Lord our God, the Lord is one. Love the Lord your God with all your heart and with all your soul and with all your mind and with all your strength." The second is this: "Love your neighbour as yourself." There is no commandment greater than these.'

Christian love isn't about feeling—it's about doing. A feeling will sometimes follow the doing. Sometimes a feeling of well-being. Sometimes a feeling of disappointment. I used to think that love was a lovely warm feeling that would take me through all the difficulties of loving difficult people, so that I and they would be washed along on a tide of love. But that mindless ecstasy happens through drugs, not through doing the will of God. Jesus didn't *feel* fantastic in the Garden of Gethsemane. He felt frightened. 'Sit here while I pray,' he said to Peter, James and John, 'and he began to be deeply distressed and troubled. "My soul is overwhelmed with sorrow to the point of death," he said to them' (Mark 14:32–34, NIV). They went to sleep—but the end of the line for him was his word of surrender. '"Abba, Father," he said, "everything is possible for you. Take this cup from me. Yet not what I will, but what you will."' (Mark 14:36, NIV).

If we want to know what the will of God is we can find out by studying the word of God: 'Be transformed by the renewing of your mind,' wrote St Paul—and to soak ourselves in the word of God, and to let it shape our lives, is what it means to love God with our mind. If we don't know his words, then we can't know his will.

Reflect

Love, once kindled in the soul, is the mother of all heroic actions; love knows how to bound and overflow—the man who has lighted his life from Christ's love is constant in trials, patient in suffering, courageous in assaults, prudent in difficulties, victorious and triumphant in action.

Rufus M. Jones, Spiritual Reformers in the 16th and 17th Centuries, Macmillan

SB

Judgment delayed

And I saw another mighty angel coming down from heaven, wrapped in a cloud, with a rainbow over his head; his face was like the sun, and his legs like pillars of fire. He held a little scroll open in his hand. Setting his right foot on the sea and his left foot on the land, he gave a great shout, like a lion roaring. And when he shouted, the seven thunders sounded. And when the seven thunders had sounded, I was about to write, but I heard a voice from heaven saying, "Seal up what the seven thunders have said, and do not write it down."

So far, everything has looked pretty bad. But at last there is a sound of hope. A mighty angel appears, signalling something of great importance, and he is crowned with a rainbow, the symbol of God's mercy. At his appearing, the seven thunders of doom sound, but their meaning is not to be written. Why? Because God has cancelled the doom they were to bring. Instead, a new hope for the world is to be announced.

The first mighty angel announced the opening of the closed scroll of history, but this angel carries a small open scroll—the message of the gospel. While the hidden purpose of God is hard to find in the history of the world, the purpose of God for salvation is open to all.

This is why judgment is put off. God has no desire to lose any of his creatures, and so the gospel is proclaimed to call people back to his love.

When I preach about evangelism, there is one thing I can count on—worried faces in the congregation. Yet this is the purpose of the church. It may sound a tall order, but we are here to bring hope to the world. In the message of Jesus which we are to share lies the only cure for the ills of the world. Only by getting straight with God can people find healing for broken relationships, respect for creation and purpose for their lives.

A prayer

Father, you have called your church to share the good news of Jesus Christ. Open my eyes to the opportunities you give for sharing that message, and give me the courage to speak out when the moment is right.

MM

Sweet and sour

Then the voice that I had heard from heaven spoke to me again, saying, "Go, take the scroll that is open in the hand of the angel who is standing on the sea and the land." So I went to the angel and told him to give me the little scroll; and he said to me, "Take it, and eat; it will be bitter to your stomach, but sweet as honey in your mouth." So I took the little scroll from the hand of the angel and ate it; it was sweet as honey in my mouth, but when I had eaten it, my stomach was made bitter. Then they said to me, "You must prophesy again about many peoples and nations and languages and kings."

Yesterday I said that people look worried when I mention evangelism—and with some good reason. Like Ezekiel before him, John found that God's word was sweet and sour. Sweet with the message of love, but a bitter pill to swallow in its message of human sinfulness. And it is like that when we proclaim the gospel; sometimes people can be upset. Yet they still need to hear the word of God.

So the message of God's love can bring opposition, and even hatred, yet without it there is no hope. We who are called to proclaim the gospel have this choice; to remain silent and comfortable, or to speak and risk pain.

The choice will depend on how much God's word of salvation means to us. John was told to eat the scroll, and he did. He made it a part of himself, so that the gospel was his source of strength and nourishment. And that is what the word of God is meant to be to us. When we read the scriptures and let them get inside us, they change our way of thinking, our way of living. And, once we have truly heard the word of God, will it even be possible to remain silent?

A meditation

The lion has roared;
who will not fear?
The Lord God has spoken;
who can but prophesy?

Amos 3:8

MM

The church militant

Then I was given a measuring rod like a staff, and I was told, "Come and measure the temple of God and the altar and those who worship there, but do not measure the court outside the temple; leave that out, for it is given over to the nations, and they will trample over the holy city for forty-two months. And I will grant my two witnesses authority to prophesy for one thousand two hundred and sixty days, wearing sackcloth."

There's not much difficulty in figuring out what the temple stands for in today's reading. The church is often compared to a building or a temple in the New Testament, and that is what it means here. John has to measure it, as a sign of God's protection, showing that God has the true measure of his church and knows and cares for it inch by inch.

But not all of the temple is measured, because that would be to remove the church from the world, and we have seen that the church is meant to share in the sufferings of the world. In fact, it is to suffer in some ways more than the world—the outer court is to be given over to the nations. Or, in other words, the church is to suffer persecution.

Of course, it is only likely to be persecuted if it is faithful to its calling. Yet, in a way, the church that compromises and refuses to proclaim the gospel will still end up trampled underfoot. It will be absorbed into the secular world and become, in the end, impossible to recognize.

But then it will not be the church, and John's message is not for any such complacent club. He is writing to those who remain faithful to Christ and know that the way of discipleship is the way of the cross. If the message of Revelation has to be summed up in one saying, it is the words of Jesus: "If anyone would be my disciple, they must take up their cross and follow me."

A prayer

Father, you have called me to follow your son on the way of the cross. Give me grace to follow him boldly, to trust in him whatever happens, and to know that, in the end, nothing can shake the people you have called your own.

MM

Call to repentance

(The two witnesses) are the two olive trees and the two lampstands that stand before the Lord of the earth. And if anyone wants to harm them, fire pours from their mouth and consumes their foes; anyone who wants to harm them must be killed in this manner. They have authority to shut the sky, so that no rain may fall during the days of their prophesying, and they have authority over the waters to turn them into blood, and to strike the earth with every kind of plague, as often as they desire.

Like the temple, the two witnesses stand for the church. They are modelled on Moses and Elijah and, like them, their message is a call to true faith and repentance. The fire that pours from their mouths is the gospel for, when the good news of Jesus is really preached, it burns people's consciences and calls them to repent of their sins.

In some circles, this passage is taken much more literally, as a prediction that, near the end of time, two great preachers with miraculous powers will appear in Jerusalem. But that misses the point John is making. This is not something that will happen one day, but a description of what is happening now. This is the mission of the church from day to day.

But don't get it wrong. It isn't saying that all Christians are called to be great evangelists. What it is saying is that, when we live our lives in the light of Christ, we witness both by word and deed to the truth of his gospel.

The unemployed person who maintains hope through faith, the single parent who strives to produce a home of warmth and love, the chronically ill person who discovers courage and joy in Christ, the poor person who shows generosity; all who struggle with adversity in the strength of God are witnesses to the gospel, and a goad to the conscience of the world.

A prayer

Father, people know that I am a Christian, and they watch what I do. Sometimes I am a good advertisement for you, and at other times I am not. But, at all times, I thank you for the privilege of being part of your work of bringing salvation to the world.

MM

Life out of death

When they have finished their testimony, the beast that comes up from the bottomless pit will make war on them and conquer and kill them, and their dead bodies will lie in the street of the city that is allegorically called Sodom and Egypt, where also their Lord was crucified . . . But after the three and a half days, the breath of life from God entered them, and they stood on their feet, and those who saw them were terrified. Then they heard a loud voice from heaven saying to them, "Come up here!" And they went up to heaven in a cloud while their enemies watched them. At that moment there was a great earthquake, and a tenth of the city fell; seven thousand people were killed in the earthquake, and the rest were terrified and gave glory to the God of heaven.

Allen Gardiner was the first Anglican missionary to South America. He had no success, and died of starvation in Patagonia. But his example led to the founding of the South American Missionary Society and a strong Anglican presence which is still to be found through that continent.

Was Gardiner a failure? In the world's eyes, yes. But, in the end, no. It is that quality of the church, which in the grace of God brings life out of death, and success out of failure, which is one of the greatest witnesses to the power of the gospel.

It is this message of hope with which John rounds off this description of the church's mission. We may sometimes feel that we have failed. Churches may close, and faith may seem to be at a low ebb in the life of our nation. But there is never a final defeat for God and his people. Even our apparent failure sows the seeds of God's final triumph.

So John pictures the death of the church's witness—a victory for the enemy. Yet God brings new life to his people, and such is the sign of his power that the inhabitants of the city (the world) finally give glory to the Lord of life.

A prayer

Father, how much I fear failure! How afraid I am of seeming foolish! But you are the God of resurrection and can build success on my failure and speak wisdom through my folly.

MM

The Lamb's triumph

Then the seventh angel blew his trumpet, and there were loud voices in heaven, saying, "The kingdom of the world has become the kingdom of our Lord and of his Messiah, and he will reign for ever and ever." Then the twenty-four elders who sit on their thrones before God fell on their faces and worshipped God, singing, "We give you thanks, Lord God Almighty, who are and who were, for you have taken your great power and begun to reign."

We end our look at Revelation as we began it, with the worship of heaven. But this is the final worship for, with the sounding of the last trumpet, God at last rules over all.

Of course, the message of the book as a whole is that God is always in charge, but this is a different kind of rule. Previously, God had been ruling despite the wishes of the people of earth. But now they acknowledge him as Lord, and heaven and earth at last are in harmony.

John's message to the church, both now and when he first wrote, is that we have a vital part to play in bringing that final rule of God to its completion. The way has been opened by the death of Christ, the Lamb who was slain for the sins of the world. And in this world, as we come to faith in him, the kingdom of God is extended. As the church bears its witness (poor, incomplete and faulty though it surely is) so God acts to draw more and more into the kingdom.

Persecution cannot stop the witness, for martyrdom itself is the greatest witness to the power of God. Adversity and opposition, and even failure and death, provide the building blocks of the kingdom of God.

The only danger to the church lies within the church itself. Complacency, lack of love, compromise with a world that opposes God, are the real dangers to the kingdom. And even they, in the end, will not be enough to prevent the final victory.

A prayer

For all the church, and especially for those who face opposition, ridicule and persecution. Pray for love, for yourself and all Christian people, and for the courage to bear witness to the love of God by word and deed.

MM

An unwilling prophet, a letter from an apostle, and another prophet

The story of Jonah is where we start this seven-week section—with the rebellious prophet totally refusing to do what God has told him to do. But finally doing it, with very bad grace and in a very bad temper. Graham Dodds takes us through Jonah's reluctant journey—and shows us the tenderness and compassion of God as we travel along the way.

The letter to the Ephesians comes next (with me)—and it's a wonderful letter. It tells us about the glory of God, about the Gospel, and about the Christian life. New life—and freedom—and the way to win the good fight of faith. We see how an apostle prays for his converts—and that shows us how to pray for our church. It also shows us what the right model is for ministry. Not a one-man band—but the whole body of the Church gifted with different gifts for the building up of the body.

Then for two weeks Henry Wansbrough takes us from the birth to the death of the prophet Samuel—and in the process teaches us about prayer and about the presence of God, awesome and powerful. We also see how disobedience can lead to depression and desperation. But through it all God is there—and his plans and loving purposes for his people never change, even though his people do.

The fruit of the Spirit

There are different kinds of gifts, but the same Spirit. There are different kinds of service, but the same Lord. There are different kinds of working, but the same God works all of them in all men. Now to each one the manifestation of the Spirit is given for the common good. To one there is given through the Spirit the message of wisdom, to another the message of knowledge by means of the same Spirit, to another faith by the same Spirit, to another gifts of healing by that one Spirit, to another miraculous powers, to another prophecy, to another the ability to distinguish between spirits, to another the ability to speak in different kinds of tongues, and to still another the interpretation of tongues. All these are the work of one and the same Spirit, and he gives them to each one, just as he determines.

In our garden we have three apple trees and a pear tree. Each year the apple trees groan with fruit and we are able to eat them from August until—well, the following April, very often. They are good apples, too, with a lovely flavour.

But the pear tree is a dead loss! For whatever reason, it produces either no fruit at all or wretched, hard, sour little pears that are totally inedible. The apple trees and pear tree *look* all right, but the former produce good fruit and the latter bad fruit. As today's Opening Sentence at Communion says, 'You will be known by your fruits'.

Jesus (see John 15:5) and St Paul (see Galatians 5:22) both suggest that the quality of the fruit depends on the life *within* the tree, or its 'sap', as we would say. And the sap of the life of the Christian tree, as St Paul argues in this passage, is no less than the Spirit of God. When he is present and able to flow freely through the tree's branches, good fruit abounds. His gifts become evident. When he is restricted, resisted or rejected, then the result is no fruit, or even worse, bad fruit. All Christian service, all Christian ministry of every kind, is simply and solely by *gift*. It is a product of the life-giving 'sap', the Holy Spirit. We can't produce the fruit of the Spirit by the energy of the flesh, but God can bring fruit from the most unlikely 'trees' when we allow his Spirit to flow into and through us.

A prayer

Dear Lord, may my life so abide in you that your Spirit may flow through every part of it and produce the good fruit of your purpose in me. Amen.

DW

On the run

The word of the Lord came to Jonah son of Amittai: 'Go to the great city of Nineveh and preach against it, because its wickedness has come up before me.' But Jonah ran away from the Lord and headed for Tarshish. He went down to Joppa, where he found a ship bound for that port. After paying the fare, he went aboard and sailed for Tarshish to flee from the Lord. Then the Lord sent a great wind on the sea, and such a violent storm arose that the ship threatened to break up.

There is a very familiar theme to the story of Jonah and it's demonstrated so clearly within the opening verses. It's the theme of rebellion. God tells Jonah to go east 500 miles to Nineveh and so he heads off west 2,500 miles to Tarshish (most likely to be in Spain).

We can almost hear God speaking between the recorded lines of the book—'Jonah, don't go to Joppa—Jonah, don't go looking for a ship—Jonah, don't waste your money on the fare— Jonah, don't get on board the ship—OK have it your own way, but don't say I didn't warn you.'

And yet this theme of rebellion is not new in Jonah's time. It's as old as Genesis, and in particular Adam and Eve. 'Eve, don't believe what the serpent is saying—Eve, don't take the fruit—Eve, don't eat it—Adam, leave it alone.' What follows in the Old Testament is the long period of wilderness years ending with Jesus, crucified on a cross. For Jonah it's a miserable three days in a fish.

There are times when I, like Jonah, find myself rebelling against God. The strange thing is that I'm not quite sure why I do it. I know in my heart that he wants the best for me and yet I still put my back against him.

The rather unpalatable conclusion of all this rebellion is that although God always provides a means of restoring the relationship, it can be very bloody. My own experience is that God is a gradual-ist. He gives plenty of warnings and lots of opportunities. However, there comes a day when the storm gathers and the sea opens. Then, whether I rebel or comply, I am reliant on his mercy.

Prayer

*Take my life and let it be
Consecrated, Lord, to thee;
Take my moments and my days,
Let them flow in ceaseless praise.*

Frances Ridley Havergal

GD

A rude awakening

Jonah had gone below deck, where he lay down and fell into a deep sleep. The captain went to him and said, 'How can you sleep? Get up and call on your god! Maybe he will take notice of us, and we will not perish.' Then the sailors said to each other, 'Come let us cast lots to find out who is responsible for this calamity.' They cast lots and the lot fell on Jonah. So they asked him, 'Tell us, who is responsible for making all this trouble for us? What do you do? Where do you come from? What is your country? From what people are you?' He answered, 'I am a Hebrew and I worship the Lord, the God of heaven, who made the sea and the land.' This terrified them and they asked, 'What have you done?' (They knew he was running away from the Lord, because he had already told them so.)

How embarrassing! Not only is Jonah rebelling against God privately, but now he is also being a public hypocrite. He says he worships the Lord and yet he is running away from him. I wonder why he broadcast it to the sailors when he got on board. Was it bravado? Or a quiet confession to one of the more sensitive-looking ones? Regardless of the reasons, he's now the cause of their possible deaths. Not that Jonah is all that bothered about the rest of the crew. There's a sort of eerie apathy from him at this point. It's almost as though he wants to be arrested by God when he goes to sleep in the midst of the storm. The captain, using his official authority, tries to encourage him into action. The sailors have a rougher justice. They cast lots and decide to interrogate him themselves. Bit by bit the odds stack against Jonah, yet still he does not repent.

There comes a point in many rebellions when turning back becomes much harder. Intransigence sets in and the rebel reinforces his or her attitude. The decision to head for Tarshish has been taken and the finding of a boat and boarding has been completed. Now Jonah waits to arrive.

But it's precisely at this moment that God decides to chip away at the rebellion: first the storm, then the captain, then the sailors. Likewise, just when we think it's safe for us to sleep in our rebellions, God begins his chiselling.

Think

Circumstance, authority and peers are some of God's tools to make Jonah obedient. What others does he use in our lives?

GD

Man overboard

The sea was getting rougher and rougher. So they asked him, 'What should we do to you to make the sea calm down for us?' 'Pick me up and throw me into the sea,' he replied, 'and it will become calm. I know that it is my fault that this great storm has come upon you.' Instead the men did their best to row back to land. But they could not, for the sea grew even wilder than before. Then they cried to the Lord, 'O Lord, please do not let us die for taking this man's life. Do not hold us accountable for killing an innocent man, for you, O Lord, have done as you pleased.' Then they took Jonah and threw him overboard, and the raging sea grew calm. At this the men greatly feared the Lord, and they offered a sacrifice to the Lord and made vows to him.

There's a joke about an evangelist who admitted that his wife was better at saving souls than he was. 'Why's that?' his friend asked. 'She's learning to drive,' answered the evangelist, 'and she puts the fear of God into more people than I could ever hope to!'

There's a sense in which we do not really repent or change our attitudes until we're frightened. A heart problem may scare us into changing our behaviour or the way we live. The possibility of losing our job may make us more careful about what we do and how we do it. The threat of military intervention often makes the aggressor at least think carefully before continuing.

The storm rages on and the sailors fearfully realize there is no option but to press Jonah for the answer to their inevitable fate. Even when he tells them, they are reluctant to kill him. It's touching how they plead with God not to hold them accountable for Jonah's sui-cide attempt. So Jonah goes to the lowest point of his life. He gives up everything. Nothing remains that is worth living for. God has apparently won. Ironically for the prophet the sailors are saved. They even worship God. But the price seemed to be the death of Jonah, one of God's precious children. Just as it appeared on Good Friday.

***

Think

What are the differences and similarities between Jonah's story and Jesus' story?

GD

Jonah's wail

From inside the fish Jonah prayed to the Lord his God. He said: 'In my distress I called to the Lord, and he answered me. From the depths of the grave I called for help, and you listened to my cry. You hurled me into the deep, into the very heart of the seas, and the currents swirled about me; all your waves and breakers swept over me. I said, "I have been banished from your sight; yet I will look again towards your holy temple."'

Bishop Richard Hare once came to our church and told us about a conference he had attended. One superb speaker made his address and everyone was impressed. So much so, in the evaluation of the address afterwards the planning team said, 'it was just like being in the presence of the Messiah'. A large Texan man on the team, who had been giving a good impression of being asleep during the evaluation suddenly said, 'Check his hands.' In all the exuberance of Christianity we must not lose sight of the fact that Jesus' body still bears the cruel marks of his victory. Jonah's experience foretells that before resurrection there will be death. Yet for him even the very act of being hurled into the watery grave is evidence of God's awesomeness. He experiences, at the hand of God, the immense and fearful power of the waves.

I hail from Hartlepool in the North East of England. One of my favourite pastimes as a child was to go to the breakwater and watch the waves burst against the rock. Thirty or forty feet high, the water would crash against the wall. Sadly for any who were mad enough to stand on the breakwater it could easily spell disaster, but for me it was exhilarating to stand so close to something so powerful.

Jonah's psalm is born out of just such an experience. He has stood in the middle of God's creative force and encountered not only his power, but also his mercy. It's in the middle of such experiences that we deepen our faith.

Activity

Write a psalm: Write one phrase for each of the following.
Praise: something about God that is wonderful
Thanksgiving: something God has done for you recently
Enquiry: a question you've always wanted to ask God
Emotion: something that makes you angry
Revelation: something that God has specifically shown you
Thanksgiving: something about God and today
Praise: something about God forever.

GD

The watershed

'The engulfing waters threatened me, the deep surrounded me; seaweed was wrapped around my head. To the roots of the mountains I sank down; the earth beneath barred me in for ever. But you brought my life up from the pit, O Lord my God. When my life was ebbing away, I remembered you, Lord, and my prayer rose to you, to your holy temple... Salvation comes from the Lord.' And the Lord commanded the fish, and it vomited Jonah onto dry land.

A couple of years ago I was broadcasting 'Thought for the Day' each Friday morning on Radio Bristol. It's never easy choosing a subject which is both topical and thoughtful. One Wednesday morning I was in the centre of Bath when I saw a fight in the main street between a traveller and two large men. I chose this for the broadcast on the Friday. I described the scene, making the point about how travellers usually appear as outcasts but for a moment had engaged our sympathy.

Less than one hour after the broadcast it was reported to me that two large men were looking for me at the church. They were determined to find me and would not be put off. As they couldn't contact me then, they were going to phone me later in the day.

All day I waited in fear and trepidation. Like the disciples in the upper room with the doors locked there seemed no end to the tension. I wanted to do some work during the day and yet I was gripped by the impending encounter. When it came, the phone call was such a relief and God was present. It was also

private so I will not say any more.

Jonah comes to the lowest place in his fear where he experiences the salvation of the Lord. It's taken considerable time and effort before he has arrived and his watershed is ironically at the bottom of the sea. It's lovely to have the mountain-top experience, but sometimes we too need to reach new depths in our lives before God lifts us up.

Pray

Where can I go from your Spirit? Where can I flee from your presence? If I go up to the heavens, you are there; if I make my bed in the depths, you are there. If I rise on the wings of the dawn, if I settle on the far side of the sea, even there your hand will guide me, your right hand will hold me fast.

Psalm 139:7—10 (NIV)

GD

Pass it on

Then the word of the Lord came to Jonah a second time: 'Go to the great city of Nineveh and proclaim to it the message I give you.' Jonah obeyed the word of the Lord and went to Nineveh. Now Nineveh was a very important city—a visit required three days. On the first day, Jonah started into the city. He proclaimed: 'Forty more days and Nineveh will be overturned.' The Ninevites believed God.

So Jonah survived the fishy grave and has now been through his 'resurrection'. To use the word 'resurrection' is not quite correct. Perhaps a better word would be 'resuscitation' because Jonah, as far as we know, still had to face death.

I preached a sermon a few Easters ago where I constructed a tomb at the front of the church out of children, adults and a white sheet. We had two people at the entrance to the tomb. One was Jesus and the other, Lazarus. The point I wanted to make was that when Lazarus came out of the tomb he came out the way he went in. In other words he had to die again. But Jesus went through death and on to a life beyond the power of death.

Jonah, on his return, finds that his old task has emerged with him. God is not going to let him off the hook. From being in a fish he becomes a fisherman however, this time he's obedient. It's not surprising considering what he had been through!

I failed English Language O Level at school. When I thought about entering the ministry, where there is so much use of language, I wondered how I would cope. Then I read about Jeremiah. He too felt like an inexperienced youth, but God showed him the message and he passed it on.

God said the same to Jonah as he did to Jeremiah, as he does to every preacher: 'proclaim the message I give you'. Simply listen, then pass on what you hear. This is the true tradition of the Church, to hear the good news and pass it on. It's what Paul talks of in 1 Corinthians 15. Not the mundane repetition of an ancient rite but the vibrant good news of God. Jonah returned from his grave for a reason. When we begin to follow Christ we are not immediately resurrected into heaven. Like Jonah, we live a risen life here on earth, and our tradition is to pass it on.

Task

Find a copy of one of the Gospels and give it to someone else.

GD

See for yourself

The next day John was there again with two of his disciples. When he saw Jesus passing by, he said, 'Look, the Lamb of God!' When the two disciples heard him say this, they followed Jesus. Turning around, Jesus saw them following and asked, 'What do you want?' They said, 'Rabbi' (which means Teacher), 'where are you staying?' 'Come,' he replied, 'and you will see.'

There are two memorable sayings in this passage. The first has become well known to us in church art and in the liturgy: echoing 'The Lamb of God, who takes away the sin of the world'. Its familiarity may blind us to its astonishing claim. In the Law of Moses, the ritual involved in forgiveness required the sinner to lay his or her hand on the head of a lamb or goat, confess his sin and then offer the animal as a sacrifice. (Leviticus 4:27–29). In this way, ritually at least, the sins of the individual and of the community could be taken away. But now, says John, God has sent his own 'lamb' and he will take away 'the sin of the world'—a cosmic sacrifice for a cosmic fault. And that 'lamb' is Jesus. His death would be sufficient for all of the world's sin—past, present and future. He would 'take it away'.

The second saying is less dramatic, but also very revealing. It is the invitation Jesus gave to the two disciples of John—one of them was Andrew—when they asked where he was staying. 'Come and see,' he replied. In one sense it is an invitation no one ought to refuse. 'Just come and have a look', he says, 'See whether you like it, whether my lifestyle, my message, my friendship, really appeals to you. You don't have to stay, or commit yourself... just *come and see*.' Sometimes we are very anxious that those we pray for and care about should become totally committed to Christ. Very well. But first, let them 'taste and see how gracious the Lord is'. Give them a chance to 'come and see'. Few who have genuinely tasted have failed to stay.

A prayer

Lord Jesus, as you opened the door of your simple lodging by Galilee and invited those young seekers to come in, draw us and those we pray for gently into the place of blessing. Amen.

DW

Missing the method

On the first day, Jonah started into the city. He proclaimed: 'Forty more days and Nineveh will be overturned.' The Ninevites believed God. They declared a fast, and all of them, from the greatest to the least, put on sackcloth. When the news reached the king of Nineveh, he rose from his throne, took off his royal robes, covered himself with sackcloth and sat down in the dust.

There are countless handbooks written on evangelism these days. Even though I find much to stimulate me in their methods of proclamation, I am still disappointed with them. The reason is that they so often miss out the vital ingredient of the direct work of the Holy Spirit. The work of the Holy Spirit is like a floodlight lighting up Jesus, directly convincing a person that Jesus is who he is. This seems to me to be the most important factor in evangelism. It's not we who convert someone but the Holy Spirit. There may be a few external signs that someone is interested in God, but what is going on deep inside is well hidden from human view.

All this is well demonstrated in Jonah's story. We may assume that Jonah preached long sermons about God, persuading, convincing, arguing like Paul the apostle, but the text doesn't support this theory. Jonah simply said what God had told him to say and we're left with the blunt, stark, statement, 'The Ninevites believed God.'

This is not the only time the Bible records such dramatic turning around. In Luke 5:27–28 we read, ' "Follow me,"

Jesus said to him, and Levi got up, left everything and followed him.' Again this extraordinary, immediate response to God is astonishing.

We've decided in our church to put aside the various methods of evangelism. There are so many, we're a little confused by them. Instead, what we do is get together and worship God, often including Holy Communion. Then we spend an hour going out and talking to people about the world, God and what it's like to live in Bath. Our contact with people is informing us as to how the Church might be more attractive. But just occasionally we meet someone who God has been speaking to directly. Like Levi or the Ninevite people, the response can be immediate and dramatic.

***

Pray

Lord, show me the way in which you want to work and help me to be open enough to be a part of it.

GD

Facing faith

Then [the king] issued a proclamation in Nineveh: 'By the decree of the king and his nobles: Do not let any man or beast, herd or flock, taste anything; do not let them eat or drink. But let man and beast be covered with sackcloth. Let everyone call urgently on God. Let them give up their evil ways and their violence. Who knows? God may yet relent and with compassion turn from his fierce anger so that we will not perish.' When God saw what they did and how they turned from their evil ways, he had compassion and did not bring upon them the destruction he had threatened.

When we turn to God, even with the smallest seeds of faith, great things happen. Sometimes in the Church we chastize ourselves too much for our lack of faith. We are so keen to try to get more of it that we forget to use the amount we have been given. However, when we do turn to God, there are tremendous effects and benefits. Guilt begins to disappear, new perspectives come into view. We find that Jesus does heal the sick and there are many people who find that problems do in fact resolve.

The king of Nineveh turned, along with his government and people, to God. He urged them on with a decree. He humbled himself and asked for mercy. God then changed his mind and turned from destroying them as they came to faith in him. The immediate benefit was compassion. The empathizing, loving, embracing care of God took hold of them.

Recently I heard Edmeia Williams, a Brazilian evangelist who told us of her faith for the street children of South America. On the surface they are cold and hard. They are angry, look fierce and will literally kill you if you threaten them. Because children under sixteen cannot be jailed they are trained to fight with machine guns and do the killing for the adults. Her experience is that if they and the adults who sponsor them come to God they reveal an inner life with a severe need of care. Even in the most vicious of people—and the Ninevites were some of the worst offenders—faith, compassion, understanding and love follow a change of heart and mind.

Jesus said the most radical thing when he told us to have faith. Faith changes the world, but most of all it changes the human heart.

Meditate

Most people are brought to faith in Christ not by argument but by exposure to it.

Samuel Shoemaker

GD

Continual care

But Jonah was greatly displeased and became angry. He prayed to the Lord, 'O Lord, is this not what I said when I was still at home? That is why I was so quick to flee to Tarshish. I knew that you are a gracious and compassionate God, slow to anger and abounding in love, a God who relents from sending calamity. Now, O Lord, take away my life, for it is better for me to die than to live.' But the Lord replied, 'Have you any right to be angry?'

Oh dear! After all that Jonah has been through, his old sin has returned. Why does he feel so angry, so displeased with God, so annoyed that God should relent towards the Ninevites? It's astonishing to think that after a major rebellion which resulted in him being a cat's whisker away from death, Jonah should now revive his first 'thorn in the flesh' and rebel again. Jonah has a big problem.

God never promises us a 'magic wand' healing from all our woes when we repent and follow him. What he does promise is that he will be there in all his power when we need him. In this situation he replies to Jonah with the devastating and yet gentle question, 'Have you any right to be angry?'

We meet people like this in our churches all the time, for instance those who have an addiction to drugs or alcohol. They may have gone through a traumatic experience to find healing, been hailed by the church as gloriously 'saved', then some time later they're trapped again in the same problem.

The length of time of healing can be proportional to the length of time of the problem. Someone who has been addicted for twenty years might take months or even years to get better rather than overnight. Of course it's right to thank God for healing but we also need to maintain care on a continual and private level.

Ironically, Jonah needed the same compassion that he was so angry about. He was incensed that it should be given to the bad Ninevites and not to God's chosen one. The truth is that God is equally generous to everyone.

The book of Jonah will end without us knowing if he was healed of his attitude. Perhaps it became a 'thorn in his flesh' for his whole life. The good news is that God still loved him.

Meditate

Here is a trustworthy saying that deserves full acceptance: Christ Jesus came into the world to save sinners.

1 Timothy 1:15

GD

Reflecting mercy

Jonah went out and sat down at a place east of the city. There he made himself a shelter, sat in its shade and waited to see what would happen to the city. Then the Lord God provided a vine and made it grow up over Jonah to give shade for his head to ease his discomfort, and Jonah was very happy about the vine. But at dawn the next day God provided a worm, which chewed the vine so that it withered. When the sun rose, God provided a scorching east wind, and the sun blazed on Jonah's head so that he grew faint. He wanted to die, and said, 'It would be better for me to die than to live.' But God said to Jonah, 'Do you have a right to be angry about the vine?' 'I do,' he said. 'I am angry enough to die.'

Some people believe that any kind of anger is wrong. I don't. The Bible says, 'In your anger do not sin' (Psalm 4:4). It's not the fact that we have anger that matters. Whether we sin or not depends on why we have it and what we do with it. Here, Jonah's anger demonstrates a bigoted, religious, exclusive jealousy. He was angry because God had compassion on the Ninevites.

The blatant contrast is between Jonah's arrogance and God's mercy. Jonah wants destruction, God wants the people restored. Jonah wants to be exclusive, God wants his creation united in him. Jonah seems literally 'hell bent' on their annihilation, wanting God to punish the heathen. We can almost hear him saying, 'Why should those who are so wicked find a place in the kingdom? They're not even God's chosen ones, they're Gentiles!' Even God's provision of a shelter from the sun for him, showing divine kindness, does not make the penny drop. God is being merciful, Jonah is being belligerent.

But before we totally castigate Jonah, we too need to examine the planks in our eyes. Can we find ourselves like Jonah, refusing to preach the kingdom? Do we form the Church into an exclusive club or get angry if a new member rocks the boat? If we do, we deny the openness which knowing Jesus is all about. Worse still, if we try to persuade God not to be merciful and pray for him to take vengeance on the heathen, then we destroy the bridge over which we ourselves must cross.

Think

In what ways do others see the mercy of God through me?

GD

Jonah, grow up!

But the Lord said, 'You have been concerned about this vine, though you did not tend it or make it grow. It sprang up overnight and died overnight. But Nineveh has more than a hundred and twenty thousand people who cannot tell their right hand from their left, and many cattle as well. Should I not be concerned about that great city?'

God's words began the book and he has the last word. They are words of great compassion on 120,000 'children' of Nineveh. They cannot tell their right hand from their left, implying that they are mere infants needing a Father.

In the parochial ministry I find more and more that 'growing up' does not come naturally to some. Sometimes people find themselves stuck in adolescence even though they may be well beyond those teenage years chronologically. It can be very wearing for the priest and congregation to continue the patient loving concern when time after time the person seems stuck in this adolescent behaviour.

The Ninevites may have been somewhat primitive in their morals, but Jonah is just as much a spiritual juvenile. His emotional sulk as he took himself out of the city was equalled by his attitude to the plant which sheltered him. He was pleased when it arrived even though he did not tend it or make it grow. But when it went, he was notably 'angry enough to die'. Gratification without responsibility is the prerogative of youth, but inevitably it doesn't last.

I feel like shaking Jonah and telling him to grow up, in no uncertain terms. Yet God reasons with him. He explains what Nineveh is like and gives him another chance. This is our God, a tender compassionate Father, slow to anger and rich in love. Even though we might be hard on others and ultimately ourselves, he is always ready to employ unconditional love in a gentle way.

This is the real point of the book of Jonah—God's unconditional love compared with our often reluctant love. We're not told what happens after verse 11 as the book ends. But because it ends here surely we're meant to infer that God is going to carry on with Jonah for a very long time helping him to find the answer to his problem.

Meditate

There is no sin small enough for it not to matter to God. There is no sin great enough that he cannot deal with it.

GD

Letting change happen

As the crowds increased, Jesus said, 'This is a wicked generation. It asks for a miraculous sign, but none will be given it except the sign of Jonah. For as Jonah was a sign to the Ninevites, so also will the Son of Man be to this generation . . . The men of Nineveh will stand up at the judgment with this generation and condemn it; for they repented at the preaching of Jonah, and now one greater than Jonah is here.

Whatever we have thought about Jonah, it is clear that Jesus regarded him as fulfilling his mission. He was a sign to the Ninevites which caused them to repent, so avoiding the impending judgment. Jesus, greater than Jonah, is also a sign of God's judgment upon every subsequent generation.

Judgment seems to be a rather distorted and frowned-upon concept in the modern-day Church. Members of my church questioned people on the streets of Bath about it. The overwhelming view was that it wasn't going to happen as the Bible says. As a student preacher at college I was once given the theme of preaching on judgment and hell in a local church. Afterwards the members of the congregation were invited to give their comments. 'It was a bit black,' said one, 'It could have been more cheerful,' said another, 'It can't be as bad as all that,' said a third, and so it went on. In our modern culture we are just beginning to realize that there are some things that really do need facing. We cannot just take the good things of life without dealing with the evil. The Ninevites realized this too and decided to change.

Jesus left us the Holy Spirit. He is the one who will 'convict the world of guilt in regard to sin and righteousness and judgment' as John 16:8 puts it.

The challenge to us is to be true disciples of Jesus who carry on his ministry with the Holy Spirit inside. We will at times need to speak out about the final judgment. In some ways it was the fear of it that drove me to believe in Christ. But let us not forget the lesson of Jonah—when God's message is preached, a change of heart is always possible.

Think

Every time we say, 'I believe in the Holy Spirit,' we mean that we believe that there is a living God able and willing to enter human personality and change it.

J.B. Phillips

GD

The mind of Christ

... No-one knows the thoughts of God except the Spirit of God. We have not received the spirit of the world but the Spirit of who is from God, that we may understand what God has freely given us. This is what we speak, not in words taught us by human wisdom but in words taught by the Spirit, expressing spiritual truths in spiritual words. The man without the Spirit does not accept the things that come from the Spirit of God, for they are foolishness to him and he cannot understand them, because they are spiritually discerned. The spiritual man makes judgments about all things, but he himself is not subject to any man's judgment. 'For who has known the mind of the Lord that he may instruct him?' But we have the mind of Christ.

Today's reading provides the theme for the day. 'Who has known the mind of the Lord? ... But we have *the mind of Christ.*' 'If I meet her today', my grandmother would say, 'I'll give her a piece of my mind'. As a child, I used to wonder what she meant. How could she give someone 'a piece of her mind?' And in any case, *which* piece? Wouldn't that leave her with less than she started with? What she meant, of course, was that she would like to convey to the other person exactly how she felt about something (usually, about something they had done that she didn't approve of!). And when the Bible speaks of Christians having 'the mind of Christ', or commands us to 'Let this mind be in you that was also in Christ Jesus', it is describing a process by which the way Jesus feels about something, or the way in which he sees it, becomes the way *we* feel about it or see it. It's almost a matter of thought transference: making his thoughts our thoughts. Now this may sound very mystical and mysterious, a process only open to exceptional saints. Yet it's a pro-cess we're familiar with in ordinary life. When two people know each other very well, eventually they begin to share each other's thoughts. At the same moment *both* say, 'Let's make a cup of tea' or 'Should we phone Auntie?' They have truly begun to give each other (and receive from each other) a 'piece of their mind'! It's no more complicated than that in the spiritual realm. If we get to know the Lord very well and spend a good deal of time with him, then eventually we shall find ourselves feeling and thinking about things in the way he does. We shall have received 'a piece of his mind'.

A prayer

Heavenly Father, as I join with other Christians today in prayer and worship, draw me closer to your Son, so that I may think and feel as he does. Amen.

DW

Something to sing about

Paul, an apostle of Christ Jesus by the will of God, To the saints who are in Ephesus and are faithful in Christ Jesus: Grace to you and peace from God our Father and the Lord Jesus Christ. Blessed be the God and Father of our Lord Jesus Christ, who has blessed us in Christ with every spiritual blessing in the heavenly places, just as he chose us in Christ before the foundation of the world to be holy and blameless before him in love. He destined us for adoption as his children through Jesus Christ, according to the good pleasure of his will, to the praise of his glorious grace that he freely bestowed on us in the Beloved. In him we have redemption through his blood, the forgiveness of our trespasses, according to the riches of his grace that he lavished on us.

In view of Paul's past record, it was astonishing that it was the will of God for him to be an apostle. He had persecuted the Church—and stood by when Stephen was stoned to death. But if God, can do such a turnaround for him, then he can do it for anyone—and any sinner can become a saint. In the New Testament *all* Christians are saints—not just a special hierarchy of special people. Everyone was (and is) special to God, and everyone has a unique and special song to sing 'to the praise of his glorious grace that he freely bestowed on us in the Beloved'. You cannot sing my song and I cannot sing yours.

Now, as I sit in my garden reading the word of God and writing these notes, I am starting to sing my song of praise to God. I don't know whether I would be singing it in prison, where Paul sang his song. But Terry Waite sang his song there—and it always has to do with the wonder and the glory of God rather than our circumstances.

A way to pray

Read the passage again and reflect on our relationship with the God and Father of our Lord Jesus Christ. Whatever we have done in the past makes no difference. It made none for Paul—except to make him sing an even more passionate and beautiful song to God-in-Christ.

SB

Now we can understand

With all wisdom and insight he has made known to us the mystery of his will, according to his good pleasure that he set forth in Christ, as a plan for the fullness of time, to gather up all things in him, things in heaven and things on earth. In Christ we have also obtained an inheritance, having been destined according to the purpose of him who accomplishes all things according to his counsel and will, so that we, who were the first to set our hope on Christ, might live for the praise of his glory. In him you also, when you had heard the word of truth, the gospel of your salvation, and had believed in him, were marked with the seal of the promised Holy Spirit; this is the pledge of our inheritance toward redemption as God's own people, to the praise of his glory.

Yesterday I read a novel by Dick Francis, the best-selling author who was the Queen Mother's jockey and who now writes superb mysteries about the world of racing. He understands people and he understands horses—and he has helped me to understand what I never had before: the relationship between a horse and its rider. I would never have understood the mystery unless Dick Francis had written about it.

It is like that with the mystery of the will of God. He reveals it to us so that we can understand and appreciate it. The Communion service itself would be a total mystery and a closed book to someone who didn't know the story of Jesus. But once we know that story, we can understand. 'Take, eat, this is my body which is for you ...' And through *that* story we understand the will of God for his world—a plan almost beyond belief: 'To gather up all things in him, things in heaven and things on earth.' We are all part of the plan whether we choose to be or not. Everything will be gathered up, including us, whether we choose it or not. But we can choose to be part of the glory, and to be a child of God through the grace of God. Then we are sealed with the Spirit—a mark that we belong to God, and a down-payment on our future glory.

A way to pray

Reflect on the mystery of the will of God—made known now through Jesus Christ. Reflect on the glory you know now—and on the glory that you will know.

SB

Power for the asking

I have heard of your faith in the Lord Jesus and your love toward all the saints, and for this reason I do not cease to give thanks for you as I remember you in my prayers. I pray that the God of our Lord Jesus Christ, the Father of glory, may give you a spirit of wisdom and revelation as you come to know him, so that, with the eyes of your heart enlightened, you may know what is the hope to which he has called you, what are the riches of his glorious inheritance among the saints, and what is the immeasurable greatness of his power for us who believe, according to the working of his great power.

This letter was written to the Church, not just to an individual, and it was probably a circular letter that went to several of the churches in Asia Minor.

Paul wanted the people of God to be mature Christians—and it might be that Christian maturity was in as short supply in his day as it is in ours. A lot of Christians are half-grown and under-nourished because we don't feed ourselves properly, either on the word of God or on the bread and wine of Communion.

Paul tackles the problem by praying—and if we will do the same for our church and for one another, then great things will happen, and we shall know 'the immeasurable greatness of his power for us who believe, according to the working of his great power'. Catherine Marshall wrote once that 'Many Christians are like deep sea divers marching bravely to pull out the bath plug.' All the power we need is there. But we need to use it. We are in a battle—and later on in this letter there will be more about the battle. But before we can fight it, we need to know what it is and how to get the strength and the power to fight.

A way to pray

Pray Paul's prayer for yourself and for your church—and begin, as he does, by being thankful (even if you don't feel it).

SB

The power of God in us

God put this power to work in Christ when he raised him from the dead and seated him at his right hand in the heavenly places, far above all rule and authority and power and dominion, and above every name that is named, not only in this age but also in the age to come. And he has put all things under his feet and has made him the head over all things for the church, which is his body, the fullness of him who fills all in all.

If we want power for living and for doing the will of God, then we can have it. An astonishing power, almost beyond believing. It is the power of God that raised Christ from the dead, and it is there for us. But we have to make the connection and let it in—except that the power is personal: not an 'it', but a 'he', the Holy Spirit of the living God. Sometimes our trouble is that we don't want that power.

It isn't necessarily comfortable to have the living God living in us, the God who made the world and all the stars in the Milky Way, and who made a new creation by raising the dead. Jesus Christ 'was crucified, dead and buried, and the third day he rose again from the dead, and sits on the right hand of God the Father Almighty'. The right hand is the place of the power of God—and through Jesus all the power of God can flow to us and through us like a river.

A river of life to give life to a poisoned and dead world. And we are the body of that Christ, so we can know the fullness of Christ, the presence of Christ, and the power of Christ for all our living and loving. If only we want it and pray for it. If only we would!

A way to pray

Will you pray for that power and that presence, for you and for the whole Church, and for your local church in particular? The world we live in is dying in the darkness—and doesn't even know that it needs the life and the love of Christ. So pray. For power, for love, and for an outpouring of the Spirit of God on the Church in our day—so that the blessing will spill over and bless the world.

SB

Alive to love

You were dead through the trespasses and sins in which you once lived, following the course of this world, following the ruler of the power of the air, the spirit that is now at work among those who are disobedient. All of us once lived among them in the passions of our flesh, following the desires of flesh and senses, and we were by nature children of wrath, like everyone else. But God, who is rich in mercy, out of the great love with which he loved us even when we were dead through our trespasses, made us alive together with Christ—by grace you have been saved—and raised us up with him and seated us with him in the heavenly places in Christ Jesus, so that in the ages to come he might show the immeasurable riches of his grace in kindness toward us in Christ Jesus.

Sin is a killer. And at the root of sin is a non-relationship, a relationship with God that we do not have. The story of Adam and Eve is the story of a broken relationship—first they hide from God, and then they hide from each other—covering up their nakedness with ineffective fig leaves. We don't want to be known—especially by God. But God created us to know him. Paul's delighted description of the glory of heaven in 1 Corinthians 13:12 speaks of the limitation of our present seeing and knowing, but says that 'then we will see face to face. Now I know only in part; then I will know fully, even as I have been fully known' (NRSV). And in Philippians 3:10 he writes that 'I want to know Christ and the power of his resurrection' (NRSV). However, even our sin doesn't mean that God stops loving us or that his will for us changes. He desires a love relationship with us far more intimate than a human marriage—and later on in this letter Paul will say that a human marriage mirrors the relationship between Christ and his Church. Now, through the love of God and the death of Christ, we are alive. Alive for love, in the richest meaning of that word.

A prayer

I am a new creation,
No more in condemnation,
Here in the grace of God I stand.
My heart is overflowing,
My love just keeps on growing,
Here in the grace of God I stand.

Dave Bilbrough (Thankyou Music, 1983)

SB

The gift of God

For by grace you have been saved through faith, and this is not your own doing; it is the gift of God—not the result of works, so that no one may boast. For we are what he has made us, created in Christ Jesus for good works, which God prepared beforehand to be our way of life.

Once I had an unpleasant and unhappy argument with a very learned theologian. 'God will save everyone,' he insisted. 'But what if they don't want to be saved?' I asked. That was several years ago, and I am learning more sense now. Arguing is fairly futile, and the theologian began to get irritated with me. 'You are saying it depends on us,' he said, 'but it all depends on God.' 'Yes,' I agreed, 'of course it does—in one sense. We cannot save ourselves. But surely we have to *receive* forgiveness and accept the love of God?'

You can't *make* somebody love you. They have to respond to your love. For me it is like the empty hands that I hold out at Communion—to be given the body and the blood of Christ. The greatest theologians in the world have argued about this issue, and Augustine and Pelagius wrangled on for years. Paul is quite clear that our salvation isn't our own doing—it is the gift of God. But gifts, have to be received—if we want them. Then we have to use them for the purpose they were made. God has made us and created us for good works—and that doesn't mean going round patronizing people. It means loving them—and the way to know what *that* means is to work out how we would want to be treated in their circumstances. Some decisions are easy to make. If we are hungry and thirsty, we shall want another person to feed us and give us something to drink. But sometimes, we don't know what the right thing is to do, or what the 'good' action is. Then we can pray for wisdom—confident that God will give it to us.

Pray

Pray for an end to futile arguments in the Church. Then think of a particular need you know—and pray for wisdom to work out how to meet it.

SB

The pain and the presence

O Lord, you deceived me, and I was deceived; you overpowered me and prevailed. I am ridiculed all day long; everyone mocks me. Whenever I speak, I cry out proclaiming violence and destruction. So the word of the Lord has brought me insult and reproach all day long. But if I say, 'I will not mention him or speak any more in his name,' his word is in my heart like a fire, a fire shut up in my bones. I am weary of holding it in; indeed, I cannot. I hear many whispering, 'Terror on every side! Report him! Let's report him!' All my friends are waiting for me to slip, saying, 'Perhaps he will be deceived; then we will prevail over him and take our revenge on him.' But the Lord is with me like a mighty warrior; so my persecutors will stumble and not prevail.

Last Sunday I was watching Thora Hird's television programme *On the Straight and Narrow*. The entrancing small boys in the Angel Voices Choir joined with the men's choir to sing a song. 'Just one voice, singing in the darkness: only one voice... Then there will be more than one voice, singing in the darkness...'

That one voice will draw other people into the light. But it isn't easy to be the voice. Not for us and not for the prophets. Jeremiah's life as a suffering servant of God was an agony. God is with him like a mighty warrior—but there is hardly ever instant success in the battle.

When Jesus sent out his disciples he gave them a warning and a promise: '...you will be dragged before governors and kings because of me... When they hand you over, do not worry about how you are to speak or what you are to say; for what you are to say will be given to you at that time; for it is not you who speak, but the Spirit of your Father speaking through you' (Matthew 10:18–20, NRSV).

When we come to communion to receive the bread and wine that are the body and blood of Christ, they can remind us of the truth: that he keeps on coming to us and that he is always with us—whatever happens.

SB

Friends with our enemies

So then, remember that at one time you Gentiles...were...aliens from the commonwealth of Israel, and strangers to the covenants of promise, having no hope and without God in the world. But now in Christ Jesus you who were once far off have been brought near by the blood of Christ. For he is our peace; in his flesh he has made both groups into one and has broken down the dividing wall, that is, the hostility between us. He has abolished the law with its commandments and ordinances, that he might create in himself one new humanity in place of the two, thus making peace, and might reconcile both groups to God in one body through the cross, thus putting to death that hostility through it.

In the temple at Jerusalem a Jew went through various courtyards to get to the inner court, where the Holy of Holies stood at the centre, veiled from everyone by a thick curtain. Only the high priest could enter the holiest place, and that only once a year. Women could come in as far as the court of the women, and Gentiles as far as the court of the Gentiles. But between the Court of the Gentiles and the rest of the temple there was a wall, with tablets set into it warning that if a Gentile went any further he was liable to be put to death. But now Paul is saying that that wall has been broken down—and so have all the walls, though he doesn't say so here. In the Gospels it says that at the very moment when Christ died the great curtain which separated the people from God in the Holy of Holies was torn from the top to the bottom—and the way into the presence was open.

Now all the walls are down, and people who were once enemies can be reconciled and know the peace of God. Now 'there is no longer Jew or Greek, there is no longer slave or free, there is no longer male or female; for all of you are one in Christ Jesus' (Galatians 3:27–28). Paul wasn't saying that a Jew was no longer a Jew, or that slavery would instantly be abolished, or that women and men were the same. He was writing of the barriers to friendship and real love between all those groups. But it all has to be worked out in our daily living and we still aren't managing it very well.

A way to pray

Pray for peace in Christ in the battle of the sexes and between ethnic groups who despise each other in our nation and in our world.

SB

An offer of peace

So he came and proclaimed peace to you who were far off and peace to those who were near; for through him both of us have access in one Spirit to the Father. So then you are no longer strangers and aliens, but you are citizens with the saints and also members of the household of God, built upon the foundation of the apostles and prophets, with Christ Jesus himself as the cornerstone. In him the whole structure is joined together and grows into a holy temple in the Lord; in whom you also are built together spiritually into a dwelling place for God.

As I write, there is a terrible lack of peace in Bosnia, Serbia and Croatia—and the peace plans that are offered aren't accepted by any of the warring groups. There could be peace—but they refuse it.

We can refuse it too, when Christ proclaims and offers it to us. When he says, 'Follow me', we can decline, and still go on walking along our own way and doing our own thing. Even as Christians we refuse to follow Christ all along the way, and refuse the peace he offers us in every area of our life. We refuse it because we don't want to obey him.

On the whole the Christian Church in the Western world is not ablaze with holiness. So the world ignores us and despises us. The holy temple that we are meant to be, indwelt by the Holy Spirit of God, and shining with the light of the world, is almost in ruins. But we can rebuild it if we will—penitent and obedient——and if we hunger and thirst for God.

Reflection

Think about any areas in your own life where you long for a deep heart peace. Then imagine the risen Christ standing before you and offering you his peace. What will it mean to you? What will he say to you? When he calls you to follow him along the way of holiness, will you do so? Listen to the words that the risen Christ spoke to a lukewarm church in Laodicea: 'Here I am! I stand at the door and knock. If anyone hears my voice and open the door, I will come in and eat with him, and he with me' (Revelation 3:20).

SB

Don't look down

This is the reason that I Paul am a prisoner for Christ Jesus for the sake of you Gentiles ... In former generations this mystery was not made known to humankind, as it has now been revealed to his holy apostles and prophets by the Spirit: that is, the Gentiles have become fellow heirs, members of the same body, and sharers in the promise in Christ Jesus through the gospel. Of this gospel I have become a servant according to the gift of God's grace that was given me by the working of his power. Although I am the very least of all the saints, this grace was given to me to bring to the Gentiles the news of the boundless riches of Christ.

William Barclay, the great Scottish commentator on the Bible, wrote that the basic sin of the ancient world was contempt. 'The Jews despised the Gentiles as worthless in the sight of God ... The Greeks despised the barbarians—and to the Greek all other nations were barbarians.' We haven't changed much. Recently I worked with Wilfred Wood, the only black bishop in the Church of England, on a book he has written for the BRF. Called *Keep the Faith, Baby!*, it was published in July 1994 at the start of the Black Anglican Congress in York. He told me of one of his small daughters, listening to television comment on an issue that involved black people and white people. 'Daddy, why do they speak about us like that?' she asked.

But Paul, a Jew who could boast that in terms of being a Jew he had got it all, spent the whole of the rest of his life after his conversion to Christ serving and working for the group of people whom he had once despised. Not that the despising had ever been right—and our despising and contempt is never right and always sinful. Paul knew the enormous preciousness of every human being in the eyes of God. Christ didn't die just for one ethnic group. Christ died for the whole world.

Pray

Pray for those who despise each other. In Northern Ireland, in Africa, and in your own country.

SB

Pray with Paul . . .

For this reason I bow my knees before the Father, from whom every family in heaven and on earth takes its name. I pray that, according to the riches of his glory, he may grant that you may be strengthened in your inner being with power through his Spirit, and that Christ may dwell in your hearts through faith, as you are being rooted and grounded in love. I pray that you may have the power to comprehend, with all the saints, what is the breadth and length and height and depth, and to know the love of Christ that surpasses knowledge, so that you may be filled with all the fullness of God. Now to him who by the power at work within us is able to accomplish abundantly far more than all we can ask or imagine, to him be glory in the church and in Christ Jesus to all generations, forever and ever. Amen.

Paul has written about the wonder of the plan of salvation, and about the purpose of God for his Church. Having set it out in its glory, he now prays that the Church will live it out. Then the glory will shine out. We can pray Paul's prayer for ourselves as individuals and for the Church as a whole. Pray it for the people in our local church—and for the leaders of the Church throughout the world. We looked earlier at the astonishing power that is available to us. The power of God who created the world and who raised Christ from the dead. Ours for the asking—if we meet the conditions. And the conditions are that we ask and pray, and that we are a holy people. We are anyway, in one sense, because we are the people of God and we belong to God. That makes us holy. But holy people need to live holy lives—and we manifestly don't. But God, can change us. He can change me and he can change you. He can change the Church. And he can change the world.

A way to pray

Pray Paul's prayer for yourself, and for your church.

SB

Entitled to say so

I therefore, the prisoner in the Lord, beg you to lead a life worthy of the calling to which you have been called, with all humility and gentleness, with patience, bearing with one another in love, making every effort to maintain the unity of the Spirit in the bond of peace. There is one body and one Spirit, just as you were called to the one hope of your calling, one Lord, one faith, one baptism, one God and Father of all, who is above all and through all and in all.

A brilliant professor whom I know spends most of his days and nights looking after his wife, who has Alzheimer's disease. He is 85 and she is 83—and his patience and gentleness is astonishing. When I go to stay with them I watch him caring for her, and doing all that has to be done for her and for the housekeeping as well. And I remember the impatience of his earlier years and I am wide-eyed at the grace of God working in him. So if he should ever try to prod me towards patience (an area where I need a lot of help!), I would listen—because he knows the way to it and he knows what he is talking about. It is just like that with Paul. Writing from the cell of a Roman prison, he was entitled to beg people to live a life worthy of the calling they had been called to. He was in far worse circumstances than theirs.

In the daily nit-picking and criticism that goes on in the average church Paul's words might shame us into repentance. 'I don't get anything out of it,' some people complain after a service. To which the reply has to be: 'And what did you put into it?' Catherine Marshall was once deeply convicted of her critical tongue and her critical attitude to other people—and she prayed for forgiveness and a new attitude. Perhaps if we do the same, God could use us more effectively—and the world would see the Christ-likeness of Christians in the Church of Christ.

A way to pray

Ask yourself, 'Is my life worthy of the calling to which I have been called? Am I like Christ? Do I make every (or any) effort to maintain the unity of the Spirit in the bond of peace? Do I need to repent?'

SB

Grow up!

But each of us was given grace according to the measure of Christ's gift . . . The gifts he gave were that some would be apostles, some prophets, some evangelists, some pastors and teachers, to equip the saints for the work of ministry, for building up the body of Christ, until all of us come to the unity of the faith and of the knowledge of the Son of God, to maturity, to the measure of the full stature of Christ.

We are beginning to get it right, thank God. We are beginning to see that the vicar or minister of a church doesn't have to possess *all* the gifts of ministry—and that God in his wisdom has given different gifts to different people. The people are 'saints' (all Christians, according to the New Testament) and the task of all the people with all the gifts is to equip one another for the work of ministry.

The task of ministry is to build up the body of Christ and to enable it (and urge it) to grow to maturity. In a church like that there will be teaching—and in the early Church that would have been done by telling the stories about Jesus, and by reading out the letters that the apostles wrote to the churches.

Many people then came into the Church out of a pagan world, and they knew nothing of Christianity. So the teachers had to tell it to them in a way they could understand—and to teach them the great doctrines of the faith in a way that they could grasp. Perhaps we need to pray that Christ will raise up gifted teachers like that in our day—because there are millions of people who are ignorant, and in almost total darkness, about the Christian story.

A way to pray

Pray for the ministry in your church—and for your own ministry to your church. Pray for Christian maturity—for yourself and for your church.

SB

Ask for God

One day Jesus was praying in a certain place. When he finished, one of his disciples said to him, 'Lord, teach us to pray, just as John taught his disciples.' He said to them, 'When you pray, say: "Father, hallowed be your name, your kingdom come. Give us each day our daily bread. Forgive us our sins, for we also forgive everyone who sins against us. And lead us not into temptation." . . . So I say to you: Ask and it will be given to you; seek and you will find; knock and the door will be opened to you. For everyone who asks receives; he who seeks finds; and to him who knocks, the door will be opened. Which of you fathers, if your son asks for a fish, will give him a snake instead? Or if he asks for an egg, will give him a scorpion? If you then, though you are evil, know how to give good gifts to your children, how much more will your Father in heaven give the Holy Spirit to those who ask him!'

'When you go to the library,' my next door neighbour said to me, 'please will you bring me back the further-education leaflet.' She has already been to a beginners' class in calligraphy, and now she wants to move on to the next stage. It is like that with prayer. We start as beginners—and we learn how to pray like a child learning to speak. Part of the prayer is simply the pleasure of being in the presence of God—just as a baby loves to be held by its mother or father. The start of a new relationship—and then the language to be learned in order to communicate. Listening—and speaking. A crying out that we are hungry and thirsty—and a quiet resting when we are satisfied. '. . .I have stilled and quietened my soul; like a weaned child with its mother, like a weaned child is my soul within me' (Psalm 131:2, NIV).

But we have to move on. The disciples must have known something about praying. But they wanted to know more and so they asked for help. Right at the heart of praying there is our Father God—far better than any human father. But we can learn something of what God is like by looking at how human fathers (and mothers) act towards their children. No human parent would give a child a snake instead of a fish. But what if the child asked for a snake, something that would damage it and harm it? Then the answer will be 'no', and the thing we long for won't be given to us. But something and someone far better, will be. We can ask for the Spirit—who is the living God himself. And day after day he will keep on coming to us, and keep on filling us with himself and the glory of his living presence. So ask—and know that to this request the answer is always 'Yes'.

SB

Our new clothes

You must no longer live as the Gentiles live... You were taught to put away your former way of life, your old self, corrupt and deluded by its lusts, and to be renewed in the spirit of your minds, and to clothe yourselves with the new self, created according to the likeness of God in true righteousness and holiness... Do not grieve the Holy Spirit of God, with which you were marked with a seal for the day of redemption. Put away from you all bitterness and wrath and anger and wrangling and slander, together with all malice, and be kind to one another, tender-hearted, forgiving one another, as God in Christ has forgiven you. Therefore be imitators of God, as beloved children, and live in love, as Christ loved us...

I have just bought a pale-pink safari jacket from Jigsaw—and when I wear it I feel great. It is new and pretty and people like it. My old safari jacket, which I loved, has worn out and had patches on it. I am sorry to see the end of it—but the time comes for buying new clothes, and they have a different feel to them from old clothes. The Bible uses different images to describe the Christian life and the Christian's relationship to God. Sometimes we are 'born again' into the family and sometimes adopted. And we are also to 'clothe' ourselves with the 'new self'.

My new pink jacket is lovely and clean at the moment and I want to keep it that way. So I don't keep it on to make the tomato sauce for my pasta—or even to eat the pasta in case it gets splashed. But if it does get a stain on it, I shall immediately sponge it clean with water. It is like that with our new self, and the stains that we make by our sinning. But when we sin we can take ourselves to the cleaners and be washed clean again in the blood of Christ. And then get on with living the new life, checking out our actions and aware that sin grieves the Holy Spirit who lives within us.

A reflection

See yourself clothed in your new self— and work out how to imitate God and live in love in every area of your life.

SB

The champagne of God

Be sure of this, that no fornicator or impure person, or one who is greedy (that is, an idolater), has any inheritance in the kingdom of Christ and of God. Let no one deceive you with empty words, for because of these things the wrath of God comes on those who are disobedient. Therefore do not be associated with them. For once you were darkness, but now in the Lord you are light. Live as children of light—for the fruit of the light is found in all that is good and right and true . . . Do not get drunk with wine, for that is debauchery; but be filled with the Spirit . . .

Perhaps the reason why the Bible isn't very popular reading these days is that people don't like what it says. Even Christians fornicate and commit adultery. Anything can be forgiven—if we *know* it needs to be. But these days, we hardly see sexual sins as sins at all. God doesn't want us to stop sinning in order to spoil our fun, but to make us really happy. After all, he invented sex—we didn't!

Chastity is tough—especially for anyone who has experienced a sexual relationship (or relationships). But it is possible, and the deprivation of it can drive us to God to find a satisfaction that is beyond all believing. Jesus called us to take up our cross daily and follow him— and this can be one of the ways to do it. The death and denial of our false self— and a flooding in of a new life that bubbles like champagne. So that we are not drunk with wine, but filled with the Spirit.

A way to pray

In silence, allow the Holy Spirit to show you your life as he sees it, in every area. Ask him to help you to repent, if you need to. Then ask him to fill you with his Spirit, and remember that on the day of Pentecost they thought that Peter and the rest of the disciples were drunk.

SB

The freedom of Christ

Be subject to one another out of reverence for Christ. Wives, be subject to your husbands as you are to the Lord. For the husband is the head of the wife just as Christ is the head of the church, the body of which he is the Saviour. Just as the church is subject to Christ, so also wives ought to be, in everything, to their husbands. Husbands, love your wives, just as Christ loved the church and gave himself up for her, in order to make her holy by cleansing her with the washing of water by the word . . . In the same way, husbands should love their wives as they do their own bodies. He who loves his wife loves himself. For no one ever hates his own body, but he nourishes and tenderly cares for it, just as Christ does for the church, because we are members of his body.

A woman I met who went to a seriously deluded house church was only allowed to read her Bible when her husband said that she could. That was what it meant (he said, and so did the other demented 'elders') for a wife to be subject to her husband. But it certainly isn't what the New Testament meant—and this (admittedly fairly tricky) passage starts off by saying to *everyone* 'be subject *to one another* out of reverence to Christ'.

In fact, the whole passage is a charter of liberation for women, because for a man in those days to love his wife as he loved his own body was really to turn his world upside down. In Jewish law a woman was a thing, not a person. She was her husband's possession and she had no legal rights at all. One of a Jew's daily prayers thanked God that he had not made him 'a Gentile, a slave or a woman'. A man could divorce his wife if she oversalted his supper or talked to a man in the street, and all he had to do was

to give her a bill of divorce properly written out by a Rabbi in the presence of two witnesses. In the Greek world and in Rome, matters were even worse—and Barclay writes that 'it is impossible to exaggerate the cleansing effect that Christianity had on home life in the ancient world and the benefits it brought to women'.

A way to pray

Reflect on what life used to be like—and be thankful for the change that Christ has brought.

SB

As if they were Jesus...

Children, obey your parents in the Lord, for this is right. 'Honour your father and mother'—this is the first commandment with a promise: 'so that it may be well with you and you may live long on the earth.' And, fathers, do not provoke your children to anger, but bring them up in the discipline and instruction of the Lord. Slaves, obey your earthly masters with fear and trembling, in singleness of heart, as you obey Christ; not only while being watched, and in order to please them, but as slaves of Christ, doing the will of God from the heart... And, masters, do the same to them.

In the ancient world they drowned children who were weak or deformed, and babies (nearly always girls) were exposed to die in the open country. The same thing is happening in our day—but not in Christian countries. The Christian faith has made a dramatic difference to children. Perhaps in our day the instruction to fathers might be a bit different. Perhaps it might be, 'Fathers, give time to your children—and listen to whatever it is they want to talk to you about.' In one family I know that always happens. The father and the mother have listened to their children ever since they could talk, and now that they are teenagers there is no communication problem between the generations.

So far as slaves go it is almost unbelievable to us that Paul should not have preempted William Wilberforce and fought against the slave trade. Instead, he offered the costly freedom of the second mile—which was to go twice as far and to give twice as much as they were compelled to do. There were probably 60 million slaves in the Roman world, and to those who became Christian Paul didn't say 'rebel'. He said act towards your boss as you would act towards Christ. But that can still go hand in hand with using all the political means at our disposal to fight against the terrible sin of slavery and of racial oppression. William Wilberforce did it, and so did Martin Luther King.

Reflect

We have a power, power that can't be found in Molotov cocktails, but we do have a power. Power that cannot be found in bullets and guns, but we have a power. It is a power as old as the insights of Jesus of Nazareth and as modern as the techniques of Mahatma Gandhi.

Martin Luther King, in William Sykes,
Visions of Love, BRF, page 272

SB

Be ready to fight

Finally, be strong in the Lord and in the strength of his power. Put on the whole armour of God, so that you may be able to stand against the wiles of the devil. For our struggle is not against enemies of blood and flesh, but against the rulers, against the authorities, against the cosmic powers of this present darkness, against the spiritual forces of evil in the heavenly places. Therefore take up the whole armour of God, so that you may be able to withstand on that evil day, and having done everything, to stand firm. Stand therefore, and fasten the belt of truth around your waist, and put on the breastplate of righteousness. As shoes for your feet put on whatever will make you ready to proclaim the gospel of peace. With all of these, take the shield of faith, with which you will be able to quench all the flaming arrows of the evil one. Take the helmet of salvation, and the sword of the Spirit, which is the word of God.

I think it was Gordon Stowell who drew a cartoon that stuck in my mind. A person was sitting on the floor looking like a child surrounded by his toys. But they weren't toys. They were the pieces of Christian armour—strewn around him, but not on him. An inset in the picture had a figure crying out 'Help!' 'Hold on,' said the caption, 'I'm coming.' But it could have been too late, because we have to wear our armour all the time.

It isn't fashionable these days to think of the Christian life as a battle but the Bible is quite clear that it is. We are fighting an evil power who has several names. One of them is Abaddon, the destroyer. To look at the destruction in our world now is to know that there is still a battle to be fought, against men who are filled with a spirit of evil instead of the Holy Spirit of love. There are only two sides in the battle—and we are on one of them. We may not be *filled* with the Spirit—but even half-filled we are on the right side. And men may not be *filled* with a spirit of evil. But even half-filled they are on the side of the destroyer.

A decision to make

Choose... this day whom you will serve.

Joshua 24:15 (NIV)

SB

Pray!

Pray in the Spirit at all times in every prayer and supplication. To that end keep alert and always persevere in supplication for all the saints. Pray also for me, so that when I speak, a message may be given to me to make known with boldness the mystery of the gospel, for which I am an ambassador in chains. Pray that I may declare it boldly, as I must speak.

Because God is with us and in us all the time, then we can pray all the time. We may not *feel* as if he is in us—but if we are Christians then he is. And we may not be filled with him—and in that case we need to set about being so, through the ordinary Christian disciplines of repentance, forgiveness and obedience. It is Love we are saying sorry to and obeying, and it is Love whom we are praying to. Love is with us and in us all the time. Love will help us to pray when we do not know what to pray for or even how to pray. In his letter to the Romans, Paul writes that '...the Spirit helps us in our weakness; for we do not know how to pray as we ought, but that very Spirit intercedes with sighs too deep for words' (Romans 8:26, NRSV).

The Spirit of God makes his home with us and in us—so we can be at home with God. I love to come home to my little house after I have been away. It seems to welcome me with open arms, and to be glad I am back again. I relax on my sofa and listen to music. I cook meals for myself and for my friends, and I do a lot of my work here. I go up to sleep in my attic bedroom at night and I wake up in the morning and look out of my window and delight in the view. Then I go down to make my morning tea, and bring it back to bed again to have my special time with God, when I tell him what I am feeling and thinking. I read the Bible, and I pray. But when I leave home I don't leave God behind—because wherever I go he comes too. We are at home in God and God is at home in us, and because of that we can pray at all times.

Paul's final prayer and blessing

Peace be to the whole community, and love with faith, from God the Father and the Lord Jesus Christ. Grace be with all who have an undying love for our Lord Jesus Christ.

Ephesians 6:23−24 (NRSV)

SB

Speak out

Scripture says, 'I believed, and therefore I spoke out', and we too, in the same spirit of faith, believe and therefore speak out; for we know that he who raised the Lord Jesus to life will with Jesus raise us too, and bring us to his presence, and you with us. Indeed, it is for your sake that all things are ordered, so that, as the abounding grace of God is shared by more and more, the greater may be the chorus of thanksgiving that ascends to the glory of God.

Believe, yes, that's all right. But speak out? That sounds like the embarrassing business of evangelism, or witnessing, or whatever we call it. It's something that many shy away from, out of fear or false humility. Yet for Paul, belief and proclamation were two sides of the same coin. There could be no secret, personal and private religion. There was only the response to God's call: a call to salvation and to mission.

Part of the problem is the way we separate our worship, prayer and devotion from our witness. Perhaps that can work when we are on our own, but never when we are in public. The way we live our lives, the extent to which our behaviour is shaped by our awareness of God, our relations with others by his love, and our conversation by his understanding—are all testimony to the faith we have.

Even more than that, our worship is a proclamation of the faith. In 1 Corinthians 11, Paul wrote that each celebration of Holy Communion is a proclamation of the Lord's death. At the very least, this means that the fact of our church worship is a statement to the world at large of the importance to us of God.

And the public celebration of the Eucharist is even more than that. It is saying that at the heart of our faith and worship is the death and resurrection of Jesus.

There's no getting away from it. To believe is to speak out, in one way or another.

MM

Her way to pray . . .

While Hannah went on praying to Yahweh, Eli was watching her mouth, for Hannah was speaking under her breath; her lips were moving but her voice could not be heard, and Eli thought she was drunk. Eli said, 'How much longer are you going to stay drunk? Get rid of your wine.' 'No, my lord,' Hannah replied, 'I am a woman in great trouble; I have not been drinking wine or strong drink—I am pouring out my soul before Yahweh.' . . . Eli then said, 'Go in peace, and may the God of Israel grant what you have asked of him.'

If one cannot pour out one's heart to the Lord without being scolded by the clergy, where can one go? Poor Hannah was pouring out her sadness at being childless, despite the special devotion and attentiveness of her husband. Just as silent reading was unknown for many centuries (St Augustine was astounded to see St Ambrose reading and to hear no sound), so prayer was normally loud and vocal. Even today there is a great variety of prayer and to despise any of it is perilous. At one time I may wish to sing for joy to the Lord, at another to creep under a rock and hide in the shelter of his wings. At one time to howl to him for grief, at another to purr gently at the warmth of his fire.

Hannah's instinct was to hide in the Lord and share with him her grief at her barrenness. To cap her sorrow she has to bear the rebuke of the Lord's spokesman, Eli. Not only is she barren; she is also misunderstood and falsely accused—and that in God's name. Such an official false accusation, allowing no redress, is among the hardest misunderstandings to bear. (And how often are clergy guilty of unfair judgments!) So her prayer and devotion have to be tested and proved. If prayer is a real adherence to God, it can put up with trials.

Prayer does not consist in the words; it is an affair of the heart. At times the words of a prayer can be false and hypocritical. Or else the words can be meaningless, like the cooings of love, an inadequate expression of cleaving to the Lord and to him alone.

Prayer

Lord, thou has created us for thyself, and our heart is restless till it rest in thee.

HW

A prayer of praise

Elkanah lay with his wife Hannah, and Yahweh remembered her. Hannah conceived and, in due course, gave birth to a son, whom she named Samuel . . . Hannah then prayed as follows:
My heart exalts in Yahweh, in my God is my strength lifted up,
my mouth derides my foes, for I rejoice in your deliverance . . .
He raises the poor from the dust, he lifts the needy from the dunghill.

Hannah's prayer after the birth of her son Samuel is reminiscent of the Magnificat of Mary after the conception of hers, when she went to visit her cousin Elizabeth. Each recognizes that all success, strength and riches come from God the Creator. Human efforts can get nowhere without God's blessing.

The theme that God's special favour rests on the poor becomes stronger and stronger in the prophets, as Israel's position becomes more and more wretched. The poor and underprivileged are the special friends of God, for their poverty drives them to recognize their dependence on him. One might say that the whole of Old Testament history was designed to teach Israel its utter dependence on God, rather than reliance on any human efforts or achievement. After all, it was only when Israel was persecuted almost to annihilation in Egypt that God intervened to rescue them and make them his people. Centuries later, it was only when they were exiled in Babylon that they returned to the original spirit of faithfulness to God. It was only when they were becoming more and more wretched under the Roman domination that Mary conceived the Son who was to deliver Israel.

But is it not too strong a contradiction in terms that wretchedness is a blessing? Not all beggars are saints. It needs the open heart of faith to turn to God in helplessness. Then we can learn by suffering and misfortune. Anyone who has really suffered bereavement or misfortune knows that to turn to God in helpless confidence brings a profound peace and enrichment.

On a human level the poor and unfortunate call forth our Christian instinct to take our share in God's work of care and concern. If the human being is nearest to God as the crown of creation, every person must share in God's creative forgiveness and mercy.

Prayer

My soul proclaims the greatness of the Lord, and my spirit rejoices in God my saviour.

HW

The prayer of quiet

Now the boy Samuel was serving Yahweh in the presence of Eli . . . The lamp of God had not yet gone out, and Samuel was lying in Yahweh's sanctuary, where the ark of God was, when Yahweh called, 'Samuel, Samuel!' He answered, 'Here I am,' and running to Eli, he said, 'Here I am, as you called me.' Eli said, 'I did not call. Go back and lie down.' So he went back and lay down. And again Yahweh called, 'Samuel, Samuel!' He got up and went to Eli and said, 'Here I am, as you called me.' He replied, 'I did not call, my son; go back and lie down.' [And so a third time] . . . Eli then understood that Yahweh was calling the child, and he said to Samuel, 'Go and lie down, and if someone calls say, "Speak, Yahweh; for your servant is listening."'

This passage, the first call of the Lord to his prophet Samuel, gives an unforgettable picture of the prayer of quiet. The clue to the understanding and love of it is the Hebrew name, which sounds like the soft soughing of the air: *Shmu-el, Shmu-el*. In the little valley of Shiloh, in the evening breeze of the shrine, was it the wind or the voice of the Lord, or the distant calling of Eli? As he dozed off and woke up, the lad would not know what he had heard. The voice of the Lord is not always clear. It demands calm, patience and careful listening. It is only too easy to imagine it in what we expect to hear, and especially in what we want to hear. More often than not, it tells us what we do not want to hear: there is no point in God intervening merely to echo our own desires, and plenty of point in God correcting and guiding them. God's message is often hard to swallow, and we need to be told it several times.

Samuel, already dedicated to the Lord in the sanctuary, showed himself alert to the Lord, sensitive, obedient (he got out of bed three times, one after another, and never once complained!) and open-minded.

Prayer

Speak, Lord, for your servant is listening!

HW

Losing the Presence

It happened at that time that the Philistines mustered to make war on Israel and Israel went out to meet them in war . . . When the ark of Yahweh arrived in the camp, all Israel raised a great war cry so that the earth resounded . . . And [the Philistines] realised that the ark of Yahweh had come into the camp. At this the Philistines were afraid; for they said, 'God has come into the camp . . . Disaster! Who will rescue us from the clutches of this mighty God? . . . But take courage . . . ' So the Philistines gave battle and Israel was defeated, each man fleeing to his tent. The slaughter was very great . . . The ark of God was captured too.

The Philistines (from whom Palestine gets its name) lived on the fertile coastal plain (the home today of Jaffa oranges). They introduced into the country iron, the metal of weapons, gradually expanding inland into the hill-country held by the Israelites. Israel tried in vain to check their advance.

The religious historians who gave us the biblical accounts of the period see the defeat of their nation as the judgment of God on the moral decline of the people. The ark was the symbol of God's presence with his people, and of his protection among them. It contained the most sacred symbols of God's love for them, the reminders of the Covenant he had made with them on Sinai. It had accompanied the people through the desert in their journeyings for forty years. Now they used it as a sort of talisman to guarantee them his protection.

The modern comparison is the use of the trappings of religion to cover a real lack of devotion or of moral seriousness. Churchgoing without real prayer or concern for others can so easily become hypocritical without our noticing it. For the Israelites the disaster of the battle was the loss of God's presence in the form of the ark. Worse than the casualties, it showed them that God was no longer with them. The child born to the wife of Phinehas just after the defeat was named 'Ichabod', which means 'Where is the Glory?', for the glory of God had left them, leaving them deserted and unprotected. It was the inevitable result of their lifestyle, forcing them to face up to the facts.

Reflect

What I want is love, not sacrifice.

Hosea 6:6

HW

The power of the Presence

Taking the ark of God . . . the Philistines put it in the temple of Dagon . . . When the people of Ashdod got up the following morning and went to the temple of Dagon, there lay Dagon face down on the ground before the ark of Yahweh . . . Dagon's head and two hands lay severed on the threshhold . . . Yahweh oppressed the people of Ashdod; he ravaged them and afflicted them with tumours . . . When the people of Ashdod saw what was happening they said, 'The ark of the God of Israel must not stay here with us, for he is oppressing us and our god Dagon.' . . . They then sent the ark of God to Ekron, but . . . the Ekronites shouted, 'They have brought me the ark of the God of Israel to kill me and my people!' They summoned all the Philistine chiefs and said, 'Send the ark of the God of Israel away; let it go back to where it belongs and not kill me and my people.'

This little story shows the awesome power of God. It also has a touch of humour, for the tumours they suffered are usually interpreted as the laughable and humiliating disease of piles! Further, it reinforces the lesson of the defeat of the Israelites in battle: this was not because their God lacked the power to protect them. He was incomparably more powerful than the chief god of the Philistines, who literally could not stand beside him. The defeat was not the fault of God's inability to protect his people; it must be that they had forfeited their right to his patronage. If they were unfaithful to him, he could not protect them. But the reaction of the Philistines is a recognition of where he really belongs, that is, protecting his own people.

The presence of God is not always comforting; it can also be threatening and frightening. If I refuse to recognize God for what he really is, I put myself at serious risk and lay myself open to the destructive power of God. So the prophets later will teach that God is a consuming fire, purging and purifying away the unworthiness and filth even of his own people, so that they eventually come before him worthy to behold him.

Reflect

It is not anyone who says to me, 'Lord, Lord,' who will enter the kingdom of Heaven, but the person who does the will of my Father in heaven.

Matthew 7:21 (NJB)

HW

Yahweh is king!

Samuel was judge over Israel throughout his life . . . When Samuel grew old, he appointed his sons as judges of Israel . . . His sons did not follow his example, but, seduced by love of money, took bribes and gave biased verdicts. The elders of Israel all assembled, went back to Samuel . . . and said, 'Look, you are old, and your sons are not following your example. Give us a king to judge us, like the other nations.' Samuel thought it was wrong of them to say, 'Let us have a king to judge us,' so he prayed to Yahweh. But Yahweh said to Samuel, 'Obey the voice of the people in all that they say to you; it is not you they have rejected, but me, not wishing me to reign over them any more.'

The difference between Israel and other nations was that the Lord and no one else was king of Israel. 'King' is perhaps the most frequent of all God's titles in the Bible, and he is acclaimed as such throughout the Psalms, the prayer-book of Israel. In moments of high exaltation he is declared king, 'Now he reigns!' So it was an act of betrayal to say that they needed another king, a mere mortal, as though God was insufficient. In fact the purpose of the Covenant was to make Israel a special people, uniquely close to God, enfolded in his love.

Samuel perceived this betrayal and was duly outraged. But God does not force loyalty from his subjects. He gives us our free will and allows us to exercise it. So Israel are allowed to put their trust in a mortal king, and to become—to that extent—like other, ordinary nations. Samuel merely lays out the evils they will suffer for submitting themselves to a king instead of remaining directly subject to God.

The scene is reminiscent of another scene in which God's kingship over Israel is denied, perhaps the most spine-chilling of all the scenes of the Passion of Christ. In the Gospel of John, as Jesus stands before Pilate, Pilate offers Jesus to the Jewish authorities as their king. They reject the offer with the awful words, 'We have no king but Caesar.' With that the special relationship with God as king of Israel is officially denied. They make themselves into one little nation, just like any other.

Prayer

Yahweh is king! Let earth rejoice.

Psalm 97:1 (NJB)

HW

A sabbath prayer

Since you have been raised up with Christ, you must look for the things that are above, where Christ is, sitting at God's right hand. Let your thoughts be on the things that are above, not on the things that are on earth—because you have died, and now the life you have is hidden with Christ in God.

Lord Jesus, your people, the Jews, keep the Sabbath, a new invention for the world. It was only with Judaism that the weekend began! The moon's month of 28 days was divided into four so that each quarter could have one day set aside for the praise of your Father, the Creator. So began that blessed day of rest and recuperation. It was not a day for football matches, horse-races, recovering from Friday night's hangover. Originally it was a day for praising your Father.

It meant not only thanking him for creating all things, which reach their completion in you, the first-born and head of all creation, but also sharing in his creative power. We are his representatives in creation, sharing his creative power, not only by the awesome work of sex and procreation (that is shared by crocodiles and rabbits too), but by shaping the creation that exists. You gave us the incomparable power of mind to make advances in medicine, to form communities which care, to develop nuclear power with all its promise and menace.

The Sabbath became a day of rejoicing, celebration, dancing, as it still is in Judaism today, a day for the family to celebrate the ongoing creation and all the talents and achievements which you have set in your creation. I thank you that you made me what I am, that you implanted in me the talents that I have, the humour, the qualities that make me lovable and give me value. I thank you even for the faults and the weaknesses, which draw me to you ever and again in sorrow and repentance.

But Saturday, the Sabbath of the Jews, is, for your Christian children, only the stepping-stone to Sunday, the Day of the Lord and the day of resurrection. This brought creation to completion when you rose from the dead to a new and fuller life, the life we share with you.

We believe that if we died with Christ we shall live with him too.

HW

God's choice

Now since the donkeys belonging to Kish, Saul's father, had strayed, Kish said to his son Saul, 'My son, take one of the servants with you and be off; go and look for the donkeys.' ... When Samuel saw Saul, Yahweh told him, 'That is the man of whom I said to you, "He is to govern my people."' Saul accosted Samuel in the gateway and said, 'Tell me, please, where the seer's house is.' Samuel replied to Saul, 'I am the seer ... You must eat with me today ... As regards your donkeys, however ... do not worry about them; they have been found. And for whom is the whole wealth of Israel destined, if not for you and for all the members of your father's family?' To this Saul replied, 'Am I not a Benjaminite, from the smallest of the tribes of Israel? And is not my family the least of all the families of the tribe of Benjamin?'

When something very special is to happen in the Bible this is sometimes indicated by such an interlocking search as here: Saul comes looking for Samuel, and Samuel is guided to Saul by the Lord. In the same way in the Acts of the Apostles the representatives of the centurion Cornelius come looking for Peter, and Peter has a vision that they are on the way. Or in the conversion of another Saul, the apostle Paul, Ananias is guided to Saul and Saul in prayer has a vision of Ananias coming to him. So this is a way of showing the special significance of this moment in the development of the history of God's people.

Throughout the Bible we come across the process of God choosing the naturally less favoured candidate, often the younger brother. So Jacob is chosen over Esau, and soon David will be chosen, so much the youngest of the brothers that he is quite forgotten by the rest of the family. Admittedly, earlier in the story we are told that Saul was 'a handsome man in the prime of life. Of all the Israelites there was no one more handsome than he; he stood head and shoulders taller than anyone else.' Saul is perhaps being modest about himself. But the principle is that God chooses whom he will, not having any regard for human achievement or merit.

Reflect

*He has pulled down princes
from their thrones and raised
high the lowly.*

The Magnificat

HW

The strange Spirit

Samuel took a phial of oil and poured it on Saul's head; he then kissed him and said, 'Has not Yahweh anointed you as leader of his people Israel? You are the man who is to govern the Yahweh's people and save them from the power of the enemies surrounding them.' . . . As soon as he turned his back to leave Samuel, God changed his heart . . . There was a group of prophets coming to meet him! The spirit of God seized on him and he fell into ecstasy with them. Seeing him prophesying with the prophets, all the people who had known him previously said to one another, 'What has come over the son of Kish? Is Saul one of the prophets too?'

This incident seems to be a rather primitive and basic sign of God's power coming upon Saul as a result of his royal anointing. When God calls someone to an office he also gives the power to fulfil it. Although it seems an odd way to show the royal power, this is the basic sign that Saul is no longer on his own, but has some power more than natural—and even eerie and unpredictable. On another occasion Saul is said to have joined the company of prophets in their frenzy, stripped off his clothes, and then collapsed naked on the ground for a day and a night. Kingship has always been an awesome thing, surrounded with an aura which is not quite human (English kings were credited with the almost miraculous power of curing 'the King's Evil'). Even today, in these days of constitutional monarchy, kingship does still carry an awesome responsibility towards the community, and demand a special charism—and special prayers from their subjects.

In the early days of Israel's monarchy these companies of prophets appear in the Bible from time to time, often with such dervish-like behaviour. But it is not clear what else they did, or what their function was. Was it simply to remind people that there are powers beyond those we can understand and control? Perhaps it was like the 'speaking in tongues' described by Paul's letter to the Corinthians, which also occurs nowadays in some gatherings for worship. Someone seems to be taken over by the Spirit and drawn to praise God in language beyond normal human expressions.

Prayer

Praise Yahweh, my soul!
I will praise Yahweh all my life.

Psalm 146:1–2 (NJB)

HW

A strange act of Love

Samuel said to Saul, 'I am the man whom Yahweh sent to anoint you as king of his people Israel, so now listen to the words of Yahweh: "I intend to punish what Amalek did to Israel—laying a trap for him on the way as he was coming up from Egypt. Now, go and crush Amalek; put him under the curse of destruction ... Do not spare him, but kill man and woman, babe and suckling, ox and sheep, camel and donkey."' Saul then crushed the Amalekites ... He took Agag king of the Amalekites alive and, executing the curse of destruction, put all the people to the sword.

The curse of destruction was part of Israel's Holy War. It was commanded also in Joshua's time, when Israel first came into the Promised Land and waged war on the earlier inhabitants, winning territory from them. Theologians have toiled to explain this un-Christian blood-thirsty act: how can a merciful God, who loves all his creatures, give such a destructive command?

There are, however, two positive aspects to it: first, the purpose of it is to prevent any mixing between Israel and its pagan neighbours. This shows the importance of the purity of the religion of Israel; it must not be contaminated by its neighbours. Indeed, it is extraordinary, and a real proof of God's care, that this one faith survived through all the upsets and distractions of history. No other faith survived. The Babylonian religions disappeared, the Egyptian religion collapsed, the Greek gods were discredited. In this we can only see the hand of God.

The other positive aspect is that we must give credit to the gradual advance and education of Israel under God's guidance. To start with, they were a primitive people, with ideas which seem to us primitive and barbaric. They had a lot to learn, and the process of learning was itself a mark of God's love. Even today we too have a lot to learn and need to remain alert to God's tuition.

Prayer

Blessed are you, Yahweh,
teach me your will ...
... the wonders of your law.

Psalm 119:12, 18 (NJB)

HW

A disobedient king

The word of Yahweh came to Samuel, 'I regret having made Saul king, since he has broken his allegiance to me and not carried out my orders.' Samuel was appalled and cried to Yahweh all night long. In the morning, Samuel set off to find Saul . . . Saul then said to Samuel, 'I have sinned, having broken Yahweh's order and your instructions because I was afraid of the people and yielded to their demands. Now, please forgive my sin and come back with me, so that I can worship Yahweh.' . . . As Samuel turned away to leave, Saul caught at the hem of his cloak and it tore, and Samuel said to him, 'Today Yahweh has torn the kingdom of Israel from you and given it to a neighbour of yours who is better than you.'

The rejection of Saul is one of the puzzles of the Old Testament. Two faults of Saul are mentioned, first that he did not wait for Samuel to perform a sacrifice at the start of a campaign. Instead, when Samuel was seriously late, and the army was beginning to slip away, he performed it himself. The second fault relates to yesterday's passage, when Saul did not destroy all the booty and prisoners from a campaign (Samuel himself proceeded to butcher the captured King Agag 'before the Lord').

Some scholars think that we have not been told the full story. The fact is, they argue, that all the stories have been filtered through the propaganda-machine of David, who took Saul's place. And Saul's repentance and plea for forgiveness do seem to be heartfelt and sincere. In fact Saul was not such a bad or unfaithful king at all, but simply did not 'control the media'; it was only the bad press that survived.

But Saul was important in Israel's history, since he repulsed the Philistines, who might otherwise have engulfed and swallowed up Israel. He also laid the foundations of the monarchy. He himself had no court organization or bureaucracy, and the remains of his palace (or rather little fortress) which have been excavated are extremely modest. But on these foundations David built his empire and became the ideal of kingship in Israel, the model for the future King Messiah.

Reflect

Samuel said: Is Yahweh pleased by burnt offerings and sacrifices or by obedience to Yahweh's voice?

1 Samuel 15:22 (NJB)

HW

A depressed king

Now the spirit of Yahweh had withdrawn from Saul, and an evil spirit from Yahweh afflicted him with terrors. Saul's servants said to him, '... Let ... your servants ... look for a skilled harpist; when the evil spirit from God comes over you, he will play and it will do you good.' ... One of the servants then spoke up and said, 'I have seen one of the sons of Jesse the Bethlehemite: he is a skilled player, a brave man and a fighter, well spoken, good-looking and Yahweh is with him.' ... David went to Saul and entered his service; Saul became very fond of him and David became his armour-bearer ... And whenever the spirit from God came over Saul, David would take a harp and play; Saul would be soothed; it would do him good, and the evil spirit would leave him.

The evil spirit is said to come from the Lord, just as the good spirit did. This is surprising, but perhaps it is because the Israelites considered God to be the direct cause of everything; there was no question of God merely allowing something to happen. In any case, Saul was certainly subject to moods of deep depression—and homicidal depression, since we hear later that he tried to pin David to the wall with his spear. Linked with the sense of his own failure was jealousy of David's rising fortunes, which no doubt deepened his depression.

One school of thought believes that David was a pert young schemer who deliberately set out to win the crown from Saul, unscrupulously building up his own power-base. Saul saw this going on and was powerless to prevent it, which only depressed him further.

We all fail sometimes, and this is often a bitter blow, sending us into the same sort of mood as Saul. Everything seems black. On these occasions it is essential to realize that there is no necessary connection between failure and loss of God's love. God can love us and value us precisely because we fail. Humanly speaking, Jesus himself was a failure, and went to his death as such. What remained of the glorious kingdom he was to found? No ardent crowds of Galilean supporters. Only eleven picked cowards, who had fled at the first sign of trouble. Jesus had only confidence in his Father to sustain him.

Prayer

Into your hands, O Lord, I commend my spirit.

HW

A desperate king

Now Samuel was dead . . . Saul had expelled the necromancers and wizards from the country. Meanwhile the Philistines had mustered and had come and pitched camp at Shunem . . . When Saul saw the Philistine camp, he was afraid and his heart trembled violently. Saul consulted Yahweh, but Yahweh gave him no answer . . . Saul then said to his servants, 'Find a necromancer for me, so that I can go and consult her.' . . . Saul, disguising himself . . . set out . . . their visit to the woman took place at night . . . The woman asked, 'Whom shall I conjure up for you?' He replied, 'Conjure up Samuel.' The woman then saw Samuel and, giving a great cry, she said to Saul, 'Why have you deceived me? You are Saul!' . . . Samuel said to Saul, 'Why have you disturbed my rest . . . ? Tomorrow you and your sons will be with me; and Yahweh will hand over the army of Israel into the power of the Philistines.'

Saul had purged superstitious practices from the land, and then shows his hopelessness by turning to just such a practice as he has outlawed. It is hard not to have some sympathy for him in his desperate state.

Was Samuel a ghost? Do ghosts exist? Can they speak? Are they channels for messages from God? This eerie story is not meant to give an answer to such questions. Christians have many different answers to such questions, and (I think) there is no sure teaching on the subject, to which all Christians must adhere. This ghost story shows the depths to which Saul has sunk, and the divinely-fated consequences for Israel.

The tragic end of Saul puts Israel back at square one with regard to the Philistines. Saul is defeated and killed on the Mountains of Gilboa, in the very heartland of Israel; they must have taken over the whole of the rich, fertile plain of Jezreel. To succeed him there remains only his incompetent son in the north, and in the south the ambitious David. Israel is again without a human leader, and utterly dependent on God. Things can only improve.

A lament

*You mountains of Gilboa,
no dew, no rain fall on you,
O treacherous fields
where the heroes' shield lies dishonoured!*

David's lament over Saul and Jonathan
2 Samuel 1:21 (NJB)

HW

A letter & a love story

There are a lot of letters in the New Testament—and the two to Timothy and the one to Titus are known as the Pastoral Epistles. From the Apostle Paul, they tell how the two men are to minister to their congregations and give them the right sort of pastoral care. Rosemary Green tells us about the letter to Titus, and shows how relevant the letter is to us.

The love story of Hosea shows us the love and the suffering of God. Some people don't like this book, because of its bluntness and frankness about sexual matters. But God is always blunt—and always loving—and through the sheer awfulness of Gomer's immorality and unfaithfulness, and the astonishing love and faithfulness of Hosea, we can see the amazing grace and the wonderful love of God. Through Hosea's broken heart we can see into the broken heart of God—and make the right connection between our sin and the suffering of God.

A prayer for the day of life

You cannot have forgotten that all of us, when we were baptised into Christ Jesus, were baptised into his death. So by our baptism into his death we were buried with him, so that as Christ was raised from the dead by the Father's glorious power, we too should begin living a new life.

Oh yes, Lord, I don't need reminding that I was baptized into your death! I am only too aware of the death that lurks in me, bursting out everywhere at unexpected times to putrify something beautiful, to spoil a relationship, to nullify an achievement. But I do need reminding that we should begin living a new life. Elsewhere, in the letter to the Ephesians, your inspired mouthpiece stresses that our resurrection with you is in the future: But when Christ is revealed—and he is your life—you, too, will be revealed with him in glory. But already we can and should begin living a new life. We can make a start.

Each week, Lord, each seventh day, you remind us of that new and risen life. The Jews had the Sabbath, and we Christians build on this. They celebrate creation; we celebrate the new creation. The Sabbath is the day of God's creation; Sunday is the day when you completed creation by rising to a new life, the fulness of life.

For us, baptism marks the beginning of that life, a tiny pledge and promise which dedicated us to new life in you. From ancient times a Christian baptistery had eight sides, to remind us of the eighth day of the week (the day after the Sabbath) when you rose from the dead. The font has eight sides to remind us also of that life you give us in baptism.

So Sunday is the day of life. Even in our pagan, post-Christian society you remind me of that by leisure, families at leisure enjoying life, children at play, released from chores, grandparents visiting the continuance of their life in the grandchildren. This ebullient, bubbling life, Lord, breaking out all around on Sunday, is the image and reflection of the greater life you have in store for us. What we see is still the life to which you died, a pale ghost of a life compared to the joy and strength in store for us in your risen life.

When Christ is revealed—and he is your life...

HW

Titus—who was he?

Before we read this letter, a New Testament jigsaw puzzle will help us to discover something about Titus himself! Although not mentioned by name in Acts he was clearly one of Paul's most trusted and loved companions; 'my true son in our common faith', 'my partner and fellow-worker', 'my brother Titus'. Titus shared Paul's concerns, his enthusiasm and his initiative (2 Corinthians 2:13; 7:6; 8:16, 17, 23).

Early in his Christian life Titus found himself at the heart of a key controversial issue: could Gentiles really be Christians without being circumcised? He was a Greek from Antioch, the first place where the gospel was shared with Gentiles as well as with Jews and proselytes (Gentile converts to Judaism). Eyebrows were raised at H.Q. in Jerusalem and Barnabas was sent to check up; he endorsed what he found and went to fetch Paul to help him teach the church. But later the argument was stirred up by men from Judea who taught: 'Unless you are circumcised according to the custom taught by Moses, you cannot be saved.' After a sharp dispute, Titus went with Paul and Barnabas and other believers to report to the leaders in Jerusalem, who decided that circumcision was not, after all, necessary (Acts 11:20; 15:1–2; Galatians 2:1, 3).

Titus' early lessons about disagreements between Christians was good training for his later ministry. When there were difficulties with the church at Corinth it was Titus who went there several times: to oversee a collection scheme, to take a tough letter, to smooth over tension between Paul and the church. When the infant church in Crete needed help to put it on its feet, Titus was again the person for the job. Paul wrote to him to give encouragement for this task.

So read these words from Paul in 1 Thessalonians 5:12–15. Reflect on our attitudes to our leaders and on the way we deal with arguments in the church.

Reflect

Now we ask you, brothers, to respect those who work hard among you, who are over you in the Lord and who admonish you. Hold them in the highest regard in love because of their work. Live in peace with each other. And we urge you, brothers, warn those who are idle, encourage the timid, help the weak, be patient with everyone. Make sure that nobody pays back wrong for wrong, but always try to be kind to each other and to everyone else.

RG

Man with a mission

Paul, a servant of God and an apostle of Jesus Christ for the faith of God's elect and the knowledge of the truth that leads to godliness—a faith and knowledge resting on the hope of eternal life, which God, who does not lie, promised before the beginning of time, and at his appointed season he brought his word to light through the preaching entrusted to me by the command of God our Saviour, To Titus, my true son in our common faith: Grace and peace from God the Father and Jesus Christ our Saviour.

Paul does write some long sentences! Though confusing at first, this opening paragraph of his letter is worth dissecting, to discover what he is saying about God and about himself and God's purposes for him.

About God. The first thing that strikes me is 'God, who does not lie'. We often do not understand what God says or why he acts as he does (or at times appears to be inactive.) But *he does not lie*; he is utterly trustworthy; he makes no mistakes. And he is eternal. Paul looks at the God who was 'before the beginning of time' and who gives an assurance of eternal life for the future. He is beyond time, yet also one who 'at his appointed time' intervened in history and 'brought his word to light'. The word—God's character disclosed to us both in the person of Jesus Christ ('the Word became flesh', John 1:14) and in the written word of Scripture—is then passed on through the preaching of people like Paul.

About himself. Paul was a man with a mission, 'a servant of God and an apostle of Jesus Christ'. He had a clear mandate to preach ('the preaching entrusted to me by the command of God our Saviour') and there was nothing he loved more than to be out and about speaking about his Saviour and encouraging God's people in the faith that makes a difference to the way we live now ('truth that leads to godliness') and to our assurance for the future. In the Bible, 'hope' is not a wishy-washy word of vague uncertainty but a strong word of confidence about the future.

A question to ponder

What is the mission that God has entrusted to you?

RG

Leadership qualities

The reason I left you in Crete was that you might straighten out what was left unfinished and appoint elders in every town, as I directed you. An elder must be blameless, the husband of but one wife, a man whose children believe and are not open to the charge of being wild and disobedient. Since an overseer is entrusted with God's work, he must be blameless— not overbearing, not quick-tempered, not given to drunkenness, not violent, not pursuing dishonest gain. Rather he must be hospitable, one who loves what is good, who is self-controlled, upright, holy and disciplined. He must hold firmly to the trustworthy message as it has been taught, so that he can encourage others by sound doctrine and refute those who oppose it.

Titus' first priority in Crete was to appoint leaders in all the churches. So Paul gives some clear guidelines for the qualities of character to look for in choosing Christian leaders, whether for full-time ordained ministry or for part-time lay leadership. He wants a person who is faithful in marriage, whose children demonstrate that they have enjoyed a wise, loving and disciplined upbringing, whose home is welcoming. Hospitality can be warm and relaxed without being lavish. I have a picture of a person who is equable in temperament and relaxed but firm with subordinates; someone who is even-tempered and temperate with alcohol. Honesty must replace greed, self-control must replace violence. 'Blameless' is Paul's overall adjective—one at whom others cannot lay any charges of immorality. 'Total integrity' is the phrase I would use. Would that our modern leaders, in church, business or politics, stuck to the same standards!

Paul is concerned too for the leader's solidity of faith and belief. I fear he turns in his grave over some modern preaching which has strayed far from Paul's biblical teaching and which undermines the faith of many ordinary people! Apologetics is an unfashionable and maybe a frightening word. It means the ability to give a reason for what we believe. In these days of much confused thinking about our faith we would do well to learn more clearly what we believe, and why; then we will be more secure ourselves and better able to explain to those who are ignorant or argumentative.

RG

Nuisance-makers

For there are many rebellious people, mere talkers and deceivers, especially those of the circumcision group. They must be silenced, because they are ruining whole households by teaching things they ought not to teach—and that for the sake of dishonest gain. Even one of their own prophets has said, 'Cretans are always liars, evil brutes, lazy gluttons.' This testimony is true. Therefore, rebuke them sharply, so that they will be sound in the faith and will pay no attention to Jewish myths or to the commands of those who reject the truth. To the pure, all things are pure, but to those who are corrupted and do not believe, nothing is pure. In fact, both their minds and consciences are corrupted. They claim to know God, but by their actions they deny him. They are detestable, disobedient and unfit for anything good.

Weaknesses in character, in behaviour, in attitudes; these are Paul's targets. He was not prejudiced against either the Cretans or the Jews; he frequently emphasized God's love for all people and his offer of salvation for all. It certainly is easy to fall into the trap of racial prejudice. 'All Australians are… All Chinese are…' while each of us wants to be an exception to other people's expectations of 'All Brits are reserved' (or whatever unflattering trait is associated with your own nation). That was not Paul's problem. But he had seen some group characteristics that he did not like and feared that corruption might spread like gangrene. So what were his concerns?

The 'circumcision group' held inflexible views that even Christians of non-Jewish backgrounds should follow all the rules of the Jewish Law. This debate had dogged the Church since the gospel first spread beyond the adherents to Judaism; in fact, we see it when Jesus challenged the Pharisees. But Paul, despite his background as a Pharisee, always advocated the freedom of obedience to Christ without submission to legalism. The parallel question for us to ask is whether our church customs are truly Christian or merely conventions of culture which inhibit our spiritual growth and become barriers to non-churchgoers discovering Jesus.

The inhabitants of Crete—where Titus was working—had a long-standing reputation for dishonesty and laziness. This behaviour had to be challenged, for a claim to know God must not be merely skin deep but should show the evidence of holy behaviour and godly attitudes.

RG

Teach and train

You must teach what is in accord with sound doctrine. Teach the older men to be temperate, worthy of respect, self-controlled, and sound in faith, in love and in endurance. Likewise, teach the older women to be reverent in the way they live, not to be slanderers or addicted to much wine, but to teach what is good. Then they can train the younger women to love their husbands and children, to be self-controlled and pure, to be busy at home, to be kind, and to be subject to their husbands, so that no-one will malign the word of God.

Paul has a great sense of order. On Wednesday we read about the selection of church leaders. Yesterday's verses were a warning against those whose teaching and lives disrupted church life. Today he moves forward again in the pattern of 'teach, train, build'. Teach the more mature people about holy living so that they may be able to encourage the younger ones to follow their example.

'Teach what is in accord with sound doctrine.' What we believe should work through into the way we live and the sort of people we are. But beware! It is possible to have an orthodox, biblical creed but still to have blind spots on the issues of life. The injustice of apartheid was fostered by the Bible-believing Dutch Reformed Church. Much closer to home, I have at times turned a deaf ear to God. When he made it quite clear to me that a particular friendship needed a major reform, I made excuses to him. The result of my disobedience was almost catastrophic, and it was only a forgiving, redeeming God who could turn it to good and give me an emotional spring-clean for which I am deeply grateful.

So look at the qualities of character Paul is encouraging for both old and young. He looks for us to be self-controlled and worth respecting; strong in faith, love and endurance; neither gossipers nor alcoholics; sexually pure, efficient in the home, loving in our relationships. We might even work through the list and assess ourselves on a scale of 1 to 10 before we pray!

A prayer

Lord, please help me to be open to change, so that even my weak spots may be transformed and that I may grow more like Jesus.

RG

The old and the new

Similarly, encourage the young men to be self-controlled. In everything set them a good example by doing what is good. In your teaching show integrity, seriousness and soundness of speech that cannot be condemned, so that those who oppose you may be ashamed because they have nothing bad to say about us. Teach slaves to be subject to their masters in everything, to try to please them, not to talk back to them, but to show that they can be fully trusted, so that in every way they will make the teaching about God our Saviour attractive.

Modern Western society has thrown into disarray the old order of relationships between old and young, men and women, employers and employees. Modern society in the East holds to more traditional values of respect for the old, of 'the woman's place is in the home', of the servile position of the employee. Yet even Eastern cultures are being disturbed by currents of change from the West. So are Paul's words just for the culture of his day or are they relevant for us, nineteen centuries later? Think about this.

A biblical faith, godly attitudes, Christ-like behaviour; these should not change. So we must not say 'Slaves? Young women stuck at home? That's not our modern way of doing things!' and throw out the baby with the bath water. For example, 'seriousness' does not imply that solemnity excludes laughter and fun, but it means that lives will be moulded by wisdom rather than by frivolity. And let those of us who are in any subservient position (and it is not healthy for any person to be 'boss' in every area of life) read the advice for slaves in the light of Jesus saying of himself 'For even the Son of Man did not come to be served, but to serve, and to give his life as a ransom for many' (Mark 10:45).

For meditation

Learn by heart those words of Jesus. Then slowly re-read the passage—and perhaps yesterday's as well. Think what bearing Jesus' attitude of self-giving service has on our own attitudes and behaviour.

RG

Courage to love

Jesus said, 'This is my commandment: love one another, as I have loved you. A man can have no greater love than to lay down his life for his friends. You are my friends, if you do what I command you. I shall not call you servants any more, because a servant does not know his master's business; I call you friends, because I have made known to you everything I have learnt from my Father. You did not choose me, no, I chose you; and I commissioned you to go out and bear fruit, fruit that will last; and then the Father will give you anything you ask in my name. What I command you is to love one another.'

It is often said that the hardest place to be a Christian is at home, for there all our failings are known, and there can be no pretence for very long. Amongst our families, or in the solitude of our own lives, love must be genuine, forgiveness absolute and compassion freely offered, or the falsehood is immediately apparent.

The second hardest place to be a Christian is in church. No, not in the easy task of church services, but in the difficult hurly-burly of Christian fellowship. It is when we see our sisters and brothers in Christ hurting, but offer no healing; when we share the 'Peace' but offer no forgiveness; when we know the loneliness of others, but give no companionship, that our faith rings hollow and our discipleship seems false.

Of course, fear is the big barrier to obeying Jesus' command to love. Fear of becoming over-involved, fear of embarrassment, fear of rejection, fear of being inadequate to the occasion.

Love requires courage. For Jesus, and for many before and since, it has required courage in the face of death. But once we set out to love, we can get that courage, for like love itself, it is the gift of God.

If we keep Jesus' commandment, and bear the fruit of love, we can ask for anything; including the courage love requires.

MM

Gospel tenses

For the grace of God that brings salvation has appeared to all men. It teaches us to say 'No' to ungodliness and worldly passions, and to live self-controlled, upright and godly lives in this present age, while we wait for the blessed hope—the glorious appearing of our great God and Saviour, Jesus Christ, who gave himself for us to redeem us from all wickedness and to purify for himself a people that are his very own, eager to do what is good.

Salvation is a huge word—available to all people, appropriated by some. Sometimes we are asked 'Are you saved?' We might answer 'I have been saved, I am being saved, I will be saved.'

The past. 'The grace of God... has appeared to all men... Jesus Christ gave himself for us...' At a particular moment around 5BC, the Son of God was born in Bethlehem. 'The Word became flesh, full of grace and truth' (John 1:14). Around AD31, in Jerusalem, he died 'to give his life as a ransom for many'. Once I accepted God's gift of salvation through Christ I could say 'I have been saved.'

The future. But the story is not finished. We recite in the Creed 'He will come again to judge the living and the dead.' Teaching about the Second Coming is rare these days, but Paul was excited as he looked forward to 'the glorious appearing of our great God and Saviour', when the world as we know it will end and not only people but 'creation itself will be liberated from its bondage to decay and brought into the glorious liberty of the children of light' (Romans 8:21). I cannot really imagine what that will be like, but I share Paul's confident hope of a glorious re-creation. So we can say 'We will be saved.'

The present. Salvation past and future; that is a powerful stimulus for our lives now. We are to turn our backs on 'ungodliness, worldly passions, wickedness'. There may not be 'big sins' in our lives, but what about the 'little sins' God minds about? We are to live self-controlled, upright, godly, pure lives, eager to do good. As we change, we are being saved.

To pray

Finish, then, Thy new creation:
Pure and spotless let us be;
Let us see Thy great salvation,
Perfectly restored in Thee.

C. Wesley

RG

Leaders in action

These, then, are the things you should teach. Encourage and rebuke with all authority. Do not let anyone despise you.

I have today been at a service for the consecration of a new bishop. He was given a Bible with the words 'Receive this book; here are the words of eternal life. Take them for your guide, and declare them to the world.' Then the Archbishop handed him his pastoral staff and charged him 'Keep watch over the whole flock in which the Holy Spirit has appointed you shepherd. Encourage the faithful, restore the lost, build up the body of Christ...' I was immediately reminded of these words of Paul to Titus about his leadership: 'These are the things you should teach.' Look back over the readings for the last few days to remind yourself about how he is to teach. The emphasis has been on uprightness of character and behaviour, rooted in a biblical grasp of the joy of knowing Christ and his salvation. We are to be Christians through and through— in what we believe, in who we are, in the way we live.

'Encourage and rebuke.' A leader needs to be able to praise and also to confront. When I am counselling I try to do the supposedly impossible, to stand in two places at the same time! I need to be alongside the other person, to listen, to understand, to encourage. But I also need to be out in front, so that I may teach, challenge, exhort, rebuke—whatever is needed to help that person move forward. Encouragement should come before rebuke; a person who feels understood and valued will be more ready to accept a reproof or a challenge than one who is made to feel 'I'm no good'.

'With all authority... Do not let anyone despise you.' A leader must not be afraid to lead, and may have to make some tough decisions. But one whose position rests on mutual respect rather than on being heavy-handed will find willing cooperation instead of sullen obedience.

Guidelines for prayer

Think of the people you know who are leaders at work, in the church, at home. They need God's help to be able to match up to his standards of leadership. Pray for them in as much detail as you can.

RG

Living in the community

Remind the people to be subject to rulers and authorities, to be obedient, to be ready to do whatever is good, to slander no one, to be peaceable and considerate, and to show true humility towards all men.

I was struck by a titbit on the radio recently. In one area the police, tightening up on speeding drivers, caught a car going at 80 mph in a 50 mph area. To their surprise and embarrassment they found the driver was their Chief Constable! His orders were 'Treat me as you would any other driver.' Perhaps he had read Paul's words! Subject to authorities? No—and yes. He broke the rules but submitted to the consequences. Humble? Yes. It is so easy to see ourselves a little better than others, thinking 'That doesn't apply to *me!*' But our relationship with God must be worked out in our relationships with other people.

Now imagine next that you are listening in on my private time with God . . .

Remind the people. 'Lord, thank you for the privilege I have of teaching others. Please may I remember to do myself what I encourage them to do.' *To be subject to rulers and authorities, to be obedient.* I suppose that means government of any sort—including at work and at school. Oh dear—my driving! 'Lord, I confess that I often drive according to my own judgment of what is safe rather than obeying the letter of the law.' And what else? I must think about that as I go through today. 'Lord, I pray for Julia, in

her dilemma when her boss tells her to do things you don't like.' *To be ready to do whatever is good.* I don't contribute much positive good in my neighbourhood. 'What do you want me to do, Lord?' It's a small thing, but perhaps picking up that rubbish on the path today fits here. But I look at my neighbours, and I can see non-believers who are much better neighbours than I am. But there's Patricia, with cancer; what can I do for her? And Sarah. 'Lord, please show me how to help her in her intense agoraphobia. I'd love her to find you as her rock and refuge. Are there practical ways I can show her my faith?'

That is a sample meditation; it could be continued phrase by phrase to the end of the passage.

RG

Grasp God's grace

At one time we too were foolish, disobedient, deceived and enslaved by all kinds of passions and pleasures. We lived in malice and envy, being hated and hating one another. But when the kindness and love of God our Saviour appeared, he saved us, not because of righteous things we had done, but because of his mercy. He saved us through the washing of rebirth and renewal by the Holy Spirit, whom he poured out on us generously through Jesus Christ our Saviour, so that, having been justified by his grace, we might become heirs having the hope of eternal life. This is a trustworthy saying.

Who deserves to be rescued by Christ? Not Paul, not me. Try reading the first two sentences as 'I' instead of 'we'. 'At one time I too was foolish...' That is a shock: 'I'm not that bad!' The Jews were furious when Jesus called them 'slaves to sin'. 'We are Abraham's descendants and have never been slaves of anyone. How can you say that we shall be set free?' Jesus replied 'I tell you the truth, everyone who sins is a slave to sin. Now a slave has no permanent place in the family, but a son belongs to it for ever. So if the Son sets you free, you will be free indeed' (John 8:33–36).

That is a wonderful commentary on today's verses. When we see that we were slaves we appreciate better God's love in bringing us into his family. Paul's theological language easily masks the immensity of God's loving rescue. 'He saved us.' Why? Not because we were any good, but because of his kindness, his love, his mercy. Grace—God's free, undeserved generosity. Justified—when he looks at me 'just as if I'd never sinned'.

Grace and forgiveness, present but often unrecognized in the Old Testament, are evident in Jesus our Saviour. 'He saved us.' How? Through the 'washing of rebirth'—being born again, in fact. That was the subject of Jesus' conversation with a puzzled Nicodemus (John 3:1–15). We are meant to experience it, not mock the phrase. Confusion can arise when we have been given in baptism the 'outward, visible sign' of being in God's family without appropriating for ourselves the 'inward, spiritual grace' of the Holy Spirit who gives us that new life.

To ponder

Do I enjoy the privileges of being an heir?

RG

Church discipline

And I want you to stress these things, so that those who have trusted in God may be careful to devote themselves to doing what is good. These things are excellent and profitable for everyone. But avoid foolish controversies and genealogies and arguments and quarrels about the law, because these are unprofitable and useless. Warn a divisive person once, and then warn him a second time. After that, have nothing to do with him. You may be sure that such a man is warped and sinful; he is self-condemned.

Paul's concern for discipline is often disregarded in our churches today. 'Gentle Jesus, meek and mild' was the one who attacked the temple traders and the hypocritical Pharisees! We rightly stress God's patience and forgiveness. But our attitude can be a cover-up for tolerance born of apathy rather than concern for a his holy love and justice. Our churches are weakened by our failure to confront sin. Paul's emphasis here is on the quarrels and pettifogging that cause division. These need to be nipped in the bud; and we must not duck out of confronting, first privately and then (if necessary) publicly, those who disrupt fellowship. I must pause at this point to ask myself: Are my own words or attitudes causing division in my congregation? Do I have a responsibility to confront anyone else about their own wrong speech or behaviour? That is difficult, and not to be undertaken before I have tested my motives; so I ask myself whether I want good for that other person and for the whole church, or personal revenge.

For meditation

'Those who have trusted in God may be careful to devote themselves to doing what is good.' Take that in bite-size pieces:

Trust. *As I look at a chair and watch other people sitting in it, do I trust that it will hold my weight? It looks all right. But I do not actually trust it until I sit in it myself and stop wondering whether it is reliable! That is a picture of trusting in God.*

Devote—*a word of whole-hearted commitment, not of intermittent superficiality.*

To doing what is good. *That is a challenge for each part of the next 24 hours, the next week . . . and for the rest of our lives.*

RG

Personal greetings

As soon as I send Artemas or Tychicus to you, do your best to come to me at Nicopolis, because I have decided to winter there. Do everything you can to help Zenas the lawyer and Apollos on their way and see that they have everything they need. Our people must learn to devote themselves to doing what is good, in order that they may provide for daily necessities and not live unproductive lives. Everyone with me sends you greetings. Greet those who love us in the faith.

We often skim over the personal messages in Paul's letters. We don't know the people and the comments appear irrelevant. **Artemas** and **Zenas** are unknown elsewhere, though Artemas might replace Titus as Paul's delegate in Crete, to free Titus to rejoin Paul for the winter. **Tychicus,** 'a dear brother, a faithful minister and servant in the Lord' (Colossians 4:7), had been with Paul in freedom in Greece and in imprisonment in Rome. From there Paul sent him as a messenger, to carry both letters and verbal news to the churches in Ephesus and Colosse; as far as we know Tychicus did not have previous responsibility in church leadership. **Apollos** was an interesting person who travelled widely. He was a Jew from Alexandria who had arrived in Ephesus as a believing but ill-taught Christian. There he stayed with Aquila and Priscilla who welcomed him and taught him, so that he became a good teacher and an effective apologist for the faith when he moved on to southern Greece (Acts 18:24–28).

Zenas and Apollos were probably travelling through Crete on their way from Greece, perhaps back to Apollos' home town. So Paul took the chance to use them as postmen. 'Look after them well before they continue their journey,' he told Titus. The Bible is full of examples of generous hospitality, examples for us to follow.

'Our people must learn to devote themselves to doing good.' Paul's last exhortation reminds us that the Cretans had a reputation for laziness, perhaps for sponging off other people. But Christians need to lead changed lives. Which of the people mentioned in these verses challenge you to change?

A prayer

Lord, thank you for lessons to learn even from the apparently dull parts of scripture.

RG

Send me out . . .

'I gave them your message, and the world hated them, because they do not belong to the world, just as I do not belong to the world. I do not ask you to take them out of the world, but I do ask you to keep them safe from the Evil One. Just as I do not belong to the world, they do not belong to the world. Dedicate them to yourself by means of the truth; your word is truth. I sent them into the world, just as you sent me into the world.'

It appears to me that the most dangerous and challenging words in the entire Bible are 'Here I am.' There is no knowing where they will lead. Being sent on an errand can be exhilarating or tedious. Sometimes I have been sent to find out about something. When I received a curate I was sent on a course to find out how to train him. It was a welcome break from the regular ministry of the church. I enjoyed listening to the lectures and was glad to be sent on the course. It was a comfortable few days spent drinking in the experience and knowledge of the experts.

When God called me into the full-time ordained ministry I was excited. I began my job with that naïve enthusiasm. Over the last eleven years the enthusiasm has changed. There have been times when I wonder why God sent me. When a young couple lose a baby or the church seems to be dividing before my eyes, I ask God the questions: Why did you send me? Why am I here?

There are times when the last thing I want is to be sent. Sometimes I'm wanting to do something else—'Don't bother me with that Lord, I'm doing your work over here, can't you see?' When I have to face the angry man or the grieving young husband—'Can't you find someone else Lord, someone who is used to this, who is so much better?'

Yet Jesus sends us as he was sent. We do not enter new avenues without his hand close by. Indeed if we stand still and do not go the hand may very well have gone on ahead.

When we hear the words at the end of Communion, 'send us out in the power of your spirit', at one and the same time we walk out into our unknown and God's known. This is the apostolic Church at work.

GD

Love's anger

The word of Yahweh which came to Hosea son of Beeri during the reigns of Uzziah, Jotham, Ahaz and Hezekiah kings of Judah, and of Jeroboam son of Joash, king of Israel. The beginning of what Yahweh said through Hosea.

God is a person who speaks his mind. What was on his mind was the idolatry, the immorality and the injustice in Israel—and it made him angry. The God who is Love does get angry. Dr Campbell Morgan explains why: 'If cruelty makes Him angry, it is because His heart is set upon kindness. If oppression stirs up His wrath, it is because His purpose for man is that he should live in peace. If the sorrows inflicted upon man by man call down his judgment, it is because the one great desire of His heart for humanity is that of its well-being and happiness.' (G. Campbell Morgan, *Living Messages of the Books of the Bible*, Pickering and Inglis.)

There wasn't much happiness in Hosea's day. Many people were extremely rich, but a lot were appallingly poor. In Britain in the 1990s things are much the same. Some people are sleeping in cardboard boxes on the streets, while others are making (or losing) fortunes on the Stock Exchange. The rest of us are somewhere in the middle wondering what on earth to do—and perhaps praying 'Your will be done on earth as it is in heaven'.

In Hosea's time, the rich were oppressing the poor and treating them unjustly. Businessmen were dishonest and traders cheated their customers with scales that gave them short weight. Those who were destitute and had sunk to the bottom of the pile were sold as slaves. As well as the loveless social injustice and dishonest business practice, the Jews were worshipping false gods and committing appalling acts of immorality in the process. So the God whose name is love told Hosea to speak to them in his name and tell them of his anger.

A prayer

Lord God, thank you that you speak your mind to us through the prophets. May we listen to what you say and do what you tell us. Make us (and make me) realize how much you love us, and how much you love the poor and the needy all over the world. Prod us (and prod me) into doing what you want us (and me) to do.
Amen.

SB

Love's suffering

Yahweh said to Hosea, 'Go, marry a whore, and get children with a whore; for the country itself has become nothing but a whore by abandoning Yahweh.' So he went and married Gomer, daughter of Diblaim, who conceived and bore him a son.

It was an astonishing thing for God to tell Hosea to do—to go and marry a whore. Some experts think that Gomer was a temple prostitute. Others think that God simply knew that she would run off with other lovers after she was married. We can't be sure which view is right.

Hosea married a wife who would be unfaithful to him. God has done much the same thing. He made us in order to have a deeply intimate love relationship with us—like a marriage. 'Your Maker is your husband' says Isaiah (54:5). The Jewish nation was the first to know this, as they heard the words of love that God spoke through their prophets—words that were not just for them but for the whole world.

A good marriage can show us a faint reflection of the love between the Creator and his creatures. And we can see it in the Song of Songs, as a man and woman tell each other about their love with intense delight. But a marriage that has gone terribly wrong can also show us the love, and the agony, of God. The other day a man told me of his wife's adultery. As he spoke, he could hardly hold back the tears. She had gone on holiday with another man and lied about it. 'But I still love her,' he said, 'I still want her back.'

In our Western world people often take adultery for granted. Television sometimes portrays it as something to laugh at. But God takes a different view. 'You shall not commit adultery' is a commandment designed to make us happy. When we break it, we usually break someone's heart—just as Hosea's heart would be broken, but would show us the heart of God in the process.

Think and pray

Do I laugh at jokes about adultery?
Do I see adultery as God sees it?
Dare I pray that he will show it to me for what it really is?

SB

A new name

After weaning Lo-Ruhamah, she conceived and gave birth to a son. Yahweh said, 'Call him Lo-Ammi, for you are not my people and I do not exist for you.'

But the Israelites will become as numerous as the sands of the sea, which cannot be measured or counted. In the very place where they were told, 'You are not my people.'

The Victorians used to burden their children with the name of a Christian virtue—Faith, Hope or Charity—and I am always grateful that I was born too late to have the name Patience inflicted on me. We have as little choice about our name as about who our parents will be. But we can have a new name when we are baptized or confirmed, and to become a Christian is to have a new parent. Whatever our parents were like and whatever they named us, we can make choices and changes in our lives—through the power of the living God who loves us.

Gomer conceived and gave birth to a son. Yahweh said, 'Call him Lo-Ammi, for you are not my people and I do not exist for you'.

Poor Lo-Ammi had a terrible name. One day I caught my breath in horror when I realized what it meant: 'you are not my people and I do not exist for you'. It was as if the Self-Existent One, always there, had ceased to be. The One whose very nature and name is 'I am who I am' was saying 'I am not...' Perhaps that is what hell will be: that God will say to someone who has persistently refused his love, in spite of a lifetime's wooing, 'I do not exist for you...' And then (after the judgement) that person will simply cease to exist.

But God will give Lo-Ammi a new start and a new name and a new life—and he will do the same for everyone. Lo-Ammi had a terrible name and a terrible mother. But God loved the child and the mother, and his love would transform them both. The horror of non-existence and non-relationship would be transformed into life and love.

A prayer

Father God, thank you that you can take anything in me—my sorrow and my sin—and give me its very opposite: joy instead of sorrow, love and righteousness instead of sin—through Jesus Christ, my Lord and your Son. Amen.

SB

Stop sinning

To court, take your mother to court! For she is no longer my wife nor am I her husband. She must either remove her whoring ways from her face and her adulteries from between her breasts, or I shall strip her and expose her naked as the day she was born; I shall make her as bare as the desert. I shall make her as dry as arid country, and let her die of thirst.

The other day in a confirmation class I asked two people to demonstrate repentance. They stood face to face, one to represent sin and the other to be the sinner. Then the sinner turned her back on sin and walked away. To repent is not only to be sorry for our sins but also to turn around and leave them behind. For Gomer, that meant leaving her lovers behind.

Hosea could have taken her to court and the judge would have found her guilty. When the God of love judges you and me to see if we have broken his law of love, the verdict is always guilty and the penalty is always death. Spiritual death is to be cut off from a relationship with God. Sin separates us like a dark cloud that cuts off the light of the sun. The sun still shines and God still loves us but somehow the sin has to be removed. Not in the way that Gomer had to 'remove her whoring ways from her face' and stop sinning. The sins that she had committed against love would not just evaporate into thin air. Something had to be done, and only God could do it.

To think about

The Christian who has heard his word of pardon from the lips of Christ upon the Cross is never in danger of supposing that God does not mind. He minds, like that. And so, as St Paul says, Christ as set forth upon the Cross shows the righteousness of God in the very act of forgiveness. This is part . . . of that which Christian tradition has stood for in its insistence that the mere appeal of love to our souls is not sufficient as an account of the Atonement—that there must also be in a true sense a propitiation toward God.

(William Temple, *The Kingdom of God*, Macmillan.)

SB

Love minds so much

And I shall feel no pity for her children since they are the children of her whorings. Yes, their mother has played the whore, she who conceived them has disgraced herself by saying, 'I shall chase after my lovers; they will assure me of my keep, my wool, my flax, my oil and my drinks.' This is why I shall block her way with thorns, and wall her in to stop her in her tracks; then if she chases her lovers she will not catch them, if she looks for them she will not find them, and then she will say, 'I shall go back to my first husband, I was better off then than I am now'; she had never realised before that I was the one who was giving her the grain, new wine and oil...'

Do you wonder how a God of love can possibly speak in this way through a prophet? Do you think that God and Hosea ought to go on pitying us whatever we do, and that our Maker ought not to mind? But how can love not mind? If the person you love most in the world came and told you that she or he had murdered a man, raped a woman, sexually abused a child, or robbed a bank, would you really not mind? You would go on loving them—but the more you loved them, the more you would mind.

So God minds most of all. God gives us everything—our life, our earth, our food and our drink. So it must provoke him if we give the credit to other sources. How would we feel if we gave someone a beautiful present and they thanked someone else for it? Multiply that by a million and we start to see what God has given us. But he doesn't give up. The things that we have been enjoying seem to slip through our fingers—perhaps when God withdraws his pity (his sympathetic sorrow for one suffering) and allows us to suffer the consequences of our actions. Then our suffering and lack of pleasures drive us back to him.

A prayer

God of love, I find it surprising that you still want someone who comes back to you just because they are hungry and have nowhere else to go. But then I remember the Prodigal Son and the Waiting Father. I am glad you are like that—and I am glad that you mind so much when we sin, because you love us so much.

SB

A godly seduction

But look, I am going to seduce her and lead her into the desert and speak to her heart. There I shall give her back her vineyards, and make the Vale of Achor a gateway of hope. There she will respond as when she was young, as on the day when she came up from Egypt. When that day comes— declares Yahweh—you will call me, 'My husband', no more will you call me, 'My Baal'.

Hosea and God are setting out to attract their beloved back. It's a second wooing—after the beloved's adultery. But the beloved is still beloved, and nothing she does will make her Lover hate her— although he will get very angry. In his beautiful commentary entitled *Love to the Loveless* (The Bible Speaks Today Series, IVP) Derek Kidner says:

'There is a right infatuation (implied in the Hebrew for "allure her") as well as a disastrous one, for true love need be no less ravishing than false: only less disappointing. The Lord now for His part will exert his charms and speak to the heart of the beloved. This is the positive and creative side of His severity, for "the wilderness" could mean either of two things for Israel: either her life in ruins or her pilgrim spirit and youthful promise recaptured. Here it offers her the second, by way of the first.'

A Meditation

Think about the place in your life that makes you most ashamed or that causes you the most sorrow or pain. Let yourself feel the shame, or the sorrow or the pain, in the loving presence of God. Then stay in the presence and ask him to make that place of trouble into a doorway of hope for you. Make it a real transaction between you and your God—and keep remembering it in faith throughout the coming weeks.

SB

Serving can be smelly!

After Jesus had washed their feet, he put his outer garment back on and returned to his place at the table. 'Do you understand what I have just done to you?' he asked. 'You call me Teacher and Lord, and it is right that you do so, because that is what I am. I, your Lord and Teacher, have just washed your feet. You, then, should wash one another's feet. I have set an example for you, so that you will do just what I have done for you.'

Some years ago I was involved in the teaching of mentally handicapped adults. One particular man in his early thirties had the most tremendous stomach upset one day. I don't need to go into the details but he was in a bad way in the middle of a session.

Fortunately there were showers on site and I took him to them. I wanted to help him as much as I could so I ran the water to the right temperature got the soap and towels ready and knocked on the changing room door. 'Are you ready?' I called. There was a grunt. I called again but there was no appearance. Eventually I went in and there he was, just as I had left him, fully clothed and reeking. I realized he was frightened, feeling embarrassed and very upset. To cut a long story short we both got in the shower and I cleaned him up. I can't say I enjoyed it at all but I shall always remember him.

The Philippians reading about Jesus taking the form of a servant always astounds me. To think that Jesus really did become as nothing for me is staggering. I know what it can cost me to do a small service for someone else, but his service was in a different league.

God sent his Son, not simply to knock on the door, although he does that, but to take the form of a servant and, so to speak, get in the shower with us. Yet this kind of modern-day parable goes on every day in hundreds of places in the world.

It strikes me that the people who do this—in homes, hospitals, or for relatives—show real servanthood. In church today, many of us will sit in pleasant surroundings with, by and large, pleasant people. That's great, and to be enjoyed, but let's not forget that Jesus washed smelly, dirty feet and told us to act like him.

GD

A new engagement

I shall betroth you to myself for ever, I shall betroth you in uprightness and justice, and faithful love and tenderness. Yes, I shall betroth you to myself in loyalty and in the knowledge of Yahweh. When that day comes, I shall respond—declares Yahweh—I shall respond to the heavens and they will respond to the earth and the earth will respond to the grain, the new wine and oil, and they will respond to Jezreel. I shall sow her in the country to be mine, I shall take pity on Lo-Ruhamah, I shall tell Lo-Ammi, 'You are my people,' and he will say, 'You are my God.'

God is making his plans for his beloved and now the transformation and the turnabout is going to begin. A betrothal is where a marriage begins, and God and his beloved are going to begin again. There will be the delight of falling in love all over again (although God never fell out of love even if Hosea did).

Now there will be a new start and a betrothal that will last for ever.

Someone I know became a Christian when he was middle-aged. He had not been either a good father or a good husband. But his new relationship with Christ transformed his other relationships and he would tell people about the dramatic change in his life. 'I've fallen in love with my wife for the first time,' he said. It was true.

When someone really knows the love of God, the blessings start to flow out from their heart like a river. Even the earth knows the difference. The child who never knew pity starts to know it. The child who never belonged begins to know the delight of belonging—and

begins to respond to the love that is flowing into his heart.

A prayer

Lord God, I marvel at the way you can transform our lives through your love. Let your love keep on flowing into my heart and never let me put up a barrier to stop it. I delight to say to you 'You are my God'. I want to know you more deeply and love you more deeply every day of my life here on earth—and then through all eternity.

SB

Love an adulteress

Yahweh said to me, 'Go again, love a woman who loves another man, an adulteress, and love her as Yahweh loves the Israelites although they turn to other gods and love raisin cakes.' So I bought her for fifteen shekels of silver, a *homer* of barley and a skin of wine . . .

Love sometimes dies in a marriage. And when it has died people will sometimes say: 'Well, once it's dead it's dead. There's nothing we can do about it.' But that isn't what God says. He says 'Go again, love a woman who loves another man, an adulteress . . .' Perhaps it might just be possible to revive love if there isn't another woman, another man. But if there is, surely that's an outrageous, impossible demand to make of someone? Yet even a secular poet knew that the demand could be made.

The Advisers

Reason says, 'Love a girl who does not love you?
Learn to forget her, learn to let her go!'
But Fate says, 'When I sent you far to find her
I had a plan whose end you cannot know.'

Reason says, 'Love like this will bring you a thousand
Unhappy days for every happy hour.'
'To give great joy,' says Fate, 'without great suffering,
Light without shadow, lies beyond my power.'

'Can you,' says Reason, 'love a girl in love with
Another man? Have you no pride, no will?'
'I am using you,' says Fate; 'have faith; be humble.
Tools are not told what purpose they fulfil.'

'What she needs,' Reason says, 'you cannot give her,
Nor she what you need.' 'No, not now,' says Fate;
'But both of you will change. When you are ready
To play your parts, you will. Be patient. Wait.'

Reason says, 'If you chase a dream through darkness,
What but confusion, misery can you find?'
Fate says, 'Before you lies a long hard journey,
But I can see the way though you are blind.'

Reason says, 'Look, there are easier paths to choose
  from
And lesser goals with greater hopes of gain.'
But Fate says, 'You are the chosen, not the chooser,
I give you, friend, the privilege of pain.'

Poem by A.S.J. Tessimond. Grateful thanks to Mr Hubert Nicholson for permission to reproduce the poem.

In the poem there is a dialogue between Reason and Fate. Fate tells the lover what to do, just a God tells Hosea what to do—and also shows him how to do it.

To think about

But Fate says, 'You are the chosen, not the chooser. I give you, friend, the privilege of pain.'

SB

We will both wait

And I said to her, 'You will have to spend a long time waiting for me without playing the whore and without giving yourself to any man, and I will behave in the same way towards you.' For the Israelites will have to spend a long time without king or leader, without sacrifice or sacred pillar, without *ephod* or domestic images; but after that, the Israelites will return and again seek Yahweh their God and David their king, and turn trembling to Yahweh for his bounty in the final days.

Gomer will have to go through a time of probation and purification and stop sleeping around. But even Hosea won't sleep with her as her husband. That was wise from a health point of view. Yet this was essentially a time for testing and for re-establishing their love and their relationship. A new courtship and a new betrothal. Just as Gomer would have to do without her lovers, so Israel would have to do without the things she relied on. Her forbidden household gods would have to go, but so also would her sacrifices to the true God. Israel had corrupted even the good things, and her worship of Jehovah was tainted with Baal worship. 'A clean break was needed, deep enough and long enough to make a new beginning possible: a pure return, in all humility, to the Lord Himself; a renewal of the marriage that had seemed beyond repair' (Derek Kidner, *Love to the Loveless*).

To think about

Imagine a man and a woman mending their broken marriage. Think of the time they would spend together . . . the things they would say and do (and not do) . . . how they would start to communicate again: to tell each other their feelings, their hurts, their hopes and their dreams.

Then transfer that mending marriage into the spiritual realm and think about that.

SB

The failure of love

Israelites, hear what Yahweh says, for Yahweh indicts the citizens of the country: there is no loyalty, no faithful love, no knowledge of God in the country, only perjury and lying, murder, theft, adultery and violence, bloodshed after bloodshed. This is why the country is in mourning and all its citizens pining away, the wild animals also and birds of the sky, even the fish in the sea will disappear.

We might think that the happy ending of Hosea chapter 3 would mean that the rest of Hosea would be an account of how he and Gomer lived happily ever after. But it isn't. It is a detailed account of the sins that are making God angry with Israel—and it also uses the picture of a father's love for his son to describe the conflict within God's heart between his anger and his love. We shall look at that next week. Today we look at the appalling list of Israel's sins and their effect on all of God's creatures.

All those sins are failures in loving. If we love someone we will not be disloyal. We will not lie to them or about them. We will not murder them or steal their possessions. We will not commit adultery and we will not be violent.

We have failed to love the earth that God told us to look after. We use it for our own ends. We cut down its trees, poison its seas and destroy its creatures. But they are God's creatures and it's God's world. We are meant to love it.

A reflection

'Love all God's creation, the whole of it and every grain of sand. Love every leaf, every ray of God's light! Love the animals, love the plants, love everything. If you love everything, you will perceive the divine mystery in things.'

Feodor Dostoyevsky, The Brothers Karamazov

SB

Rejected priests

But let no one denounce, no one rebuke; it is you, priest, that I denounce. Priest, you will stumble in broad daylight, and the prophet will stumble with you in the dark, and I will make your mother perish. My people perish for want of knowledge. Since you yourself have rejected knowledge, so I shall reject you from my priesthood; since you have forgotten the teaching of your God, I in my turn shall forget your children.

The priests were the equivalent of our clergy. Their task was to know God and to pray—and to enable other people to know God and to pray. But they were doing their job so badly that God was going to give them the sack. They were going to lose their jobs.

In Ezekiel, God says he will do the job himself. 'I myself will be the shepherd of my sheep... says the Lord God. I will seek the lost, and I will bring back the strayed, and I will bind up the crippled...' (34:15, 16a). Years later the man Jesus walks in the land of Israel, where the sheep and the lambs feed in the hills and the valleys, and says: 'I am the good shepherd. The good shepherd lays down his life for the sheep' (John 10:11).

To think about

If I am a Christian, I am 'in Christ'. He lives in the Father's presence. Therefore so do I. 'To him who loves us and has freed us from our sins by his blood and made us a kingdom, priests to his God and Father, to him be glory and dominion for ever and ever. Amen'
(Revelation 1:5b, 6).

In Christ all Christians are priests. Am I being what I am? Do I realize what I am, in Christ?

SB

Equality in sin

Old wine and new wine addle my people's wits, they consult their block of wood, and their stick explains what they should do. For an urge to go whoring has led them astray and whoring they go and desert their God; they offer sacrifice on the mountain tops, they burn incense on the hills, under oak and poplar and terebinth, for pleasant is their shade. So, although your daughters play the whore and your daughters-in-law commit adultery, I shall not punish your daughters for playing the whore nor your daughters-in-law for committing adultery, when the men themselves are wandering off with whores and offering sacrifice with sacred prostitutes, for a people with no understanding is doomed.

Instead of looking to their God to guide them the people of God were throwing a stick down on the ground and letting it point them to the way they were to go. Perhaps the so-called Christian countries who read their horoscopes so assiduously come into the same category.

What Hosea says about the prostitute daughters of Israel is astonishingly advanced. There isn't one sexual morality for men and another for women. The feminist movement got that truth right even though they sometimes got their practice wrong. 'Men are promiscuous,' they said, 'so we will be promiscuous too.' One of them even wrote bizarrely about her 'right to catch VD'. But God says through Hosea that there is one law for men and for women. The men should have been setting a good example. Instead, they were setting a bad one. Therefore their daughters wouldn't be punished for following it. *They* would. Because they had failed to understand, their whole society was doomed.

To think about

In the Western world, we live in a sex-mad society. Who has got it right? The world which worships sex or God who created sex?

SB

The light of the world

God in his mercy has given us this work to do, and so we are not discouraged. We put aside all secret and shameful deeds; we do not act with deceit, nor do we falsify the word of God. In the full light of truth we live in God's sight and try to commend ourselves to everyone's good conscience. For if the gospel we preach is hidden, it is hidden only from those who are being lost. They do not believe, because their minds have been kept in the dark by the evil god of this world. He keeps them from seeing the light shining on them, the light that comes from the Good News about the glory of Christ, who is the exact likeness of God. For it is not ourselves that we preach; we preach Jesus Christ as Lord, and ourselves as your servants for Jesus' sake. The God who said, 'Out of darkness the light shall shine!' is the same God who made his light shine in our hearts, to bring us to the knowledge of God's glory shining in the face of Christ.

A way for us to reflect on today's passage is to apply it to our own life—and to be drawn into worship as we contemplate the wonder and the nature of the Good News. We may not all be preachers in the strict sense, but each one of us is a light in the world. So pray that the Spirit will bring into the light anything that you have hidden in the darkness—so that your light will shine more brightly. Think about the people you know from whom the gospel seems to be hidden. Pray for them— that they will start to hate the darkness they are living in, and long for the light. Pray that they will see the glory of the light of Christ, who is the exact likeness of God—'a friend of sinners', and 'a man of sorrows'. Reflect on the glory of God—shining in the face of Christ, and praise God for the day when he called you out of darkness into his marvellous light (even if you don't know what day it was) and made you a new creature and a new creation—just as millions of years ago he commanded the light to shine in the darkness and created the worlds.

SB

God's faithful love

I shall go back to my place until they confess their guilt and seek me, seek me eagerly in their distress. Come, let us return to Yahweh. He has rent us and he will heal us; he has struck us and he will bind up our wounds; after two days he will revive us, on the third day he will raise us up and we shall live in his presence. Let us know, let us strive to know Yahweh; that he will come is as certain as the dawn. He will come to us like a shower, like the rain of springtime to the earth.

In the Song of Songs, the beloved ignores her lover and can't be bothered to open the door to him. Then when she longs to see him he isn't there, so she has to go searching for him. The beloved Israel will not seek her lover God for the best of motives. She will return to him because she is in distress—just as the prodigal son returned to the waiting father. The prodigal son hadn't realized the tenderness and the love that would flow out to welcome him. Israel did know—and it made her sin against love all the worse. She knew that the love of God was as certain as the sun's rising. She knew that in the warmth of the sun, and with the spring rain falling on her dry earth, new life would start to grow again. It would all happen as she pressed on to know God in the mutual knowledge of one another that the marriage relationship signified.

A prayer

Lord God, I thank you for your faithful love—a love that I can utterly rely on and that never fails me. Thank you that you are always there for me, as certain as the dawn and as refreshing as the spring rain. I praise you that '. . .the path of the righteous is like the light of dawn, which shines brighter and brighter until full day' (Proverbs 4:18). Let the light of your love shine on me and on all your church, and don't let us hide from your light in the darkness of sin.

SB

Like morning mist

What am I to do with you, Ephraim? What am I to do with you, Judah? For your love is like morning mist, like the dew that quickly disappears. This is why I have hacked them to pieces by means of the prophets, why I have killed them with words from my mouth, why my sentence will blaze forth like the dawn—for faithful love is what pleases me, not sacrifice; knowledge of God, not burnt offerings.

Yesterday we saw how confident Israel was in the love of God if she returned to it. But God is less confident of her love. Ephraim and Judah were two of the tribes of Israel, descended from two of Jacob's sons. It is as if God shakes his head in despair and perplexity. They say they will love him, and their love starts to rise in their hearts. But it is like the morning mist. Sometimes I look out over the fields very early in the day and watch the morning mist, like a white cloud that has come down to earth and is resting on the trees and the earth. Exquisitely beautiful, it drifts gently along with the wind—and then, as the sun gets warmer, it vanishes. And that is just how morning mists are meant to be. But it isn't how the lovers of God are meant to be. Our love is meant to be like the love of God. Like the verse from Proverbs that we prayed yesterday. God's love 'shines brighter and brighter until full day'—and the reason why the path of the righteous is like the light of dawn is that they are getting to know God better and better.

A way to pray

Remember a morning mist that you once saw and look at it in your mind's eye. Then ask the Holy Spirit to help you to look at your love for Christ as it now is. Be still, and wait in silence for a few moments.

SB

The harvest of love

Ephraim is a well-trained heifer that loves to tread the grain. But I have laid a yoke on her fine neck, I shall put Ephraim into harness, Judah will have to plough, Jacob must draw the harrow. Sow saving justice for yourselves, reap a harvest of faithful love; break up your fallow ground; it is time to seek out Yahweh until he comes to rain saving justice down on you. You have ploughed wickedness, you have reaped iniquity, you have eaten the fruit of falsehood.

As a Jewish heifer walked over the grain to thresh it she would have enjoyed herself—because the law said that she wasn't to be muzzled. So she could eat what she wanted. But life was going to get tougher for Ephraim. God was going to discipline him, and Judah and Jacob would have to plough and to harrow. But the whole point of it is a rich harvest.

Israel has been planting the wrong seeds and reaping the wrong harvest. God desires a crop of love and of justice—and justice is the expression of love in society. We can usually work out what justice is by putting ourself in the other person's place. The way Jesus put it was to say 'whatever you wish that men would do to you, do so to them' (Matthew 7:12).

Fallow ground does not bear a crop—but sometimes it is right to leave it fallow. But now God wants a crop. The ploughing will probably hurt, and the planting will probably be exhausting. But the word of God has to take root in us and abide in us. 'By this my Father is glorified, that you bear much fruit, and so prove to be my disciples' (John 15:8).

To think about

'Why should I start at the plough of my Lord, that maketh deep furrows on my soul? I know He is no idle husbandman. He purposeth a crop.'

('The Loveliness of Christ', from The letters of Samuel Rutherford, *Samuel Bagster and Sons Ltd*).

SB

The father's sorrow

When Israel was a child I loved him, and I called my son out of Egypt. But the more I called, the further they went away from me; they offered sacrifice to Baal and burnt incense to idols. I myself taught Ephraim to walk, I myself took them by the arm, but they did not know that I was the one caring for them, that I was leading them with human ties, with leading-strings of love, that, with them, I was like someone lifting an infant to his cheek, and that I bent down to feed him.

One human relationship is not enough to show us how God loves us. The love between a husband and a wife shows us something of the love. The love of a father for his son shows us something else—and there is heartache in both the loves. This son has gone away from the father, just as the prodigal son went away. Hosea tells us what goes on in the father's heart as he yearns for his son. He remembers when his son was a little boy, just out of babyhood and learning to walk. The father helped him—probably proud of his first, wobbling steps. He put a leading string on him—to lead him in love along the right way. He picked him up to cuddle him and bent down to feed him. That is what God did for Israel—but Israel didn't know who was looking after him.

To think about

Do I realize how God has looked after me and led me all the days of my life—except when I have turned away into my own way? Is God yearning after me because I have gone away from him? Am I like the eldest son in the story of the waiting father, living in the father's house but not enjoying the father's presence and all the benefits? Or have I come home to the Father—and has he made his home in me? Jesus said 'If a man loves me, he will keep my word, and my Father will love him, and we will come to him and make our home with him' (John 14:23).

SB

The father's love

Ephraim, how could I part with you? Israel, how could I give you up? How could I make you like Admah or treat you like Zeboiim? My heart within me is overwhelmed, fever grips my inmost being. I will not give rein to my fierce anger, I will not destroy Ephraim again, for I am God, not man, the Holy One in your midst, and I shall not come to you in anger.

In the verses that occur before today's reading the Father God has spoken through Hosea of the dire things that are going to happen to Israel because of her actions. Then the Father's heart is seized with compassion and he realizes he cannot do what he said he would do. If we start to get on our theological high horse and say that this is absurd because God cannot change then we shall miss the point. We shall also miss the point of most of what the prophets said and a good deal of what Jesus said.

Right at the heart of the universe is an enormous heart of love—the love of God and the sacred heart of Jesus. And a heart that loves can be broken. Perhaps it had to be 'made flesh' in order for that to happen. The incarnation is a mystery we shall never fathom. But we shall know far more about God by listening to the love stories in the Bible, and the stories about lost things and lost creatures that are found and rejoiced over, than we ever shall by studying the concept of God and knowing the Greek-based words that describe him as omniscient, omnipotent, omnipresent.

To think about

'Jesus found him. The man did not find Jesus; Jesus found him. That is the deepest truth of Christian faith; Jesus found me. Our fellowship with Him is rooted in His compassion.'

(William Temple, *Readings in St John's Gospel*, Macmillan).

SB

Lover and creator

I shall cure them of their disloyalty, I shall love them with all my heart, for my anger has turned away from them. I shall fall like dew on Israel, he will bloom like the lily and thrust out roots like the cedar of Lebanon; he will put out new shoots, he will have the beauty of the olive tree and the fragrance of Lebanon. They will come back to live in my shade; they will grow wheat again, they will make the vine flourish, their wine will be as famous as Lebanon's. What has Ephraim to do with idols any more when I hear him and watch over him? I am like an evergreen cypress, you owe your fruitfulness to me.

The Lover who is also Creator has beautiful plans for his beloved people. The divine physician will cure them of their disloyalty, and when the time is ripe he will walk on the earth along the dusty roads of Galilee and be the friend of sinners. The Lover who suffers when his beloved people sin will love them with all his heart—and one day on a hill outside Jerusalem the world will see how much that is and how much he suffers. Hosea showed us something of the love at the heart of the universe when he showed us his heartbreaking love for his wife.

The Creator God who loves you and me and the whole world desires a response from us—not just a once for all commitment of our life to him, but a continuous response of love that grows deeper and deeper every day of our life, until finally he possesses the whole of our heart. Nothing less will ever satisfy him—and nothing less will ever satisfy us.

To think about

'All that I am I give to you, and all that I have I share with you, within the love of God' (From the Marriage Service, The Alternative Service Book).

'Love is the cosmic energy that flames from the constellations and is concealed in the abyss of the atom; is whispered by the Holy Spirit in the heart, and placarded before men's eyes upon the Cross. It offers to us all that it has, and demands from us all that we can give.'

(Bishop Lumsden Barkway in the introduction to Evelyn Underhill's An Anthology of the Love of God, A. R. Mowbray & Co Ltd).

SB

The gospel of Luke

For the next six week Marcus Maxwell takes us through the first twelve chapters of the Gospel of Luke, and apart from Remembrance Sunday (at the start of week 46) the readings from Luke are on Sundays as well as weekdays.

Luke sets out his reasons for writing at the start of his Gospel: 'I too decided, after investigating everything carefully from the very first, to write an orderly account for you . . . so that you may know the truth concerning the things about which you have been instructed.'

The four Gospels are unique in all the world—and although some of the stories and some of the material is the same (particularly in the first three, the Synoptic Gospels) each Gospel is different. So as we read each one we discover different things about the good news (which is what gospel means: *god* = good, *spel* = news). The good news about God, about Jesus Christ and the kingdom of God, and about the love of God and the forgiveness of sins.

In a few weeks' time it will be Christmas. As we look ahead to that the Gospel of Luke is a good preparation, because it starts with the birth of Jesus, and says much more about it than the other Gospels. Our last reading from Luke, in chapter 12, points us to what is known as the second coming of Christ. So that makes a good lead in to Advent, when the Church looks back to his first coming, as a baby in Bethlehem, and looks ahead to his second coming in glory.

Learning the faith

Since many have undertaken to set down an orderly account of the events that have been fulfilled among us, just as they were handed on to us by those who from the beginning were eyewitnesses and servants of the word, I too decided, after investigating everything carefully from the very first, to write an orderly account for you, most excellent Theophilus, so that you may know the truth concerning the things about which you have been instructed.

Luke begins by dedicating his work to someone—a common practice in those days. We don't know who Theophilus was, perhaps a wealthy Christian or Gentile enquirer, or even a fictitious person who represents the enquiring believer (Theophilus means God-lover). But the point of the dedication is clear. Here is a book which sets out in an orderly way the events which are the basis of Christian faith.

Luke knows that ignorant Christians are weak Christians. I remember reading an account of a journalist who went into a church and asked some of the worshippers to explain their faith. None could. What point, asked the journalist, is there to a belief that its followers don't understand?

Of course, Christians are not all meant to be great theologians. We don't ask the average believer to debate their faith with a professor of philosophy. But it is still important for us to be able to explain our faith to others—and to ourselves.

Obviously, we can never interest others in the faith if we can't say what it means. But just as important is our own understanding. Faith is not just blind; it must relate to the world in which we live. Only by knowing something about it can we begin to act out our faith in daily life. So here Luke gives us a start—an account of the work of Jesus, and what it means.

Think

How ready are you to learn about things that interest you, sports, hobbies, and so on? How does that compare to your interest in learning about the things of God?

MM

Spirit of prophecy

Once when [Zechariah] was serving as priest before God and his section was on duty, he was chosen by lot, according to the custom of the priesthood, to enter the sanctuary of the Lord and offer incense. Now at the time of the incense offering, the whole assembly of the people was praying outside. Then there appeared to him an angel of the Lord, standing at the right side of the altar of incense. When Zechariah saw him, he was terrified; and fear overwhelmed him. But the angel said to him, 'Do not be afraid, Zechariah, for your prayer has been heard. Your wife Elizabeth will bear you a son, and you will name him John. You will have joy and gladness, and many will rejoice at his birth, for he will be great in the sight of the Lord. He must never drink wine or strong drink; even before his birth he will be filled with the Holy Spirit. He will turn many of the people of Israel to the Lord their God. With the spirit and power of Elijah he will go before him, to turn the hearts of parents to their children, and the disobedient to the wisdom of the righteous, to make ready a people prepared for the Lord.'

Amidst the wonder and doubt he felt, I suspect that Zechariah was worried. Prophets are all right when they are dead and gone, and their words are safely written down and respected as Scripture. It's another thing entirely to have to cope with the word of God being spoken here and now.

Yet if God is real, then his words are not just the words of the past. We should (and do) give a special place to the Bible, and it should be the check on our teaching and thinking today. But we also need to hear the living word of God. And where can we find that?

The answer is, wherever the Spirit of God is at work. The one who inspired the prophets of old is the one who is at work in the Church, and in the hearts and lives of Christians. And his task now, as ever, is to inspire us to speak of God, and to 'make ready a people prepared for the Lord'.

Pray

Lord, I may not be a prophet, but I have your Spirit. So guide my life and words to be a call to readiness for the coming of Jesus into the lives of those around me.

MM

God's favour

In the sixth month the angel Gabriel was sent by God to a town in Galilee called Nazareth, to a virgin engaged to a man whose name was Joseph, of the house of David. The virgin's name was Mary. And he came to her and said, 'Greetings, favoured one! The Lord is with you.' But she was much perplexed by his words and pondered what sort of greeting this might be. The angel said to her, 'Do not be afraid, Mary, for you have found favour with God. And now you will conceive in your womb and bear a son, and you will name him Jesus. He will be great and will be called the Son of the Most High, and the Lord God will give to him the throne of his ancestor David. He will reign over the house of Jacob forever, and of his kingdom there will be no end.'

What a wonderful person Mary must have been, to be chosen by God! Or so we are often told. But Luke doesn't say that. (Nor does Matthew.) We assume she must have been very pure and pious, because she 'found favour with God'. But isn't that because we tend to think that God's favour must somehow be deserved?

What the story actually tells us is that the angel appeared out of the blue and announced God's favour to Mary. She may well have been a wonderful person, but she may not have been. (In fact the only qualification we are told of is that she was engaged to a man of the house of David.) She wasn't chosen because she was wonderful. She was wonderful because she was chosen by God.

God came to Mary to give her Jesus, and that made her great. In a different but just as real sense, God comes to us with the gift of Jesus. And if it is the gift that makes Mary great, it is the same gift which makes us great!

It may seem very arrogant to put ourselves on a level with the mother of Jesus. But it is God who *gives* his favour, not we who earn it. This is the wonder of the grace of God: that he comes to us, the undeserving, with a gift beyond understanding.

Meditate

You have more in common with Mary than you may have realized!

MM

Spirit of life

Mary said to the angel, 'How can this be, since I am a virgin?' The angel said to her, 'The Holy Spirit will come upon you, and the power of the Most High will overshadow you; therefore the child to be born will be holy; he will be called Son of God. And now, your relative Elizabeth in her old age has also conceived a son; and this is the sixth month for her who was said to be barren. For nothing will be impossible with God.' Then Mary said, 'Here I am, the servant of the Lord; let it be with me according to your word.' Then the angel departed from her.

Yesterday we saw God's gift to Mary as similar to his grace to us. Today the similarity becomes even stronger. New life is coming to Mary—the presence of Jesus. Of course, Mary's experience is unique; only she will bear the child Christ. But the new life which is the presence of Jesus comes to all Christians, as they open their hearts to the grace of God. In that sense, Mary is the Christian, and her experience is ours.

A new life and a new creation are taking place in Mary, and how does this happen? By the power of the Holy Spirit. It is the wind/Spirit who swept over the waters of chaos at creation (Genesis 1:2) who comes to create again; the breath/Spirit who was life to Adam (Genesis 2:7) who stirs new life into being.

And this is the work of the Holy Spirit in all Christians—to bring about a new creation (2 Corinthians 5:17) and a new birth (John 3:5–6). It is by the overshadowing of the power of the Most High that we are born again.

So this is the characteristic work of the Holy Spirit, to recreate and bring to life. It is not for nothing that when the Spirit hits the Church, we speak of renewal. The Holy Spirit is the wind of change.

Pray

Father, I fear change, and I fear new birth, for there is pain in both. Give me the grace you gave to Mary, that your new creation and rebirth will continue in my life and my church, so that we may be renewed in the image of Christ.

MM

The heart of worship

Mary said, 'My soul magnifies the Lord, and my spirit rejoices in God my Saviour, for he has looked with favour on the lowliness of his servant. Surely, from now on all generations will call me blessed; for the Mighty One has done great things for me, and holy is his name. His mercy is for those who fear him from generation to generation.'

Have you ever seen a child receive some delightful gift? The look of wonder and joy, and often of gratitude. The hugs and kisses, and thanks. If we are cynical, we dismiss the thanks—real love isn't bought, we say. But if we are cynical, we miss the point, and forget our own experience.

Haven't we ourselves been suddenly bowled over by some surprise joy—a gift, a moment of exquisite beauty or wonder? And haven't we suddenly wanted to cry aloud our thanks and praise and love to the giver? When we recognize the giver as God, then we have discovered the heart of worship.

Mary's hymn of praise begins with her own experience of God, and her awareness of what he has done for her. So it is with our worship. We begin with what God has done. Of course, we rarely come into church full of the joy of salvation! That's why many churches use a liturgy which sets out the basis of our worship.

Some Christians feel that liturgical worship is a kind of second best—that it cannot truly be 'led by the Spirit'. But that fails to recognize what is going on. In liturgies we hear Scripture and sermon and recite the Creed, all reminders of God's mighty acts in history ('as he promised to our ancestors'). We confess our sins and receive his forgiveness, and to all this we respond in prayer and praise. And hopefully we learn to recognize the hand of God on our own lives, and give thanks for that too. Just as Mary recited the acts of God, we can learn much from such reminders.

Reflect

Take time to remember what God has done, both in the great events of the Bible and history, and in your own life. Make them the basis of your own time of worship and praise.

MM

Manifesto

He has shown strength with his arm; he has scattered the proud in the thoughts of their hearts. He has brought down the powerful from their thrones, and lifted up the lowly; he has filled the hungry with good things, and sent the rich away empty. He has helped his servant Israel, in remembrance of his mercy, according to the promise he made to our ancestors, to Abraham and to his descendants forever.

The second half of the Magnificat may pose at least two problems. First, it doesn't seem all that religious—it's more like some sort of revolutionary manifesto. Secondly, it says God has *done* all these things, when it is obvious that he has not!

The first problem isn't a problem with Mary's song—it's a problem with us. When we read the Bible, we meet a God who is very concerned with people's everyday, material lives. He cares about justice and compassion for the poor, and is angered by abusers of power and hoarders of wealth.

The notion that religion is all about immaterial, 'spiritual' things is a heresy that has no place in true Christianity. Yet it is a comfortable heresy, because it allows us to be 'Christian' with no challenge to our values and our way of life. Mary sees it differently. The coming of Jesus into the world is the turning upside-down of human values, and a challenge to the way we see the world.

That answers the second problem. No, these things are not yet reality, but the fate of the oppressors, the heedless rich and the self-reliant is sealed. When God chose to be born incarnate of a Jewish peasant girl, to save the world through the mystery of the crucified Lord, and to conquer death in a garden, he opened the way to a true new order. Those who belong to him must indeed see the song of Mary as a challenge to the old ways, and a call to a new set of values.

Think

What difference does the coming of Christ make to your values, your idea of success and prosperity, your lifestyle?

MM

The humble lifted high

In that region there were shepherds living in the fields, keeping watch over their flock by night. Then an angel of the Lord stood before them, and the glory of the Lord shone around them, and they were terrified. But the angel said to them, 'Do not be afraid; for see—I am bringing you good news of great joy for all the people: to you is born this day at the city of David a Saviour, who is the Messiah, the Lord. This will be a sign for you: you will find a child wrapped in bands of cloth and lying in a manger.' And suddenly there was with the angel a multitude of the heavenly host, praising God and saying, 'Glory to God in the highest heaven, and on earth peace among those whom he favours!'

When Matthew tells of the birth of Jesus, he sets it against the background of Herod and the Magi. The contrast is made between earthly kings and the King of kings. Luke gives us the shepherds, who out of all the people of Israel see the angels and for a brief moment glimpse the worship of heaven.

Yet in each case the point is the same—the Messiah comes to the humble and poor and is born in a stable rather than a palace. No doubt we've all heard that in a dozen Christmas sermons, but there's another way of looking at it.

Probably the shepherds were no more religious or prayerful than anyone else. In fact, probably less than many. Yet they were the ones who saw the angels. When we pray and worship, perhaps we do so with too little expectation. We think of the great saints and mystics, or the writers of paperback books on 'How God Really Blessed Me and My Church', as the ones who have great experiences of God. But it isn't true. We are as likely (or as unlikely!) to glimpse the reality of heaven as anyone else. In our worship we are lifted high by the God who is no respecter of persons, and we too may hear the angels sing.

Think

What do you expect from your worship? What effect would (or does!) a close encounter with God have on you?

MM

Out of the desert

In the fifteenth year of the reign of Emperor Tiberius, when Pontius Pilate was governor of Judea . . . the word of God came to John son of Zechariah in the wilderness. He went into all the region around the Jordan, proclaiming a baptism of repentance for the forgiveness of sins, as it is written in the book of the words of the prophet Isaiah, 'The voice of one crying out in the wilderness: "Prepare the way of the Lord, make his paths straight. Every valley shall be filled, and every mountain and hill shall be made low, and the crooked shall be made straight, and the rough ways be made smooth; and all flesh shall see the salvation of God."'

We don't know what John was doing in the desert of the Judaean wilderness, but it is a fair bet that he was preparing himself for the task he knew God would give him. At last the word of God came to him, and he emerged, like the great prophet Elijah, to be a 'troubler of Israel'.

The desert is a place of great significance in the Bible. It is a place of terror and mystery, the abode of demons. Yet at the same time, it is the place where God is near, and where people return to their religious roots. It was in the desert that God shaped the Israelites during their wanderings with Moses, and in the desert that God made his covenant with his people. So the desert is a place both of desolation and of deep spiritual experience.

We use the term to describe those times in our lives when God seems far away, and prayer appears empty—the desert experience. It is at times like that when we wonder whether our faith is worthwhile. Yet it is our desert experiences that often draw us closer to God.

As we persevere through our dry spells and difficulties, God meets us afresh, and gives us a new insight into him and a renewed experience of his presence.

It is perseverance when prayer is hard that shapes our faith and deepens our experience of God.

Meditate

God uses the desert of the heart as he used the desert of Sinai—to shape and toughen his people, so that, like John, they may hear his voice clearly.

MM

Troubler of Israel

John said to the crowds that came out to be baptized by him, 'You brood of vipers! Who warned you to flee from the wrath to come? Bear fruits worthy of repentance. Do not begin to say to yourselves, "We have Abraham as our ancestor"; for I tell you, God is able from these stones to raise up children to Abraham. Even now the axe is lying at the root of the trees; every tree therefore that does not bear good fruit is cut down and thrown into the fire.'

Centuries earlier, King Ahab had called Elijah the 'troubler of Israel'. Like Elijah, John came with a message which was hardly calculated to bring comfort.

The sermons we hear and preach are much more polite and temperate, and that is probably a good thing. Yet when the word of God ceases to be troubling, we have ceased to listen. John challenged the complacency of his listeners, their self-satisfaction and sense of well-being. And that is the first task of the gospel, and the first stage of the Holy Spirit's work in bringing renewal.

As long as people are satisfied with the way things are, they will never respond to the message of the gospel, for it is a call to repentance and a promise of new things to come. Whether we are hearing the good news of Jesus for the first time, or striving to grow as Christians, we need what someone once called a 'holy dissatisfaction'—a sense that things are not as they should be, and need to change.

If we have that, then God's change will not be far away, and new life is coming. If we have not, then we have the most effective barrier in the world to the grace of God.

This means that when the Church receives complaints—about criticizing the government, about challenging expectations of baptism enquirers, about evangelism, or whatever—then there is a fair chance that it is doing its job. For only the troubled heart seeks for the peace of God.

Think

Where do you need to be challenged in your Christian life? What challenge does your church present to its local community?

MM

Baptisms

John answered all of them by saying, 'I baptize you with water; but one who is more powerful than I is coming; I am not worthy to untie the thong of his sandals. He will baptize you with the Holy Spirit and fire. His winnowing fork is in his hand, to clear his threshing floor and to gather the wheat into his granary; but the chaff he will burn with unquenchable fire' . . . Now when all the people were baptized, and when Jesus also had been baptized and was praying, the heaven was opened, and the Holy Spirit descended upon him in bodily form like a dove. And a voice came from heaven, 'You are my Son, the Beloved; with you I am well pleased.'

Later, in prison, John was to doubt that Jesus was the Messiah. Perhaps it was the depression of being locked up, but perhaps it was also because the judgment of fire had not come. Jesus certainly brought the power of the Spirit, but the sweeping away of sin and sinners did not happen.

But then, Jesus was a strange Messiah. He brought healing and the presence of God, but the judgment he reserved for himself. If he underwent a baptism for repentance, it was to identify with sinners. And the judgment against sin was a judgment he would bear on behalf of those sinners as he hung on the cross.

Of course, he himself saw a final judgment, but he had changed the rules. It would not be a separation of sinners from righteous people, but a separation of those sinners who had accepted the grace of God from the sinners who had not.

Meanwhile, Jesus' baptism marks the beginning of his ministry. As he accepts the burden of human sin, he also receives the power of the Holy Spirit. No work of God can be carried out by merely human strength. It must be led and empowered by the Spirit of God. And the first step to receiving God's power is to accept the will of God. That's as true now as ever it was.

Think

Do you feel that your Christian life lacks power, and the experience of the Spirit? Could it be that you want the power and experience, but not the work to use them in?

MM

Led into temptation

Jesus, full of the Holy Spirit, returned from the Jordan and was led by the Spirit in the wilderness, where for forty days he was tempted by the devil. He ate nothing at all during those days, and when they were over, he was famished. The devil said to him, 'If you are the Son of God, command this stone to become a loaf of bread.' Jesus answered him, 'It is written, "One does not live by bread alone."'

'And lead us not into temptation...' We pray that prayer often enough, don't we? Yet that is exactly what happens to Jesus. The Spirit leads him to a confrontation with the devil; an encounter which takes the form of severe temptation. Jesus emerges victorious, but it is not without a struggle, as he faces the possibility of abusing his power for his own ends, rather than God's.

I seem to spend half my time feeling down in the dumps, and far away from God. Temptations come, and sometimes I resist, and sometimes I give in. And in it all, I often wonder where God is, what he is playing at, and why I even bother. That, of course, is the real temptation— 'Why bother? Why keep on trying to serve God, to live by Christian standards? Why not take the line of least resistance?'

The answer, of course, is that a faith which isn't tested is no faith at all. If we are kept safe from all opposition, all temptation, we are not really choosing to serve God, or learning to know him. We are simply sliding along well-greased grooves.

God could have made the path smooth and easy for Jesus, but that would have been pointless. It was by Jesus's free choice of service and sacrifice that salvation became possible. God could make the path easy for us, but we would not be free children. We would be pets in a gilded cage.

It is as we choose to cling to God in the times of difficulty and darkness that our relationship with him grows and is strengthened. And of course, as we choose God, we find that we do indeed have the strength to hang on. Because it is God, through the Holy Spirit, who gives us that strength.

Think

What hard times have you faced? How did you respond? And what did you learn about God?

MM

Ruler of the world

Then the devil led him up and showed him in an instant all the kingdoms of the world. And the devil said to him, 'To you I will give their glory and all this authority; for it has been given over to me, and I will give it over to anyone I please. If you, then, will worship me, it will all be yours.' Jesus answered him, 'It is written, "Worship the Lord your God, and serve only him."'

God is the creator of the world, and for all its troubles, he is at work in it at all times. This is a fact we celebrate in our worship and acknowledge in our mission. Yet there is another face to the world which we forget at our peril.

In the second temptation, the devil offers Jesus the nations of the world. It isn't an empty offer, for in a real sense they are his to give.

Good and evil are not just matters of individual actions and attitudes. They get built into the systems of thought, economics and politics which wrap the world in an invisible net. And because they are of human origin, they are flawed like their creators, and become systems which oppose God and the message of the gospel with an almost living malevolence.

The result is that the world is not a neutral place in which we can practise our faith. It is a place where faith comes hard, and obedience to God is opposed. Later in Luke's Gospel Jesus compares himself to a robber invading a strong man's home, and we too need to remember that we are part of an invading force, called to bring the gospel into hostile territory.

None of this means that all is hopeless, nor that there is not good in the world (it is God's after all). But it does mean that we are strangers in a strange land, and where we take the teaching of Jesus seriously we can often expect a rough ride.

Think

Where do you see the hand of God at work in the world? And where does it most look like the devil's domain?

MM

Body and soul

When [Jesus] came to Nazareth, where he had been brought up, he went to the synagogue on the sabbath day, as was his custom. He stood up to read, and the scroll of the prophet Isaiah was given to him. He unrolled the scroll and found the place where it was written: 'The Spirit of the Lord is upon me, because he has anointed me to bring good news to the poor. He has sent me to proclaim release to the captives and recovery of sight to the blind, to let the oppressed go free, to proclaim the year of the Lord's favour.'

How should we interpret the passage that Jesus took as his manifesto? Should we look for a spiritual meaning, and speak of spiritual sight for those who are blind to the reality of God, and freedom for those held captive to sin and oppressed by failure?

Or should we see a call to action in the physical world, a statement of concern for the poor, revolution for the oppressed, reform for prisons?

Both ways of looking at the gospel have their champions, and both, if we insist on a choice, are wrong. They are wrong because the choice itself makes a distinction between physical and spiritual, the everyday world and religious life. It is a distinction we see every time someone complains about the vicar preaching politics, or refuses to sign a petition on human rights because the gospel is simply about personal salvation.

The passage itself doesn't give a hint of that distinction, because in the Bible it doesn't exist. We think of body and soul, physical and spiritual, as separate things.

But the Bible does not. It sees both as one. Humans do not have souls—they are souls, for we are spiritual animals. What happens to us spiritually affects us physically and vice versa.

So the gospel is a call to recognize our spiritual poverty and turn to the riches of God. And it is a call to aid the poor. It preaches release from the oppression of sin and an end to injustice in the world. Anything less is only half the good news.

Think

Which 'side' of the gospel do you prefer to stress? Why?

MM

Local hero

They said, 'Is not this Joseph's son?' He said to them, 'Doubtless you will quote to me this proverb, "Doctor, cure yourself!" And you will say, "Do here also in your hometown the things that we have heard you did at Capernaum."' And he said, 'Truly I tell you, no prophet is accepted in the prophet's hometown . . .' When they heard this, all in the synagogue were filled with rage. They got up, drove him out of the town, and led him to the brow of the hill on which their town was built, so that they might hurl him off the cliff. But he passed through the midst of them and went on his way.

In the other gospels, the rejection of Jesus at Nazareth is because his neighbours know him too well. They can't believe a local lad could do so well. But I think Luke tells the story a bit differently. Jesus's own town is quite ready to believe—up to a point.

They speak well of him, and are impressed at first. 'Come on, they say, let's see you do your stuff.' Only when he explains that this is the wrong understanding of a prophet's work do they get angry—not with his claims for himself, but with his refusal to perform for them.

I think they wanted to make a fuss of Jesus—local boy makes good, roll up and see! But there were to be no special favours for Nazareth. And so they got angry—'Who does he think he is, anyway? What's Capernaum got that his own town hasn't?' and so on.

If I'm right, there's a terrible warning for us in all this. As the Church, we think of Jesus as ours. We know him and we serve him, so we have a special claim on him. But we don't. Jesus is for everyone, and woe betide those who want to keep him for themselves!

Yet still we fence Jesus off from everyone, hiding him behind religious jargon, impenetrable church services, music which has no connection to popular culture. Then we have the nerve to complain that no one seems interested in religion any more. Perhaps they would be interested in Jesus, if only he wasn't hidden from sight behind the strange trappings of religion.

Think

How easy is it for a stranger in your church to see Jesus? Or do they need to learn a new language first?

MM

Retreat and advance

At daybreak [Jesus] departed and went into a deserted place. And the crowds were looking for him; and when they reached him, they wanted to prevent him from leaving them. But he said to them, 'I must proclaim the good news of the kingdom of God to the other cities also; for I was sent for this purpose.' So he continued proclaiming the message in the synagogues of Judea.

Quite often we see Jesus getting away from it all for a while, and probably praying. He knew the importance of spiritual refreshment. It is impossible simply to keep going at anything without a rest, and our spiritual life is the same.

For some of us, special retreats provide the needed spiritual refreshment. For most, it is Sunday worship that gives the new strength we need to follow God through the week (though I hope going to church isn't going into a deserted place!). And that's why allowing our worship to tail off is soon followed by ineffectiveness in our spiritual lives.

The retreat from the hurly-burly is not an end in itself, though. Jesus would not remain where he was, but went on with his task. Once he was refreshed through prayer, it was time to get on with the task. 'I was sent for this purpose,' he said. And we too are sent for the same purpose—to proclaim the good news.

As with Jesus, so for us the proclamation of the gospel springs from the time we spend with God, alone in our prayers or together with other Christians in church.

Perhaps another point we could reflect on is the way Jesus did not allow himself to be side-tracked. It might have been tempting to stay where he had such a good welcome. But he had a job to do. We can learn from that. Don't we, and our churches, so easily spend our time and energy on things that are not part of our central task?

Meditate

Come to me, all who labour and are heavy laden, and I will refresh you . . .

MM

Saints and sinners

[Jesus] . . . saw a tax collector named Levi, sitting at the tax booth; and he said to him, 'Follow me.' And he got up, left everything, and followed him. Then Levi gave a great banquet for him in his house; and there was a large crowd of tax collectors and others sitting at the table with them. The Pharisees and their scribes were complaining to his disciples, saying, 'Why do you eat and drink with tax collectors and sinners?' Jesus answered, 'Those who are well have no need of a physician, but those who are sick; I have come to call not the righteous but sinners to repentance.'

I know of an elderly gentleman who left his church, never to return, when someone told him that he was a sinner. It was an extreme case, but it is the perfect illustration of the attitude of the Pharisees in this passage. Of course, you may say, we know that we are sinners, and that Jesus came to save us. That's what makes us Christians. And I'm sure that my old chap knew it too. But on that one occasion, he *knew* it. And there's a world of difference.

Modern Bible scholars tell us that the Pharisees were not really self-righteous, and that their teaching was really very similar to that of Jesus; that they are given an unfair press in the Gospels. I believe that—up to a point. When we look at the writings of the Pharisees, they are far from being the rigid legalists of the Gospels. Just as when we look at the teaching of our Church, we find that we are all sinners saved by the grace of God.

But in practice, I think the Pharisees were much as Jesus met them, and much as we are. We pay lip service to our need for God's forgiveness, but at heart think we have an awful lot to our credit simply by being good church-goers.

Jesus did not call the righteous—because they would not respond. Only those who really know, in their heart of hearts, their need of God's grace can truly repent. We have a special name for those who know the depth of their sinfulness—we call them saints.

Pray

Give us true repentance, and make us saints.

MM

Renew the Church— but not yet!

He also told them a parable: 'No one tears a piece from a new garment and sews it on an old garment; otherwise the new will be torn and the piece from the new will not match the old. And no one puts new wine into old wineskins; otherwise the new wine will burst the skins and will be spilled, and the skins will be destroyed. But new wine must be put into fresh wineskins. And no one after drinking old wine desires new wine, but says, "The old is good." '

What a confusing passage! Is Jesus in favour of the new or the old? What we should realize is that the last bit, about preferring old wine, is an ironic comment on the Pharisees. Because they have such a good knowledge of the old ways, they are not interested in trying the new.

Looked at in that light, Jesus is saying that the new order he brings cannot be contained within the old faith of Israel; it goes beyond the old boundaries.

There's an important lesson here for us. We too can be tempted to defend our old ways of worship and faith to the death, while God himself may be wanting to do something new.

Recently a senior clergyman in our diocese told me sadly that some churches were thriving and growing but most were in decline. When I asked what was the difference between the two types, he said, 'Vision'. Whatever their churchmanship, the growing churches were open to change, and wanted something new. The dying ones did not.

Looked at in that light, there is only one option for us. We must be thirsty for new wine. It is not an easy thing to do, for there is comfort in the mellow old wine, while the new is too robust for some tastes. But we must develop the taste, for otherwise we join the Pharisees—staunch defenders of an age that is past.

Pray

Father, give us a vision for new things, a thirst for new wine, so that we will grow and move forwards in the footsteps of Christ.

MM

The purpose of the law

One sabbath while Jesus was going through the grainfields, his disciples plucked some heads of grain, rubbed them in their hands, and ate them. But some of the Pharisees said, 'Why are you doing what is not lawful on the sabbath?' Jesus answered, 'Have you not read what David did when he and his companions were hungry? He entered the house of God and took and ate the bread of the Presence, which it is not lawful for any but the priests to eat, and gave some to his companions?' Then he said to them, 'The Son of Man is lord of the sabbath.'

One Easter day, we had three communion services. Normally the evening one would be evening prayer, but it seemed right to cater on this special day for those who couldn't come in the morning. Only a couple of the twenty or so present took communion, and they said they felt uncomfortable doing it on their own. But the rest had had their communion already, and somewhere they'd been taught only to receive the sacrament once in a day.

As a result the important aspect of eucharistic fellowship was diluted. It was the classic case of tradition taking the place of love and common sense.

The same thing happens in our reading. There were good reasons for the law against working on the sabbath, but the Pharisees had taken it too far. Jesus understood the true point of the law, whether it was God's law or human law—that it is there to serve people, and to protect their well-being.

The disciples broke the letter of the law, by doing what was technically work, but obeyed its meaning (probably without giving it much thought) by meeting their simple need for food.

Christians, like the Pharisees, can get a reputation for being against things, when really we should be for people. The laws and traditions of church and state are good only when they serve us. When they stop doing so, they need to be rethought in the light of Jesus' attitude.

Think

Are there traditions and rules you keep that have long lost their meaning and purpose?

MM

Do it now!

On another sabbath he entered the synagogue and taught, and there was a man there whose right hand was withered. The scribes and the Pharisees watched him to see whether he would cure on the sabbath, so that they might find an accusation against him. Even though he knew what they were thinking, he said to the man with the withered hand, 'Come and stand here.' He got up and stood there. Then Jesus said to them, 'I ask you, is it lawful to do good or to do harm on the sabbath, to save life or to destroy it?' After looking around at all of them, he said to him, 'Stretch out your hand.' He did so, and his hand was restored. But they were filled with fury and discussed with one another what they might do to Jesus.

It was late at night, I was tired, the house was warm and it was raining hard. The phone rang. 'Will you come and see a lady at the hospital? She's unconscious, and I don't think she'll wake up.' I asked whether she was likely actually to die in the night, and the nurse said no. So I said I'd go in the morning. In the morning I went, and the patient had died.

The patient had been alone and unconscious. Could my visit and my brief prayers have done any good? I don't know. But I know that my delayed visit did no good at all. I don't put off calls these days.

We have all put off some good we could do, and perhaps sometimes we've missed the moment. The Pharisees would not object to treating an emergency on the sabbath, but unnecessary work, which could as well be done tomorrow, was forbidden. The man's hand had been lame for years. One day would make no difference. But Jesus saw it differently. If there is an opportunity to do good, to do God's work, it must be seized at once. Who knows what tomorrow will bring?

Our motives for delay are usually less worthy than those of the Pharisees—laziness, fear of involvement, fear of commitment. But God sends us opportunities for the present, not the future. Often they don't come again.

Pray

Lord, help me to recognize your moments, and to seize them as they come.

MM

Patriarchs

Now during those days he went out to the mountain to pray; and he spent the night in prayer to God. And when day came, he called his disciples and chose twelve of them, whom he also named apostles: Simon, whom he named Peter, and his brother Andrew, and James, and John, and Philip, and Bartholomew, and Matthew, and Thomas, and James son of Alphaeus, and Simon, who was called the Zealot, and Judas son of James, and Judas Iscariot, who became a traitor.

One of the strange facts about the Gospels is that the names of some of Jesus' twelve disciples differ in various lists. Probably this means that some of the twelve played little important role in the early Church, and were overshadowed by the more active ones. Or perhaps they remained with Jesus' followers in Galilee, which soon became a backwater in Church history. Or perhaps some of the legends of long missionary journeys, and martyrdoms in distant lands, have a spark of truth to them. We really don't know.

What is important, however, is that the number is remembered quite well. There were twelve. It was one of the most significant numbers in the Jewish faith, for it was the number of the tribes of Israel.

By choosing twelve disciples, Jesus was stating clearly that the old people of God must be renewed. His followers were to be the nucleus of a new people of God.

As time went by, the amazing discovery was made that this new people of God was to be defined not by birth into the descendants of Abraham, but by faith in Jesus Christ. We who follow Jesus can claim the title of 'God's people'.

That means that, like Israel, we are called to be a 'light to the nations', a witness to the presence of the living God in our midst.

These days the Church seems (at least in the West) to be more concerned with its inward troubles than its outward witness. The sad thing about the Decade of Evangelism is that we have to have one—because we forget what it means to be God's people.

Think

Make a list of ideas you associate with the phrase, 'People of God'. How does your local church measure up? And what can you do to improve it?

MM

Seeds of destruction

Now during those days he went out to the mountain to pray; and he spent the night in prayer to God. And when day came, he called his disciples and chose twelve of them, whom he also named apostles: Simon, whom he named Peter, and his brother Andrew, and James, and John, and Philip, and Bartholomew, and Matthew, and Thomas, and James son of Alphaeus, and Simon, who was called the Zealot, and Judas son of James, and Judas Iscariot, who became a traitor.

Yes, I know it's a dull passage to read twice, but more needs to be said about the disciples—and about the Church which looks to them as its first members.

Yesterday, I said we need to rediscover what it means to be the people of God, and I believe that. But there is one common idea about that rediscovery, or renewal, which we adopt at our peril. And that is the idea that the Church should be a collection of pure and holy people.

All through history, there have been two conflicting views about the Church, summed up in the question, 'Society of saints, or school for sinners?'

I remember once going with a friend to a little church in Liverpool, where we were greeted at the door with a request for our letter of introduction from our church; proof that we were worthy to enter the hallowed portals. We didn't have one, but could quote the name of a well-known leader of that denomination, so we were allowed in. That's an extreme example, but there are more and more churches, of all denominations, suggesting that we should beware of letting in any but 'real' Christians.

But I don't think that's the right approach, because the twelfth disciple was Judas Iscariot. In her series of plays, *The Man Born to be King*, Dorothy Sayers pictured Jesus recognizing the danger in Judas, but offering him his chance for salvation. And that, I think, is close to the truth. We can never be sure that our church does not carry a similar threat within it—in fact we can be sure it does. But we are here, like Jesus, to offer the chance of salvation. And that means opening the doors to all.

Think

What barriers do we raise around the Church? Which ones are necessary, and which deny people their chance?

MM

In remembrance . . .

For I received from the Lord what I also delivered to you, that the Lord Jesus on the night when he was betrayed took bread, and when he had given thanks, he broke it, and said, 'This is my body which is for you. Do this in remembrance of me.' In the same way also the cup, after supper, saying, 'This cup is the new covenant in my blood. Do this, as often as you drink it, in remembrance of me.' For as often as you eat this bread and drink the cup, you proclaim the Lord's death until he comes.

To remember is to bear in mind, and not to forget. Every Sunday in almost every church in the world is a remembrance Sunday, as people remember the events of the first Good Friday and the first Easter Sunday. The words differ slightly, but not much. The worshippers eat the bread and drink the wine of communion, and hear again the words that Jesus spoke on the night before he died—and the eating and the drinking are to be 'in remembrance of Me'.

This Sunday is another Remembrance Sunday—and on this day we remember the dead of two world wars and of other wars as well. Most of us cannot remember them in the days when they were alive on this earth—but then we can't remember Jesus Christ in that way either. Yet we believe that he is alive—and that all those who died in Christ are alive in him. Alive now—and that one day we shall see them again. We can say thank you for that, and give praise to God for it.

But perhaps there is another sort of remembering that we should do on Remembrance Sunday. A remembering of the agony of war, and the hideous cruelty that men have inflicted on one another throughout the years. There can be 'a just war', they say—a war fought for the right reasons, to put down evil. War can bring out the good in us—but it can also bring out the worst. 'Our Father . . . Forgive us our sins, as we forgive those that sin against us . . .'

A prayer to reflect on but not to pray

Lord that made the dragon, grant me thy peace,
But say not that I should give up the gold,
Nor move, nor die. Others would have the gold.
Kill rather, Lord, the Men and the other dragons;
Then I can sleep; go when I will to drink.

C.S. Lewis, 'The Dragon Speaks', in *Poems*

SB

True happiness

And [Jesus] lifted up his eyes on his disciples, and said: 'Blessed are you poor, for yours is the kingdom of God. Blessed are you that hunger now, for you shall be satisfied. Blessed are you that weep now, for you shall laugh. Blessed are you when men hate you, and when they exclude you and revile you, and cast out your name as evil, on account of the Son of man! Rejoice in that day, and leap for joy, for behold, your reward is great in heaven; for so their fathers did to the prophets.'

It seems ridiculous to list the worst disasters—hunger, poverty, sorrow and exclusion from society—and then say that those who suffer them are happy, or blessed. And we know that Jesus did not see suffering as good in itself, for he went out of his way to relieve it wherever he could.

In these beatitudes (so much starker than Matthew's) Jesus takes up an old biblical theme—that those who have nowhere on earth to put their trust must put it in God alone; and that God will deliver those who trust in him. The truth in this is that it is usually wealth and health that turn us away from God. When all is going well, we are less likely, in our selfishness, to pray or seek God's guidance. It's when things get rough that we remember our Lord and return to him. So true blessedness is found by those who, pushed to the edge, return to the one who alone loves and cares for them utterly.

But there's more to it than that. These words are for the disciples, and they are a warning that following Jesus is not easy. It is a rocky path, and there will be opposition from those who don't want to hear the gospel, or who, on hearing it, want nothing more than to remove all reminders of its challenge.

This is a lesson that many churches are learning today. As we begin to take the Decade of Evangelism seriously, and to make our voice heard, we find that those who spoke well of the Church, and who perhaps contributed to the odd fund (but never came to worship) have become less sympathetic. It's a good sign. The Church has ceased to be part of the landscape, and the challenge of the gospel is beginning to bite.

A thought

Is your church just local scenery, or does it make others uneasy?

MM

Gospel of doom

'But woe to you that are rich, for you have received your consolation. Woe to you that are full now, for you shall hunger. Woe to you that laugh now, for you shall mourn and weep. Woe to you, when all men speak well of you, for so their fathers did to the false prophets.'

'I don't mind the good news of the gospel, it's accepting the bad news that is difficult.' So said a friend of mine when he was wrestling with the step of faith that would plunge him into Christian discipleship.

What he meant was that it is good to be told that God has an infinite love for you, that he wants you to spend eternity with him, that he has resources of strength and support for your life here and now. It is less palatable to be told that you must change your way of life, stop doing enjoyable but hurtful things—in short, pay the cost of discipleship.

Luke gives us not only a set of beatitudes, but their downside—a set of woes to those who do not accept the strange blessings of the kingdom. They are a statement of judgment of the ways of the world. Those who have become prosperous and well-fed at the expense of the poor will find in the end that they have gained only emptiness. Those who have found happiness on the world's terms will find that all too often that happiness is swept away as the systems of the world collapse in the light of God's judgment. And then there are those who have found popularity by ignoring the call of God to challenge the wrongs among which they live.

Of course, not all human success and well-being is wicked. But the course of life may often be easier for those who compromise (and which one of us does not?) with the demands of a world that ignores God.

The woes remind us that while we are called to count the cost of following Jesus, in fact there is no choice. Failure to follow him in the end leads literally to nothing.

A prayer

Lord, deliver me from compromising with the world and seeking success and happiness at the expense of knowing and obeying you.

MM

Foolish love

'But I say to you that hear, Love your enemies, do good to those who hate you, bless those who curse you, pray for those who abuse you. To him who strikes you on the cheek, offer the other also; and from him who takes away your coat do not withhold even your shirt. Give to every one who begs from you; and of him who takes away your goods do not ask them again. And as you wish that men would do to you, do so to them.'

The late F.F. Bruce once wrote that there are two types of hard sayings of Jesus: those that are hard to understand, and those that are hard to do. Today's reading is both.

It's hard to understand, because it sounds as though these verses are just telling us to lie down and be doormats. And we know that that does no good at all. Those who simply remain passive in the face of evil provoke further abuse. The torturer and the schoolyard bully are both provoked by weakness, and their evil increases.

Yet retaliation also fuels violence and abuse. As we look at the news from Northern Ireland, don't we see the continuing spiral of revenge? Someone is killed, and someone else is killed in retaliation, which provokes a vengeance murder, which leads... and so on.

Jesus's answer, it seems to me, is more radical either than revenge or passivity. He tells us that those who are secure in the strength of God can turn that strength towards their aggressors—but in love. The answer is not to do nothing in the face of evil, but to do good. Reach out to those who hurt with forgiveness and help. It's hard, though, and needs the strength that can come from God alone.

It also takes practice. We need to get into the habit of forgiving the small hurts and injustices that come our way each day. When we can do that, we shall be ready for the great acts of love. Perhaps the best thing we can do for those we feel have wronged us is to pray for them— not that God will make them nice to us (which is really praying for ourselves) but that God will meet their needs, and heal their hurts.

A prayer

Pray for someone who has hurt or offended you.

MM

Clear sight

He also told them a parable: 'Can a blind man lead a blind man? Will they not both fall into a pit? A disciple is not above his teacher, but every one when he is fully taught will be like his teacher. Why do you see the speck that is in your brother's eye, but do not notice the log that is in your own eye? Or how can you say to your brother, "Brother, let me take out the speck that is in your eye," when you yourself do not see the log that is in your own eye? You hypocrite, first take the log out of your own eye, and then you will see clearly to take out the speck that is in your brother's eye.'

This passage is a good example of the way the Gospel writers tended to work. There are three sayings (which Jesus may have said at separate times), two of them linked by the theme of vision, and one in between that is meant to explain the others. The saying about the blind man tells us that those who claim to lead (the Pharisees?) can be useless unless they have a clear vision of the path. Before they can see clearly, they need to be learners, listening to Jesus, so that they in turn can be reliable teachers. Then they will be able to help others with their problems. Seen in that light, the saying about the speck in the eye is not just a warning not to judge others, but a statement about what we need if we are to be of help to others.

I remember a woman who used to proclaim the gospel in a loud voice at every opportunity. But she was well known to be a miserly, grasping person who did little to ease the living conditions of tenants in the dilapidated houses that she let out. Not surprisingly, no one took her seriously. Even worse, many people were put off the Christian faith by her. True Christian witness is not simply telling people about Jesus, but letting them see what a difference he has made to us. We need, not just for our own sakes, but as a prelude to evangelism, to bring our needs to Christ and let him heal us.

A thought

What difference does knowing Jesus make to you? That is the difference others will see, and find attractive.

MM

Standing firm

'Why do you call me, "Lord, Lord," and not do what I tell you? Every one who comes to me and hears my words and does them, I will show you what he is like: he is like a man building a house, who dug deep, and laid the foundation upon rock; and when a flood arose, the stream broke against that house, and could not shake it, because it had been well built. But he who hears and does not do them is like a man who built a house on the ground without a foundation; against which the stream broke, and immediately it fell, and the ruin of that house was great.'

I was watching a television programme recently, in which we were told that many Italian politicians were worried by the popular swing in opinion against the Mafia. They were worried because they had been helped to power by Mafia money or influence, in return for turning a blind eye to crimes. They had taken an easy route to the top, but were to be swept away by the flood of outrage.

It's not an unusual story. Short-cuts and easy options are always tempting. Whether it is the simplicity of the easy lie to get us out of trouble, petty pilfering at work ('everyone does it') or discrediting a rival for promotion, there is a price to pay. It may be the price of uneasy vigilance lest anyone find out, or a guilty conscience or, even worse, the death of conscience.

The worst short-cut is the one Jesus warns against: ignoring God. God makes difficult demands, for integrity, honesty and love. He calls for total commitment and wholehearted obedience. The short-cuts we take to avoid God's demands are summed up by the old, ugly word, 'sin'.

And in the end, the short-cuts come to nothing. Because at last we have to face the flood of God's judgment, and there the foundation of our lives is laid bare; it is Christ or nothing. And while we know that following Jesus is usually a matter of repeated failures and forgivenesses, we need to remember the very real difference between failure and not bothering to try at all.

A thought

At its very root, what do you really base your life on?

MM

New life

[Jesus] went to a city called Nain, and his disciples and a great crowd went with him. As he drew near to the gate of the city, behold, a man who had died was being carried out, the only son of his mother, and she was a widow; and a large crowd from the city was with her. And when the Lord saw her, he had compassion on her and said to her, 'Do not weep.' And he came and touched the bier, and the bearers stood still. And he said, 'Young man, I say to you, arise.' And the dead man sat up, and began to speak. And he gave him to his mother. Fear seized them all; and they glorified God, saying, 'A great prophet has arisen among us!' and 'God has visited his people!' And this report concerning him spread through the whole of Judea and all the surrounding country.

Nowadays, miracles are looked on with some disbelief. Apart from a few sections of the Church, even those who claim to believe in miracles demand almost impossible evidence for modern claims. (Those in the Bible are safely distant, and no real threat—though they can still be explained away if need be!) Perhaps the idea of miracles threatens us, both by upsetting our cosy, safe view of the world and, even worse, by suggesting that God doesn't mind his own business (or that his business can be very disturbing!)

As to whether miracles *can* happen, the answer seems obvious. If God is the creator, then he has the power to do unusual things occasionally. The real point that many people miss is that miracles have a purpose beyond mere amazement. They make a point about God.

Today's story has two points. The grieving mother is a widow, one of the poorest classes of people in the ancient world; without her son, she would be destitute. Jesus' action affirms the Old Testament view of God as the one who sides with the poor and the oppressed.

Secondly, it is a statement about the power of Jesus to bring new life. It is an acted sermon of the need of all people for that life. Yesterday we saw the need to follow Jesus' teaching. Today we see the power that makes following him possible—the new life that comes only from him.

For meditation

In him was life, and the life was the light of men

John 1:4

MM

Welcoming the rejected

There was a rich man who was dressed in purple and fine linen and lived in luxury every day. At his gate was laid a beggar named Lazarus, covered with sores and longing to eat what fell from the rich man's table. Even the dogs came and licked his sores. The time came when the beggar died and the angels carried him to Abraham's side. The rich man also died and was buried. In Hades, where he was in torment, he looked up and saw Abraham far away, with Lazarus by his side. So he called to him, 'Father Abraham, have pity on me and send Lazarus to dip the tip of his finger in water and cool my tongue, because I am in agony in this fire.' But Abraham replied, 'Son, remember that in your lifetime you received your good things, while Lazarus received bad things, but now he is comforted here and you are in agony.'

The Bible tells us to 'love our neighbour' and that may seem easy when our neighbour is very much like us—a decent, respectable, deserving kind of person. But supposing the neighbour is a beggar covered in sores? That was the challenge which the rich man in this story failed to accept.

It isn't, of course, a parable about being kind to beggars. Its central thrust is that what we do during this life determines where we are in the next one. But, by choosing two such contrasting characters as a naked beggar and a well-dressed rich man, Jesus was undoubtedly inviting his hearers to consider how they would have acted in the same circumstances.

As we join in worship in church today, and especially as we come to Communion, we are reminded of the beggar who longed 'to eat what fell from the rich man's table'. Every Sunday we say that we are not worthy 'so much as to gather up the crumbs' from the Lord's Table—but it is not easy to put ourselves in the position of beggars. Perhaps we shall never really value our neighbour until we have seen ourselves as the poor man at the gate, rather than as the rich man living it up inside.

A prayer

Heavenly Father, you invite us to your table as we are. Help us to welcome those whom the world rejects, seeing them through your eyes. For Jesus Christ's sake. Amen.

DW

Extravagant love

One of the Pharisees asked [Jesus] to eat with him, and he went into the Pharisee's house . . . And behold, a woman of the city, who was a sinner . . . brought an alabaster flask of ointment, and standing behind him at his feet, weeping, she began to wet his feet with her tears, and wiped them with the hair of her head, and kissed his feet, and anointed them with the ointment. Now when the Pharisee who had invited him saw it, he said to himself, 'If this man were a prophet, he would have known who and what sort of woman this is who is touching him, for she is a sinner.'

The common view of religious people is that they are all about being good. Since Christianity teaches that we should be good, that is a fairly understandable view. Unfortunately, it is a view sometimes held by Christians—who ought to know better. And it leads to the idea that we should somehow insulate ourselves from people who are not all that good.

The Pharisee (whose name was Simon) was probably not a bad man at all. I dare say that, like many Pharisees, he was devout and caring. But like many devout people, he disapproved of sinners. If Jesus was really a holy man, he ought to put as much distance between himself and this woman as possible!

Yet, of course, the whole point is that Jesus came to bring hope and forgiveness to sinners. In a way, Simon's problem is not that he sees the woman as a sinner, but that he fails to realize that he himself is a sinner, and needs the forgiveness Jesus can bring. Rather than wishing Jesus would reject her, he should be joining her!

Of course, Simon's sins were probably not as notorious or spectacular as hers. Most people's aren't. But that doesn't mean that they do not need forgiving and healing—just that it is *more difficult* to have them forgiven. Not because they are worse, but because they are often not recognized as sins in the first place. Paradoxically, the great sinners seem to have a better chance of repentance, for at least they know they are sinning!

A prayer

Father, open my eyes to my mundane sins so that I can seek your forgiveness, and never let me set myself above others who also need your help.

MM

Gratitude

Jesus answering said to him, 'Simon, I have something to say to you.' And he answered, 'What is it, Teacher?' 'A certain creditor had two debtors; one owed five hundred denarii, and the other fifty. When they could not pay, he forgave them both. Now which of them will love him more?' Simon answered, 'The one, I suppose, to whom he forgave more.' And he said to him, 'You have judged rightly.'

The story makes a fairly obvious point. Gratitude is in proportion to the gift. That point alone should have been enough to make Simon think again; what tremendous gift of forgiveness had the woman he so despised received from Jesus? Her response was surely that of someone who has had a great burden lifted. Perhaps part of his trouble was that she was not only a sinner, but that she was an intruder. Here was the Pharisee, the well-known religious person, sitting down for a cosy religious chat with an interesting new preacher. There were no doubt intriguing points of theology to clear up, little details of worship to be discussed, and the exact nature of God's kingdom to be addressed. Then came the disturbance, embarrassing and noisy, to upset the polite tea party and interrupt the important and serious talk of God. But of course, what was really going on was far more important and much more to do with God. This was no little religious event; this was the tempestuous meeting of a lost soul with the saving power of God. We can learn a lot for our churches from this story. We all too easily become religious clubs. Taking God seriously, yes, but treating him as our own preserve, or our own talking point, all done with quiet decorum. Woe betide anyone who disturbs us. We often get defensive when newcomers alter our normal routine, yet we should rejoice when strangers disturb us and new faces threaten our little enclave. For it could well mean that God is once again at work, bringing forgiveness into the lives of the lost, and pouring blessings into our arid worship.

A thought

How readily do we welcome intruders who come to meet Jesus?

MM

The roots of worship (1)

Turning toward the woman [Jesus] said to Simon, 'Do you see this woman? I entered your house, you gave me no water for my feet, but she has wet my feet with her tears and wiped them with her hair. You gave me no kiss, but from the time I came in she has not ceased to kiss my feet. You did not anoint my head with oil, but she has anointed my feet with ointment. Therefore I tell you, her sins, which are many, are forgiven, for she loved much; but he who is forgiven little, loves little.' And he said to her, 'Your sins are forgiven.' Then those who were at table with him began to say among themselves, 'Who is this, who even forgives sins?' And he said to the woman, 'Your faith has saved you; go in peace.'

It's pretty clear that the woman had already met or heard Jesus, but whether her worship is thankfulness for forgiveness, or a demonstration of need, is hard to tell. It doesn't really matter, though. She knew that Jesus was the answer to her need, and that knowledge called forth worship. For worship it certainly was, in the original sense of the word: a recognition of the worthiness of Jesus to receive all the thanks and praise she could muster. This is what Christian worship always is, a response to the grace of God. And as with this forgiven sinner's extravagant gesture, worship reflects the strength of our feeling for God. This is where the strength of more informal, 'charismatic' worship lies, and it is good that this style of worship has come to play a part in so many churches today. The opportunities for informal prayer and confession, the songs and choruses that focus more on feelings than on doctrine enable us to express genuine love and devotion, and to let the worship affect us at a level other than the mental one alone. For that matter, this is just why many 'traditional' worshippers express a dislike for modern worship songs and for 'open' prayer. It's not that the music is any worse or the prayers any less genuine, but they challenge us to respond emotionally to God.

A thought

How do you feel about God?

MM

The roots of worship (2)

Turning toward the woman [Jesus] said to Simon, 'Do you see this woman? I entered your house, you gave me no water for my feet, but she has wet my feet with her tears and wiped them with her hair. You gave me no kiss, but from the time I came in she has not ceased to kiss my feet. You did not anoint my head with oil, but she has anointed my feet with ointment.'

We often hear how rude Simon the Pharisee had been—failing to greet Jesus with a formal kiss, anointing and foot-washing. But he wasn't rude at all. All those gestures of welcome were reserved for the very honoured guest. Jesus was a guest, but he was not one to get VIP treatment. The fact is that Simon didn't feel half as strongly about Jesus as the forgiven woman. While it is important to express our feelings to God, they can be a poor guide to our relationship with him. There are many times when we feel little, or feel wrongly. And it is then that we can wonder whether our worship is genuine. When we come to church out of a sense of duty, with a strong desire to be somewhere else (like in bed!) our response to God needs to be guided and helped. It's no good faking an emotional high (we can never have one to order), yet the fact remains that God is still worthy of our praise and thanks. This is where churches with a well-constructed liturgy win out. There in the order of service the facts of what God has done are set out, and our need for forgiveness and our response of praise are presented in order to remind us of our true standing with God. The liturgy takes hold of us and enables us to say to God, 'Even though my feelings are far from appropriate, none the less you have forgiven me, love me and care for me, and deserve all my love and praise.' In time, the woman with the ointment would calm down, but the fact would remain: she had met Jesus, and new life was hers. And that meeting with Jesus, and his new life within us, is the basis for all our worship.

Next time you are in a service of worship but feel less than worshipful, let the service carry you along and concentrate on the facts of what God has done. The feelings will follow.

MM

Filthy lucre

Soon afterward [Jesus] went on through cities and villages, preaching and bringing the good news of the kingdom of God. And the twelve were with him, and also some women who had been healed of evil spirits and infirmities: Mary, called Magdalene, from whom seven demons had gone out, and Joanna, the wife of Chuza, Herod's steward, and Susanna, and many others, who provided for them out of their means.

At our last church we had a stewardship campaign, aimed to get people to take their giving more seriously. It was successful and well supported by most, but some staunch church members were very opposed to it. It was, they said, interfering in a matter of individual conscience, unspiritual and nothing to do with the real preaching of the kingdom, and so on.

It's amazing how, as soon as money is mentioned in church, people 'come over all spiritual'. Yet money is a spiritual matter. The Bible is quite clear about that. Its use is a reflection of our faith and our commitment to God, not to mention our love (or as we used to say, our charity).

Jesus relied on money just as we do. It is impossible to be a wandering prophet and healer while holding down a job as a carpenter, or a fisherman or tax collector. So Jesus and the Twelve had a support group who seem to have helped (probably part-time) with the travelling ministry, but who were mainly important for their financial contributions. In a male-oriented society, it is not surprising that this group contained women, who could help in this way without drawing too much adverse comment (though it is likely that men contributed too).

So next time someone complains about how the Church today is bogged down in finances, point out this passage to them. The preaching of the kingdom has always needed financial support, be it for missionary work or just keeping the parish church going. And it is nothing to be embarrassed about that we help to give that support; it is a part of our discipleship and worship.

A reflection

Think and pray about your contribution to the Church's mission. How well does it reflect your service to God?

MM

STARTED Nov 22 97

Seeing the secrets of God

And when his disciples asked him what this parable meant, [Jesus] said, 'To you it has been given to know the secrets of the kingdom of God; but for others they are in parables, so that seeing they may not see, and hearing they may not understand...'

Jesus has just told the famous parable of the sower, and then this strange saying follows. Surely the point of the parables is that they are stories that are easy to understand? Instead of the dry sayings of theology, here are lively stories to engage the imagination and bring the gospel to life. Yet Jesus quotes God's words to Isaiah (Isaiah 6:9–10) in which the words of the prophet are meant to bring judgment on an unrepentant people. If we take these words literally, the parables are to *stop* people understanding!

Well, not exactly; they are the secrets of the kingdom given to the disciples. They are only a mystery to others.

I don't think Jesus was using a special language that could only be understood by insiders. I think the difference lies in the people who hear. For those who are hungry for the word of God, who know their need for him and are seeking some form of spiritual fulfilment, the parables, and all the teachings of Jesus, are a life-saving message. They speak to the heart and give new hope and faith.

Yet there are others who may well know what the point of the stories is, yet in whom there is no answering spark. The message is understood and rejected.

So they hear and do not hear, see but never truly understand. There are those who are insulated from the word of God, by self-righteousness, by complacency, by indifference. For such, these are indeed words of judgment.

A prayer

Father, where I am complacent, shake me; where I am indifferent, awaken me, where I am self-satisfied, challenge me, that I may hear your word, and let it take root in me.

MM

The proof of faith

When Jesus had finished saying all this in the hearing of the people, he entered Capernaum. There a centurion's servant, whom his master valued highly, was sick and about to die. The centurion heard of Jesus and sent some elders of the Jews to him, asking him to come and heal his servant. When they came to Jesus, they pleaded earnestly with him. 'This man deserves to have you do this, because he loves our nation and has built our synagogue.' So Jesus went with them. He was not far from the house when the centurion sent friends to say to him: 'Lord, don't trouble yourself, for I do not deserve to have you come under my roof. That is why I did not even consider myself worthy to come to you. But say the word, and my servant will be healed. For I myself am a man under authority, with soldiers under me. I tell this one, "Go", and he goes; and that one "Come", and he comes. I say to my servant, "Do this", and he does it.' When Jesus heard this, he was amazed at him, and turning to the crowd following him, he said, 'I tell you, I have not found such great faith even in Israel.' Then the men who had been sent returned to the house and found the servant well.

Today's theme is 'The proof of faith' and this story offers the most telling proof possible. The centurion—not even a Jew—has no doubt that Jesus can heal his servant. Indeed, he utters one of the great statements of faith in the Gospels: 'Say the word, and my servant will be healed'. He knows what it is to exercise authority (v. 8) and he recognizes in Jesus an authority greater than anything he has encountered before. His faith is uncomplicated by theology or tradition. His servant needed a miracle, and here was the one who could provide it.

In one sense the 'proof' of faith in this story is the miracle, of course. But its real proof, as Luke relates the event, is in the centurion's words—they were what provoked Jesus to say, 'I have not found such great faith even in Israel.'

The 'proof', the 'test' of faith is within the believer. Faith recognizes who Jesus is and whose authority he has.

A Prayer

Dear Lord, give me the gift of faith, so that I may trust where I cannot see and believe where I cannot know, for Jesus Christ's sake. Amen.

DW

Apprentices

And he called the twelve together and gave them power and authority over all demons and to cure diseases, and he sent them out to preach the kingdom of God and to heal. And he said to them, 'Take nothing for your journey, no staff, nor bag, nor bread, nor money; and do not have two tunics. And whatever house you enter, stay there, and from there depart. And wherever they do not receive you, when you leave that town shake off the dust from your feet as a testimony against them.' And they departed and went through the villages, preaching the gospel and healing everywhere.

The word disciple means 'learner', so we are not surprised when we find Jesus' disciples listening to his words, asking about the meaning of parables and being pulled up short when they misunderstand. But today's reading may seem more unusual to us.

We are possibly more used to the idea of the apostles going out into the world to preach the gospel after the resurrection. Here we see them doing exactly that, at a time when they were far from fully trained. This seems peculiar to those of us who think of learning as being about words and books, or even tapes and videos. However, if we think about apprentices, who learn on the job, the picture becomes clearer. Jesus is teaching the disciples by letting them do the job.

In fact, there are many jobs we can only learn by doing them, be they bricklaying or surgery. And the most important one of these is the job of being a Christian. We can have all the book learning and Bible knowledge in the world, but it is meaningless until we begin the practical business of actually living our lives by it. It is as we actually pray, try to forgive those who offend us, haltingly mention our faith to our friends, and to act by the standards we learn from God that we discover what Christianity really is.

To give one small example, there are many people who, when asked to do something in church (perhaps merely read a lesson or lead prayers), will say 'I couldn't possibly do that!' But until they try, they will never know. Much worse, of course, is when we say the same about God's command to love our enemies or to share our faith. Until we try, we will never learn how.

A thought

Are you an on-the-job learner—or only a theorist?

MM

Church triumphant

After this the Lord appointed seventy others, and sent them on ahead of him, two by two, into every town and place where he himself was about to come . . . The seventy returned with joy, saying, 'Lord, even the demons are subject to us in your name!' And he said to them, 'I saw Satan fall like lightning from heaven. Behold, I have given you authority to tread upon serpents and scorpions, and over all the power of the enemy; and nothing shall hurt you. Nevertheless do not rejoice in this, that the spirits are subject to you; but rejoice that your names are written in heaven.'

Traditionally, the Church in this world is described as the 'Church militant' (still fighting) and those who are with Christ in heaven as the 'Church triumphant' (enjoying the final victory). This is true enough, but it can sell us short. In today's reading, the disciples find that they have power over the forces of evil, and Jesus rejoices that their mission has cast Satan out of heaven. That is, the powers of darkness can no longer reign unchallenged, for a great force is arrayed against them: the followers of Jesus.

Jesus tells us that we must count the cost of following him, that we must bear our cross, and expect suffering and opposition. It is no light matter to serve God. But if we are to expect trouble, we are reminded here that we are also to expect victory.

Because we so often seem to fail, to fall short of what we are called to do and to be, we can get into the habit of thinking of ourselves as almost useless. We may, for instance, see a small congregation gathered in a large parish and think at best of a small outpost defending the faith in a gallant last stand. It's not true. That small congregation has been given the authority to tread down the powers of darkness and to proclaim the word of God. It is a spearhead aimed at the heart of the enemy. Whether we are many or few, we have the foe outnumbered, for Jesus is on our side.

A thought

Are you tempted to think defensively about your faith? Remember whose authority you have.

MM

Pattern for prayer

He was praying in a certain place, and when he ceased, one of his disciples said to him, 'Lord, teach us to pray, as John taught his disciples.' And he said to them, 'When you pray, say: Father, hallowed be thy name. Thy kingdom come. Give us each day our daily bread; and forgive us our sins, for we ourselves forgive every one who is indebted to us; and lead us not into temptation.'

It was common for rabbis to give their disciples a particular prayer, which marked them as belonging to that rabbi's school, and was usually used to round off the daily worship. John the Baptist seems to have done the same with his disciples, and Jesus was happy to do so when he was asked. The two versions, in Matthew and Luke, show how the prayer was used in the early church. Luke is probably closer to the original, but Matthew's is better adapted for liturgical use, with 'deliver us from evil' balancing the final request. A later editor added the liturgical doxology, 'thine is the kingdom, the power and the glory'. This is a prayer that lives in the worship of God's people.

Yet it is worth noting that the request was not for 'a prayer' (though that may well be what was meant), but 'teach us to pray'. And as we look at the Lord's prayer we discover not only a simple intercession, but a pattern for our prayers as a whole.

In our prayers we praise God and ask for his rule to extend over all the earth. This in fact means putting ourselves at his disposal; if his kingdom is to come, it will come as God uses us to help bring it.

We bring him our daily needs, too, for God is not only interested in purely 'spiritual' things. He cares about all areas of our lives, and our daily welfare. Indeed, the least 'churchy' person you will ever meet in church is God.

We confess our sins and receive his forgiveness, but we must remember that forgiveness is meant to be shared. The unforgiving are not forgiven.

And, of course, we need God's help and strength to live our lives as he would wish.

A prayer

Pray to God through the Lord's prayer, and relate each section to your own life and to the needs of the world. When you pray it in church, remember that vast areas of life are summed up in each phrase.

MM

Wilful unbelief

Now he was casting out a demon that was dumb; when the demon had gone out, the dumb man spoke, and the people marvelled. But some of them said, 'He casts out demons by Beelzebul, the prince of demons'; while others, to test him, sought from him a sign from heaven. But he, knowing their thoughts, said to them, 'Every kingdom divided against itself is laid waste, and a divided household falls. And if Satan also is divided against himself, how will his kingdom stand? For you say that I cast out demons by Beelzebul. And if I cast out demons by Beelzebul, by whom do your sons cast them out? Therefore they shall be your judges. But if it is by the finger of God that I cast out demons, then the kingdom of God has come upon you.'

When I let my children stay up late to watch television, I know that they will still demand just a few minutes more when bed-time finally comes.

We can see the same sort of thing happening in today's story. Jesus casts out a demon and heals a dumb man, but some still ask for a 'sign from heaven'. What had he already given them? 'Ah, but he might really be in league with the devil . . .'

We can understand it better if we think again about my children. They don't really want to watch the television programme; that's just an excuse for not going to bed. And I suspect that Jesus' critics weren't serious about his satanic involvement. It was just an excuse to avoid facing what Jesus meant. They had seen the power of God at work, and his kingdom had arrived. But the kingdom brings a challenge to conversion, to repentance and commitment.

The same thing happens today. Peo-ple hear the gospel, know it rings true, and then perhaps spend years thinking of ways to avoid the challenge. Even worse, Christians do the same. We hear God speak, through the Bible, a sermon or a book or whatever, and make ourselves thoroughly miserable finding ways to avoid acting on what we know to be right. In the end, though, there's only one course of action—to give in to God.

A thought

How do you avoid God's challenges?

MM

Empty vessels

'When the unclean spirit has gone out of a man, he passes through waterless places seeking rest; and finding none he says, "I will return to my house from which I came." And when he comes he finds it swept and put in order. Then he goes and brings seven other spirits more evil than himself, and they enter and dwell there; and the last state of that man becomes worse than the first.'

Of course, this is not the whole story, or Jesus would hardly have bothered performing exorcisms. In fact, it is a parable, taking the popular idea of demon possession, and the desert as the haunt of evil spirits. What it's really about is the fact that we are all made to be filled with the presence of God.

Those who do not know God will attempt to fill the spiritual emptiness with other things. Sometimes the demonic nature of these is obvious—excess alcohol, drugs, pornography, shallow sexual encounters. Usually, though, they are not so obvious—a creeping sense of disillusionment, failure, inadequacy or fearfulness. For many there is the hopeless struggle against petty sins; the failings which we despair of ever correcting, but know to be wrong and unworthy of us.

All these God can put right. He can enter into lives like a new broom and leave us, for a while, sparkling clean. And most Christians, looking back to their earliest encounters with the Lord, can remember that. But all too often it is only a memory. All too soon, the demons return, often worse than ever.

The reason is that though we are emptied of the rubbish, we fail to be filled with the good things of God. Perhaps it is through fearfulness, a sense of unworthiness, or just plain ignorance. Whatever the reason, we cut God off in mid-flow.

The answer, of course, is to let God in, through our prayer and worship. To follow through with him and not be satisfied with what we have now, but to desire more of him. Being filled with God's Spirit is not a one-off event, but a continuous process. When we remove ourselves from the flow, the emptiness returns.

For meditation

Be filled with the Spirit.

Ephesians 5:18

MM

Keep your eyes open!

'Let your loins be girded and your lamps burning, and be like men who are waiting for their master to come home from the marriage feast, so that they may open to him at once when he comes and knocks. Blessed are those servants whom the master finds awake when he comes; truly, I say to you, he will gird himself and have them sit at table, and he will come and serve them. If he comes in the second watch, or in the third, and finds them so, blessed are those servants! But know this, that if the householder had known at what hour the thief was coming, he would not have left his house to be broken into. You also must be ready; for the Son of man is coming at an unexpected hour.'

The question of when Jesus will return in triumph and judgment has been the happy hunting-ground of fools and cranks throughout the history of the Church. Some Christians have been obsessed by the need to calculate and predict it, despite words such as Jesus speaks here. Others have reinterpreted it as something entirely different. But all of these seem to me simply to be ways of avoiding what Jesus really says: be ready!

The point is not whether or when the second coming will happen, but our attitude in the meantime. Jesus's question is really, 'If I come today, what will I find you doing, and will it glorify me?'

I came across a story that summed it up beautifully. Sometime during the last century, an eclipse of the sun happened during a session of a state senate in America. There was instant confusion, with some crying out that the end of the world was here. Many members fled to the doors, until one man stood up. 'I do not know whether this is the Lord's return or not,' said the senator, 'but if it is not, then we have business to attend to, and if it is, then he will expect to find us doing our duty.' The session continued by candlelight.

A prayer

Lord, give me grace to live my life in such a way that at any time I would not be ashamed to meet you face to face.

MM

God comes to us

When an angel came to Joseph in a dream, to reassure him about the baby who was going to be born to Mary, he spoke to him about the names of the child. 'You are to name him Jesus', the angel said, 'for he will save his people from their sins.' And he reminded the worried Joseph about the prophecy of Isaiah: 'Look, the virgin shall conceive and bear a son, and they shall name him Emmanuel,' which means, 'God with us' (Matthew 1:21–23).

Through this season of Advent, and then at Christmas, David Winter gives us different readings to show us the different ways in which God is with us, and the different ways in which he comes to us. As creator, as law-giver, and as redeemer. We read about the true light that gives light to every man coming into the world, and about the birth of the baby Jesus. We see the glory of the Lord that shone around the frightened shepherds; as they worship God so do we. And we join in with the song of the angels, and say, 'Glory to God in the highest heaven . . .'. Then, on the last day of the year, we pray for ourself and for the rest of the world:'Lord God, give me a vision like Simeon's, of your love in Jesus touching and changing the whole world. And help me to share in making that love known. Amen.'

Sheep and goats

'When the Son of Man comes in his glory, and all the angels with him, then he will sit on the throne of his glory. All the nations will be gathered before him, and he will separate people one from another as a shepherd separates the sheep from the goats, and he will put the sheep at his right hand and the goats at the left.'

This is one of the best known and least understood sayings of Jesus! At the day of judgment, it seems, Jesus (the 'Son of Man') will divide people into two categories, the 'sheep' 'inheriting the kingdom' (v. 34) and the 'goats' departing into 'the eternal fire prepared for the devil and his angels' (v. 41). And the acid test will be whether they fed the hungry and thirsty, clothed the naked and visited the sick and the prisoners. Do it, and you go to heaven. Neglect to do it, and you go to hell. The message seems both simple and stark.

But those who know their New Testament will detect a problem. Eternal life is God's gift to those who trust in his Son, not a reward for acts of charity. Surely this passage introduces a completely different criterion for salvation, one based, apparently, entirely on works?

In fact, it does nothing of the kind. In the preceding passage (vv. 14–30) Jesus has set out the terms for the judgment of his disciples in the story of the 'talents'. This passage is about the judgment of the 'nations' (*ethnoi*, in Greek)—the Gentiles, the people without the revelation of God. They will be judged on their response to the 'members of Christ's family' (v. 40), his 'brothers and sisters'. In welcoming, feeding and receiving them, they will be welcoming, feeding and receiving Jesus himself. The corollary is stark. In rejecting them they are rejecting him. The choice is theirs.

A prayer

Father of all, I remember on this Advent Sunday all those who have never known your love shown in Jesus. In whatever guise he comes to them—in the poor, the starving or the oppressed—may they welcome and receive him. Amen.

DW

God comes——as Creator

These are the generations of the heavens and the earth when they were created. In the day that the Lord God made the earth and the heavens, when no plant of the field was yet in the earth and no herb of the field had yet sprung up—for the Lord God had not caused it to rain upon the earth, and there was no one to till the ground; but a stream would rise from the earth, and water the whole face of the ground—then the Lord God formed man from the dust of the ground, and breathed into his nostrils the breath of life; and the man became a living being.

For the weeks of Advent we shall be looking at the various ways in which God comes to us. During this week, the readings will reflect how he comes to us as our Creator. It was his words ('Let there be light') that sparked the universe into existence. It was by his will that sea, land and sky came into being, the birds flew in the sky and fish swarmed in the depths of the sea. He sent rain to enable the grass to grow and provide food for the animals.

And then, as the culmination of it all, the Lord brought into being the crown of his creation, 'humankind'—in its two representations, male and female (1:27). We are made from what already exists ('the dust of the ground') yet we are different. We are 'living beings'. We exist, and we know we exist, just as God exists and knows he exists.

If you read on through this chapter you will see, and perhaps be moved by, the gentleness and care of God's dealings with these new creatures of his. From the beauty of their environment (vv. 8–9) to the provision of food (v. 16), creative work (v. 15) and companionship (v. 18), he is 'on their side'. We miss the whole point if we get hung up on issues of biology, anatomy—or gender roles! This Creator cares for his creatures. The one who made us, loves us. That's how God comes to us as Creator.

A prayer

Lord God, my Creator, thank you for your loving care. Help me today to put myself into the hands of the one who made me . . . and loves me. Amen.

DW

The Creator honours us!

O Lord, our Sovereign, how majestic is your name in all the earth! You have set your glory above the heavens. Out of the mouths of babes and infants you have founded a bulwark because of your foes, to silence the enemy and the avenger. When I look at the heavens, the work of your fingers, the moon and the stars that you have established; what are human beings that you are mindful of them, mortals that you care for them? Yet you have made them a little lower than God, and crowned them with glory and honour.

Mortal man: insignificant, but glorious! That seems to be the message of this Psalm. God is majestic—indeed, so majestic that, as C.H. Spurgeon pointed out, no words could express it, so it is left as an exclamation mark: how majestic! In comparison, humankind is puny and insignificant. The moon and the stars tower above us in the night sky, immense and unchanging. The heavens 'declare the glory of God', in their size and their beauty. Besides them, mortals seem to be nothing—and certainly not worth the thought or care of God himself—the God who can use helpless babies to declare his praise or defeat his enemies (according to which translation you chose of the baffling verse 2!).

Yet God has honoured us! He has taken this puny, two-legged creature and given him an honoured place in his scheme of things—a place, apparently, just below his own ('a little lower than God'). And that honour was confirmed in the incarnation, for when the Son of God came as a son of man he paid the human race the highest honour he could, and gave it the greatest dignity in the universe.

During the Second World War the two royal princesses were wandering in Windsor Great park when a game-keeper stopped them. 'Who are you two?' he asked. 'Oh, we're nobody,' replied Princess Elizabeth, 'but our daddy's the king.' We may often feel without dignity—nobodies, in eternal terms. But God has made us somebodies. Our Father, our Creator, is the King.

A prayer

Lord, when I feel that I am nobody, help me to remember who made me. Amen.

DW

Worthy of our worship

For the Lord is a great God, and a great King above all gods. In his hand are the depths of the earth; the heights of the mountains are his also. The sea is his, for he made it, and the dry land, which his hands have formed. O come, let us worship and bow down, let us kneel before the Lord, our Maker! For he is our God, and we are the people of his pasture, and the sheep of his hand. O that today you would listen to his voice!

As we think of the way God comes to us as Creator, this Psalm reminds us that the proper response to that is worship. When we consider that all the splendour and power of creation are his—the earth's depths, the mountains' heights, the sea's vastness—it should evoke in us nothing less than awe. The world is 'hand-made' by God, and before this display of his power we are called to 'bow down and worship'.

In Hebrew the word for 'worship' is associated with the idea of falling down, of prostrating oneself before a person of authority and majesty. So here we are called to 'bow down' and 'kneel' before the awesome power of our Creator.

But the universe is not just 'hand-made'. It is 'hand-held'. It is not only because we recognize God's power that we are drawn to worship him. The one whose hands made the universe is 'our God'. We are 'the sheep of his hand'. We are the 'people of his pasture'—enfolded in his protection, loved and cared for.

So both out of respect for his power and in response to his love, let us 'listen to his voice', because it is a voice calling us to obedience and faith. And let us do it 'today'—the word here is urgent and insistent. Draw near and listen, because the voice is the voice of 'our God'.

A prayer

Lord God, our God, we thank you for your power revealed in creation and your love revealed in your care for your flock. Help us today to draw near and listen to your voice. Amen.

DW

The potter and the clay

You will say to me then, 'Why then does he still find fault? For who can resist his will?' But who indeed are you, a human being, to argue with God? Will what is moulded say to the one who moulds it, 'Why have you made me like this?' Has the potter no right over the clay, to make out of the same lump one object for special use and another for ordinary use?

This is not an easy passage! The picture is vivid enough, and very familiar in the ancient world. The potter worked with the clay, taking a handful of it and throwing it on to his wheel. But although all the clay was the same, what emerged from the work of his hands could be very different. The same clay and the same hands might make a simple ornament for cooking or household hygiene, or a splendid ornament, to be glazed and decorated for a rich man's dinner table. The difference was not in the basic material, but in the potter's intention.

St Paul is using this analogy to illustrate the mysterious working of God's will in the calling of Israel, but it obviously has a much wider application. The maker has power over what he makes and the important thing for the creature is to accept that the maker knows what he is doing! That is not always easy, especially when we see other creatures, formed (as it were) from the same clay, being chosen for what seem to us more honoured or attractive purposes.

As we saw on Monday, the biblical picture of humankind is of a being made from 'the dust of the ground'. Add water, and you've got... clay! The message is simple: we all have the same origin, we are all part of what God has made. But each of us is also shaped by the potter's hands for a particular purpose, and our joy and fulfilment will come from discovering and recognizing what that is, whether it be 'great' or 'small'.

A prayer

Lord God, master potter, shape me to your purpose, and help me to find my joy in being what you have intended me to be. Amen.

DW

A proper humility

Then the Lord answered Job out of the whirlwind . . . 'Where were you when I laid the foundations of the earth? Tell me, if you have understanding. Who determined its measurements—surely you know! Or who stretched the line upon it? On what were its bases sunk, or who laid its cornerstone when the morning stars sang together and all the heavenly beings shouted for joy?'

We are considering the way God comes to us as Creator, and here, in his final answer to the desperate questions of his servant Job, we seem to have a rather peremptory coming. It's as though God is saying to Job, 'This is how it is. Take it or leave it!' As Job could never understand the mind of the Creator, or even begin to fathom how he worked, his questions (and the answers of his wretched 'advisors') were 'words without knowledge' (v. 2).

Yet God went to great lengths to remind Job of the wonder, intricacy and order of what he had made, as chapters 38–41 reveal. He was not, as it were, trying to explain the inexplicable, but to evoke in Job a proper sense of awe.

In our modern world, in which science has done a great deal to unlock and sometimes explain the 'wonders' of creation, there may be a danger of our lacking a proper humility in our approach to these questions. In my experience, this is seldom so with scientists themselves. As they probe the mysteries of origins, or explore structures and systems in the creation, even those who have no religious faith are often (and I use the word deliberately) awestruck by what they find. As that outstanding physicist—and now Anglican priest—John Polkinghorne has written, 'There has grown up a widespread feeling, especially among those who study fundamental physics, that there is more to the world than meets the eye.' I think that was the conclusion Job eventually came to, as well!

A prayer

Lord God, as you come to me in the wonder and order of what you have made, give me the priceless gifts of holy humility and godly awe. Amen.

DW

Made—and remembered

But now hear, O Jacob my servant, Israel whom I have chosen! Thus says the Lord who made you, who formed you in the womb and will help you: Do not fear, O Jacob my servant, Jeshurun whom I have chosen . . . Remember these things, O Jacob, and Israel, for you are my servant; I formed you, you are my servant; O Israel, you will not be forgotten by me. I have swept away your transgressions like a cloud, and your sins like mist; return to me, for I have redeemed you.

God comes to us as Creator, not only in the sense that he made everything that is ('maker of all things, seen and unseen') but also, as we are reminded here, in a personal and individual sense. I am what I am because God has made me thus. The Lord 'formed me in the womb'—he made me *me*, as the children's chorus says.

These words are addressed to the people of the Old Covenant, the people of 'Jacob' and 'Israel' ('Jeshurun' is an alternative name for Israel). He made them to be his 'servants'—a privilege as well as a responsibility. He made them a nation. But he also made them as precious individuals, each one formed in his or her mother's womb according to the will of the 'potter' (as we saw yesterday).

And what God has so wonderfully made he never forgets! 'You will not be forgotten by me.' Even a mother may be forgetful of the child she bore, but 'I will not forget you' (Isaiah 49:15). He will forget our transgressions and sins (v. 22), but he will not forget those he has made, shaped and redeemed. That is a promise to treasure, whether we are the people of the Old or the New Covenant.

A prayer

Help me, heavenly Father, to recognize how much you value me for what I am, because this is how you have made me. Thank you for your unfailing love. Amen.

DW

The encouraging scriptures

For whatever was written in former days was written for our instruction, so that by steadfastness and by the encouragement of the scriptures we might have hope. May the God of steadfastness and encouragement grant you to live in harmony with one another, in accordance with Christ Jesus, so that together you may with one voice glorify the God and Father of our Lord Jesus Christ.

Today is 'Bible Sunday', so called because of the splendid Collect for this day in the Book of Common Prayer, which is based on these words of St Paul in Romans. The 'scriptures' he wrote about were, of course, those of what we call the Old Testament, and his claim is that those scriptures were written for our 'instruction'. He was reminding the Roman Christians of this in the context of their reaction to various disputes going on in the church about dietary laws, and the observance of special days. He doesn't say (as we might have expected him to, in a way) 'just look in the Bible and find out whether they or you are right'. He says, look in the Bible and see that these petty disputes about minor matters destroy Christian harmony and make it impossible for you to glorify God with united voices.

That's a good message for the Church in every age. There is a great temptation for all of us to use the Bible as a stick with which to beat other Christians from whom we differ over this or that. But the scriptures are not given to divide us, but to unite us. And they do that by reminding their readers that the God of the Bible is a God of 'steadfastness and encouragement', and we are to read them as witnesses of that.

Sometimes we may find it hard to think of the God of the Old Testament as 'encouraging'... we may feel that he often appears to be a judge and punisher of human frailty. But the Jews didn't read their scriptures like that. To them, God was a 'rock', utterly reliable, who desired only the best for his people. We might not always understand or appreciate his methods, but we should never doubt his motives.

A prayer

Blessed Lord, who hast caused all holy scriptures to be written for our learning; grant that we may in such wise hear them read, mark, learn and inwardly digest them, that by patience, and the comfort of your holy Word, we may embrace and ever hold fast the blessed hope of everlasting life, which thou hast given us in our Saviour Jesus Christ. Amen.

Collect, Second Sunday in Advent

DW

The right kind of 'fear'

Then God spoke all these words: I am the Lord your God, who brought you out of the land of Egypt, out of the house of slavery; you shall have no other gods before me . . . When all the people witnessed the thunder and lightning, the sound of the trumpet, and the mountain smoking, they were afraid and trembled and stood at a distance, and said to Moses, 'You speak to us, and we will listen; but do not let God speak to us, or we will die.' Moses said to the people, 'Do not be afraid; for God has come only to test you and to put the fear of him upon you so that you do not sin.'

This week we are thinking about the way God comes to us as law-giver—probably not the most popular of his advents! Yet the Bible is quite clear that God is the source of all moral authority, that his Law is perfect, just and good, and that it is a priceless gift to the human race. In this passage we read of the giving of the ten commandments through Moses. This Law, so awe-inspiring that it was accompanied by thunder, lightning and trumpets, was given by the one who 'brought them out of the land of Egypt'—their saviour and deliverer. So it was not the arbitrary command of a distant tyrant, but the instructing word of a caring saviour.

The people would have preferred a 'human' message—'Moses, you speak to us!' But he reassured them: God had come as law-giver not to make you be fearful ('Do not be afraid...') but to teach you to fear properly ('to put the fear of him upon you'). That is not a contradiction. 'Fear' of God is reverence and respect not only for who he is but for what he stands for. If they learnt to reverence him, then they would not sin. God's Law was not given to condemn them, but to 'deliver them from evil'.

A prayer

Lord God, holy and true, teach me to show my love for you by living in accordance with your loving will. Amen.

DW

The delightful decrees

With my whole heart I seek you; do not let me stray from your commandments. I treasure your word in my heart, so that I may not sin against you. Blessed are you, O Lord; teach me your statutes. With my lips I declare all the ordinances of your mouth. I delight in the way of your decrees as much as in all riches. I will meditate on your precepts, and fix my eyes on your ways. I will delight in your statutes; I will not forget your word.

On the whole, laws aren't popular! Put up a sign saying 'Do not walk on the grass' and everyone seems to be consumed with an immediate desire to do exactly that. We don't like being told what to do, how to behave or what to avoid. I suppose 'laws' are a threat to our self-sufficiency. What we want to be is masters (or mistresses) of our destiny, not followers of someone else's rules.

So it seems a bit strange for the Psalmist to be singing the praise of God's laws (his 'statutes', 'decrees' and 'precepts'—it all amounts to the same thing), in quite such extravagant terms. God's 'Word' is rich, a treasure, a delight. His sole concern is to meditate on it, fix his eyes on it—and declare its truth to others.

But the Psalmist sees the laws as more than simply rules made up of words. They represent the very nature of God himself. 'With my whole heart will I seek you'—it is God himself, his character and beauty and goodness, which is represented by the 'words' of his statutes and decrees. To 'treasure' them in his heart would be the best way to counter temptation and sin, for they would plant there something of the holiness of God himself.

A prayer

Almighty Lord, help me to treasure in my heart all that you will and command, so that my life is shaped, not by what I want, but by what your will is for me. Amen.

DW

'Wondrous things'

Deal bountifully with your servant, so that I may live and observe your word. Open my eyes, so that I may behold wondrous things out of your law. I live as an alien in the land; do not hide your commandments from me. My soul is consumed with longing for your ordinances at all times.

As a child I remember singing a simple chorus based on the words of verse 18. It said, 'Open thou mine eyes, that I may behold, Wondrous, wondrous things, Out of thy law.' I can't recall whether I felt I knew what 'wondrous' meant—it's not a word used habitually by seven-year-olds. But that was how the Psalmist saw God's Law—as full of 'wondrous things'... things that evoke wonder, admiration, awe.

We may find it hard to share that degree of enthusiasm. He was writing about the Law, the Torah, the command-ments which shaped the life and religion of Israel. We are accustomed to thinking of them as restrictive and burdensome, not full of 'wondrous things'. But for the people of Israel they were the glorious truths that separated them from the pagan tribes around them (v. 19). They spoke of a holy, just and also merciful God.

When we come to our own Bible reading as Christians, we can learn something from this reverence and wonder. The scriptures reveal to us, in story, history, poetry, symbol and teach-ing, what God is like. If we read them but fail to see God in them, they aren't doing us much good! Jesus rebuked the scrip-ture readers of his own day for searching the scriptures but failing to come to him to whom they bore witness (John 5:39–40). The Bible is a means to an end, not an end in itself. It points us to God, not to itself. As we look for the witness to God in what we read—prayerfully, intelli-gently and imaginatively—we shall, like the Psalmist, see wondrous things in it.

A prayer

Dear Lord, you have shown us yourself through the words of men and women handed down to us over the centuries. Open our eyes to see you in what you have inspired, and teach us to value it. Amen.

DW

363

A pathway to the good life

Teach me, O Lord, the way of your statutes, and I will observe it to the end. Give me understanding, that I may keep your law and observe it with my whole heart. Lead me in the path of your commandments, for I delight in it. Turn my heart to your decrees and not to selfish gain. Turn my eyes from looking at vanities; give me life in your ways.

Recently I listened to a distinguished Jewish rabbi speaking about the Law, the Torah. He explained that Christians often misunderstood how the Jewish faith regarded the Law of God. Because, he claimed, of the Greek word used for 'law' in the New Testament (*nomos*), which means regulation or decree and has entirely legal overtones, we regard the Law as basically negative. It tells us what not to do. Keep the law—OK. Break the law, you get punished. Simple.

But, he said, that is not how Jewish teachers see the Law. And he instanced scriptures like today's reading to back up his point. The Torah is a positive, not a negative thing, a 'way', a 'path'. Most of all, it is a 'teaching'—it's not there to provide a stick with which we can be beaten, but to teach us the way of God. As he said, you don't teach effectively by constantly hitting the pupil, punishing them for getting it wrong. What you say is, 'Look, do it this way!' And that, for him, is the model of the Law of God—it is a path leading to life (v. 39) ... a delightful path (v. 35), a way of understanding (v. 34). And the Psalmist's prayer is not so much that he may slavishly keep it, but that the Lord will 'teach [him] the way of [his] statutes'.

I hear an echo of this idea in the words of Jesus, 'If you love me, you will keep my commandments' (John 14:15). Love for God doesn't start from obedience, but from devotion. But if we love him, what better way can we show it than by delighting in his will?

A prayer

Heavenly Father, in your patience and mercy teach me, a rather stubborn and wilful pupil, the loving and gentle way of your commandments. Amen.

DW

Law written on the heart

But this is the covenant that I will make with the house of Israel after those days, says the Lord: I will put my law within them, and I will write it on their hearts; and I will be their God, and they shall be my people. No longer shall they teach one another, or say to each other, 'Know the Lord,' for they shall all know me, from the least of them to the greatest, says the Lord; for I will forgive their iniquity, and remember their sin no more.

We have seen over the last few days a very attractive picture of the way in which the people of Israel could respond to God's Law. As he came to them through his commandments and precepts, and as they responded to them, so a wonderful new way of living opened up for them. That is the spirit of Psalm 119, of course—the Law of God is good, and it changes us.

But in practice that ideal was not often attained. Under the influence of the surrounding Canaanite nations, the Israelites constantly tended to drift away from the Law of God. Far from finding it a delight, they found it an irksome restraint on their freedom to live as other peoples did. That is the background to the message of the great prophets of the times of the exile. It was because they had turned their backs on the good and holy Law of God that they were now suffering.

This prophecy of Jeremiah marks a watershed in the history of Israel. It speaks of a 'new' covenant, not based on the observance of an externally applied rule (as the law of Moses was), but on a change of heart. The Law of God—so wholesome and life-giving—was to be written not on tablets of stone but on the very hearts of the people. They would do God's will not because he commanded it (though he did), but because through a conversion of heart they knew the Lord and had experienced his forgiveness (v. 34).

It was this 'new covenant' that Jesus was to seal with his blood (Luke 22:20). The people of the new covenant are still people of the Law, but theirs is to be an inner obedience of the heart... in response to the love and mercy of God.

A prayer

Lord, write your will on my heart, so that I may know its lifegiving strength. Amen.

DW

Doers of the word

But be doers of the word, and not merely hearers who deceive themselves. For if any are hearers of the word and not doers, they are like those who look at themselves in a mirror; for they look at themselves and, on going away, immediately forget what they were like. But those who look into the perfect law, the law of liberty, and persevere, being not hearers who forget but doers who act—they will be blessed in their doing.

We have been thinking this week of the God who comes to us as law-giver. We have seen that this is not a negative or restrictive idea. The Law of God is good and perfect, and the world would be a better place if we all lived by it. But the experience of Israel (and of all the rest of us, for that matter) is that we simply can't do it unaided. The 'law of liberty', as James calls it, doesn't seem to liberate us from evil. Like the person in today's passage looking in a mirror and failing to do anything about what he sees, we look into God's perfect Law and do nothing about it. Knowing the Law isn't enough, says James. We have to do it.

Perhaps the mirror illustration can help us here. Let's suppose we are just getting dressed in the morning, prior to inflicting ourselves on the rest of the public. We look in the mirror, and see that our hair is unkempt, there's a nasty spot on the tip of the chin, and a large dollop of junior's very early breakfast seems to have lodged on the left ear. Now there are really only two courses of action open to us. The mirror, like the Law, has done its job in showing us what needs attention. We can say, 'I can't be bothered', or 'There's not time', or 'No one will notice anyway', and walk out of the house as we are. Or, of course, we can wash and comb our hair, deal with the spot and clean up the deposited baby food.

When God has shown us his will, the choices are broadly the same. What James is saying is, 'Don't just talk about it. Do it.'

A prayer

Lord God, help me not only to hear what you are saying, but give me grace to do it, for Jesus' sake. Amen.

DW

The one who is to come

When John heard in prison what the Messiah was doing, he sent word by his disciples and said to him, 'Are you the one who is to come, or are we to wait for another?' Jesus answered them, 'Go and tell John what you hear and see: the blind receive their sight, the lame walk, the lepers are cleansed, the deaf hear, the dead are raised, and the poor have good news brought to them. And blessed is anyone who takes no offence at me.'

John the Baptist's question seems at first sight quite reasonable. Israel had been waiting for 'the one who is to come' for centuries. There had been plenty of disappointments and false dawns. At first, he had no doubt that Jesus was 'the one', but perhaps the experience of his own arrest and imprisonment, and news that the message of Jesus was not what some people had expected, had combined to plant a few doubts in his mind. So he sent his disciples with a direct question. Are you 'it' ... or does the waiting go on?

It's a question many sincere believers find themselves asking in moments of darkness, depression or tested faith. Is Jesus really 'the one'? Might not some of these new ideas be nearer the truth? Or could it be that my own faith is a kind of self-deception? There are not many Christians who have not, at one time or another, asked themselves the question, at least.

And the answer given here is the only one that will do. 'Go and tell ... what you have heard and seen.' Look at the evidence. See what he has done. Remember the times when he has been real to you,

when he has comforted, reassured, forgiven or encouraged you. Read again the Gospel stories, and ask yourself whether history has ever shown us anything like this man—at once so strong and so gentle, so commanding and yet so loving. People may 'look for another', but where is there anyone remotely like this?

A prayer

Lord Jesus, at the time when I am tempted to doubt you, draw near to me and show me once again, in your patient mercy, who you are and what you have done for me. Amen.

DW

I have come to deliver you

Then [the Lord] said, 'Come no closer! Remove the sandals from your feet, for the place on which you are standing is holy ground.' He said further, 'I am the God of your father, the God of Abraham, the God of Isaac, and the God of Jacob.' And Moses hid his face, for he was afraid to look at God. Then the Lord said, 'I have observed the misery of my people who are in Egypt; I have heard their cry on account of their taskmasters. Indeed, I know their sufferings, and I have come down to deliver them from the Egyptians, and to bring them up out of that land to a good and broad land, a land flowing with milk and honey.'

This week we shall be thinking of the God who comes to us as redeemer, and we begin with this marvellous scene before the bush in the desert that burnt but was not consumed. Moses had fled from Egypt, leaving behind his people, the Hebrew slaves, at the hands of their persecutors. Now, far away in the desert, at the foot of Mount Horeb, comes this great moment of destiny. The God of Israel is about to act decisively to deliver his people from slavery—and Moses is his chosen human instrument to do it.

The words of God from the burning bush set out the principles of redemption. It's worth concentrating on the verbs: 'I have observed... I have heard... I know... I have come down to deliver them and to bring them to a good land.' What God is about to do is his response to what he has heard, seen and understood about their plight. Whatever they may have felt about it, he had not abandoned his people. He was fully aware of their situation, and had been waiting for the right moment to act. And when he acts, it is not simply to rescue them (though that would have been marvellous) but to bring them out of darkness into something wonderful beyond imagining—a land 'flowing with milk and honey'. That is 'redemption'.

A prayer

Almighty God, help me to believe when things are dark that my Redeemer knows, understands and will deliver me and bring me to the place he has promised. Amen.

DW

The God of comfort

Comfort, O comfort my people, says your God. Speak tenderly to Jerusalem, and cry to her that she has served her term, that her penalty is paid, that she has received from the Lord's hand double for all her sins. A voice cries out: 'In the wilderness prepare the way of the Lord, make straight in the desert a highway for our God. Every valley shall be lifted up, and every mountain and hill be made low; the uneven ground shall become level, and the rough places a plain. Then the glory of the Lord shall be revealed, and all people shall see it together, for the mouth of the Lord has spoken.'

We are thinking this week of the God who comes to us as 'redeemer'. To 'redeem' something is to 'buy it back', to restore it to its rightful owner. The most common use of it in previous generations was in connection with the pawn shop, where people left articles of value, like a gold watch or a ring, as security for a loan. When they repaid the loan, the watch or ring was 'redeemed'—the owner got it back. God redeemed the Israelites from Egypt when he restored to them their freedom and brought them to the Promised Land.

But now, when this prophecy was written in the sixth century BC, the people of Israel are again in captivity, this time in Babylon. For the prophet, they are there because of their wilful disobedience and compromise. But God has not forgotten his promises to them—and now the time of their deliverance is at hand. The time for harsh words of judgment is over. The prophet is to 'speak tenderly' to Jerusalem, to tell her that the price of her sin has been

paid. In fact, they should start the preparations now for the triumphal arrival of their deliverer.

As with Israel in Egypt, there is a divine 'moment', a time of redemption. God keeps his promises, but until that moment we have to learn to trust him.

A prayer

Heavenly Father, help me to trust you in the times of waiting, and to believe that you never turn a blind eye to the suffering of your people—even when it's been well deserved. Amen.

DW

The conquering shepherd

Get you up to a high mountain, O Zion, herald of good tidings; lift up your voice with strength, O Jerusalem, herald of good tidings, lift it up, do not fear; say to the cities of Judah, 'Here is your God!' See, the Lord God comes with might, and his arm rules for him; his reward is with him, and his recompense before him. He will feed his flock like a shepherd; he will gather the lambs in his arms, and carry them in his bosom, and gently lead the mother sheep.

Most of us could sing the last verse in that passage! Handel set those words to a gentle, dancing kind of melody, full of pastoral delight. And, indeed, it is a picture of a gentle Shepherd-God caring for his flock with motherly attention.

But it's preceded by a quite different picture, isn't it? The God who comes to deliver the captive people of Jerusalem is a God of power and might, whose arm is strong and who brings with him both reward and penalty. It's astonishing to move straight from that embodiment of awesome authority to the image of the gentle, caring shepherd.

But they aren't two different Gods! The whole point of the prophecy is that God's power and love are both aspects of his nature. Without the mighty power he could not deliver Israel from the grip of the military might of Babylon. Without the gentle care he could not restore his chastened flock to a proper relationship of love and trust in him. As God was then, so he is now. Sometimes we see— we need to see—his power and author-ity. He is the one who rewards and recompenses... sin is not simply to be overlooked. It has to be dealt with. But sometimes we see—and, again, we need to see—his gentle love restoring the sinner and leading us back into his fold.

A prayer

Lord God, help me in times of rebellion to recognize your authority, and in times of repentance to recognize your restoring love. For Jesus Christ's sake. Amen.

DW

A wonderful inheritance

Blessed be the God and Father of our Lord Jesus Christ! By his great mercy he has given us a new birth into a living hope through the resurrection of Jesus Christ from the dead, and into an inheritance that is imperishable, undefiled, and unfading, kept in heaven for you, who are being protected by the power of God through faith for a salvation ready to be revealed in the last time.

Not far from our home in Oxfordshire stands Blenheim Palace, home of the Dukes of Marlborough. It's a magnificent building in a splendid setting of gardens and lakes. When an eldest son is born to the Duke, he inherits all that! From the moment of his birth, it is potentially his. He doesn't have to earn it, or pay for it. It is his by right of birth.

It's some such idea that Peter has in mind as he writes these memorable words. He's writing to Christians scattered across the Middle East, many of them ordinary, poor people—even slaves. But they are 'inheritors' of a fortune, he tells them—an imperishable and unfading fortune, which is kept, not in a Swiss bank, but in heaven. Nothing can take it away from them, because God is protecting his investment in them until the moment ('the last time') when it will all be theirs. All they have to do is keep on trusting him, and in the risen Lord Jesus—and even that faith is protected (v. 5). They have been 'born again' into this 'living hope'—and that, too, is God's gift (v. 3).

This is how God redeems his people of the new covenant. We, like Israel of old, were in captivity—not to Egyptians or Babylonians, but to death itself. But, through the resurrection of Jesus, God redeemed us, set us free, gave us a completely new life in a new environment... a life that goes beyond earth, into heaven itself. That's some inheritance!

A prayer

Lord God, we thank you for the great deliverance you have won for us through the death and resurrection of your Son. Keep us firm in our faith in him and protect your investment in us, until the day when our salvation is complete in your presence. Amen.

DW

Christ will come again

'There will be signs in the sun, the moon, and the stars, and on the earth distress among nations confused by the roaring of the sea and the waves. People will faint from fear and foreboding of what us coming upon the world, for the powers of the heavens will be shaken. Then they will see "the Son of Man coming in a cloud", with power and great glory. Now when these things begin to take place, stand up and raise your heads, because your redemption is drawing near.'

This is part of what is called the 'little apocalypse'—the book of Revelation presumably being the big one! It contains various prophecies of Jesus about the 'end times', what the Jews called the Day of the Lord, when God's power and justice would be demonstrated to the whole world. Jesus connected this event with his own return—the 'Son of man' coming in power and great glory. And that in turn relates to a prophecy of Daniel, in which a 'son of man' is given by God authority over the whole world (Daniel 7:13–14). It's not helpful to press the details of such visionary language, but there seems no doubt that Jesus foresaw the 'day of the Lord' as the final vindication of God's justice, and that he would be a central figure in that event.

On that day everyone would see justice done. In that sense, it would be a day of judgment. Without such a day, it seems to me, God's 'justice' is a nonsense and human history intrinsically unfair. If there is a God, and he is good, then surely in the end he must put right the evil that has defiled his creation for so long? That is what a day of judgment is all about.

But for Christ's disciples this would not be a day of dread or fear, but an occasion to 'lift up their heads'. At last their redemption was to be complete—redeemed not only from the effects of sin (through forgiveness), but from its presence . . . brought into a kingdom where truth, justice, love and mercy are supreme. That is the true Advent message. That is hope.

A prayer

Lord God, when I think about the day of judgment, help me to remember that you are a God of perfect justice and mercy . . . and the God who sent Jesus so that we should not perish, but have eternal life. Amen.

DW

Redemption of the earth

I consider that the sufferings of this present time are not worth comparing with the glory about to be revealed to us. For the creation waits with eager longing for the revealing of the children of God; for the creation itself was subjected to futility, not of its own will but by the will of the one who subjected it, in hope that the creation itself will be set free from its bondage to decay and will obtain the freedom of the glory of the children of God.

As we come to the end of Advent, and of our reflections on the ways in which God comes to us, this is a stirring call to enlarge our vision. It's very easy to think of God's final victory simply in terms of our own salvation as individuals, or even just as the salvation of humanity. But Paul's vision is much greater than that. God's plan is nothing less than the redemption of everything that exists—the whole creation! At present, creation itself is in slavery: what he calls 'bondage to decay'—that's to say, everything grows old, everything is finite, nothing is eternal . . . not even rocks and mountains.

But at the time of the 'revealing' (v. 19)—literally 'apocalypse'—everything will 'obtain the freedom of the glory of the children of God'. When God acts to bring in his reign of justice, peace and love the whole creation will be transformed, in the same way as the love and grace of God has already transformed his 'children'—those who are 'in Christ'.

It's a mind-blowing thought! And it goes far beyond the idea of God just plucking a few 'brands from the burn-ing' and abandoning everything else. And we—the 'children of God'—are part of the plan, the models of what he is to bring about in everything, everywhere. I think this is what lies behind Paul's language elsewhere when he speaks of God being 'all in all' (1 Corinthians 15:28). In the end, God will be seen to be the ruler and redeemer of all that he has made. That is the real Advent hope. It is that for which we wait patiently (v. 25) and in 'joyful hope'.

A prayer

Lord God, help me not to set limits to your power and love, but to wait patiently and joyfully for your redemption to be revealed. Amen.

DW

Born to save

Now the birth of Jesus the Messiah took place in this way. When his mother Mary had been engaged to Joseph, but before they lived together, she was found to be with child from the Holy Spirit. Her husband, Joseph, being a righteous man and unwilling to expose her to public disgrace, planned to dismiss her quietly. But just when he had resolved to do this, an angel of the Lord appeared to him in a dream and said, 'Joseph, son of David, do not be afraid to take Mary as your wife, for the child conceived in her is from the Holy Spirit. She will bear a son, and you are to name him Jesus, for he will save his people from their sins.'

The problem with familiar stories is precisely that—they're familiar. And we always tend to miss what is right under our noses! Most Bible readers will be aware that the two accounts of the nativity (in Luke, and here in Matthew) are by no means identical. Luke's story is Mary's; Matthew's is largely Joseph's. There are a number of apparent inconsistencies and even contradictions between the two accounts, and it seems futile and unrewarding to try to harmonize them down to the last detail. It is probable that the aim of the two writers was quite different, and even that they are writing in completely different genres.

What they do agree on are the important central truths about the coming of God's Son into the world. They agree that the child was 'conceived of the Holy Spirit' rather than of a human father— the problem addressed by Matthew in this story of Joseph's dream. They agree that the birth took place at Bethlehem, the city of David. They agree that Mary was his mother and Joseph was, or became, her husband. And, most importantly of all, that the angelic messenger insisted that he should be called 'Jesus'—literally, 'saviour' or 'deliverer'— 'for he will save his people from their sins'. That, after all, was the object of the exercise: the birth of the Saviour.

A prayer

Heavenly Father, as I celebrate the birth of your Son, help me to remember the simple central truth, that you sent him to be our Saviour. And help me to be infinitely grateful for that. Amen.

DW

The light of the world

The true light that gives light to every man was coming into the world. He was in the world, and though the world was made through him, the world did not recognise him.

The man Jesus said to his followers, 'I am the light of the world'—and they obviously believed him. John wrote this Gospel because he believed that, and he wanted other people to believe it too. 'Jesus did many other miraculous signs in the presence of his disciples, which are not recorded in this book', he writes, 'But these are written that you may believe that Jesus is the Christ, the Son of God, and that by believing you may have life in his name' (John 20:30–31).

If some of the things that Jesus said about himself were not true then he was either a liar or suffering from megalomania, a condition defined by Webster's Dictionary as 'a delusional mental disorder that is marked by infantile feelings of personal omnipotence and grandeur'. Jesus made stupendous claims for himself, and his followers endorsed them and believed them.

When John says that Jesus is the 'true' light he isn't using a word that means true as opposed to false, but a word that means 'real' or 'genuine' as opposed to unreal. All the genuine enlightment in the hearts of all people all over the world shines out of the heart of God. 1 John 1:5 says that 'God is light; in him there is no darkness at all.' And all the time the light is shining—and it has been shining ever since God made the world—and all the time the Word of God is being spoken. The Word that can be read in the whole of creation—and the Light that gives light to all people. God loves the whole world—even though it doesn't return his love. The start of John's Gospel says that the Light who is also the Word is has come into the world and has become a human being.

A prayer

Lord Jesus Christ, you are the light of the whole world, and you are the light of my life. I remember and wonder at your word to us who believe in you: 'You are the light of the world.' As I pray now, show me how to do what you have told us to do: 'Let your light so shine before men that they may see your good works and glorify your Father who is in heaven.'

SB

Born for us

He came to that which was his own, but his own did not receive him. Yet to all who received him, to those who believed in his name, he gave the right to become children of God—children born not of natural descent, nor of human decision or a husband's will, but born of God.

Perhaps we have got a bit tired of listening to carols—played to us on the radio and at railways stations ever since November. But there is still something special about them for most of us—and the wonder of the Christmas story can start to come alive again. And sometimes the words themselves can come alive with the glory of the Christmas message. 'No ear may hear his coming; but in this world of sin, Where meek souls will receive him, still the dear Christ enters in.' For those of us who are Christians there can be a fresh awareness of the truth and the glory, and a fresh entering in to us of the Spirit of Jesus—to renew us in our weariness, or our hopelessness, or our sheer overwork that has somehow dried up our spiritual life. For those of us who are not Christians there can be a receiving of Christ for the first time.

On Christmas Eve the church is always filled with people, some of them who only come on that night, and who have come on from their parties. They have been eating and drinking party food and wine. Now they hold out their hands (some of them very unsure of what they are doing) and take the bread and the wine of communion. Some people disapprove of the outsiders coming in like this. But I don't believe Jesus disapproves. He loved outsiders, and sinners. And perhaps as some of them receive the bread and wine they receive Jesus into their hearts for the first time, and know his forgiveness and his love. Then they know the wonder of the new birth—and of Christ born again in their hearts.

A prayer of thanksgiving

Light and life to all he brings,
Risen with healing in his wings.
Mild he lays his glory by,
Born that man no more may die.
Born to raise the sons of earth,
Born to give them second birth.
Hark! the herald-angels sing,
'Glory to the new-born King'

Charles Wesley

SB

Starring role

In that region there were shepherds living in the fields, keeping watch over their flock by night. Then an angel of the Lord stood before them, and the glory of the Lord shone around them, and they were terrified. But the angel said to them, 'Do not be afraid; for see—I am bringing you good news of great joy for all the people: to you is born this day in the city of David a Saviour, who is the Messiah, the Lord'.

The shepherds were religious outcasts in Jewish society, because their work prevented them from taking part in the great temple feasts and ceremonies. It is typical of the way God acts all through scripture that the most momentous announcement of history was made to a group of frightened men living on the fringe of respectable society. And the angel makes it absolutely clear that the good news is for them. 'I am bringing you good news.' They were being entrusted with a message of joy 'for all the people'. The news of the birth of the Messiah and Saviour of the world was to be entrusted to them, and to no one else. That may be an important lesson for us, too, because God has entrusted to his followers in each generation the same message 'for all the people' ... and very often we've kept it to ourselves!

Of course, in one sense the shepherds were the 'right' people, because all of this was happening in the town of David, and David was the most famous shepherd boy in Israel's history. He may well have been keeping the sheep on the very same hillside when the call came for him to meet the prophet Samuel and be anointed king of Israel (1 Samuel 16:11). It was hard for his father, Jesse, to accept that such an honour was to befall his youngest son, the shepherd boy. Luke, who all through his Gospel has an eye for the downtrodden and the outcasts of society, must have enjoyed giving the shepherds the starring role on that first Christmas night.

A prayer

Lord, I thank you for the good news of a Saviour, which someone in the past shared with me, and I am now called upon to share with others. Let me not, for false humility, fear or pride, be found guilty of keeping it to myself. Amen.

DW

The astonishing sign

'This will be a sign for you: you will find a child wrapped in bands of cloth and lying in a manger.' And suddenly there was with the angel a multitude of the heavenly host, praising God and saying, 'Glory to God in the highest heaven, and on earth peace among those whom he favours!'

The word 'sign'—*semeion*, in Greek—is a very significant one in the Gospels. It means much more than a signpost or direction—the angel was saying more than that the shepherds would find the baby by looking for a manger. It carries the idea of meaning, understanding, key to the evidence. In some mysterious way, the fact that the baby was wrapped in bands of cloth and lying in a manger was the clue to the whole story.

Of course, it must have been a great help in identifying which particular baby was the promised Messiah, because however few or many babies there were that night in Bethlehem, there could surely only have been one lying in a feeding trough. But the picture offers us much more than that. You could say that it shows that when God became man, he did it properly! He didn't pay us a brief visit, nipping back to the glory of heaven at the first opportunity; nor did he do it the comfortable way (after all, future kings are usually born in palaces). The manger provided the first clue to what kind of a Messiah Jesus was to be—not a conquering king riding in to sweep away the Romans and restore the throne of David, but a 'Son of Man' sharing our trials and deprivations, one with the human race in all its suffering and sorrow. It was to be hard for people to accept this, and I suppose it still is. But there is the 'sign' for us: the Son of God, lying helpless in a feeding trough. 'Lo, within a manger lies/ He who made the starry skies.'

A prayer

Lord, help me to see and understand the signs of your grace and love, especially today in the humility of the coming into our world of the Lord Jesus. For his sake, Amen.

DW

The shepherds' reward

When the angels had left them and gone into heaven, the shepherds said to one another, 'Let us go now to Bethlehem and see this thing that has taken place, which the Lord has made known to us.' So they went with haste and found Mary and Joseph, and the child lying in the manger. When they saw this, they made known what had been told them about this child; and all who heard it were amazed at what the shepherds told them. But Mary treasured all these words and pondered them in her heart.

I suppose the shepherds could have declined to go to Bethlehem! After all, it was a pretty bizarre instruction, and involved leaving the sheep in their fold out in the fields. Not only that, but they must have wondered whether they weren't suffering from some mass hallucination. Still, they went, mainly, it seems, because they were convinced that it was 'the Lord' who had 'made this known' to them. And their reward was to be the first people, other than the parents, to see with their own eyes the Messiah Jesus. It was, they discovered, exactly as the angel had foretold—and their story seems to have reached a few ears beyond the stable, too ('all who heard it').

The shepherds eventually went back to their flock in the fields 'glorifying and praising God' (v. 20), but Mary's reaction was a more reflective one. She 'treasured all these words and pondered them in her heart'. Assuming that she was herself Luke's informant about the story of the birth of Jesus, this may well have been how she recalled feeling at the time—there had been so much to absorb, such profound feelings, such tests of faith. Now, with the baby asleep beside her, was the time to treasure the experience, and ponder on its meaning.

A prayer

Heavenly Father, as another Christmas passes, help me like Mary to treasure the event and in quietness to reflect on what it means for me, and for your world. Amen.

DW

God's 'last word'

Long ago God spoke to our ancestors in many and various ways by the prophets, but in these last days he has spoken to us by a Son, whom he appointed heir of all things, through whom also he created the worlds. He is the reflection of God's glory and the exact imprint of God's very being, and he sustains all things by his powerful word.

It's very helpful to move from the manger in the stable, where we were yesterday, to this magnificent hymn to the glory of the Son of God. Neither picture can properly be understood without the other. The baby in the feeding trough is the reflection of God's glory. The one through whom God created the worlds, and who sustains them in being, is also the baby in the feeding trough. This is the true measure and glory of what the incarnation means.

This passage also puts Bethlehem in its historic context. God has always communicated with his human creatures. He has never left them without witnesses. All down the ages, the prophets spoke 'in many and various ways'—I like J.B. Phillips' rendering, 'glimpses of the truth'. What they had to say was true, but necessarily incomplete. But now, in these last days, God has spoken his final, complete and authoritative 'word'. He has given us (J.B. Phillips again) 'the truth in his Son'. In a proper sense of the word, there is nothing more to say, because God can't do more to reveal himself to human beings than to become one of them.

Jesus is 'the exact imprint of God's very being'—the Greek word is *karakter*. Jesus shows us the very 'character' of God, the inner truth of God's nature. 'He who has seen me has seen the Father' (John 14:9). God in his patience continues to speak to us, but Jesus is his final word.

A prayer

Lord God, help me to see your character in the person of Jesus—and help me to hear and believe what you say to me through him. Amen.

DW

Love revealed at Bethlehem

In this is love, not that we loved God but that he loved us and sent his Son to be the atoning sacrifice for our sins. Beloved, since God loved us so much, we also ought to love one another. No one has even seen God; if we love one another, God lives in us, and his love is perfected in us. By this we know that we abide in him and he in us, because he has given us of his Spirit. And we have seen and do testify that the Father has sent his Son as the Saviour of the world.

Just before Christmas last year we had a wedding in church. The young couple were very keen to have carols sung, instead of the usual wedding hymns, and among them they chose 'Love came down at Christmas'. So, immediately after the blessing of the newly-married bride and groom, we sang it—first verse a solo, and then everyone. Frankly, there was hardly a dry eye in the place. 'Love came down at Christmas, love all lovely, love divine . . .' Jon and Abi knew that the words referred to Jesus, but they also knew that they were experiencing in their own relationship something of a reflection of Bethlehem love: 'All that I have I give to you, and all that I am I share with you.' They had learnt the vows by heart and the words seemed to come home with special meaning at that season of the year. The measure of God's love is the extent of God's giving, and at Bethlehem and Calvary he gave himself. That is the real test of love.

'The Father has sent his Son as the Saviour of the world': that is really the message of the incarnation in a nutshell. At Bethlehem God's plan and purpose was put into action—and it was a purpose fuelled only by love. 'In this is love . . . that he . . . sent his Son.' And the only proper response to love is . . . love.

A prayer

Heavenly Father, teach me what love really means: to give rather than to take. And for love of you, help me to show love to others, for Jesus Christ's sake. Amen.

DW

God's adopted children

But when the fullness of time had come, God sent his Son, born of a woman, born under the law, in order to redeem those who were under the law, so that we might receive adoption as children. And because you are children, God has sent the Spirit of his Son into our hearts, crying, 'Abba! Father!' So you are no longer a slave but a child, and if a child then also an heir, through God.

'Born of a woman' is a common biblical expression meaning simply 'ordinary humanity'. And that is how God sent Jesus to us, not with trappings of glory but as an ordinary human being. Indeed, there were a few extra handicaps, because he was born into that very legal system from which he was to deliver us—'born under the law'. He identified not only with the humanity of the whole race, but with the particular 'bondage' of one nation, the Jews. And it is by that identification, at every level, that he was able to be our Saviour.

The result of the redemption Christ brought us is our 'adoption' into God's family. Being adopted, we share in the family privileges. We can call God 'Abba'—'daddy'. We are heirs to all the riches of heaven. We have the Spirit of Jesus living in our hearts.

All of this came about because at precisely the right moment—'the fullness of time'—God sent his Son. It is that 'moment' that we have been celebrating over the past week, the decisive action of God in history which we call the 'incarnation'. It happened at a point in time (though we don't know the exact date) and at a place on the map, Bethlehem in Judea. It was a real event, with real consequences. Indeed, the shock waves from Bethlehem have not yet subsided!

A prayer

Lord God, I give you thanks and praise for the wonder of the coming of your Son into our world as the fulfilment of your divine plan. I ask you to help me to appreciate more and more fully what it means to be your adopted child, a member of your family and an heir of your kingdom... and to be grateful. Amen.

DW

Saviour of the whole world

Guided by the Spirit, Simeon came into the temple; and when the parents brought in the child Jesus, to do for him what was customary under the law, Simeon took him in his arms and praised God, saying, 'Master, now you are dismissing your servant in peace, according to your word; for my eyes have seen your salvation, which you have prepared in the presence of all peoples, a light for revelation to the Gentiles and for glory to your people Israel.'

The 'Song of Simeon', known to many of us by its opening words in Latin (*Nunc dimittis*), makes a fitting conclusion to our thoughts on the incarnation, which is the theme of this first Sunday after Christmas. The elderly Simeon was one of those 'true Israelites' who had faithfully watched and waited for the coming of the Messiah. Now at last his patience was to be rewarded, because he was enabled to recognize the baby carried by Joseph and Mary as the 'one who was to come'. This 'song'—a weaving together of many different phrases and ideas from the Old Testament—looks far beyond the narrow nationalism that had cramped the expectations of the Jews for so long. God's salvation, Simeon declares, is for 'all peoples' (echoing the angels in Luke 2:10) and to reveal the truth of God to all the nations (the *ethnoi*, the Gentile races). But it will also, of course, bring 'glory' to the particular people to whom the Saviour is entrusted, 'your people Israel'. Nothing could bring together more beautifully the promises God had made to Abraham—'in you shall all the nations of the earth be blessed'—and the words the angel had spoken so recently to the shepherds.

The coming of Jesus is for the whole world. That is why each Gospel, in its different ways, ends with the disciples being sent out to carry the good news to the corners of the earth. 'Go into all the world, and make disciples of every nation.' The command remains and the task is not yet completed.

A prayer

Lord God, give me a vision like Simeon's, of your love in Jesus touching and changing the whole world. And help me to share in making that love known. Amen.

DW

Notes from BRF

If you have enjoyed reading and using *Day by Day* volume 3 you may wish to know that similar material is available from BRF in a regular series of Bible reading notes, *New Daylight*, which is published three times a year (in January, May and September) and contains printed Bible passages, brief comments, and prayers.

For further information, contact your local Christian bookshop or, in case of difficulty, The Bible Reading Fellowship, Peter's Way, Sandy Lane West, Oxford, OX4 5HG.